D0617167

WITHDRAWN

CIRCLE
OF
FIRE

ALSO BY JOYCE EGGINTON

Police photograph of the charred circle on the nursery rug, left by the fire that surrounded the infant carrier. The partially melted carrier, at the rear, had been in the center of this circle, but was moved back before the picture was taken.

JOYCE EGGINTON

CIRCLE
OF
FIRE

Murder and Betrayal
in the "Swiss Nanny" Case

HIGHLAND PARK PUBLIC LIBRARY
494 Laurel Avenue
Highland Park, IL 60035

WILLIAM MORROW AND COMPANY, Inc.
New York

364.1523
R579e

Copyright © 1994 by Joyce Egginton

All rights reserved. No part of this book may be reproduced or utilized in any form or by any means, electronic or mechanical, including photocopying, recording, or by any information storage or retrieval system, without permission in writing from the Publisher. Inquiries should be addressed to Permissions Department, William Morrow and Company, Inc., 1350 Avenue of the Americas, New York, N.Y. 10019.

It is the policy of William Morrow and Company, Inc., and its imprints and affiliates, recognizing the importance of preserving what has been written, to print the books we publish on acid-free paper, and we exert our best efforts to that end.

LIBRARY OF CONGRESS CATALOGING-IN-PUBLICATION DATA
Egginton, Joyce.
Circle of fire / by Joyce Egginton.
p.   cm.
Includes index.
ISBN 0-688-10564-5
1. Murder—New York—Westchester County—Case studies.   2. Riner,
Olivia.   3. Arson—New York—Westchester County—Case studies.
I. Title.
HV6533.N5E35   1994
364.1'523'09747277—dc20   94-28829
                                                CIP

Printed in the United States of America

First Edition

1 2 3 4 5 6 7 8 9 10

BOOK DESIGN BY KATHRYN PARISE

For those treasured people in my life
who encouraged, sustained, and endured me
from the concept to the completion
of this book:

Stephen-Paul, Shirley,
John, and Stephen

AUTHOR'S NOTE

The research for this book was begun in the belief that this was an entirely different story. Before and during her trial, Olivia Riner seemed to be innocent of the murder of Kristie Fischer. As the media reported it, this was a classic tale of an uninvolved stranger, falsely accused by a tightly knit community unable to contemplate the evil in its midst. When she was acquitted, it was persuasive to believe that justice had been done.

It was a good story, the stuff that headlines and television talk shows are made of. And were. Books take longer, and in the painstaking process of probing and unraveling, a different set of truths emerged. What follows is, I believe, the real story behind the Olivia Riner case, one that raises troubling questions about the intrusion of certain sections of the media into the course of criminal justice, and the potential for trial results to be influenced by the quality of defense an accused person can afford. This is also the story of a decent, law-abiding American family, deeply shaken by a hideous tragedy, who believed that the judicial system and the media would treat them fairly, and found themselves betrayed.

It became possible to tell it in such depth because members of the extended Fischer family opened their hearts and homes to me, and gave me their trust. I am deeply grateful to all of them. Additional thanks are due to Jan Menting for his constant support of this project, and for his detailed drawings and photographs of the house he designed: the most important exhibit in this case, which the jury never saw.

I am indebted to Alexandra Chciuk-Celt for her skilled translation of Karl Jaspers's medical dissertation, *Heimweh und Verbrechen;* to all the members of the Mount Pleasant Police Department, past and present,

9

named in this book; to those journalist colleagues who generously shared their insights and information, especially Marlene Aig, Patrice Johnson, Mary Meenan, Alex Philipiddas, and George Simor; to my agent, Jane Cushman, who had the vision to see from the beginning that there was much more to this case than was then being reported; and to my editor, Robert Shuman, for his unfailing support, encouragement, and suggestions.

Yet another dimension to this book was provided by the professional insights of two New York City clinical psychologists and psychotherapists: Dr. Stephen Paul, director of Incarnatus Institute, and Dr. Herry O. Teltscher. My profound thanks to them for sharing their wisdom, their time, and their understanding of this case. Both of them helped me, immeasurably, to put the pieces of the puzzle together.

On several occasions, Olivia Riner was approached for an interview, directly and through her attorney, but did not respond.

—J.E.

CONTENTS

PART ONE

THE FIRE

1

Most days Bill Fischer went home to lunch. As the senior partner in the family business, he could pick his time, and this was usually late, after the employees had eaten. At about one-thirty on this damp and gray afternoon, December 2, 1991, he walked around to the back of the auto-repair shop, climbed into his Chevrolet Blazer, and made the familiar five-mile drive from North White Plains to Thornwood: left on Route 22, up the hill, then left again onto West Lake Drive and over the long stone bridge across the reservoir. This took him into the village of Valhalla, and it was a curiosity of local geography—to become of crucial importance later in the afternoon—that West Lake Drive, the long winding road where he lived, would soon seem to disappear and merge into Columbus Avenue. It could be found again with difficulty by taking an illogical turn to the right, but the easiest way to the Fischer house was to stay on Columbus most of the way, and then, just past the Rose Hill Shopping Center, make two sharp right turns back onto the far end of West Lake Drive which, by now, had meandered through Valhalla into the neighboring village of Thornwood.

Bill Fischer had lived in this part of Westchester County for most of his forty-seven years, seeing it develop, without losing much of its rural character, from a scattering of hamlets into a center of light industry and an exurb of New York City. He had grown up in the old Colonial-style house next to Fischer's Garage, where his father and sister, Barbara, still lived; white frame with a front porch and a big kitchen, which at times of rejoicing, grief or stress was still the family gathering place for up to four generations of Fischers. Virtually all family decisions of importance were made around Barbara's kitchen table. Bill's current

15

home on West Lake Drive was very different. It was built by his former father-in-law, Jan Menting, who as a contemporary artist and designer had a strong sense of light and space; its large skylights and plate-glass windows were intended to let nature into the living room. Set exactly in the middle of a one-acre parcel of land, the house was farther back from the street than its neighbors, surrounded by a generous landscaping of bushes and trees to give it a sense of peace and isolation. It was a pleasing place to come home to. On fine days Bill would fix a sandwich for his lunch and eat it sitting on the deck, enjoying the still greenness of his surroundings.

Over the years he had added improvements to the house—skylights, an upper deck, and deeper closets. In his spare time he was usually doing some kind of carpentry or electrical work, and kept his building materials with the organized precision of a man whose livelihood depends upon the skilled use of his hands. During lunch breaks he would often do a little work on a current project before driving back to the repair shop. In the murder trial in which he would be a leading witness, a trial as yet beyond his imagining, the prosecuting counsel would describe Bill Fischer as a careful craftsman who knew at any given time what tools and supplies he owned, and exactly where to find them.

These last few weeks he had driven home for his early afternoon breaks with more joyous anticipation than he had felt in a long time. For almost three years after his first wife moved out he had often come into an empty house; although his two grown children, Troy and Leah, still lived there, they were usually at college or working. But more than a year ago Bill Fischer, a man of deliberate actions and few words, surprised his family by introducing into the household Denise, a slender, pretty woman who shared his love of outdoor pleasures—hiking in the woods, cycling, camping, cross-country skiing—who had the same quiet ways that he had, but who was not afraid to express her opinions with a disarming directness which he seemed to admire. Bill let it be known that she had become an important part of his life. He met her as a customer at his garage; she was eight years younger than he, both her parents were dead, she had long been divorced from an early and childless marriage, and she seemed very much alone in the world. She lived a few miles away and worked as an accountant with a company in the nearby town of Stamford, Connecticut.

Their wedding was so quiet that Bill did not even mention it to his younger brother, Bob, who was his partner at the garage. All that most people in the family knew, after the event, was that he and Denise went off to Nantucket one weekend and got married. Soon Bill was renovating the upstairs den into a new master bedroom and, after Troy moved out, turning his son's old room into a nursery for the coming baby. When Leah, his younger child, was twenty-two, William Fischer caused even more amazement among his relatives by becoming a father again. And on this December afternoon he was hurrying home not just for lunch, but to spend a little time with his new baby daughter.

If asked, he would have said that he wanted to make sure that Olivia Riner, the Swiss au pair who had been with the family for almost six weeks, was managing all right on her own now that Denise had gone back to work. But that wasn't a serious concern. Olivia had already shown herself to be so dutiful and solicitous of the baby that he and Denise had felt confidence in this twenty-year-old young woman who seemed to be the perfect baby-sitter.

No, he wasn't worried about Olivia. It was Kristie he wanted to see.

Kristie Rebecca Fischer was born in White Plains Hospital on September 11, 1991. An early snapshot of her shows an engaging infant with a delicate fair complexion, the vivid blue eyes of both parents, Denise's cute little upturned nose, and the perfectly formed features of a newborn who has escaped a traumatic journey down the birth canal.

Denise had a difficult pregnancy. Years earlier she had suffered several miscarriages, and bringing this first baby to term in her fortieth year required a lot of caution. It was even more scary than she had anticipated—she was normally so healthy—but her blood pressure shot up, she was ordered a lot of bed rest, and the birth had to be by cesarean section. She wanted Bill to be with her through labor and delivery, and he was anxious to be supportive, having missed out on the experience when his older children were born. Eight years ago his sister, Barbara, also had a third child in her late thirties, and her husband, Jim Donnelly, had shared his feelings about how memorable it had been for him, how immediately and deeply he felt involved in the miracle of new life by being present in the delivery room.

Even when the doctors decided upon surgical intervention, Bill stayed at his wife's side, and in a role reversal that touched him deeply, he was the first to be given their new daughter to hold.

"He saw them taking her out of me," Denise related. "Normally they would give the baby to the mother to hold, but I was too weak, so he held her in his arms when she was only two minutes old."

She asked Bill to choose a name for her, and he suggested Kristie. Denise added Rebecca.

On this December afternoon, almost twelve weeks later, Bill let himself into his house and went straight to the nursery. He never locked the front door during the day. Theoretically, anyone could walk in, but no stranger had ever done so, not in his twenty-two years of living there. The front door led directly into the family room, at the opposite end of which was a short, narrow corridor with doors on the left opening on to a laundry room, bathroom, and nursery, in that order; and on the right, a utility room, Olivia's room, and Leah's room. The living room, kitchen, and master bedroom were upstairs.

Pausing at the nursery door Bill came upon a domestic scene of such rectitude and innocence that he must have felt amply reassured about the care his new daughter was getting. Olivia was sitting on the floor with her back to him, folding some freshly laundered baby clothes. Kristie was lying on the rug beside her, looking pink and clean and happy, playing with the mobiles on an infant jungle gym. Olivia did not seem startled by Bill's appearance. She would surely have heard the front door open and close, and the sound of his footsteps on the vinyl tiles of the corridor outside the nursery. There was such resonance to that flooring, laid directly on concrete, that anyone walking around this downstairs area could be heard through most of the house.

Olivia looked up as he walked into the room. "Hi," Bill greeted her.

He bent down and spoke to Kristie, feeling a flood of tenderness toward her when she recognized his voice. She gave him a big, happy smile, a smile he would never forget or afterward be able to recall without tears coming to his eyes. She was so precious to him, this baby who was growing more alert, more responsive, more of a personality every day. He could not have imagined, before she was born, how special this renewed experience of fatherhood would make him feel. He had remained on friendly terms with his first wife, Grada, and had only recently confided to her, without intending the remark to hurt, that he was enjoying this baby so much more than he had enjoyed their two; not that he had loved them less, but because in his twenties he had been too ready to take his babies for granted, too concerned with working hard to support them, too immature to appreciate the wonder of them. Now he had so much more to give a child: financial security, and time for loving. The only thing missing was his youth.

Sometimes he worried about the arithmetic that would make him seventy when Kristie reached the age that Leah was now. It pained him to think there might come a time while she was still young when he might not be there for her, and he resolved to make every day count. It never crossed his mind that she might not always be there for him.

He smiled back at her and went upstairs to the kitchen to fix himself lunch.

While he was eating, reading the newspaper, he heard Kristie fussing a little. Olivia was clearly taking care of her because the whimpering soon subsided as she fell asleep. He and Denise had been struck by this young Swiss girl's devotion to their baby, and by her uncomplaining willingness to spend the day alone with her in a house which was half a mile from the neighborhood shopping center, and not within walking distance of anywhere else. Olivia looked younger than her age, with her hair worn straight down her back, her scrubbed complexion, and her teenage style of dressing: always jeans, sneakers, and a sweatshirt. But she seemed to be very responsible and self-sufficient. Before they contracted to sponsor her one-year stay in the United States, Denise had been concerned that this girl might become bored and homesick, and she telephoned Olivia's home in the small town of Wettingen, near Zurich, to warn her of the possibility: "It's real countryside where we live. You can't walk into town. You won't see many people around, and we will be at work all day. It's very quiet. What will you do when you are alone in the house with the baby?"

"I shall talk to her," Olivia replied in her softly accented English. Denise had been impressed with that response.

Since then Olivia had given the Fischers no reason to doubt her competence or sincerity. "We felt we had found the perfect nanny," Denise said.

At about 2:45 P.M. Bill prepared to return to work. Stopping by the nursery he saw Kristie peacefully asleep, strapped into the reclining infant seat where she often napped in the daytime. It was well padded, and sturdy enough to rest firmly on the floor in such a position that Olivia, relaxing in her bedroom across the hallway, could easily watch the baby. Right now she was sitting at the desk by her window, reading.

Bill hesitated by the nursery's open door, tempted to go inside for a last close look at his daughter. But fearful of waking her, he turned toward Olivia's room.

"I'm leaving now," he said. "See you later."

She acknowledged the comment, and went back to her book.

Later, blaming himself, Bill Fischer said again and again that if he had noticed anything in the least bit wrong he would not have left the house that afternoon.

2

It was hard to tell whether Olivia was happy. She gave the impression of a dutiful, serious child who lived in a world of her own. She had none of the poise or instant friendliness of Bill's elder daughter, Leah, who at that time was the other member of the household. At twenty-two Leah had a sophistication which Olivia did not remotely possess, and probably never would. Their chronological ages were close; otherwise, they might have grown up on different planets.

Denise had been reassured to find that Olivia "wasn't the kind of baby-sitter who would have her coat on, waiting to get out of the house the minute we got home." She was allowed the occasional use of a family car; even so, it was hard to imagine where in the Thornwood area a girl like Olivia might want to go. Certainly not to the bar by the railroad station or the neighborhood McDonald's, which were popular meeting places for local young people. In an attempt to give Olivia a change of surroundings, Leah proffered a couple of invitations—to go shopping with her in the nearby town of White Plains, and to see a movie—but both times the response was a monosyllabic no. There was no explanation, no suggestion that Olivia would enjoy a later, or a different kind of, invitation. Just no. Leah took this as a rebuff and did not ask again.

So far as Bill and Denise could tell, Olivia was content to spend her evenings at home, having polite conversation with the family over an evening meal, then retiring to her immaculate little room. They were delighted to see how neat and clean she kept it, unlike Leah, who with the best of intentions was always promising to tidy up. The mess really bothered Denise. They asked Olivia about her life in Switzerland and learned that she was an only child who seemed to be devoted to her

21

father and somewhat critical of her mother, whom she compared unfavorably with herself. Her mother was a cigarette smoker; Olivia detested the habit. Her mother liked to go into town to shop for clothes; Olivia preferred the simple life of the countryside. She said she loved animals and amply demonstrated this by playing affectionately with Bill's dog, Snuffy, and the Fischers' four cats. They all took to her instantly, as to an old friend, which was another mark in her favor. In a household of so many pets, animals were believed to be excellent judges of people, with an instinctive attraction to those who are kind and trustworthy.

In her free time Olivia enjoyed reading thrillers, and was currently immersed in a German-language copy of Thomas Harris's recent bestseller *The Silence of the Lambs*. She also kept a diary, a thick volume with a mock-leather cover and a lock. Not that she need have worried about privacy. No one else in the house spoke German.

Her isolating activities seemed to be at odds with her stated desire to learn about America, which she had visited twice before, as a tourist to New York City and to Disney World. Thornwood had so much less to offer, but knowing that the agency which sent her was putting her in touch with other au pair girls in the area, the Fischers told themselves that she would soon make friends and become more adventurous.

Olivia was physically small, with dark blond hair and features which were interesting rather than pretty. The nose was a little too long and sharp, the chin too pointedly determined for her face to be truly feminine; when she pulled that long lank hair back behind her ears it could have been the face of a sensitive boy. Yet when she smiled one of her rare unselfconscious smiles, her eyes would sparkle and she could look vivacious, almost stunning. More often she had a downcast expression, with a way—when spoken to—of looking up behind lowered eyelids like a child who has been scolded, and isn't sure whether it is yet permissible to speak. The straight bangs of hair which fell almost to her thick dark eyebrows intensified the impression.

She was naturally shy, the more so because she still felt awkward about expressing herself in English. But although her syntax was sometimes strange, she had a good command of the language, and no difficulty in making herself understood. When anyone in the family used a word or phrase which was new to her she would always interject to ask its meaning. There was a forthrightness about her which at best could be refreshing, at worst judgmental. Lacking insight into how middle-aged parents might feel about the only child they were likely to have, it was her first impression that their concern for Kristie was excessive, and that she was being spoiled. Sometimes when Denise ran to pick her up at the first whimper, Olivia would look quizzical and faintly disapproving. But after a few weeks of helping to look after this baby, she too seemed to be drawn into a loving, protective relationship toward her. Both Bill and Denise came to feel that she really cared for their child.

What else was there in her life? No boyfriend back home, and a prudish attitude toward men, which was unlikely to invite romance. Leah had a steady boyfriend, John Gallagher, who saw her almost daily, and obviously loved her. Leah also had her own car and a closet full of clothes, some bought for herself, others passed on by her fashionably dressed mother—more clothes, her father and John teased her, than most girls dream about. Was Olivia envious? Did she feel like Cinderella when the three adults drove off to work in their separate vehicles, leaving her stranded in this house, without transportation, and with only a baby to talk to?

Denise worried about this. For the first few weeks of Olivia's stay in their home she had been there with her, giving Olivia companionship, reassurance, and the freedom of mornings off. But last week, finishing her maternity leave, she had eased herself back into her job by working for three full days, then taking the Thursday and Friday Thanksgiving holidays. Today, the following Monday, December 2, was the beginning of Olivia's first full week alone with Kristie. If she was intimidated by the prospect of all those days of loneliness looming ahead of her, five days a week for the next eleven months, Olivia gave no hint of it. She seemed calm and confident about being left with the baby.

After Bill returned to work that afternoon there was one known caller at the house: a delivery man bringing a supply of propane gas which had been ordered. Bill had warned Olivia to expect this, to avoid her being alarmed when a large truck backed up the driveway. After filling the outside tank, the driver stopped by the front entrance to leave his delivery note. He did not knock, but peering through the glass-paneled door he observed the flickering glow of a television screen. Outdoors it was drizzling, and with the daylight fading he could not see whether anyone was in the family room watching TV. But nothing about the house struck him as unusual. He made a note of his delivery time, 4:20 P.M., and drove off.

Shortly after five o'clock the telephone rang at Fischer's Garage. Dennis Spinelli, a senior mechanic, picked up the extension at the back of the shop.

"Meester Fischer, Meester Fischer." The voice was female, excited, and foreign. Dennis thought he knew who it was. There was a Spanish lady who had been a customer for years, and no matter who answered the phone she always asked for Mr. Fischer in that urgent tone. There were three Mr. Fischers, two Williams and a Robert: Bill, his brother, Bob, and their father, Willie, who, although long since retired, often strolled across from the house next door and found himself something to do around the garage. Normally Dennis would have dealt with the caller himself to avoid bothering any of them, but there was such panic in her voice that he called across to Bill.

"I think you had better take this," he said.

Bill put down his tools and walked into the office to pick up the phone.

It was Olivia, hysterical. "Fire, fire!" she cried.

Unable to tell whether she was reporting a small accident or a major explosion, Bill did not waste time calming her down enough to find out. It went through his mind that having got herself to a telephone, a neighbor's perhaps, she must be safe and would have Kristie with her.

"I'll be right there," he assured her. "Have you called the fire department?" He thought of the list of emergency numbers which Denise had pinned up by the kitchen phone.

At that point an operator cut in and told him that yes, the fire department had been notified, and help was on its way.

Bill hurried across the workshop and out to his truck.

"I've got to go," he called out to Dennis. And drove off.

Dennis had worked for the family, father and sons, long enough to know that Fischers rarely wasted words or felt the need to explain themselves. He asked no questions and went back to his work. Bob Fischer had already left for the day, so Dennis finished the job that Bill had been working on, locked up the garage for the night, and went home.

At the house next door, Barbara Donnelly wondered why her father was taking so long to come to dinner. He had been over at the shop, and at about five o'clock she had called across to ask Bill to tell Willie that his meal was ready. When he eventually came in, Willie Fischer explained, "Billy never told me. He had an emergency. Had to go home."

24

"What kind of an emergency?" she asked, concerned.

"I don't know," he said, and settled down to his food.

Bill drove home as fast as he dared, worrying all the way about how a fire could have started on a damp day like this. It must have ignited within the house. Only a few days earlier he had been working on the first-floor wiring. He was always so careful, but maybe this time he had been negligent and had omitted some safety precaution. He was appalled at the thought.

The first fire truck was already there when he reached the house. So was John Gallagher's elderly Ford pickup truck. John, who was an auto mechanic, worked for a nearby Jaguar dealer, and on the nights when Leah was not going to her classes, it was his habit to drive directly from work to the Fischer house to spend the evening with her. Tonight he had arrived before Leah, and within seconds of Olivia's telephone call to Fischer's Garage. As Bill got out of his van, John came running toward him from the house. His eyes were streaming and he looked ready to collapse.

"Mr. Fischer, you'd better get over there," he gasped.

Olivia was standing outside the front door, by the patio, sobbing. In the background Bill saw his next-door neighbor, George Fries, and a lot of activity in the Fries house. He hoped that Kristie had been taken there. Olivia would not have stood outdoors with her, not in weather like this. Kathryn Fries must be looking after her. A kindly woman and a grandmother; the baby would be safe with Kitty. His own home looked intact. At first glance he saw no flames, only smoke, and firemen walking in and out, so it had to be all right to go inside. He ran up the driveway only to be blocked near the front entrance by a fireman.

"You don't want to go in there," the man said.

There was such a grave tone in his voice that Bill, suddenly fearful, tried to brush past him and into the house.

"You don't want to go in there," the fireman repeated, not budging.

Bill stopped, trying to grasp what he wasn't being told. Suddenly he realized why John Gallagher looked so shocked and defeated, why Olivia was alone, and why she was still crying. Kristie must still be in the house, and no one was trying to rescue her because she was dead. In the horror of that moment he could think of only one possible cause of the fire, an electrical fault, and only one person who could have caused it.

"Oh, my God," he said to himself, "I have killed my own baby."

25

3

"What happened?"

Bill was standing next to Olivia on the patio, trying to take in the horror of the scene. Her response to the question was different from the story which she later told to the police, but as he recalled it—and he was sure he remembered correctly because Leah heard it too—Olivia said that in the late afternoon, while Kristie was still sleeping, she started to feed the cats. In bad weather like this they were fed indoors from four little bowls set out in the laundry room which was near the nursery. Before putting out their food, Olivia said, she closed the nursery door to keep the cats away from the baby. A few minutes later she smelled smoke, went to investigate, and saw a fire on the bed in her own room across the hallway. Then, she said, she realized there was another fire in the nursery but she couldn't open the door . . .

"After that," Bill related, "I do not remember what she said." The emotional overload was more than he could handle. Through the daze he became aware that Leah had arrived and was standing at his side listening to Olivia's story, and that a policeman was trying to shepherd them out of the way of the firefighters to the Fries house next door. Bill refused to leave the area, and Leah insisted on staying with him. Denise would soon be arriving home from work, and he wanted to be there to comfort her. He began to move toward the street to watch for her car. As he did so, John Gallagher—soot-stained and shaking—walked across to the place where Olivia was still standing. He was not feeling kindly toward her.

"Did you tell Bill Fischer?" he asked.

"Yes, yes, yes," she sobbed. He turned his back on her and walked

26

away. It was beyond his comprehension that she had failed to save the baby.

Almost three months previously John had been one of the first to see Kristie, minutes after she was born. He made a point of finishing work early that September afternoon and dashed to pick up Leah so that they could be at White Plains Hospital for the birth. They arrived there shortly after five o'clock, and reached the maternity floor only five minutes before Kristie was helped into the world. After a while Bill came out to them in the waiting room, all smiles, carrying his newborn daughter. He handed her to Leah, who held her awkwardly, as though fearful she might break. It was a thrilling moment for her. She adored babies, and many of the tensions and resentments about having to deal with a stepmother had diminished during Denise's pregnancy. Both she and Troy were delighted at the prospect of a tiny sibling; he, too, visited the hospital that evening to see his new half sister. It was typical of Leah's warmhearted enthusiasm that over the preceding weeks she had shopped for layette items, and had organized a surprise baby shower for Denise, despite the fact that Denise already had more clothes than any infant was likely to need.

"Before this baby was born it was all Leah would talk about," John Gallagher recalled.

Having been around the Fischer household for four years as Leah's steady boyfriend, John was almost part of the family. At the hospital Bill asked if he, too, would like to hold the baby.

"No way," John smiled. "She looks too fragile for me to touch. I'll wait until she's older."

That evening, telephoning his mother to tell her the news, he had sounded so excited. "Mom, she's cute. And she has such tiny little feet."

On his visits to the Fischer house over the ensuing weeks, John, like Leah, watched Kristie's development with childlike delight. He had not been around a baby since his two younger brothers and sister were born, too long ago for him to remember, and he was fascinated by the exploratory movements and the infant shape of Kristie. After her death, memories of those visits kept painfully flooding back to him. "Once I went to the house and she was lying on the living-room floor playing with a mobile, and she would hit these little objects, and then I would hit them, and she would hit the same ones. She had these tiny little legs which did not match her body, and I would sit and play with her feet and her fingers. She had Denise's hands to a T, tiny little hands. But some grip, though, for a little gal. And I can remember being in the kitchen and hearing her crying on the monitor—not much, just fussing. She was a very good baby.''

On the night of the fire he left the repair shop of White Plains Jaguar at about 5:00 P.M. feeling frazzled. He and a colleague sometimes did private repair work in their spare time, and they had just had words over a job they had scheduled for this evening. John had postponed the arrangement because he was having trouble with the driving mechanism of his truck, his only means of transportation, and needed to fix that instead; the income-producing job would have to wait until tomorrow. His friend had not been pleased. John intended to go ahead with his own repair, and in what was left of the evening he and Leah would visit his mother. Carol Gallagher was due to go into the hospital for throat surgery the following morning, and they both wanted to spend some time with her tonight, to wish her well. Leah had reminded him of the plan when they spoke on the telephone during the day. So they arranged to meet at Leah's home, and later to make the thirty-minute drive north to the Gallaghers' house in the village of Mahopac, most likely in Leah's Toyota.

Leah, who had a secretarial job in White Plains, usually arrived at the house on West Lake Drive a few minutes before John, close to 5:15 P.M., but today she was delayed at her office for ten minutes. John looked for her car when he drew up by her home, noted that it was not yet there, and so parked in his usual spot, at the end of the long driveway close to a tree, partly on the grass so that the family members could drive past him. There was a carport close to the house, but no garage.

He did not want to go into the house with only Olivia there. During recent visits he had exchanged a few words with her, but there was an awkwardness between them and he wasn't in a mood to make stilted conversation while worrying whether his presence was unnerving her. It was more comfortable to wait in his truck until Leah arrived. Perhaps he would have a cigarette. He needed to calm down after that argument with his colleague, and there was a rule against smoking in the Fischer house. Both Bill and Denise were resolute nonsmokers.

He arrived at just about the same time that Bill was leaving his garage in response to Olivia's urgent call. Knowing nothing of this, John might have sat out there for several more minutes before becoming aware of the crisis. But on the passenger seat beside him there was a bag of auto parts for the repair job he intended to do that evening, and as he made the sharp left turn from West Lake Drive on to the Fischers' driveway the bag fell to the floor. He braked, bent down to pick it up, and from this unlikely vantage point saw out of the corner of his left eye what appeared to be a burst of orange flames coming from the far side of the house, the side of the nursery. He pulled his head up, peered over the dashboard, and realized that the flames were real. He ran toward the house, thinking: "I hope that girl knows there's a fire. I hope she has got the baby out."

Olivia opened the front door as he reached it, crying, "Fire, fire!" Through the door, which was almost solid glass, he had seen her scurrying around the family room with a fire extinguisher in her hand. Now she held it limply at her side, dangling it from her fingers, as she stood in the doorway, motionless.

"Where's Kristie?" he yelled. He was shouting to be heard over the alarm noise of a downstairs smoke detector.

"She's in the room."

"What room? The baby's room?"

"Yes." Her voice was panicky and her body was quivering. In answer to his questions, she told him that she had telephoned the fire department, and had called Bill at his garage, which was much closer than Denise's office.

Grabbing the fire extinguisher from her, John dashed across the family room and down the hallway to the nursery. The door was shut. He twisted the knob to the right and left but it would not yield. He tried again. It was not merely stuck, but locked. There was a gap under the door, and inside the nursery an area of close to twelve inches of vinyl tile, the same brown tile as in the hallway, before the area rug began. From within the room John could see the reflection of flames on the floor's surface.

Frantic, he shouted to Olivia, "Why did you lock the door?" He did not think that anyone else would have done it. There was no answer. She had not followed him back to the nursery, but was now outside on the patio, nervously watching him from a safe distance.

"Why the hell did you lock it?" he yelled. No answer.

The door was a new one, of the mass-produced hollow-core variety.

HIGHLAND PARK PUBLIC LIBRARY

It had been one of Bill Fischer's last renovations to the nursery, and he had hung it only about ten days previously, not entirely to his own satisfaction. He had bought the door from a local lumberyard, planed it to fit, and cut a hole to insert the locking mechanism, using the old door as a template. But the new hinges were a little short, with the result that the locking mechanism barely reached the strike plate on the doorjamb. It was still possible to lock the door, but the lock was not really secure.

When the new door was in position Bill had painted it with polyurethane, cleaning his brushes with paint thinner taken from a can in the storage closet off the family room. He kept most of his supplies there, including other flammable liquids like the charcoal lighter fluid he used for the outdoor barbecue, all of the cans tightly capped and neatly lined up on the shelves. Olivia had watched while he worked on the door, wrinkling her nose and muttering "Ugh!" at the smell of the chemicals.

After the painting was done Bill had been tempted to correct the fault with the latch, but decided against it because he could not imagine why anyone would need to lock a nursery door.

It was a keyless lock of the kind often used in bathrooms, secured on the inside of the room by turning a little grooved button in the center of the knob. In the unlocked position the groove would be horizontal; locked, it would be vertical. It is a weakness in the design of these locks that if anyone turns the button to the vertical position with the door open, and then closes the door upon leaving the room, no one on the outside can get in. And that was the situation which John Gallagher found when he tried to enter the nursery.

He was a rangily built twenty-six-year-old, six feet two inches tall and 155 pounds, too slim to be powerfully strong. Bracing himself against the opposite wall of the narrow hallway, he gave the door a sharp kick close to the latch, and the ill-fitting lock yielded instantly. It required very little force; in his words, "the door popped right open." He did not even splinter the wood.

He was so traumatized by what he saw in the nursery that he could barely speak of it that night, not even when the police questioned him, certainly not to Leah when she tried to comfort him. Kristie was lying in her infant seat on the rug, so totally engulfed in flame, so horribly destroyed by it, that at first he was not sure whether what he was seeing was human. He wanted to believe that the charred and disfigured shape with its shreds of seared undershirt and cloth diaper was the remains of a doll, and he looked across to the crib in the vain hope of seeing Kristie there, knowing before he looked that it would be empty. If she had been in that crib he might have saved her. Although the smoke was overwhelming and the fire was spreading up one wall, there was only this one fire in the nursery and none of the furniture had yet been damaged. The sole source of the flames that he had seen from his truck was this inexplicable blaze on the rug: an almost perfect circle of fire with Kristie in the middle like a sacrificial offering. Whoever was responsible must have locked the door to delay any rescue attempt.

The pin on the fire extinguisher had already been removed. He sprayed in short bursts, directing the foam around the baby, as close as he dared without letting the powder touch her. He sprayed the rug, the curtains, and the walls. There was less than ten seconds' worth of chemical left in the pump but it was enough to put out the fire around the baby. As the flames died down he knelt beside her, hoping against all logic that she was still alive. The heat had been so intense that the gray plastic shell of her infant seat was melting and twisted, gluing it to the rug.

"I looked at her, saw how badly burned she was, and knew I was too late," he said, describing the scene months later. "She was already dead. It was horrible. I cannot get the sight out of my mind. I felt like I had been put in somebody's nightmare. And I will never ever forget the smell. It was not the smell of the accelerant which started the fire, or of the melting plastic of that infant seat. It was the smell of burning flesh. I almost got sick to my stomach. I had to get out. I could only hold my breath for so long. And all I could think about was how the Fischers would feel when they got home."

In the house next door the fire-department pager was sounding urgently. George Fries, one of Thornwood's volunteer firemen, was at home with his wife, Kitty, when the alert was broadcast: a house fire at 5 West Lake Drive, Thornwood. Normally he would dash to headquarters, get into his kit, and join the others on the truck. But this was the home of his immediate neighbors, whom he had known for more than twenty years. Without stopping to put on protective clothing, he grabbed a flashlight and ran outdoors, skirting the bushes which separated the two properties. Kitty, who was cooking dinner, watched anxiously through the kitchen window and saw John Gallagher emerge from the

Fischer house and say something to her husband before George hurried inside. She also noticed a young woman standing alone on the patio. She watched the girl for a few minutes, puzzled because she did not appear to be showing any reaction to the crisis, either by attempting to help or by running away; she seemed to be immobilized, as though in shock. It was cold out there, and this girl was wearing only a sweatshirt with her slacks and sneakers. Kitty put on a jacket and hurried across to see if she could help. She had never met Olivia, but guessed that this was the baby-sitter.

"Where's the baby?" she shouted to the girl.

Olivia did not respond. She was shaking.

"Where's the baby?" Kitty asked again. Still no answer.

The older woman took off her own coat and put it around the girl's shoulders. With George inside the burning house, she was very concerned for his safety, praying for the Thornwood fire truck to arrive. It seemed to be taking forever. In the meantime, she did not know what to do about this mute young woman. After a few minutes she repeated the question, more gently this time. "Where's the baby?"

Finally the girl gave her an answer of sorts. Without a word she raised a hand and pointed to the house.

George Fries came face-to-face with John Gallagher as John stumbled out of the house, coughing and choking. He was stripping off his work shirt and using it to wipe the soot and sweat from his face. Tears were running down his cheeks.

"What happened?" George asked.

"There is a fire in the nursery and it does not look good for the baby," John replied. He could not bring himself to use the word "dead."

"Is she still in there? Which room is it?"

"Third door on the left-hand side."

When George Fries entered the nursery, about two minutes after John had left it, the flames had been quenched. There was a great deal of heavy smoke, and the only illumination came from a small night-light by the window which Olivia had put on earlier, the last time she set Kristie down to sleep. Even with his flashlight it was not possible to see across the room, and crouching low he had to grope around. He felt for the crib, expecting to find the baby there, carefully ran his hands around the interior, and realized it was empty. Turning to leave the room, still keeping close to the ground, he almost stumbled into the blackened shape on the floor which had been at the heart of the inferno.

He was so shaken by this experience, thinking of his own small grandchildren, that when he saw John Gallagher outside the house he, too, could not say the word.

"Did you see the baby?" John wanted to know.

"Yes, and it does not look good." After a pause, he asked: "Would the cats have been indoors?"

"Yes, most likely."

"Well, it looks like one of them didn't make it either."

John felt as though the second wave of an avalanche was hitting him. Oh, no, he thought, not that too. The cats were more important to Leah than to anyone else in the family. He hoped it wasn't O.J., the marmalade cat, her own special pet. Later he would be relieved to discover that in the smoke-filled darkness, what had looked to George Fries like an incinerated animal was the remains of a white teddy bear, a favorite from Leah's childhood, which she had recently given to Kristie. It had been a deeply meaningful gift, a personal treasure which Leah had intended to keep forever. At the time of the fire the bear must have been on the rug close to the baby.

"I was in shock," John recounted later. "I was blown away. I could not believe what was going on around me. I was thinking: Jesus Christ, what happened here? Was it an electrical fire? Or an arsonist? My head was spinning."

With a sympathetic glance at him, George Fries suggested: "Why don't you go and sit down for a while?"

As they spoke, a second volunteer fireman, Frank Yerks, came running up the driveway. He, too, had come directly from his home, only a block and a half from the Fischers' house. The fire truck was on its way, but George Fries was fearful that the house might explode before it could get there. In the meantime, he knew it was important to have another witness to the scene in the nursery before that scene disappeared.

"Come inside with me," he said to Yerks. "There's a dead baby in there. I want you to verify this before the whole place goes up."

Seconds later Yerks hurried out of the house.

"Oh, my God," he was saying. Beyond that he was lost for words.

Within the next few minutes the Thornwood fire chief arrived in his car, followed by the first fire truck, followed by Bill Fischer, followed by Leah.

After she had told Bill her halting, incomplete story, Olivia was led across to the Fries house. An ambulance worker accompanied her, sat her down, and offered oxygen. She watched him with a kind of bewildered interest, as though she did not really belong in this scene and couldn't understand why she was there. She was no longer hysterical or hyperventilating as she had been when the paramedic first saw her on the patio; in fact, Kitty was struck by her self-control as she sat demurely at the kitchen table, with the borrowed gray quilted jacket still around her shoulders, making occasional little whimpering sounds but not attempting to speak or move.

John, meantime, went back to his truck, let down the tailgate to serve as a bench, and there in the cold and gathering darkness he, Bill, and Leah sat side by side, waiting for Denise.

4

At the time of the fire there was no 911 emergency telephone system in the area. The procedure which Denise had explained to Olivia was to make a direct call to the Mount Pleasant police at 769-1998 or, if the number was not at hand, to dial the operator and explain the emergency. The second option would inevitably take longer. To obviate this, Denise duplicated the list of emergency numbers by the kitchen phone, and put the second copy on Olivia's desk. A separate telephone line had been installed for her, listed in the Westchester directory under the name of Kristie Fischer.

At about 5:10 P.M., while the nursery fire was raging, Olivia tried to call the police from the phone in her room. But she could not make her desk light work, or see well enough without it. Just when she needed it most, the bulb had blown. She took the list to the family-room telephone, but was so panicky that she dropped it, gave up, and dialed 0.

She gave the operator the correct address in Thornwood, one of several villages in the Mount Pleasant police district, but was transferred to police headquarters in the neighboring town of Pleasantville. This was common procedure because the telephone company's switching station for the area was in Pleasantville. This conversation was recorded:

Pleasantville police officer: "Police department."

Olivia: "Hi. Fire."

"Where is this, ma'am?"

"Five West Lake Drive."

"Where?"

"In Thornwood."

"What's the address?"

"West Lake Drive."

"What number on West Lake Drive?"

"Five."

"Five West Lake Drive, you have a fire?"

"Yes."

"Okay, I'll get 'em out. I'll send the fire department. What's your name?" He assumed her to be the homeowner.

"Riner." She pronounced it the Swiss-German way, REENER, which the officer misheard.

"Leland?" he queried.

"REENER," she repeated. By now she was crying, and her words were getting swallowed by sobs.

"What's your phone number?"

Hearing her distress, an operator broke in: "769-5939."

Recognizing the Thornwood exchange, the officer repeated: "5939. Five West Lake Drive. Okay, I'll send the fire department."

Olivia: "Yes."

"Okay. Bye."

"Bye," Olivia replied. In this whole conversation she had said nothing about a baby being in danger, just as she failed to report this to Bill after the operator came back on the line and asked if she needed to call anywhere else, and put her through to Fischer's Garage. For all any of them could tell, she might have been reporting another of the nuisance fires which from time to time were set around the neighborhood merely for the sport of it: blazes in trash cans, on rubbish piles, and in disused barns. Fires serious enough to threaten human life were rare in rural Westchester.

While the Pleasantville police officer was getting essential information from Olivia, his colleague was telephoning Mount Pleasant police headquarters. This officer passed on the message with the correct address but with the garbled name of Leland.

"This is yours, isn't it?" he asked.

"I think so," replied the Mount Pleasant desk sergeant. "I'll check."

The sergeant was being cautious. All he needed to do to call out the volunteer firemen of any local village was to press the three appropriate keys of the police encoder which would activate the pagers in their various homes. The Thornwood code was 69P, and as soon as he punched that out, a tone alert would sound in the home of every Thornwood fireman, followed by his broadcast message giving the location of the fire.

But the address he was given did not sound right. One end of West Lake Drive formed a T-junction with Nannyhagen Road in Thornwood; the other end terminated about four miles south in Valhalla, by the bridge across the reservoir. From his knowledge of the Thornwood end, he doubted that there was a number 5. He had friends living in that section, across the street from George and Kathryn Fries who were at the third house on the left, number 27. It did not make sense to him that the Thornwood numbers could go as low as 5, and he wondered whether it was the Valhalla firemen he should be calling out.

He looked in the telephone directory and in the office Rolodex file for the name of Leland on West Lake Drive, but there was no such listing. With valuable minutes slipping away he decided to call back the number the operator had given and check the address. Olivia picked up the phone.

"Yes?" she said nervously.

"All right," the sergeant began. "What's your address?"

"Five West Lake Drive," she stated for the third time, unaware that she was now dealing with a different police department.

"Five West Lake Drive," he repeated. "What street is that near?"

"Nannyhagen Road."

"You're near Nannyhagen?" He sounded dubious.

"Nannyhagen, yes." It was a well-known street in the village, its curious title being a derivation of Nannahagen, the former name for Thornwood. This origin was so far forgotten that sometimes the street name was spelled as two words, Nanny Hagen, as though it commemorated a person.

"How far off Nannyhagen?" he pursued.

"What?" She was beginning to sound frantic.

"How far are you off Nannyhagen?"

"It's the next street, and then you come"—the next phrase was inaudible—"to Nannyhagen and West Lake Drive is on the right, right."

He knew what she meant. She was trying to give directions from the Mount Pleasant police headquarters on Columbus Avenue, but that did not resolve his doubt about number 5.

"Yeah. How far in on West Lake?" the sergeant inquired, still wondering if she meant all the way into Valhalla, or whether this was a prank call and a fake address.

"What?" she asked.

"How far in on West Lake?"

"Five."

Did she mean five houses? "The first house?" Not hearing her reply, he repeated the question. "The first house?"

She was becoming harder to understand as her voice rose in panic. "The first, the corner, and then the second," she said, and then another phrase which he could not grasp.

"Is it right near Nannyhagen?" he persisted.

"Yes"—then a few more words which were muffled by her sobs. "Nannyhagen."

Now he, too, was beginning to sound frustrated. "Ah, boy," he said. "Do you have any smoke in the house?"

"Yes," she cried, almost shrieking.

Again he could not discern her answer. He tried once more. "Is there any smoke in the house?"

"Yes," she repeated.

"Okay."

"Good."

She must have thought she had finally got through to him. His next question turned her tears into hysteria.

"Ma'am, I don't have a Five West Lake Drive. Can you tell me exactly where the house is?"

"The baby's in the room!" she screamed, by now frantic. It was her first mention of anyone being trapped in the fire, and it spurred him into action.

"All right," he said. Only then did he punch out the code which set off the pager in George Fries's home, and in the homes of volunteer firemen throughout Thornwood. By that time John Gallagher must have been pulling into the driveway, perhaps even running toward the house.

After she hung up the phone, Olivia acted with a rare presence of mind. She went upstairs and put on all the lights to direct the fire trucks to the house. Unlit, the place was hard to find after dark, being set back from the road and surrounded by shrubbery. But with the electric lights streaming through the skylights and the upstairs plate-glass windows, it stood out like no other house in the neighborhood, like illuminated crystal, like a beacon in the night.

Most people in Olivia's situation, with a baby trapped in a smoke-filled room, would not be so aware of the fire department's needs as to go upstairs in a burning building and put on lights. Most people would have a different, overwhelming priority: to rescue the baby. The first rule in fire emergencies is to get everyone out of the burning building;

38

the second is to call the fire department. Anything beyond that shows more composure and logic than most people can summon in a crisis. But the instinct to rescue a child in peril is basic. There were two ways into that nursery—through a door which wasn't so securely locked that it could not be kicked open, or by going outside and breaking a window which was less than two feet from the ground. Olivia attempted neither.

Given her state of panic, putting on the upstairs lights was an extraordinary inspiration, especially after her experience with the lamp in her room, which she thought to be a power failure. Or perhaps she was carrying out an emergency procedure so well learned that it came to her automatically: the kind of professional response to crisis that most people don't know about. If so, it was all the more remarkable that she did not try to save Kristie.

Not until many months later, when the information could do her no harm, did it become known that Olivia Riner was a fireman's daughter.

The house where Kristie died had been given the unlikely number of 5 by the man who built it, Bill Fischer's former father-in-law, Jan Menting. Back in 1955 he and a friend bought two acres of farmland fronting on West Lake Drive, running from the Fries property line to the corner of Nannyhagen Road. They halved it, and the friend took the corner lot, positioning his house in such a way that it made sense to give it a Nannyhagen Road address. The Fries house, a standard Cape Cod already in place on the other side of the Menting property, had been designated as 27 West Lake Drive, allowing for a downward numbering of more houses than were eventually built in the space.

In this time of minimal zoning and haphazard postwar development, Menting was left to pick his own house number, any odd figure from 1 to 25. He chose 5 because he liked the way it sounded with the street name, thus creating the only address on that side of West Lake Drive which did not have a double-digit number. The oddity was barely remarkable on this long meandering road with its confusing gap in the middle, and its method of house numbering which defied the laws of arithmetical progression.

If there had been a computerized address system in the Mount Pleasant police department, the desk sergeant could have resolved his doubts in a second. This was one of many pieces of technology the department had been requesting for years, always to be refused by the town board on grounds that it would cost too much. There never seemed to be enough money to update the department's equipment, sometimes not even enough for basic office supplies. And it did not help that the police chief and the town board supervisor were frequently and publicly at odds. Often the Mount Pleasant police department seemed to be a pawn in a personal vendetta, functioning despite the town government rather than with its aid and approval.

But even if a computerized system had existed that day, Kristie's death was inevitable. She was lost as soon as the flames started licking around her, which must have been happening when Olivia picked up the telephone. Prompter police action would not have saved her, but it would have minimized the damage to the house and allowed for more evidence of arson to be preserved. And who knows where that might have led?

More important by far, the way events unfolded, John Gallagher would not have been first on the scene. George Fries and Frank Yerks, and probably most of the Thornwood fire department, would have arrived ahead of him; thereafter no one else would have been admitted to the house. John would have been spared a sight he would never forget, and a great deal more besides.

That night, too traumatized to sleep, he thought that nothing more terrible than the events of this evening could happen to him. But there was worse, much worse, to come.

5

The town of Mount Pleasant is not a town in the literal sense, but an administrative area covering twenty-eight square miles. At its hub the three adjoining villages of Thornwood, Valhalla, and Hawthorne are so interdependent as to be essentially one community. Thornwood has the two neighborhood shopping centers, Valhalla has the town hall and police headquarters, and Hawthorne the railroad station on a commuter line to New York City. All three share the same public high school. The traffic among them is quiet but constant, and the community so stable that almost everyone knows everyone else, especially of the same generation. Most likely they went to school together.

Although much would be made of it later, it was not unusual that the first police officer on the fire scene and the lieutenant in charge that night both knew John Gallagher. Scott Carpenter, a rookie patrolman, had worked for the same construction company as John's brother Michael. John used to work for the same towing company as Scott's brother Jeff. Back then, about four years earlier, John often gave Jeff a ride to the Carpenter family home, and there would be an exchange of pleasantries. "How's the job going?" "How's Mike?"

The lieutenant, Louis Alagno, was the popular swimming coach in a Mount Pleasant summer program. As a teenager, John was on his team. They knew and liked one another, but it was a casual acquaintance. As time passed some of the youngsters coached by Alagno had their inevitable brushes with the police. John Gallagher amassed some speeding tickets, rather more of them than most. Otherwise he impressed Alagno as a decent, hardworking young man. "The only thing negative about John Gallagher," he commented, "is that he's a hot-rodder. Got a lead foot."

41

The three of them came together at the fire scene, among the mess of hoses and floodlights and trucks which were accumulating across the front lawn. Scott Carpenter had been out in his patrol car cruising the neighborhood when Robert Gardiner, the desk sergeant who had so much trouble understanding the location of the fire, sent out a radio call to all police in the area. Carpenter, one of the youngest patrolmen in the department, was about two minutes' drive from the Fischer house when he got the message. He arrived there shortly after Gregory Wind, the Thornwood fire chief, and before the first fire truck. Fries and Gallagher had left the house, and Wind had gone in immediately after them.

"I recognized the chief's vehicle, the Blazer, in the driveway," Carpenter recalled. "I pulled up in the roadway to leave room for the fire trucks to come in. In the front yard I saw Greg Wind looking so upset that he was almost like a zombie. Something had disturbed him very much. He told me: 'There's a dead baby in the house.'

"I ran to the house and in at the front door. There was so much smoke rising I couldn't see a thing. I got about twelve feet into the building, hoping to find the room where the baby was, but I couldn't even see a door, so I had to turn around and leave. At this point I ran into John Gallagher. He was nervous, pale, and sick-looking.

" 'There's a dead baby in the house,' he said. "I asked him to stick around, and he did. He must have waited about one and a half hours until I could take his statement. Later I saw him staying close to the Fischers, and him and Leah hugging a lot."

Carpenter tried to call police headquarters on his portable radio but Sergeant Gardiner on the desk could not understand him. There was a lot of difficulty with transmission to police headquarters that evening.

"You are coming in all broken up," Gardiner complained.

Carpenter ran to the corner house and used the neighbor's car phone. "There's a D.O.A. baby and we need detectives," he reported. On his way back he was relieved to see another police officer, Robert Miliambro, in the Fischers' front yard; he too, had been touring the neighborhood in a radio patrol car. Then Carpenter noticed Olivia standing on the patio, crying loudly. He asked her what happened and she replied at some length in a language he did not understand. The only word which came through to him was "cats" and she said it several times. He was probably hearing *Katze*, the German word for a single cat, but he had no background in foreign languages. What was all this about cats? he was wondering, as it kept punctuating her sobs.

He went back into the house with Miliambro. They separated, groping through clouds of smoke, searching for the baby. Miliambro found the nursery and called Carpenter to join him. The door was wide open, as John Gallagher had left it, and the carpet around Kristie was still smoldering. So were the remnants of her clothes. The burn pattern on the carpet formed a circle round the melting infant seat, as though an inflammatory liquid had been carefully poured to enclose the baby in flames. This fire was no accident.

"Let's be certain of what we have here," said Miliambro, desperately hoping that the fragile remains in the infant seat were not human. "Let's make sure it isn't a doll."

Reluctantly they moved a little closer.

"I didn't see how that baby could be alive, but I leaned over to check for vital signs," Carpenter related. "You want to save a baby's life, and when it turns out you can't . . ." He left the sentence unfinished. "It was lousy, to say the least. I never imagined, in a lifetime, to see anything like that."

Miliambro closed the nursery door behind them, unaware that the latch was still in the locked position, the way John Gallagher had found it. Outside the house he spoke to Fire Chief Greg Wind who was taking command of the arriving firemen.

"There's a crime scene in there," Miliambro said. "The fire in that room has been fully extinguished, so keep the guys out of it if you possibly can." The warning was barely necessary. Still shaken by what he had seen in the nursery, Wind was not eager to have his firemen share the experience.

Outside the house an ambulance worker had been giving Olivia oxygen. She no longer seemed to need it, and had entirely stopped crying. Fifteen minutes ago she was babbling hysterically in German. Now she was quiet and self-controlled.

Carpenter was amazed at the speed of the transformation. Again he asked her what had happened, not expecting to be understood. "But she spoke English. God strike me dead if I am lying, but she spoke English. It really took me aback. And I thought it was weird that she wasn't crying any longer. Suddenly she seemed normal."

He interviewed her briefly. "She said that she had just fed the cats, and that one of them had run away. Then she said she found a small fire on her bed. She noticed that the baby's door was closed, but did not appear to be concerned about it. She never once asked about the baby. She seemed more concerned about the cats.''

At Miliambro's suggestion Carpenter led her across the lawn to the Fries house and asked her to wait there. So far as they both could tell, she was the only witness to whatever happened in the nursery, and they did not want her talking to anyone else until a detective arrived to interview her. They need not have worried about her leaving. She had nowhere else to go.

Several of the Mount Pleasant police officers were also volunteer firemen. The most experienced was Sergeant Brian Dwyer, with twenty-five years in the fire service, twenty-two of those years as a full-time officer in the Mount Pleasant police department. There were four generations of volunteer firemen in his family. His grandfather and father had served as Thornwood's fire chief, and so had he; now his son was also a volunteer. There was very little about firefighting that Brian Dwyer did not know.

He was off duty as a police sergeant, and on call as a fireman when the beeper sounded at his Thornwood home. He hurried to the village firehouse, got into his kit—boots, waterproofs, and helmet—and was the senior man on the first fire truck to reach the Fischers' home. For the next hour he functioned in his dual capacities, switching from fireman to police officer and sometimes doing both jobs at once until Police Lieutenant Louis Alagno, who by that time was in command, put him in charge of collecting evidence. "From now on you're on the clock," Alagno told him.

In fact, Dwyer's role as a police officer was implicit from the beginning. As soon as he jumped out of the Thornwood fire truck, Robert Miliambro took him aside and into the house to see the dead baby; if Dwyer had been any other volunteer fireman, Miliambro would have kept him out.

With Dwyer at his side, Miliambro went to open the nursery door which he had carefully shut when he left with Scott Carpenter a few minutes earlier. He was surprised to find it locked. Noting the type of lock he realized what had happened. He had a similar mechanism on a bathroom door at home, and a four-year-old son who sometimes locked himself in and became too panicky to turn the little grooved button and let himself out. Miliambro was familiar with the trick of releasing the lock from outside the room by inserting a long thin nail into the small hole at the center of the knob. He removed the metal filament from his ballpoint pen, used it as a probe, and let Dwyer into the nursery.

On this visit they both noted a second, smaller burn pattern on the carpet near the nursery door. Nearby, about six inches from the baby's foot, was a one-liter plastic seltzer bottle, Vintage brand, empty and partially melted, and a charred wooden box of Diamond kitchen matches. They left these items undisturbed, to be photographed as evidence.

In Olivia's room they saw the remains of another strange fire. There was a burn area about two feet square in the middle of her bed, part of it penetrating the bed covers down to the mattress. Someone had put out this blaze with a fire extinguisher, leaving a residue of chemical foam around the scorch marks. Nothing else in the room was damaged. Although this fire, too, appeared to have been deliberately set, there was no evidence of an intruder. As in the nursery, the window in Olivia's room was closed and latched. In common with the other downstairs bedroom windows it had two clear glass panes, the right pane immovable, the left positioned on a track so that it could be slid across. In both the nursery and Olivia's room the center fastening was in the locked position.

Later Dwyer noticed a sizable hole in the nursery window, which must have been caused by a heat break, not only because of the closed latch but also because the shattered glass was outside the house. If anyone had broken in, the shards would have been inside the room. This explosion in the nursery probably happened seconds before the arrival of John Gallagher, and the orange flare which he saw from his truck would have been flames from around the baby pouring out of that hole.

At the end of the hallway Leah's door was closed. One of the first priorities of firefighters, once they are able to get inside a building, is a search-and-rescue mission which involves checking every room to make sure that no one is trapped, and that there are no extension fires behind furniture or in closets. Routinely, firemen smash windows to throw out smoldering furnishings, take off their gloves and feel the walls for heat spots, and thoroughly vent a building of smoke. Leah's closed door aroused the suspicions of the first firemen who came into the house, but their attention was drawn away from it to the body in the nursery, and for a while everything else was of lesser importance.

It is rare for small-town volunteer firemen to see a burn fatality, and in this case the size and helplessness of the victim magnified the sense of shock. Whether or not they actually saw Kristie, and several of them eventually had to, the knowledge of what lay inside the nursery, not to be moved until someone came from the Medical Examiner's office, dominated the consciousness of every fireman present that evening, coupled with a feeling of helplessness that they had all arrived too late to save this baby. Having recovered his own equilibrium, Fire Chief Greg Wind felt very protective about the men on his team.

"I have a lot of young guys, aged eighteen and up," he said. "I was very concerned about their well-being, but it was the fathers who were most upset." He was one of them, with a small daughter whose name was poignantly close to that of the dead baby: Krista. The coincidence, along with the memory of the scene in the nursery, would disturb him for months.

Structurally, this did not appear to be a major house fire, the worst damage coming from the three hoses which were swamping the downstairs area. The fire on Olivia's bed and the fatal blaze in the nursery had been extinguished before the first firemen arrived. What remained for them, so it seemed at the time, was to deal with the quantities of smoke and smoldering material by pouring water, opening windows, and bringing in ventilation fans.

In an initial quick check around the house, one fireman, James Lawrence, tried to open Leah's door, found it locked, and made a mental note to recheck during a later, more thorough search. He had just come away from seeing the baby's body, and was still in shock. At that stage no one noticed that the latch on Leah's door was similar to the one for the nursery, and that it, too, had been locked from the inside. In fact, Leah never latched her door in the daytime, let alone locked it, because she was more concerned about the cats being trapped in her room than she was about them sleeping on her bed. She habitually left her door sufficiently closed to forestall comments about her untidiness, and sufficiently ajar for a cat to squirm around.

While Jim Lawrence was standing in the hallway, Thornwood's second assistant fire chief, Joseph Rod, went up to Leah's door and tried the knob. Rod had just noticed char marks toward the top of the door, and was suspicious.

"It's locked," Lawrence remarked.

Joe Rod's reaction was the same as John Gallagher's had been, about forty minutes earlier. Without hesitating to think what danger might be on the other side, he kicked the door in. It yielded easily, not in this instance because of a fault in the locking mechanism, but because within the room, out of his vision, part of the door had burned away.

Both men were startled by a rush and roar of intense flame which leaped out of the doorway and chased them down the hall. Grabbing each other by the arm, they ran for their lives. Unknown to anyone at the scene, a third, unrelated fire had been burning in Leah's room all this time, at least forty-five minutes, until it had exhausted all the oxygen and subsided to a mass of smoldering residue, ready to burst into an inferno as soon as fresh air was let in.

The door to Leah's room, unlike the one to the nursery, fit tightly on all sides. If either her door or her window had been slightly open, the fire would have behaved differently. It would have been attracted to the source of fresh air, and thus discovered sooner. Flames would have fanned down the corridor or outside the house in search of more oxygen, like the blaze which poured through the hole in the nursery window.

The kind of flash fire which chased Joe Rod and Jim Lawrence down the hallway happens only when all the oxygen in a room has been consumed, the remaining gases become superheated, and a new source of air is suddenly let in. In Leah's room the explosive force of this chemical reaction was so great that it blew out a window, and flames went sheeting up the outside of the house to the roof.

There were several moments of confusion before all hoses were directed to this new fire. One hose which was already snaked down the center hallway from the fire truck proved to be too short to reach into Leah's room, and there was a frantic rush to replace it. Then the sudden powerful force of water drove the flames back into her walk-in closet, which was separated from the nursery closet, immediately behind it, by a thin wooden partition. Fueled by Leah's clothing, the fire raced through this partition and emerged out of the open doorway of the baby's closet, starting a second blaze in the nursery. As soon as the firemen trained their hoses on this, each hose dousing the room at the rate of twenty-five gallons a minute, the crime scene which the police had been so anxious to preserve became thoroughly contaminated. The force of water dislodged some of the smaller furnishings, the empty soda bottle, and the matches, created piles of debris, and washed away any footprints or fingerprints an arsonist might have left behind.

The evidence of the heat break in the nursery window also became confused as Brian Dwyer, fighting the fire from outside the house, smashed out the rest of the broken pane with the end of his folding ladder to make enough clear space for another hose to be brought in. As he did this, a curtain rod fell to the floor. Now there were shards of glass on the nursery carpet as well as on the ground outside, leaving Dwyer with a visual memory which would later cause him, and the case for the prosecution, a great deal of trouble.

Only Kristie's pathetic remains were carefully avoided.

Out in the front yard, some distance away from all the excitement, Leah sat on the tailgate of John Gallagher's truck weeping for her baby sister, unaware that all the memorabilia of her twenty-two years was going up in flames, and that virtually nothing would remain of her considerable wardrobe but the clothes she was wearing.

6

That night the Mount Pleasant police department was short of the staff it most needed. Of its two lieutenants, one was out of town. The other, Louis Alagno, had struggled through an eight-hour shift feeling terrible, and at 4:00 P.M. had gone straight home to bed. He did not know it then, but he had pneumonia. Of the three detectives, one was off sick, another was about to start his vacation, and the third, Bruce Johnson, had finished his day's work at 4:30 P.M. When George Fries called the police department to report what he had seen in the nursery, the desk sergeant, Robert Gardiner, had to telephone Lou Alagno and Bruce Johnson at their homes and ask them to come straight back on duty.

In fairness to himself, Alagno should have declined. He had a fever of 102, and the dampness of this December day was turning into a steady rain which would become heavier during the evening: the kind of rain which soaks to the skin and chills to the bone. It was foolhardy for him to be outdoors in such weather. But it was part of his job to take charge of a crime scene, and a matter of pride for him to be there. So he got out of bed, hurriedly dressed, and walked to 5 West Lake Drive which was around the corner from where he lived.

At his home in the neighboring village of Valhalla, Detective Bruce Johnson had just changed into comfortable clothes, sneakers and a flannel shirt worn loosely outside blue jeans, ready to spend a quiet evening with his wife and two school-age daughters. Gardiner's call came before he had a chance to eat. He flung on a jacket, and strapped his pistol on his hip in a way which was not too obvious, creating an awkward bulge under his shirt. Then he got into his car, stopped off at the police department to pick up videotape recorders and a camera, and drove to

49

the fire scene. He knew exactly where to find it. He had grown up seven houses away from what used to be known as the Menting house, regarding it as a local landmark because, in his opinion, its contemporary lines did not fit in with the Cape Cods and Colonials and split-levels of the immediate neighborhood. There was a pond at the back of the property where as a boy he used to skate with Dick Menting, who was close to his age, forty, and he had memories of Dick's older sister, Grada, who became Bill Fischer's first wife. It felt strange to be going back after all these years, in the role of police detective.

Lou Alagno was there about ten minutes before him, and had already determined that there were two witnesses to be interviewed: John Gallagher and Olivia Riner. Alagno remembered Gallagher from the swimming team and the speeding tickets, and told Scott Carpenter not to let him leave without getting a written statement. This was standard procedure. He had learned that the nursery fire was already raging when Gallagher came upon it, whereas Olivia was there when it started. He decided that interviewing her would be a detective's job.

"At this stage she was not a suspect, but the best witness we had," he said.

When Bruce Johnson arrived at about 5:40 P.M., Brian Dwyer took him, as he had already taken Louis Alagno, around the outside of the house to the broken nursery window and invited him to peer through the hole. The fire in Leah's room had not yet erupted, so the hole was exactly as Dwyer had found it: about a foot across and jagged at the edges. Johnson, who was tall and heavily built, bent down, warily stuck his head through the hole and beamed his flashlight into the room. The beam fell upon the ravaged infant carrier, on the charred body of its occupant, and on a nearby plastic toy which had melted into a shapeless glob against the wall.

As a detective he was trained to observe and remember as much detail as possible. As a father he would afterward wish that he wasn't. His strongest memory of the scene, the one he could not afterward shake no matter how hard he tried, was the position of the baby's arms: outstretched, with the tiny fingers clenched in defenseless anguish. He hoped she had not suffered; that the smoke overcame her before the fire. He stepped back, straightened up, and checked for footprints on the windowsill and on the muddy earth below. There were none. But near his feet were fragments of glass from the heat break, and he noted that the window was latched. It was beyond his comprehension how anyone could have broken in without a trace and committed so outrageous a crime.

"I'm going to let Brian do the crime scene and select the evidence, and you can do the interviews," Alagno told him. "You'll find the baby-sitter in the house next door."

Again Johnson was on familiar territory. Kathryn Fries was the town clerk of Mount Pleasant; he knew her well. He walked across the Fischers' front lawn and around the stone wall into the Fries house, where he found Olivia sitting quietly at the dining table. Scott Carpenter was with her, keeping watch, and there were at least three ambulance workers in orange jackets, carrying oxygen tanks and tubes, ready to leave. Olivia was still a little tearful but essentially calm.

Johnson sat next to her, catty-corner at the table, and pulled out his notebook. "I'm a police detective and I'd like to ask you some questions," he told her, as Carpenter left.

She answered quietly, telling him her name, her home address in Wettingen, and the fact that she had arrived in the United States to live with the Fischers on November 1, a little more than five weeks ago, and four days before her twentieth birthday. He found her English quaint but comprehensible, and she seemed to have no difficulty understanding him.

He asked her to tell him what happened and this was her story:

From the time Bill finished his lunch break she was alone in the house with the baby and the four cats (he always took the dog to work with him in the mornings, as company for his father). At about 5:00 P.M. she fed the animals in the laundry room; then Oliver, the black cat, went to her room, where he liked to sleep on the bed. After a few minutes he came running out into the hallway, "very angry." She went to see what had disturbed him, and found a circle of bright orange fire burning fiercely in the middle of her bed. She used a hand gesture to indicate flames between twelve and fifteen inches high. Upstairs in the kitchen there was a fire extinguisher, one of three in the house. She ran to get it, pulled the pin with some difficulty, and was able to put out the fire before it spread beyond her bed. She noticed that her bedroom window was open about ten inches, although she had left it closed.

Then she went to check on the baby and found the nursery door not only shut but locked. She was positive that she had left it open. Although Johnson did not know it until later, this significant detail differed from her earlier account to Bill Fischer, in which she herself had closed the nursery door to keep out the cats. She told Johnson that she saw smoke coming from under the door, and telephoned for help. She had no idea how the fires started, or how the door became locked, and she neither heard nor saw anything suspicious before Oliver's warning of the blaze on her bed.

It was an odd tale. He was struck that she seemed to have made no attempt to rescue the baby, either by trying to force the door or by going outside and breaking the nursery window. That window was barely two feet from the ground, as he remembered from having to stoop to put his head through the hole. Had she been so traumatized by the fire on her bed that she was unable to tackle another one? But surely, he argued to himself, it would be instinctive for a person in charge of an infant to try to save that child from certain death. Wouldn't there be a rush of adrenaline which would compel the adult to take action, regardless of personal danger? The effort might not be successful, but this girl had not even tried.

Olivia did not ask Bruce Johnson whether Kristie had been rescued. Nor did she mention hearing her cry or choke, although, as he would later discover, a working monitor in the baby's room was directly connected to a receiver in hers. He was privately thinking that if Kristie had sensed danger, Olivia would surely have known. In the confined space of that downstairs area the baby's screams would have filled her ears. Johnson decided to go back next door and take another look at the layout. He wondered if she was telling the truth about being alone in the house, or if she was covering up for someone else who should not have been there.

At about 7:00 P.M. Brian Dwyer came looking for him. For the past hour there had been so much activity at the Fries house that Dwyer's arrival was scarcely noticed. "It was a busy, busy evening," Kathryn Fries recalled. "I was going back and forth, and many of the firemen were coming in to call their wives. There was a tremendous amount of in and out."

Bustling around, she had overheard some of Olivia's story, and she, too, was puzzled by the obvious omission. "She was talking about the cats, how she was feeding them in the laundry room, and how one cat came running. But she never mentioned the baby. I thought it strange."

Dwyer's arrival broke the tension. Still dressed as a fireman, he was now a full-time police officer.

"Joe Butler has arrived," he told Johnson. "I think you should come over and talk to him."

Joseph Butler, the arson investigator from the Westchester District Attorney's office, was a welcome sight at any fire scene. He had an encyclopedic knowledge about the causes and behavior of fire, and such a love of his work that it would have been a crime to speak the word *retirement* in his presence. Whatever his age, and it must have been in the seventies, he had the energy and enthusiasm of a man who was half that. His familiar stocky figure, dressed in a fire chief's full kit and imperturbable as rock, commanded the respect of every police officer and firefighter in Westchester. Most of them assumed that he would be around forever.

In the next half hour at the fire scene Bruce Johnson gathered several important pieces of information. He learned from Joe Butler that all three fires were separately and intentionally set by the ignition of a liquid accelerant. Butler could tell from the pour patterns that the arsonist had worked from inside the house, moving deliberately from room to room. With a professional scorn, he described the criminal as an amateur. An experienced arsonist, he said, would have chosen a single, more volatile device, igniting it from outside the building to minimize the chance of being caught.

By the time Butler arrived, the fire in Leah's room had been extinguished, leaving a mass of charred and smoldering rubble with globs of melting foam rubber dripping from her mattress. He pointed to the elliptical pour pattern on the carpet around the bed, similar to the one which encircled the infant seat on the nursery floor. More flammable liquid had been used in Leah's room than anywhere else, and the ensuing fire had left almost nothing worth salvaging.

The smaller, localized blaze in Olivia's room was very different. In the center of the large circular burn on her bed there was a smaller area, roughly one foot square, which the fire had not penetrated so deeply, as though some item lying on top of the bedspread had protected it. During the evening Butler would develop the theory, one from which he would not be shaken through the long investigation ahead, that what had covered that area on Olivia's bed had been the infant carrier with the baby in it; that there something happened to Kristie which caused her to be taken to the nursery and a larger fire set to obliterate all evidence of whatever that something was.

Bruce Johnson went into the nursery and saw the partially melted plastic soda bottle, and the charred box of matches. He took video photographs of the body, working in a routine, mechanical way to avoid dwelling on those tiny outstretched arms. Like many small-town police officers, he did another part-time job in his off-duty hours: His was the unusual one of funeral director. He was therefore inured to dealing with the dead. But this case was unlike any in his experience.

"The worst sight you can ever see is a burn victim, and it is compounded when it is a child," he observed. "Even in my other work, you see a dead child and it hurts your heart."

In the laundry room he saw confirmation that Olivia had indeed fed the cats. Their four feeding bowls were empty, but in the sink, covered in soot from the fire, was an empty cat-food can which someone had recently washed out. The Fischers were conscientious about saving containers for the town's recycling program, and Johnson's attention was drawn to a blue plastic bin in which there were about eighteen empty one-liter soda bottles, clear plastic with opaque blue bottoms, similar to the partially melted bottle on the nursery floor. More empty soda bottles filled a plastic wastebasket nearby. He mentally filed that piece of information, wondering what to make of it.

Outside it had begun to rain heavily. Among the volunteer firefighters he saw his brother Brian, who had driven the fire truck from the neighboring village of Valhalla; also his mother, Phyllis Johnson, a Thornwood fire commissioner for the past twenty years, the first woman in the county to be elected to such a post. She had come as an observer. Johnson barely had time to say hello to each of them as he hurried on his way.

Checking around the house, he noticed that while the nursery and Leah's windows were latched, one of the two panes in Olivia's bedroom had been slid across to the fully open position. At first this looked like evidence of the break-in which her story suggested. But a couple of firemen told him that it was they who had opened the window, and that initially they had found it closed.

He stopped to speak with Scott Carpenter, who repeated what John Gallagher had just told him about the locked nursery door and the fire around the baby. Sitting beside his friend's brother in a parked patrol car, smoking one of his cigarettes, Carpenter had elicited the story in painful detail. Gallagher had choked up badly as he told it, and Carpenter had felt concerned about him; he looked so dazed and sick.

As soon as the statement was written and signed, Carpenter had been glad to let him go back to Leah. Then Alagno gave him an even more painful task.

"I had to ask the Fischers for information about the deceased," Carpenter recalled. "Who the doctor was, her full name and birthday. That was horrible. I didn't like doing it one bit."

Returning to the house next door, Bruce Johnson found Olivia still seated at the dining table. He had asked her to wait there and she had taken the request literally; in half an hour she had not stirred. He repeated his questions about the events leading up to the fire, and she retold her story in the same chronology, but with a difference. This time she was not in the laundry room when Oliver ran out of her bedroom in fright. She was sitting in the living room, playing with O.J., the marmalade cat. The rest of her tale was repetition. With the layout of the house now in his head, Bruce Johnson could see no way that a person in the laundry room could miss hearing an intruder moving between Olivia's room, Leah's room, and the nursery. That laundry room had a louvered door which was undoubtedly left open for the cats, and it faced on to the same short, narrow hallway as the three bedrooms. No one could prowl around the area without being seen or heard. Olivia's latest account about being in the living room was a little more believable. Sitting there preoccupied, perhaps watching television or dozing, she just might have been oblivious to an intruder. It was unlikely, but remotely possible. He wondered if she had thought of this in his absence, and changed her tale to fit.

They were barely fifteen minutes into this second conversation when his attention was diverted by the sight of Lieutenant Louis Alagno entering the Fries house by the back door, ushering in a very distressed couple. The man was sobbing and the woman crying hysterically. He did not need to be told who they were.

"Olivia did not see them," Johnson recounted. "She was sitting with her back to them. I knew I had to get her out of there quickly because I wanted to avoid a confrontation at all costs. I didn't want one of them yelling at her, 'Why didn't you try to save our baby?,' although it might have been interesting to watch her reaction. But she was under control, we had a rapport going, and I didn't want anything to break it.''

He led her to the front door, explaining that he would like to continue the interview in his office. She did not demur. From the beginning his manner toward her had been quiet and affable, his normal style, and he was making a conscious effort to inspire confidence. He assessed her as a compliant but reluctant witness who knew more than she was telling, but who might be more forthcoming provided she felt safe.

He took her by the elbow and guided her to his car, having asked Scott Carpenter to accompany them. The two officers sat in the front seats, with Olivia alone at the back. Nothing was said on the short drive to police headquarters. Carpenter was curious to know why Johnson was taking her in for further questioning after he had been told to let John Gallagher go, but this was not the time to ask.

It was almost 8:00 P.M. when Johnson sat Olivia down beside his desk in the detectives' office and began a more probing interrogation. He was becoming increasingly suspicious about the inconsistencies in her story, and the more time he spent with her, the more his image of her changed. By about 8:30 P.M. he had ceased to think of her as an innocent bystander and while still addressing her politely as Miss Riner was artfully framing the kind of questions that he would put to a suspect.

7

In Joe Butler's opinion, anything that could go wrong that night, did. "It was Murphy's Law at its best," he summed up.

When he wasn't on a fire call he worked normal business hours in the Westchester County District Attorney's office in White Plains, and that Monday, December 2, he finished as usual at 5:00 P.M. He drove straight home to the small town of Peekskill, and was eating his dinner when the telephone rang.

"It was Fire Control at the Fire Training Center in Valhalla, and they told me I was wanted for a fire in the town of Mount Pleasant," he recalled. Through most of his long career he would have been out of the house and on his way within a few minutes, but recently the rules had changed. "Because of budgetary problems there was a new policy in the District Attorney's office which severely restricted my movements. I was not to go out on a fire call, other than between nine and five, unless there was a death, or over a million dollars' worth of property damage. Up to last year I had responded to any emergency, at any hour of the day or night, seven days a week. But I am under union contract, and this involves overtime. So when I got this call I had to stop and ask what was the story."

"We think there's a death but we're not sure," the Fire Control dispatcher told him.

"What do you mean, you're not sure?"

"All we have is a report of a possible D.O.A."

That did not help Joe Butler make a decision, but he was used to the ambiguous ways of bureaucracy.

"I can tell you right now that unless there is a verified death or a

57

sizable property loss, I cannot go," he told the dispatcher. The temptation to leave it at that must have been strong, with the remains of his dinner getting cold.

"But here's what I'll do," he added, affably. "I'll make contact with my office, see what they think of the situation, and get back to you."

He telephoned John Keating, chief criminal investigator in the District Attorney's office, who was not pleased.

"Is there a death or isn't there a death?" Keating wanted to know.

"I don't know. I'm not at the fire scene," Butler told him. Although frustrated, he could understand Fire Control's uncertainty. There had been enough occasions in his experience when a fire victim was too deeply trapped under debris or too horribly maimed to be recognizably human.

"Well, you can't go there unless they know there's been a death," Keating reminded him.

Butler returned to his meal. He was still trying to finish it when the Fire Control dispatcher called back. "We have it confirmed that there's a D.O.A."

"Okay, I will respond immediately." After more than fifty years in the business, the language of the police blotter came naturally to him, and he spoke it with deliberate clarity, as though editing himself for the record before letting the words come out.

Before leaving home Butler was supposed to notify his superior of his decision, but when he called back to the District Attorney's office, Keating had left for the day. Anxious not to lose any more time, he drove the twenty miles to Thornwood, reaching the fire scene at almost 7:00 P.M. The trunk of his car was always packed with his white waterproof suit, yellow fluorescent pants and helmet, which he hurriedly put on over his clothes when he reached the Fischer house. His immediate task was to establish whether this was arson, and if so, whether a life had been lost as a direct result of the criminal action, or independently of it. Unlike the volunteer firemen and the more seasoned police, he was able to walk around the nursery without flinching. Not that the sight failed to disturb him, but in his experience of thousands of fires he had seen so much worse. In a preliminary attempt at identification he even touched the baby, gently trying to slip a pencil between her abdomen and the edge of the diaper. He hoped to confirm that this was indeed a female infant, like the baby who was missing. He had known strange things to happen at crime scenes. But the diaper was too firmly pinned to be pushed aside. Visually he could not understand why the firemen had any doubt in their minds about this being a human life, but emotionally he realized that they had not wanted to believe what they saw. Hence the report of "a possible D.O.A." He paced around the room with professional curiosity, documenting the details in his mind. It was not his practice to take notes. Tomorrow he would write his report from memory, the way he always did.

What he saw was clearer proof of arson than he had expected.

"On the rug was a distinctively placed flammable liquid which I would attribute to a pour and not a throw," he observed. "The maximum burning on the baby was on the right-hand side of the body where the liquid had puddled. There had been another fire coming from the closet which had left marks high on the wall near the window, but there was not much burned in the room except near the baby."

That meant someone had gone into the room and virtually walked around the baby, dribbling flammable liquid in a circle which enclosed her as she lay in the infant carrier on the rug. It was a carefully executed, purposeful act. No one leaning through the window or standing by the door, flinging fluid from a bottle while preparing to run away, could have achieved this result. Whoever set the nursery fire intended to kill Kristie, or else to destroy all evidence of something which had already happened to her.

After examining the damage in the other two rooms, Joe Butler came to his firm conclusion that the baby was initially burned in Olivia's room while her infant seat was resting on the au pair's bed. Finding a spare infant seat nearby, he was able to fit it almost exactly over the burn pattern on the bedspread.

"I do not think the baby died in the position in which she was found," he said. "I think that whatever happened in the au pair's room was critical, and that the probable cause of death was accidental, or not planned. And after that happened the baby was moved to the nursery, and the nursery fire set. The police and I immediately thought of crib death as a possibility. Or that the infant might have been dropped."

In this scenario he surmised that the blaze in Leah's room was started in the expectation that it would merge with the nursery fire, creating so much damage that the baby would seem to be a chance victim of a major disaster. "Someone might anticipate that the whole house would burn down, and that it might be impossible to tell exactly how the baby died," Butler observed.

He was distressed that it had taken so long for the third fire to be discovered. "It is unfathomable to me that no one entered Leah's room earlier. Firemen are supposed to open all doors as soon as they get in a building. But this was an emergency situation, and these were volunteers.

"Volunteers should not be involved with murder," he added.

And yet in a rural community, this was how it had to be. The police could not take control of a crime scene until the firemen declared it safe; in the meantime, the firemen must, of necessity, have sole, free access to a burning building. Professional firemen were trained to watch for details which might prove invaluable to a police investigation, like whether windows were open or closed, and the position of latches, before they began to change the scene by smashing out frames and breaking down doors. But volunteers were trained to concentrate on putting out a fire because in the sporadic experience of most of them, it was all they were ever required to do.

Paul Chrystal, the Westchester County fire coordinator, later explained: "Most volunteer firemen never see a crime scene. In a case like this they would see it as their mission to completely extinguish the fire, and to do what is necessary in opening up walls, digging behind them, getting rid of any smoldering furniture, applying water to the main fire, pulling down damaged ceilings and walls, and throwing out any burned debris. If this is not done the fire can consume the house."

The fact that the main fabric of the building was saved was a tribute to the energy they expended over almost two hours. But the upheaval created in the process left very little untampered evidence for the police.

It took Joe Butler less than an hour to establish that, in the phraseology of his formal report, "there was no plausible, natural, mechanical, electrical or accidental causation for this fire which was deliberately set with the use of a flammable fluid as an accelerant." Furthermore, he felt certain that Kristie's death was murder. He judged that about three pints of volatile liquid had been used, most of it in Leah's room, a small amount on Olivia's bed, and the contents of the soda bottle in the nursery. He smelled the twisted, empty bottle and decided that it had contained a petroleum-based distillate which could not be identified without a laboratory test.

The police had already put in a request for the medical examiner to come to the scene. Joe Butler was appalled to learn that instead of making a personal trip for an on-site examination, the medical examiner had sent one of his investigators, William Fazzalaro, with a van to transport the body to his laboratory. When Butler arrived Fazzalaro was already standing there, anxious to get on with the job.

"Do not move this body," Joe Butler told him. "Before you touch it I must notify my office and find out what they want to do about it."

Fazzalaro looked uneasy. "I have a problem," he said. "I have two other pickups to make tonight in different parts of Westchester."

"Would it be convenient to do one of them first, then come back here?" Butler inquired. He was anticipating a delay, but nowhere near as long as it would turn out to be.

"I think it would be more practical for me to wait," Fazzalaro replied.

Butler recounted: "He thought I would get clearance immediately. But I could not use the phone in the house because it was not working, so I went across the street to a neighbor. I called John Keating but he was not at home. I could have put a beeper call out for him, but I would have had to stay at that number until he got back to me and that would have meant too much time loss. So I called the assistant district attorney on duty, but he was not at home either so I had to send a beeper call to him. In the meantime, I tried to get three other ADAs. Then I called Fire Control to tell them of the situation. I was there on the phone at least an hour. It was terrible. An ADA called back fairly soon, and I told him of the situation, that the medical examiner's man wanted to move the body. He said, 'Well, I don't know what to tell you. I'll have to call one of my superiors for advice.'

"I was then advised to called ADA James McCarty. I could not get him immediately, had to beep him, and when he called back I told him the situation—that there was a dead baby and that the scene involved arson. McCarty said, 'Stay where you are. I'll get back to you.' It was maddening. The police department thought I had disappeared, and I had told them not to move anything. The firemen were champing at the bit because this was delaying cleanup and they are all volunteers. Even after they finished at the scene they were going to have to go back to the firehouse and wash off their tools and equipment, which was likely to keep them busy for most of the night.

"McCarty called me back and said, 'I will come. But don't let anyone move the body. I want to look at it first.'

"So that was more delay. Meantime I am making other calls to try and get my boss and to make the necessary notifications. I got back to the scene between nine and ten P.M. after at least an hour of relatively wasted time. The medical examiner's man was still waiting, and I had to tell him that he could not take the body until an ADA showed up. It was about ten P.M. before McCarty arrived with a woman assistant district attorney from the Domestic Violence Unit because someone had brought up the question of possible child abuse. I took them through the house and they finally agreed that the body should be moved."

In the meantime, Lieutenant Louis Alagno, the police officer in charge, had been feeling every bit as frustrated. He, too, wanted the medical examiner to come personally, concerned that important evidence might be lost if the body was moved before a pathologist saw it. Before the recent wave of economies a doctor would have come without question, but this was a delicate situation. The medical examiner made his own decisions. The police could recommend and request, but not insist.

Alagno asked Fazzalaro to telephone his office. "Tell them I want the medical examiner to come out here," he urged.

Minutes later Fazzalaro returned from making the call, with a report that the medical examiner would not be coming. He himself did not have a very clear picture of what this case was about; hanging around outside the house he was picking up the story in bits and pieces. He spoke briefly with Bill and Denise Fischer, told them who he was and why he was there, but otherwise stayed in the background. At times like this his could be a very lonely job, trying not to add to people's grief by making himself obvious, or to let the pain of it get to him personally. Finally, after a chilling three-hour wait, he went through the grisly mechanics of his task in conditions of extreme difficulty. Working in near darkness, sometimes ankle deep in water, inadequately clad for the cold, wet night except for the waterproof boots he had remembered to bring, he made his diagrams, took his photographs, and as best he could, checked the body for trauma. It is arguable whether a pathologist would have done much better, but Louis Alagno would always blame himself for not being more insistent.

"I think a forensic pathologist might have picked up additional information by viewing the scene," he said months later. "I am disappointed that I did not jump up and down and stamp my feet and demand that the medical examiner come. I had no way of forcing him to be there. But in retrospect, I am sorry that I accepted his decision not to come."

While Fazzalaro went painstakingly about his business, Alagno watched impatiently, sickeningly conscious of the fever which was racking his body. He felt an almost personal affront when the other man produced a small wooden case with a handle on top, not unlike a tool box, and prepared to wrap the dead baby in a sheet before putting her inside. What was going through Alagno's mind was the pathos, the unspeakable tragedy of somebody's child, so recently full of joy and promise, being consigned to that tiny box. It looked too small to hold a human life. At a professional level he was also thinking, with rising indignation: Why didn't this man bring an adult-size body bag so he could take the infant seat with the baby still in it? Maybe there are clues in that seat, in the way it is burned, in the way the baby is positioned, which could be important to a forensic pathologist.

But Fazzalaro had been told only that there was a dead infant to be picked up, so it had made sense to him to bring an infant-size box, especially since he needed space for two other bodies in his van.

Joe Butler shared Lou Alagno's silent outrage. "I had never seen a box that size for transporting a body," he commented later. "Normally they would bring a stretcher or a body bag, and they would take whatever is connected to the body. I could not believe that such a critical piece of evidence as that carrier would be left behind."

As Bill Fazzalaro gently lifted Kristie's body from the infant seat, a portion of her cloth diaper fell off. It was a section of gauze which had escaped the fire because she had been lying on it; the pressure of her body against the back of the seat had left this fragment of fabric essentially intact. Sergeant Brian Dwyer, one of the small group of police officers in the room, picked it up and instantly recognized an unexpected but familiar odor. He passed it to Officer Robert Miliambro.

"What does that smell like to you?" he asked.

"Paint thinner," Miliambro promptly replied.

Dwyer nodded. Paint thinner was exactly what he had in mind.

Joe Butler had an interesting observation to add. Whatever was on the diaper was not the same flammable liquid which had been in the soda bottle on the nursery floor. They had distinctly different smells. In his experience arsonists did not encumber themselves with more than one kind of accelerant, not if they were bringing it into a building from outside.

After Bill Fazzalaro had made a discreet departure with his little wooden box, Dwyer and Miliambro went through the house together, taking videos and photographs, and searching for evidence.

It was an eerie scene. There was no electricity in the house and the firemen's floodlights cast bright beams and long shadows through the gutted building as they moved from room to room, picking their way over sodden debris. Outside it was still raining heavily, and bitter cold. In the wreckage of the family room the two men soon found the closet by the stairway where Bill Fischer kept some of his construction supplies. They were impressed by its orderliness, with clearly labeled cans of oil and paint placed side by side in logical arrangement. These were all so neatly positioned that it came as a shock to see a two-liter white plastic flask, rectangular in shape, lying awkwardly on its side on the floor of the closet. It had contained paint thinner and was almost empty.

On a shelf above there were two containers for other flammable liquids. One was a white plastic flask for A & P charcoal lighter fluid which the Fischers used for their barbecue grill; the other a one-quart metal can of Coleman appliance fluid for camping stoves. Both were virtually empty. With a carelessness that was alien to Bill or Denise Fischer, the last person to use the Coleman fluid had failed to screw on the cap, and had set it loosely on top of the can as though too hurried, or too preoccupied, to be bothered.

The two officers picked up the containers and carefully placed them in their cylindrical one-gallon metal evidence cans for laboratory testing. The burned box of kitchen matches and the partially melted soda bottle were put in separate cans.

They looked indecisively at the infant seat which Bill Fazzalaro had left behind. "What about the baby carrier?" they asked Joe Butler, who, as a representative of the District Attorney's office, was nominally in charge. Clearly it was too large to go in an evidence can. Also it would have to be cut away from the rug into which it had melted.

"No need for that," Butler replied, meaning that since Fazzalaro had not taken it with the baby, he saw no reason to send it to the laboratory for separate analysis. He knew the plastic would not yield any trace of a volatile substance. The only chance of finding that kind of evidence was on porous material like cloth. And in his judgment, the best place to find it was on that scrap of diaper because whatever flammable liquid had been poured over or into the seat would have pooled where the baby was lying.

Nevertheless, Butler assumed that the police would take the carrier for their own collection of evidence, but Dwyer and Miliambro understood him to mean that they should leave it behind. They were uneasy about this, but had too much respect for Butler's expertise to question what they thought to be his decision.

"The way Joe Butler was thinking was that we had the flammable liquid and the diaper and the pour pattern, and the infant carrier would not help any more," Miliambro interpreted. From an arson investigator's viewpoint, that was true. But murder was not Butler's territory, and the police officers at the scene did not realize that he was leaving those judgments to them. Afterward Butler was appalled that the carrier was left behind that night.

"It would be normal police work to take it," he said. "When I saw them gathering up lab samples in the nursery I presumed they would also take what they needed for themselves. I never dreamed they would leave that infant carrier. Obviously I did not make myself clear to them, but I didn't assume that I had to take seasoned policemen by the hand and tell them what to secure as evidence."

Concentrating on his own job, Butler had no sense of the awe in which Westchester policemen held him. This sturdy gnome of a man with his shiny bald head and twinkling blue eyes was a legend among the law enforcement officials of Westchester County. He was thorough, energetic, a bit ponderous, and so knowledgeable that no police or fire officer ever questioned his judgments. What they heard him say that night became incontrovertible, to the extent that when two police officers were going through the wreckage the following morning and one of them again suggested taking the infant seat as evidence, the other replied, "Joe Butler said not to." And that ended the discussion. Afterward they would regret leaving the seat glued to the charred remnants of the nursery rug, to be seen and wept over by Bill and Denise Fischer when they returned to rescue what was left of their belongings. But it continued to remain there until later in the week when it was realized that there would probably be a murder trial, and that it would be important for a jury to see this horribly heat-deformed object which had so recently cradled a living child.

8

Mount Pleasant's police chief, Paul J. Oliva, had finally made the decision to retire. He had been thinking about it for three years, ever since that unexpected heart attack which was frighteningly similar to the one that killed his father at the age of fifty-four. Oliva had made an excellent recovery and was now as feisty as ever, but there were a lot of pressures in his job and he did not want to push his luck. He had the timing carefully worked out. Last month, November, he had celebrated his sixty-fifth birthday, and if he stayed on the job until the end of March he would qualify for a higher pension; in the meantime, he believed he had made his succession secure by having his two lieutenants, Louis Alagno and Michael Mahoney, take the New York State civil service examination for police chief. Both earned top scores, and both had worked their way up through the ranks of the Mount Pleasant police department. As Oliva saw it, they were the only members of his department qualified to succeed him. Having thus done all he could to ensure that his own exacting standards would be upheld, he felt confidence in letting the town board decide which lieutenant to promote.

The news of his retirement decision was not yet public, but he intended to share it with Town Supervisor [Mayor] Robert F. Meehan next week, when they sat down together for the police department's wage-contract negotiations. He did not care for Meehan, a Republican attorney who was a generation younger than himself; the mistrust was mutual and sometimes publicly expressed. But if he didn't observe protocol, he suspected that Meehan might fill his place with a candidate who was not in the Oliva tradition. Most members of the police department were, having known no other chief. Over his forty years in the Mount Pleasant police department, twenty-five of them at its head, Paul Oliva had built up a reputation for straight dealing and a demanding standard of professionalism. These qualities stood out in an area where some local police departments were reputedly open to corruption. Oliva was widely respected among his peers, stubborn, suspicious of any authority but his own, a man who ran the department like his private fiefdom. Resenting outside interference, he would fearlessly put himself on the line to defend his officers when he believed them to be right. If they erred, he might never let them forget it.

Like many of them he had grown up in this neighborhood, with deep ties to the community and personal loyalties which went back to grade school. Essentially he was a blue-collar type and proud of it, with the heavy facial features of his Italian forebears and a laconic way of expressing himself, peppered with mild expletives. As an administrator he sometimes had his critics, but in one area he could not be faulted.

"He is an excellent, excellent cop," said Bruce Johnson, who was trained by him. "He is from the old school, a cop's cop, self-taught, with a good sense of judgment and a nose for criminal investigation."

In his own twenty years as a Mount Pleasant police officer, Johnson had amassed a collection of Oliva stories. The best of them had to do with other murder investigations. "In June of '86 there was a contract murder in a house across from the Methodist Church. There was this Hungarian roofer and sider who fought with his wife for years, then paid three thousand dollars to have her killed by a Puerto Rican guy from the Bronx. This guy stabs the wife eighteen times while the husband is sitting in the back family room calmly eating pigs' knuckles. After he has done the job this little five-foot-nothing Puerto Rican runs off through the woods because his getaway car hasn't shown up. Then he goes to the volunteer firehouse down the street, covered in blood, and asks to use the men's room. Says his car had broken down and he had to change a tire, except there is no car and he has a loaded gun on him. He had thrown his knife in the woods where we found it later.

"We arrest the two of them, and the next day we are at the house processing the crime scene. While we are in the garage Paul Oliva shows up. Thought he would take a ride down there; it was a nice day. I am standing talking to him when he notices a small hole in the sheet rock of the garage ceiling. 'Pull that down,' he says. So the patrol officer starts pulling it down and fifty thousand-odd in bills falls out. Singles, tens, twenties, fifties, hundreds, all in a brown paper bag. The Hungarian guy had a cash business, and was hiding money. He and the Puerto Rican are now in jail, doing twenty-five years to life.

"Another time, a couple of years ago, Oliva was at his vacation cottage on the Connecticut shore. Sees a black guy throw a paper bag into the river there, has a feeling that he's up to no good and takes a hard look at him. Next day he reads of a homicide in Bridgeport, goes to the local authorities, they look in the water and pull this gun out. Oliva gives a complete description of the guy, and they arrest him for murder. It's like he has a sixth sense."

If Louis Alagno had begged off sick on the night of the Fischer house fire, Paul Oliva would have gone out and taken charge of the crime scene instead. He was not the kind of police chief to distance himself from his staff behind an oversize desk. The investigative side of the job had drawn him to police work in the first place and it still invigorated him to be out in the field. In his early years the Mount Pleasant police department was so small that none of the officers had the title of detective; whoever was on duty took on the responsibility. Oliva had changed that by sending Bruce Johnson, among others, to whatever training courses became available, from F.B.I. to county level. He wanted his detectives to be well versed in all types of crime, from petty larceny to murder. But when it came to solving a complex case it was still the inborn sagacity and the sixth sense of Paul Oliva which was most likely to be on target, to the extent that smaller police departments in the county called on him for advice. At the home of the homicidal Hungarian he alone noted that discreet hole in the garage ceiling, and guessed why it was there.

On the evening of December 2, 1991, Lieutenant Louis Alagno walked the seven hundred yards from the Fischer house back to his own, to the nearest available telephone, and called Paul Oliva at home. The police chief had finished work for the day before Olivia Riner's emergency call came in and was spending a quiet evening with his wife at their carefully maintained ranch house in the neighboring village of Valhalla. Minutes after Alagno's call he was back in his office.

Bruce Johnson was already in the detectives' room down the corridor, questioning Olivia. It was a sparsely furnished room with four metal desks placed back to back in pairs, vinyl tiling on the floor, and a general impression of drab monotony. The police department furnishings, unlike those of the municipal offices which occupied the larger part of the same building, were a low priority on the Mount Pleasant town budget, and it showed.

Johnson was seated at his desk in a swivel chair with Olivia in a straight-backed chair to the side of him. He swung around slightly to face her, and in the brightness of the recently installed neon strips was startled to notice that her eyelashes were singed, the right one rather more than the left. He had not been able to see this in the subdued lighting of the Frieses' dining area, and it instantly recalled a memory for him, that of preparing to make a barbecue in his own backyard and not being sufficiently cautious. As he put it: "How many times have I lit my stupid gas grill and it poofed up in my face and singed my eyelashes and mustache." He remembered the immediate reaction of needing to rub his eyes. And he saw that Olivia's eyes were still quite red.

The combustion which causes singed eyelashes is an entirely different phenomenon from that of being burned by flames, which, he conceded, might have happened to Olivia when she extinguished the fire on her bed. That kind of contact would most likely singe her long hair, perhaps also her eyebrows and the bangs which covered her forehead. But it would not singe her eyelashes alone. Singed eyelashes meant only one thing to him—that she bent over an incendiary liquid and the vapors had risen and pooled, as they automatically will, in her eye sockets. She would not have been aware of this until a source of flame, like a lighted match, ignited those vapors and caused combustion. To Johnson, singed eyelashes were the mark of someone who had lit explosive material, not of a person using an extinguisher to douse the fire.

Bruce Johnson was not yet ready to draw Olivia's attention to her eyelashes, especially since she seemed unaware of their ragged appearance. He would not let this conversation end without photographing them as evidence, but there was the delicate matter of timing. If he brought out his camera now she would realize that he suspected her. If he delayed too long she might rub her eyes and remove the evidence. His impression that she had guilty knowledge of the crime was getting stronger by the minute, and he knew that his best chance of getting her to tell him about it was to maintain a friendly, inquiring manner. Most young people of his experience, especially first-time offenders, would eventually blurt out a confession if you acted fatherly and talked to them long enough. He decided to risk postponing a question about the eyelashes until later in this interrogation.

Again he asked her to describe the events leading up to the fire. This time he led her back to Bill Fischer's arrival home for lunch, and took her step by step through that afternoon. Some of it seemed to be trivia—how often she changed the baby, what Kristie was wearing—but he elicited every possible detail, knowing that any one of them might be significant. This was standard investigative procedure, to have a witness account for every moment of questionable time, and to watch for gaps and discrepancies. He was impressed by her awareness of time, how she was able to tell him almost exactly when Bill came in, and when "the propane man," as she called him, brought his delivery, even though she had not gone to the front door when he left his note.

She recalled going upstairs to the kitchen shortly before Bill's arrival at about 1:45 P.M., and preparing an eight-ounce bottle of formula. She took it down to the nursery and sat on the floor feeding Kristie while Bill ate his lunch in the kitchen. After the baby had taken about five and a half ounces, Olivia burped her, then put her in the infant seat on the rug with a rolled-up cloth diaper to prop one side of her head. Soon Kristie fell asleep, in the position where Bill saw her when he stopped by the nursery on his way back to work.

After he left, Olivia said she sat in her bedroom reading and writing until about three o'clock, or shortly thereafter, when the baby wakened. She offered her the remainder of the eight-ounce bottle, and Kristie drank most of it. She changed the baby's diaper, but not the rest of her outfit, which she described as a light-green one-piece suit with ruffles and white stripes at the wrist, worn over a white undershirt.

"It wasn't dirty so I left it," she said.

She then carried the baby upstairs and put her in a little play swing while she took a smaller, four-ounce bottle of formula from the refrigerator and warmed it. After a while she went back downstairs and sat in a reclining chair in the family room with Kristie in her arms, feeding her the contents of this second bottle. While doing so she heard "the propane man" make his 4:20 P.M. delivery. Kristie soon fell asleep, and at about 4:30 P.M. Olivia put her back in her carrier near the nursery window. She was now positive that she left the nursery door open.

Bruce Johnson's naturally benign expression betrayed none of his incredulity. Remembering the infancy of his daughters, he was thinking: How on earth could a three-month-old baby ingest twelve ounces of formula in less than two and a half hours? He wondered whether Kristie regurgitated the excess and choked to death, whether the nursery fire was a cover-up for an act of carelessness or stupidity that Olivia was afraid to admit. He could not believe that anyone, much less this timid girl, would deliberately burn a living baby. Something must have happened to Kristie before the fire, something she was concealing from him. He pressed on with his questions.

Olivia did not react like any young person he had ever met, even allowing for the fear she must have felt in this alien place, traumatized by whatever she had seen of the fire, caught up in a legal system she did not understand. Even conceding all that, she was strange. He was used to young people who act affronted when interrogated about a crime in which they deny involvement: a defiant how-dare-you-suggest-I-did-it attitude. This girl sat passively still except for the constant twirling of her hands in her lap, a child's hands twisting a sodden tissue. Part of him felt sorry for her. In a quiet voice which rose a little with each denial, she protested that she had no idea how the fires started, or how the nursery door became locked, although she was certain that she was alone with the baby. The mystery became more mysterious when she volunteered, "If anyone else was in the house I would either hear or see them from any place I would be downstairs." Those were her exact words as Johnson carefully remembered them.

He made few notes during this extended conversation. Note taking was not a practice Paul Oliva encouraged. In Oliva's reasoning: "A seasoned police officer is trained to observe, to keep information in his head. Nothing wrong with not writing it down at the time; he will do his report later, and most cops do it from memory. Otherwise, the other side can subpoena his notes. Every police officer is supposed to have a memo book but very few of them do. They rely on their memories which are usually pretty damn good."

Johnson worked the Oliva way, listening and watching intently. Although Olivia Riner's knowledge of English was mostly limited to the present tense, much of it in direct translation from the German, he felt no need for an interpreter. She understood him adequately, and when the meaning of an English word eluded her she was not too shy to ask.

Throughout this interview a woman civilian dispatcher sat in the room, a police requirement when a female is being interrogated. On several occasions Johnson stopped his questioning to inquire whether Olivia would like anything to eat or drink, or to have the dispatcher, Betsy Hoagland, take her to the ladies' room. But every time she refused. Again Johnson privately marveled, not only at her inner fortitude but because he had rarely interrogated a suspect who did not grasp at every opportunity for a break. Her refusals were a relief to him, delaying the time when he would have to photograph those eyelashes. It would be too risky to let her leave the room and perhaps look in a mirror before he secured that picture.

Johnson had her go over and over the story, and all her versions tallied until she finished telling about giving Kristie that second bottle of formula, putting her into her infant seat on the nursery rug, and going into the laundry room to feed the cats. She said that at first the cats were loudly scrapping, but after they were fed, Kabuki and Fleetwood meowed to be let outside, and Oliver went to his favorite sleeping place in her bedroom. From then on the narrative shifted back and forth, as it had done earlier, with no satisfactory account of that crucial half hour before the fire. There was the version in which she was in the laundry room when Oliver came rushing out of her room to warn her of the blaze on her bed. And there was the version in which this happened while she was sitting in the living room with the television on, playing with O.J. Johnson was amazed at how much time she seemed to spend in that laundry room, with no other washing to do than the baby's and her own.

Her stories became consistent again when she told about finding and extinguishing the fire on her bed, hearing the two downstairs smoke alarms go off, and discovering that she could not open the nursery door. Johnson asked whether she tried to punch or kick a way in, or if she had thought of going outside and breaking the window.

"The door was locked," she told him, as though that ruled out any possibility of a rescue attempt.

He reminded her of the heavy metal fire extinguisher she had been holding and inquired whether she thought of using it to bash a way into the nursery.

"The door was locked," she repeated.

But behind that flimsy door was a fire and a baby, he was thinking. A baby for whom she was responsible. He doubted if he would ever forget those tiny clenched fists and pleading little arms, and tried to reject the thought that Kristie might have been burned alive. It was too horrible. He kept wondering whether Olivia would inquire about the baby's fate, but either she already knew or she did not want to know. Watching her intently, he observed that whenever he put an innocuous question about the baby she answered directly, even in some detail, as though trying to be helpful. But when he asked about the baby in relation to the fire, she shrank into an attitude of avoidance and withdrawal. Her voice sank to a whisper, and her head bent so far forward as to hide her face behind the lank curtain of hair which fell about her cheeks. Several times Johnson raised her chin with his hand, not merely to hear her better but to try to make her look at him. Even then she would gaze in another direction as though she was mentally somewhere else.

"She had a thousand-yard stare," commented Lou Alagno who saw her later that night.

"All the time I was interviewing her there was no emotion, no eye contact, and her body language was that she was lying," Johnson recalled. "She just sat there with this stoic stare. Most of the time it was as though she was not really there, as though there was someone else in her body. She did not show any sign of panic, shock, or anxiety. She was talking in a monotone, all the way through. I don't believe that she thought I suspected her, not at that time. I had read John Gallagher's statement and had ruled out him, along with the family members, simply because of the layout of the house. It was so small. There was no way that they, or anyone else, could have come in without her knowing. And she herself was admitting in her broken English that she would have heard or seen if anyone else had been downstairs. She was adamant about that.

"I asked her what she thought happened. She said she did not know. I asked if she was covering for someone, and she said no. I was sitting there trying to rationalize: Maybe she had a boyfriend come in. But then I thought: She has only been here a month. How the hell could she have developed that kind of relationship in a month? It was very important for me to know where she was when the fire started, but I could never get a definitive answer. She was either feeding cats in one room or playing with cats in another. I knew she was withholding something because that part of her story kept coming out differently."

Johnson was about an hour into this session with Olivia when the police chief arrived. Paul Oliva went straight to his office off the same first-floor corridor as the detectives' room, to wait there until the officers who had been at the fire scene were ready to report to him. Police protocol constrained him from walking into the detectives' room and listening to the interrogation, but after a while Bruce Johnson stopped by the chief's office, leaving Olivia in the brief custody of Betsy Hoagland. Johnson summarized what she had told him, and what he had observed. When he described her singed eyelashes the chief became excited. Oliva had a ready understanding of the dynamics of combustion.

"Bruce, that could be the most crucial piece of evidence in this entire case," he exclaimed.

Back in the detectives' room, Johnson asked Olivia where she was standing when she put out the fire in her room. Was she at the side of her bed, or at the foot of it? At the foot, she replied. Johnson was thinking: But the bed has a footboard at waist level to a person of Olivia's height. She could not have bent over it low enough to get her eyelashes singed. No way. And surely no one would lean directly over a substantial blaze with a fire extinguisher in hand, spraying chemical foam. It would be instinctive to turn the head away. He looked for burns on her hands and saw none.

"If she had told me that she was at the side of her bed when she put out the fire I might have believed that was how she got her eyelashes singed," he related. "But I asked where she was standing again and again, and she was dead sure."

She told him that she became aware of the fire in her room shortly after 5:00 P.M. Johnson tried repeatedly to get her to account for the previous half hour after she put Kristie down to sleep, but her accounts continued to vary. She returned to a consistent story when describing the fire on her bed and the locked nursery door, and gave an accurate report of her conversation with the desk sergeant in the Mount Pleasant police department who argued that 5 West Lake Drive did not exist.

She told of John Gallagher's arrival, and how he broke into the nursery "with his feet." She noticed that Leah's door was also closed, but was not alarmed by this because it seemed to her that Leah usually left it shut. She said she was not familiar with Leah's room, having entered it only once to borrow an iron which Leah had been using. Apparently she had no idea that another fire was raging there. It was only from under the nursery door that she said she saw smoke.

By this time a small group had gathered in the police chief's office. Louis Alagno and Joe Butler had come in from the fire scene, along with two assistant district attorneys. Butler told them why he was convinced this was arson, explaining how the fires were probably set. Bruce Johnson stopped by on his way to refreshing himself with a can of soda from the lunch room, and filled them in on Olivia's story.

"She keeps denying any knowledge of the fire," he told them.

They all assumed that Kristie was dead before the blaze began. The thought that a living baby was deliberately set on fire was unacceptably abhorrent to everyone in the room.

"We could not believe that anyone would do that," Paul Oliva related. "Our understanding went along the lines that something must have happened to the baby before the fire. We assumed this girl did not intend to kill the baby. We heard Joe Butler's theory about the infant seat having been on the girl's bed when that fire was set, but I did not agree with him because there would have been burns on her from picking it up and taking it to the nursery.

"We discussed it back and forth, trying to figure what the hell happened. This was a twenty-year-old girl, not much more than a child herself. We had some checks and balances with the father coming into the house for lunch, and the gas man's delivery. But there was still a lot of time unaccounted for. We wondered if she was doing something with someone who came in the house. We even thought she might have been raped, and was ashamed to say. I told Bruce to have her clothing checked.

"We went over what we had: the matches left at the scene, her admission that she was alone in the house, her statement that she gave the baby twelve ounces of formula which sounded more like she was trying to explain away time than an actual fact, her conflicting accounts of where she was when the fire started. But most of all, the singed eyelashes."

Back in his favorite role of detective, Oliva picked up on a clue which everyone else had missed. "This girl calls the police and is screaming fire," he remarked to the others. "She has already put out the fire on her bed. How the hell does she know that a fire is raging behind a locked door in the other room?"

"Because she saw smoke coming from under it," someone suggested.

"The fire was near the window," Oliva countered. "And smoke goes up. It does not come out at the bottom of a door unless the room is saturated. And when a fire is really raging the smoke is minimal." The police chief had not yet heard John Gallagher's account of seeing flames, not smoke, reflected on the tiled floor beneath the nursery door, even after Olivia had telephoned for help.

All this added up to a persuasive collection of circumstantial evidence, in addition to the direct evidence of Olivia's singed eyelashes. There was a strong feeling in the room that she was the arsonist.

Louis Alagno commented: "If this girl had said that she fell asleep in front of the TV and was wakened by the smoke alarm in the hallway, there could be some doubt about her involvement. But the fact that she said she was alert and busy around the house, there's no way she could not have heard an intruder."

Paul Oliva was faced with a decision which might have waited until tomorrow if Olivia Riner had not been a foreign citizen. If she were an American he might have let her go, keeping a careful watch on her while his department tried to find more evidence. It must surely exist among the ashes of that fire, but the search could not begin until daylight. He dared not take that risk with Olivia, and could not hold her overnight without charges. This left him no option but to have her arrested. Who knew what friends she had who might spirit her off to Kennedy Airport and on the next plane to Switzerland?

Bruce Johnson was in his office down the corridor, still trying to extract a confession, when shortly after 10:00 P.M. his private line telephone rang. It was Brian Dwyer calling from the fire scene to tell him about the odor of paint thinner which he and Robert Miliambro had just smelled on the fragment of Kristie's diaper. Dwyer thought that the diaper had been saturated with the chemical. Johnson muttered a quick thank-you and rang off, not wanting Olivia to hear of this dramatic discovery. He went back to the chief's office for another brief conference, returned to the detectives' room, advised Olivia of her legal rights, and at 10:30 P.M. told her that she was under arrest for arson.

9

_____

For the past twenty-five years it has been essential U.S. police procedure to read what has become known as the Miranda warning at the time of an arrest. Like most detectives, Bruce Johnson had the words committed to memory. They were also printed on a white card which he took from his desk drawer and handed to Olivia.

"You have the right to remain silent and refuse to answer questions. Anything you do say may be used against you in a court of law. You have the right to consult a lawyer before speaking to the police, and to have a lawyer present during any questioning now or in the future. If you cannot afford to hire an attorney, one will be provided for you without cost.

"You can decide to stop answering questions at any time. Do you understand each of these rights that I have explained to you?"

"Some I don't," she told him.

"What don't you understand?"

"Some words."

"What words don't you understand?"

"What's remain?"

"Be quiet, you can just be quiet."

"What's court of law?"

"That is the, ah, the American judicial system."

"The lawyer?"

"The lawyer is someone who can represent you for legal purposes. Now with reading these, do you understand these now?"

"Can I—?"

"Sure."

"What's afford to hire?"

"If you don't have money the court will appoint an attorney for you."

"Oh."

"If you have money and want to hire your own attorney—"

"Yes."

"You may do so."

"Oh. Decide?"

"Decide?"

"Yes."

"It's a yes or no. It's up to you whether you, you can decide to stop or to, to answer questions or not answer the questions."

"That all?"

"Yes." He turned the card over. "On this side, do you understand all those?"

"I think I do, yes."

"Okay." Continuing with the formal warning, he added: "Having explained these rights to you, do you wish to still talk to me? I'm going to ask you the same questions I have been asking since I've seen you."

"I can't say anything different."

"You can't say anything different?"

"No."

"So you wish to still discuss it with me?"

"I can talk, but I can't say anything different."

"Okay, okay. You can talk but you're not going to say anything different, right?"

"Yes."

Months later it would be argued whether, coming as she did from a disciplined society which encouraged cooperation with the police, Olivia really understood that she did not have to say another word. A more experienced traveler would have insisted upon being put in touch with the nearest Swiss Consulate, but her behavior continued to be compliant and unprotesting. After formally charging her, Bruce Johnson again inquired whether she wanted food, drink, or to go to the bathroom, and again she declined. It was beyond his comprehension how she could hold out for so long. From time to time he himself needed a break.

On the ledge behind his desk was the dual-cassette tape recorder, which he had just switched on. Being closest to him, it picked up his voice more strongly than hers, so that when the tape was played back some of her answers were inaudible. During the next fifty-seven minutes, all of them now on the record, he had her go over the afternoon's events once more.

She seemed almost eager to tell him the domestic details of her day, as in her description of Bill arriving home for lunch: "He come into Kristie's room and talk with her. . . . Then he go upstairs and she begin drooling badly, but not very, very much. . . . Sometimes she make noises and then you take the mobiler away"—she was referring to a toy mobile—"and try to put her on her stomach, but then she like it that way, and then she don't like it. And then I put her on the shoulder and then she got quiet. She looks around. She eats her finger. . . ."

And again when she prepared the first of the two bottles of formula: "I take the bottle with eight ounces and she eats about five, five and one half ounces. Then she make . . . two big burps. Then she was playing a little bit, and she was a little bit not really hungry. She wanted a little bit to eat. I give her a little bit, then she sleep and I put her in the seat. . . . And then I give her the pacifier. . . . And then I go in my room. And the door is open. . . . I can look from my room if it is all right. She sleeps where I can see her. When you go in room, sometimes she wakes up. Bill looks in room and see that she is sleeping and then he waitens, quiet, like he wants to see her and says 'See you later.' "

She had a precise memory about Kristie waking up and being fed the second bottle that afternoon: "I go upstairs and put her in the swing because I want to make another bottle. . . . And then she was in the swing, and she was happy in the swing, and . . . I take the bottle with me downstairs . . . and I go upstairs and put her out from the swing and I go downstairs to the living room. And I make TV on because she likes, she likes the sound . . . and then she a little bit hungry so I give her a bottle. But she don't really want to drink. She wants to go on shoulder, so take her on my shoulder. And then she was a little bit more hungry and I give her the bottle . . . and then I play with her, talk with her, and then she sleep in my arms."

It sounded so innocent and dutiful. Responding to Johnson's questions, Olivia went on to tell how she put Kristie back in the infant seat on the nursery rug before feeding the cats in the laundry room. In this final version she had let two of the four cats out of the house and was in the living room playing with O.J. and watching TV when "I see Oliver run out from my room and I go to look why and I see fire in my bed."

She described running upstairs to the kitchen for a fire extinguisher, conveying the panic she felt when she was not immediately able to make it work. "I pull the ring out. I don't know what work where. Who from who. I took, I took out and I try to make it the first time. It doesn't go. I don't know why. At first it doesn't, and then it goes . . ."

After putting out the fire, she said, "I try to make the light on in my room because it is dark. . . . The light didn't go, and then . . . I see the door from Kristie's room is locked, closed. And I try. It's locked. I try. It's locked." With every successive word "locked" her voice rose a little higher. "Then I run and then I see the smoke. The smoke. And I run for my room and look for telephone number. A little note for the telephone numbers. And then around, around the living room for a phone to call operator and tell him fire. And then I tell another man and tell him fire and give him address. And he asked me many times . . .

"And then the telephone rings. The man say he has no address for Five West Lake Drive. Don't get it and I must tell him where the others is. Where the house is and I tell him near from Nannyhagen Road. The first house. Then I put it down. And then, so maybe they can find it, it's dark, and I run upstairs and make light. All the lights I make."

As soon as she got back downstairs, she opened the front door to let Oliver out. Then John Gallagher arrived, and O.J. scampered out of the house as John ran in.

"What did he say to you?" Johnson asked.

"Oh, I don't know what he say. I was very nervous. I don't know what John say."

"Did you tell him there was a fire?"

"Yes. I say fire and he, he say he sees the smoke because he runs and says fire and I say Kristie's in the room, in her room. And he runs inside . . ."

Olivia remembered the next few seconds differently from John. He had said that he saw the baby surrounded by fire the instant he kicked the door open. She stated that he immediately came back out of the nursery, asking whether Kristie was in her crib. "And I say no, in the car seat. And he goes back." She gave the impression of him fumbling around in a smoke-filled room. In John's description there was no mistaking where the baby was, and it was his use of the extinguisher which created the smoke. A minor discrepancy, Johnson acknowledged, but it added to the confusion of her tale.

"Prior to John coming up the driveway, there was nobody in the house with you?" he asked her.

"I see nobody. I don't see someone."

"You had nobody over for coffee or tea or—"

"No."

"There was nobody in the house?"

"No."

He repeated the question several times, always getting a negative response.

"Then you don't know how the fire started on your bed?"

"No."

"And you don't know how a fire started in Kristie's room?"

"No, I don't."

"And her door got closed?"

"No."

"And the smoke coming out from under Kristie's door?"

"Yes, I see only smoke."

"What color smoke was that?"

"It was darken. I, I think was the same color like mine because it was dark there. I don't make the light on. I don't know."

The taping finished at 11:37 P.M. Toward the end of it Betsy Hoagland went off duty and another civilian dispatcher, Marie Solimando, took her place in the detectives' room. Middle-aged and motherly, she had a regular job on the desk which insulated her from the ugly side of police work. Now she was suddenly flung into it, called in on her day off, willing but unprepared.

"They phoned me late that evening and said they wanted me because there was a female prisoner. We have only one woman police officer and she was on vacation. I live just up the hill, and if there's a chance of overtime I am there. I had no idea of what I was going into, and I was very upset when I found what had happened to that baby. I was sitting in the detectives' room shaking, trying to hold back the tears. But this girl was not weeping. She was just very quiet, and looking down a lot. Bruce was being very patient with her, speaking to her softly. There was no yelling and screaming, just questions. Her whole behavior struck me as odd because she was not that upset. My God, if I was watching someone's child and that child just got hurt I would be devastated."

After turning off his tape recorder, Bruce Johnson ventured the question that had been on his mind for more than three hours: How did Olivia get her eyelashes singed? She looked startled, thought for a moment, then said it must have happened when she put out the fire in her room. Once more he asked where she was standing, and she confirmed that she used the extinguisher from the foot of her bed. Marie Solimando walked across to take a look, and noticed that the singed ends of her lashes were an ashy white. Johnson brought out his Polaroid, took a shot of Olivia's face, waited for the result, wasn't satisfied with it, and took more photographs with his 35mm camera.

Olivia's ordeal was far from over. Next he told her to undress and left her alone with Marie. Scott Carpenter had already been sent back to the Fischer house to bring her a change of clothes, and what he picked out—heavily patched blue jeans and a black sweatshirt with a bizarre logo in front—did not improve Olivia's downcast, almost sullen appearance when she was photographed at her arraignment the next day.

"If the outfit didn't coordinate, I'm sorry," Carpenter remarked tartly. He had taken what came first from her considerable collection of pants and casual tops. Returning to the Fischer house the following day, Bruce Johnson would be amazed to find about twenty-five pairs of jeans in her wardrobe, but not one skirt. Even so, she clearly put some thought into her daily style of dressing down. After Marie Solimando had drawn the window shades in the detectives' room Olivia removed her black pants, a hooded purple shirt, and purple canvas sneakers, which together made an interesting outfit. Then she took off her underwear. Marie folded the clothing and put it in a brown paper bag. Subsequent laboratory analysis would find no traces of flammable liquid or sexual activity on anything Olivia was wearing; however, the tests for accelerants were not considered conclusive because there was a delay of several days before they were carried out.

While she changed, Johnson had another conversation with his chief. They were joined by Sergeant Brian Dwyer, just back from the fire scene with news of his discovery of the disturbed and emptied cans of paint thinner and other accelerants in Bill Fischer's storage closet. Everything was pointing to this arson being an inside job, and to Olivia Riner as the culprit. Bruce Johnson still hoped to get a confession that night. In common police experience, only the most hardened criminals hold out through hours of interrogation. Usually there comes a point of exhaustion when the guilty give in.

"Let me take a shot at her," Paul Oliva offered. He had been itching to do so all evening.

They went back to the detectives' room and tackled the prisoner together, Bruce Johnson playing the tough guy and Paul Oliva acting avuncular. It was their strategy that, needled by Johnson's change of attitude, Olivia might confide in the chief. Soon Brian Dwyer joined in the questioning; three strong men verbally battering a shy young girl who had only a limited knowledge of their language and their laws. She continued to give direct answers until the questioning got close to the fire in the nursery; then again she looked into her lap, letting her hair fall forward and screen her face.

"I questioned her for six hours," Johnson recounted. "For four of them I was very gentle with her, and for two I acted like a bastard. But nothing worked."

He could not relate her behavior to anything he had ever seen. "I was watching her carefully, and sometimes she seemed to be almost in a trancelike state. I would ask a question, and she was out there someplace, so I would have to repeat it. But she always had an answer."

Dwyer concurred: "It was like the fire didn't happen and the baby was not involved." He added: "The thing that got to me that night was her lack of concern about the baby. At the first sign of fire you would have expected her to grab the child and run screaming to a neighbor, not to look for a fire extinguisher and a telephone."

Shortly after midnight Bruce Johnson told her that Kristie was dead. Not in so many words, but harshly and directly. "Did you kill the baby?" As Paul Oliva remarked, there is no delicate way to put that question.

Her denial was vigorous, conveying no sense of grief or shock. He pressed on, enumerating the ways Kristie could have died, assuming her dead before the fire started.

"Did you drop the baby? Did you strike the baby? Did you suffocate the baby? Did the baby choke?"

The answer was always a vehement no, yet Johnson kept returning to the same questions. Repeatedly he asked whether the baby choked, thinking of the unusual amount of formula Olivia had fed her.

He asked whether she was sexually attracted to anyone in the Fischer family, or to John Gallagher; whether she was jealous of Leah or anyone else. All these suggestions were firmly denied. He accused her directly of setting fire to the house, and she protested: "I didn't light no fire." Again and again she said this, her fractured English emphasizing her negative response. Was she covering for someone else, even (in a question he would come to regret) John Gallagher? No, no, no, she told him. She didn't light no fire, and she didn't know who did. In a house where she believed herself to be alone with a baby and four cats, bedrooms were set ablaze and doors locked as if by some supernatural force. Representing herself as the conscientious baby-sitter, too watchful to doze or to slip out of the house, she allowed for no possibility of a human error which might have let a criminal steal in.

In the course of the evening Bruce Johnson had learned a little of Olivia's background, but nothing to suggest a motive or a sense of her emotional state. She told him of her former job in Switzerland as a clerical assistant to a pediatrician, said that she enjoyed looking after babies, and that she loved Kristie very much. Yet she seemed utterly untouched by the infant's death. He judged that she was too alert to be in shock.

From midnight on his tactic was to interrogate Olivia for fifteen or twenty minutes, to leave her to think things over for a bit while the three officers conferred in another room, then to come back and renew the questioning. This achieved very little. She kept telling them that she couldn't say anything different. And didn't.

After a while the others gave up, leaving him to continue interrogating her alone. He was running out of steam, but she looked alert enough to go on all night. At 3:00 A.M. he conceded defeat. In all these hours he had been unable to establish any kind of rapport with her. It helped him to know that Paul Oliva had done no better.

"None of us could get close to her," Johnson remarked months later. "But I had no doubt that she was guilty. Her, or someone else inside her."

His last words to her, at about 3:30 A.M., were "Olivia, you need help." Then he drove home to Valhalla, utterly exhausted.

Olivia spent the rest of the night in the female holding cell at the end of the hallway from the detectives' office. It was a very small room with blank walls on three sides and iron bars on the fourth, a toilet and washbasin behind a screen, and a bare wooden bench which was scarcely wide enough to serve as a cot. No blankets or pillow were provided. The New York State Department of Corrections does not require these comforts for overnight prisoners.

Olivia did not show outrage, anxiety, fear, or frustration at being locked in this place: none of the usual emotions which police experience from those who claim to be innocent. She stretched out on the bench and lay quietly on her stomach, her head turned away from Marie Solimando who sat on the other side of the bars, keeping an uneasy watch.

It was close to 4:00 A.M. when Paula Johnson heard her husband's car turn into the driveway, and the garage door rumble open, followed by Bruce's tread on the stairs: the sound of a heavily built man trying to come in quietly. She had been sleeping fitfully as she always did when he was out on a difficult assignment. She was worrying not only about his safety but also about the tragedy which had summoned him back to work almost eleven hours earlier. What he explained to her at that time was all he had been told—that there was a house fire in Thornwood in which an infant had perished. All evening Paula had been privately praying: "Please don't let this be a family I know." She had lived in the area since she was twelve, and had a lot of acquaintances. Some police wives would have driven to the scene to find out, but she would not embarrass her husband by getting in the way. The Johnsons had a close and caring marriage which respected each other's need for space.

She smelled the smoke on his clothing as he came into the bedroom, and was instantly reminded of a house fire which had happened years earlier, next to their former home. The same kind of odor had clung to her neighbor's clothes, and she had not forgotten it. She hoped Bruce would dump his in the laundry before coming to bed. Keeping the thought to herself, she asked him about the fire, and the name of the family. He told her Fischer, which was not familiar to her, and she felt relieved.

"It was a baby," he said. "And this is looking more and more like an arson case."

When she awoke again at 7:00 A.M. he was lying quite still, staring at the ceiling.

"Did you sleep?" she asked.

"No. I don't even know why I bothered coming home." He got up and began to prepare for another long day at police headquarters, knowing that his investigation had barely begun.

10

Bad news travels even faster in a society where young people carry personal pagers. At about 6:30 P.M. on December 2, Michael Gallagher was beeped by his girlfriend Jennifer, who lived very close to the Fischers. She told him about the fire, and how his brother John had tried to rescue the baby. John had just walked across to her house, crying so hard he could barely speak. Michael, who was visiting a friend in the next village of Hawthorne, rushed to Thornwood to find his brother still sobbing incoherently, and Leah in the same state, sitting on the tailgate of John's parked truck.

The news was quickly relayed to Mahopac where Carol Gallagher was expecting John and Leah for dinner. Instantly her concern for the two of them overwhelmed her nagging worry about the throat surgery she was to undergo the following day.

"Johnny tried saving the baby, but she was dead," Mike, her youngest son, told her on the telephone.

"How's he doing?" she asked.

"Not good. He'll call you tonight."

For the rest of the evening she waited anxiously, knowing that it would be useless to try calling the Fischers. There would be so much confusion in that house even if the telephone was working.

As the mother of four young adults still living at home, all of them with friends frequently coming and going, Carol was used to minor chaos and crises. Her husband, also named John, and their three sons were all auto mechanics, which meant that men in grimy work clothes were constantly wandering into her well-kept kitchen, raiding the refrigerator for a can of beer, or fixing a sandwich. Most days the broad driveway to the Gallaghers' small rural house resembled a parking lot,

86

with cars that belonged there and cars being worked on, and in the early mornings vehicles often had to be juggled around before Carol could get out her own to drive to her work as a payroll supervisor.

In the face of all this, she had become virtually unflappable, but on the night of the fire it was difficult for her to stay calm. For all of his twenty-six years her oldest son had been very close to her. She knew about the sensitivity that he covered with flippancy and bravado, and how badly his experience in the Fischers' nursery would have affected him. It was about 11:30 P.M. when he telephoned.

"Mom." It was a tone of voice from his childhood, when he had something difficult to tell her and didn't know how to begin.

"Yes, Johnny. Are you all right?"

"I'm all right." He did not sound convincing.

"Are you sure?"

"Yes."

"What happened?"

"Mom, she set the baby on fire. Olivia set the baby on fire."

Carol was shocked. "I can't believe that," she told him. "I can't believe that anyone would do such a thing."

Now he was sobbing again. "Mom, that little tiny baby. I was there when she was being born."

"Are you sure it was Olivia?"

"It had to be. There was nobody else in the house. Everything of Leah's was burned out."

"Where is Olivia now?"

"She's at the police station. Mom, I tried putting the fire out but I couldn't."

He told her not to expect him that night. He wanted to stay close to Leah, who, along with Bill and Denise, had taken refuge with Bill's sister, Barbara, and her husband, Jim Donnelly, at the family home next to Fischer's Garage. It was the obvious place for them to go, not just because Barbara and Jim could be counted on in a crisis but also because, in an almost spiritual sense, Fischers of their generation still thought of this shabby old house of their childhood as home.

"Please do me a favor," Carol told her son. "Call me again in the morning before I leave for the hospital."

Later she recalled that "the hardest part of that whole conversation was sitting in my kitchen hearing him crying, and not being able to put my arms around him."

His morning telephone call missed her by a few minutes. Accompanied by her twenty-two-year-old daughter, Renee, Carol had already left for the hospital, feeling more worried than she cared to admit, on account of John. The surgery to remove vocal polyps was considered unpleasantly routine, but the timing could not have been worse. Just when she was most anxious to be supportive to her son, she was told not to use her voice for the next two weeks. Advised to stay in the hospital overnight, she insisted on returning home that evening in the belief that even her silent and groggy presence might be of help. Renee had made her the thoughtful gift of a slate, as a means of communication.

The following morning, Wednesday, she was lying on the living-room couch when John and Leah walked in. John still looked shaken. Leah's face was deathly white. Together they had been sifting through the ruins of the Fischer home, trying to salvage a few belongings. The essential structure of the house was still standing, but heavy smoke damage had left pathetically little worth rescuing, particularly in Leah's room.

"How are you feeling?" John asked his mother.

Carol wrote on the slate: "I am okay. How are you?"

A little boy again, he replied: "Mom, hold me and hug me."

She got up, hugged him, and tried to say something comforting, but the words would not come. She mouthed the question to Leah: "Are you all right?"

"Yes," Leah replied, uncertainly.

Picking up the slate again, Carol wrote: "Is there anything I can do for you?"

"No," Leah replied. "Is there anything we can do for you?"

Carol recalled: "It was about three weeks later. Maybe a month. We were all sitting around talking one night, my husband, myself, and the kids. I don't think Leah was here. Johnny was sitting on the couch. Somehow the conversation came up about Olivia, I don't remember how. And that was when he described what happened. He said: 'I went into that room and bent down to get the baby, and, Mom, I saw flames coming out of her eyes.' "

PART TWO

THE FAMILY

11

Even before she learned of the fire, Barbara Donnelly had been dreading this week. This was Monday, and Wednesday would be the first anniversary of Kim Marie's death. The pain of it had become so much part of her that she had almost forgotten what it was like to live without it. And in a way she did not want to let it go. She and Jim clung to Kimmy's memory, knowing there would never be another child. Kimmy was the last of their three, born on the brink of their middle age, so precious to them because her coming had been a surprise. A gift fashioned by God himself, Sister Laura had said in her eulogy at the funeral. On this gray Monday in December, a year after her death, it seemed beyond coincidence and the worst of fate's cruelties that a similar tragedy should shatter the lives of Barbara's brother Bill and his wife, Denise.

In the Donnellys' living room, where Bill and Denise and Leah and John took refuge on that night of the fire, there was a photograph of Kimmy on top of the large television set, a studio portrait of a pale and delicate child wearing a blue and white pinafore dress and a little pink turban which she had fashioned for herself. The photographer had captured a wistful expression and a sweet, uncertain smile, creating an image so enduringly present that whenever the family watched TV Kimmy became part of the scene. Kimmy presiding over the talk shows and the ball game and the evening news. Kimmy still smiling at them when the program was over and the screen had gone blank.

"You can see where her hair was beginning to grow back," Jim would remark to visitors, pointing to a wisp of brown below the turban. It seemed all the more poignant that parts of her were getting better when so much of her was dying.

91

She was ill, on and off, from the time she was three. At first it was thought that a virus had left her anemic, or that she had mononucleosis. For the next four years she was in and out of hospitals, and toward the end, mostly in. While treating her at home Barbara learned a lot about platelets and blood counts and the effects of chemotherapy. All this time she kept asking the question: Why Kimmy? Could she have been cured if the correct diagnosis had been made at the beginning? And was it merely a clustering of the statistics which made the figures for childhood leukemia in this part of Westchester seem abnormally high? Was there an environmental cause? Something they should have known about or done differently? Or was it the arbitrary nature of the Almighty? Barbara sometimes suspected this, and said so bitterly. Jim was the one with the strong church affiliation, and because of it she had kept her promise to bring up their children as Roman Catholics. She had been grateful for the comfort of the church during Kimmy's last illness, particularly in the presence of Sister Laura, who sat with the child day after day, helping her to rejoice in the life that was left to her and, as the days ran out, preparing her to die without being afraid. Death is not a topic to be avoided on a children's cancer ward.

This nun fulfilled her ministry so beautifully that one day Kimmy made a drawing of butterflies, and happily explained to her mother that they used to be hairy worms. She said that they turned into brightly colored butterflies after they died, and became more free and lovely. Soon after this Barbara took her daughter to a toy store to select anything she wanted for her seventh birthday, and Kimmy chose a little pink plastic suitcase. Was she sure that was enough of a present? she was asked. Kimmy was sure. Then what would she like to put in it? The child replied that where she was going she would not need anything in her suitcase. Nine weeks later, with her parents at her hospital bedside, she quietly fell into a final sleep.

It was beyond Barbara's understanding that God would let her die when so many people were praying for her: everyone at the Holy Name of Jesus Church in Valhalla, and at Kimmy's school, and all those friends and neighbors. While Barbara's faith had wavered, Jim became a regular churchgoer again. He would get mad at God, so helplessly enraged that he would want to yell at Him; then day after day he would go alone to an early mass, hoping to find healing and peace. Barbara repressed her anger, and held on to the hurt.

Like all the Fischers, she did not show her feelings. Of the three in her generation she was the middle child, Bill the eldest, and Bob the baby. There was no mistaking their sibling relationship. They all had well-proportioned bodies which tended to a muscular leanness, fresh complexions, and light blue eyes of a rare intensity. Their faces were like portraits in pastels, softly blurred at the edges, but their eyes were drawn with a firm hand and a brilliant crayon, the color of aquamarine. People remembered those eyes long after the faces had been forgotten. Their father, Willie, had Fischer eyes, and Kimmy inherited them. "The brightest, bluest eyes you ever saw," in Sister Laura's description.

In her early childhood, and through all the periods of remission, Kimmy and her maternal grandfather were frequent companions. By now in his seventies, he had been a widower since middle age. Barbara had nursed her mother through terminal cancer, and shared the two-family house with her parents almost from the beginning of her marriage to Jim. After his wife died, Willie moved downstairs to give Barbara's growing family the larger apartment. He was quiet, gentle, proud and self-sufficient; characteristics which were evident in his children. They called him Dad or Poppy, but he was Willie to everyone else, and had the name embroidered on the Fischer's Garage work shirts which were still his everyday attire, even though he was supposed to be retired.

For as long as she was well enough, Kimmy lived in his shadow. Illness had caused her to drop out of school in the middle of first grade so she lost the opportunity to form childhood friendships, and there was no one of her age group in the family. Willie lovingly filled the gap. She followed him around the garage workshop where he loved to putter, fixing things, and she helped him with gardening. On fine days he took her to the boatyard at Mamaroneck where he kept his elderly fishing boat, *Billy Boy II,* and they would go out on Long Island Sound together. He also owned a small rowboat, and delighted her by naming it *Kimmy.*

In the intensity of caring for Kimmy, Barbara and Jim's older children had to take second place. Jimmy, who used to be the baby of the family, was going through the growing pains of adolescence when Kimmy's illness struck. In early childhood he had been the focus of his parents' attention because he had been so tiny and premature at birth that they feared he might not survive. Now, as a strapping teenager, he needed a different kind of support, but they had little time to give him because they were taking turns keeping all-night vigil in a hospital room. One relative likened Jimmy to "a lost soul looking for someone."

Debra, the oldest, was better able to deal with the stress, and courageously volunteered for a bone-marrow transplant in the hope that it would help her sister. Her type matched Kimmy's, and Barbara's didn't. Barbara minded about being rejected, wanting to do more when she was already doing so much. She kept watch at Kimmy's hospital bedside for weeks on end, with Jim relieving her in the evenings so that she could get some fresh air. Even then she was afraid to go far, and would stand on the sidewalk outside the hospital nervously smoking the cigarette she had been craving all these hours, and not enjoying it. Jim organized his days off for Wednesdays, her bingo night, to let her go home and have a game with her women friends while he stayed overnight at the hospital in her place. The one positive thing to come out of all this was a mutual respect for the strength of their marriage.

"In the children's cancer ward we saw marriages torn apart before our eyes," Jim recalled. "There would be group meetings to try and help the families, and mostly it was the husbands who could not handle it well. A little girl in one family had to have her leg removed, and her father had not visited her for five months."

Willie Fischer was another who had his problems with hospital visiting, but Jim was understanding about that. "My father-in-law does not like hospitals. He put his brother in the hospital and his brother died. He put his wife in the hospital and she died. He did not have a good relationship with hospitals. If he would come to see Kimmy in the hospital it was an event. And that was not because it was Kimmy. It was because of how he felt about hospitals."

Kimmy went into remission for eleven months after the bone-marrow transplant. Then, when recovery seemed most likely, the symptoms returned. Barbara sometimes wondered how Debby felt about the ultimate failure of the surgery, but there were so many things that people in this family could not talk about, so much unspoken pain. It seemed easier to deal with that way. Putting it into words might have forced them to stop pretending that the hurt was bearable. All of them suffered vicariously through onslaughts of radiation, chemotherapy, and the agony of watching this frail child endure from one painkilling injection to the next. Some memories would last their lifetimes. For two days Kimmy lost her vision, and wailed in terror: "Mommy, they have taken away my eyes!" Then there was the hesitant offer of a new treatment. "The doctor said it might help, or that it might kill her because her heart was very weak," Jim recounted. "Well, Jesus, what kind of decision is that to make?"

There were also some comforting memories. As the Donnellys' money ran out, Kimmy's illness became the focus of local charities. It was amazing, and profoundly touching, how many people cared. One organization sent the family on a vacation trip to Florida so that Kimmy could have her wish to see Disney World. She loved the experience and wanted to go back, but was never again well enough. Another group, Friends of Kim Marie, was formed to help with medical expenses. Several other friends organized a benefit concert, and one of them drove around the neighborhood with a big sign on his car, "We Love You, Kim." Everything possible was done to make this child comfortable and happy because so little could be done to make her well.

When Debby was married to Edward "Rick" Huntington, the ceremony was delayed while her father got six-year-old Kimmy out of the hospital for a few hours to be her sister's flower girl. The permission was at first refused because of Kimmy's low blood count that day, but with the insistently persuasive tongue of his Irish ancestors, Jim argued until her doctor reluctantly gave consent. Meantime Debby sat at home in her white bridal gown, waiting. Willie had gone out fishing. In all the excitement and tension the family had forgotten to tell him the time of his granddaughter's wedding.

Someone drove to the boatyard to get him, and Kimmy was painfully helped into her bridesmaid's dress. With it she wore a brown wig which had been styled for the occasion, the tresses intertwined with satin combs and sprigs of baby's breath. She was so excited, and they were all so proud that she managed to walk down the aisle alone. A friend of the family walked behind her, just in case. The Donnellys did not know it then, but she was coming out of remission for the last time. The cancer had spread to her knees. Soon after the wedding she lost the use of her legs, and never walked again.

Debby's wedding was also the occasion of an awkward first encounter between the two women in Bill Fischer's life: Grada Fischer and Denise Verrant. They were bound to meet sometime, and it was probably easiest in a crowd of people who were trying to be happy. Grada's marriage to Bill had lasted for twenty-two years, and no one had been more surprised than Barbara when her brother came to tell her it was ending. From what the extended Fischer family had seen, the two of them got along fine. No hint of discord, no other loves in their lives. It was a shock to their relatives to realize that Grada had been waiting for the youngest child, Leah, to reach eighteen so that she could lead her own life and develop a career. To their intense surprise she moved out of the Thornwood house, rented a studio apartment in New York City, and went to work for a small lecture agency, where she did so well that she was soon managing it.

She had no quarrel with Bill. "He is a very nice person," she said. "But it was a marriage going in different directions. I became more business oriented and culturally oriented. Bill is a loner and an outdoors man. We did not have anything in common anymore, and once the children were grown we no longer had them. We split up as amicably as any couple can split up. I had known him since I was fifteen and saw no reason to close off the relationship." It was an easily arranged divorce in which Bill bought Grada's half share of the house.

After she left, Leah and Troy continued to live there with their father. Two years later Denise came into Bill's life and moved into the household. They were clearly committed to one another, but marriage had not yet been mentioned. Inevitably there was friction with Bill's children. Troy moved out, but Leah chose to stay. And here they all were at a wedding, Grada concerned about Leah's welfare in this unconventional situation, and Denise feeling her way along the edges of an extended family which still loved Grada. Barbara and Jim were particularly close to Grada at this time, since with typical generosity she let them use her Manhattan apartment whenever Kimmy was in a nearby hospital.

Kimmy made one more public appearance before she died. In the privacy of the family she received her First Communion, followed by a larger gathering to celebrate her seventh birthday. The entire event was held in the Valhalla ambulance headquarters because a church ceremony might have been too exhausting for a child in a wheelchair. Barbara, still harboring her personal doubts about God, was grateful for what the sacrament meant to Kimmy. And, unexpectedly, to herself. "Although I was not Catholic I needed for her to make her Communion because I knew what was coming," she said.

Debby missed the event. About to have her first baby, she telephoned Kimmy from the hospital birthing room. "She was mad at me because it was her First Communion and I could not be there," Debby remembered. When Kimmy put down the phone the guests gathered around to ask: "What did she have?"

"She didn't have it yet," Kimmy replied. "She just called to say happy birthday."

Barbara and Jim's first grandchild, a boy, was born at 9:20 on that evening of September 30, 1990. After the party they went to see him. It was an irony and a blessing that a new life should come into the family as Kimmy with her birthday pink suitcase was preparing to leave it. The baby was named Edward James which was soon abbreviated to E.J. Kimmy died on December 4. Jim and Barbara felt a kind of bleak relief that the "do not resuscitate" order which they had agonized over signing was not needed. "As it turned out, she did it her way," Jim said, with evident pride. "She just went to sleep after the show."

Willie took her death very hard, shutting himself in his room for two days until he was reminded to get ready for the funeral. He dressed, attended the service, then quickly excused himself, pleading a bad headache. Over the ensuing weeks he lost weight, aged perceptibly, and never mentioned Kimmy. "He had not felt able to visit her in the hospital, and was totally devastated," Grada said.

There was an open casket at the funeral, with Kimmy in her white Communion dress, and a cherished toy dog, Petey, seated facing her. Her uncle Bill, who had donated blood to try to save her, felt torn apart by the pathos of the sight. Debby drew comfort from the fact that her little sister looked better than she had looked in months. Barbara wanted to touch her, but couldn't. She had always felt such antipathy to the presence of death. She went through the day in a daze, silently staring ahead when friends and neighbors lined up to tell her how sorry they were. Afterward she remembered only crowds of faceless people, with no idea of how many or what they said. Jim was struck by the fact that "when you lose a child everyone worries about the mother, and has nothing to say to the father." He added: "It happened to me."

At Gate of Heaven Cemetery in Hawthorne, he and Barbara had already chosen a plot in a quiet valley, a place with flowers and trees where Kimmy would have enjoyed playing if she had been alive and well. And if all those other graves had not been there. There was a bench nearby where they could sit and feel close to her.

The day of the funeral was bitter, with a cutting wind. Leah shivered as they left the graveside.

"It's so cold to leave her here," she remarked to Bob's wife, Betsy.

"She isn't here," Betsy said firmly. "She's with God."

Leah seemed to be absorbing the thought. Her religious upbringing, like that of her parents, had been minimal. If God existed she couldn't accept that He had that much power over people's destinies. But it was an interesting idea. Bleakly, they all walked back to their cars for a family gathering at Barbara and Jim's house. The atmosphere there was one of deep sadness and irreplaceable loss. Barbara was very quiet. Like her father, she turned her grief inward. Jim kept busy, finding things to do.

"Emotions were very high," Debby remembered. "At that time I was still living at home, but I was twenty-three and I had a three-month-old child, and my father told me to go to my room because I had a row with my cousin Theresa."

Over the next few months it helped Barbara greatly to have her new grandson in the household. E.J. had such a startling resemblance to Kimmy in infancy that it was hard to tell their baby pictures apart. He even started to walk in the same funny way that she had done, teetering on his toes. The similarities were uncanny. And Barbara loved little children, even when she was not related to them. She had worked as an assistant in a nursery school, and from time to time earned extra money by looking after the children of working mothers in her own home. One of them was her nephew Christopher, an arrangement which had worked so well that Betsy wished it could have lasted longer, except that Kimmy became too ill for Barbara to continue. "My wife is happiest when she is taking care of children," Jim said. "She is like Mary Poppins. She can get kids to do things that their parents can't get them to do."

Early the following summer word went round the family that there would soon be another child. The way Bill told it was: "Denise is pregnant, and we are going to get married." He had always been a man of few words. The Fischer clan was less surprised about the unorthodox order of events than they were about Bill becoming a father again after twenty-two years. Fischers were very tolerant of one another's eccentricities. But Barbara couldn't resist teasing her brother, as he had teased her when she unexpectedly became pregnant with Kimmy at the age of thirty-eight. "So who's the dummy now?" she asked him.

When Kristie was three days old, Barbara and Jim visited Denise in White Plains Hospital. It was a Saturday evening and various friends were gathered around, eager to hold the new baby. When Jim's turn came the others were grouped in conversation around Denise's bed. Somebody asked who would be the godparents. Denise, who had long since turned away from her Roman Catholic upbringing, replied that she did not believe in imposing religion on a child, that there would be time enough for Kristie to decide about that when she was older.

Jim stood apart from them with the baby in his arms. Out of his own bitter experience he knew that there is not always time enough, that children can die. Denise, ecstatic over the birth of a beautiful, healthy daughter, was looking to the long future. Kristie learning to walk and talk. Kristie going to school and college. This child would have nothing but the best; Denise would see to that. Even before Kristie's birth she had assembled a lavish layette of clothes which she had pleasure in buying, clothes lovingly saved and passed down from her own family, clothes from the baby shower which had been Leah's generous surprise.

There was a paper cup of water on Denise's hospital bed table. On a compulsion which he did not fully understand, Jim turned away from the others, dipped his finger into the cup, made the sign of the cross on the baby's forehead, and quietly said the words of the only sacrament which a layperson can administer.

"I don't know why I did it," Jim recalled. "But I knew I couldn't let that baby out of my arms until I had baptized her. Afterward I wondered if I had done it right, if it would count. Then I went on a big guilt trip because I had done something behind the parents' back that they might not approve of. I went to speak to my priest about it, and he said it was all right."

He told Barbara about the baptism on their way home from the hospital. He thought she might be critical, and was pleasantly surprised when she said she felt relieved.

The following spring Debby and Rick moved out of the Donnellys' house to a place of their own in the nearby town of Ossining. Barbara took a part-time clerical job to help with the budget; Kimmy's medical expenses had drained their savings, and without E.J. in the house she was glad of another interest to fill her time. She still thought constantly of Kimmy, especially as the first anniversary of her death approached, obliterating all thoughts of Christmas. She used to love Christmas, and all the planning to make it a time for children in the family to remember. Now she dreaded it.

After serving dinner to her father on the evening of December 2, she went to work for a couple of hours. Willie returned to his basement apartment and, as usual, went to bed early. Barbara came back home at about 8:00 P.M. and was surprised to see Jim standing at the front door, anxiously waiting for her.

"What's the matter?" she asked.

"Your brother's house caught on fire," he told her.

Her mind flashed back to her father's remark when he came in for dinner, about how Bill had suddenly left work to deal with an emergency. At the time she had been concerned, but not seriously because her father did not seem to think there was anything to worry about.

"What?" she asked again, incredulous.

"Your brother's house caught on fire," Jim repeated. "And the baby is dead."

12

By the time Barbara and Jim reached West Lake Drive the blaze had been extinguished, but the fire trucks were still there and a lot of cleaning up remained to be done. They parked nearby and asked a fireman where they could find the family. Directed to the home of George and Kathryn Fries, they walked along the street in front of Bill's property to the house next door. At another time in her life Barbara would have felt impelled to take the route across her brother's broad front lawn to see for herself how badly his house was damaged. But tonight she could not bring herself to look at it. All she could think about was the dead baby.

They found Bill, Denise, Leah, and John Gallagher in the Frieses' basement family room where the larger Fischer family was gathering. Kathryn Fries was bustling round, serving coffee and snacks. Somehow she was managing to produce food out of a kitchen made chaotic by a steady stream of firemen coming in at the back door to use the telephone, the bathroom, or to beg a drink of water.

"What happened?" Barbara asked her brother.

"I don't know if it was an electrical fire, or what," he told her.

She was full of questions. "Where's Olivia?"

"She's at police headquarters."

"Why?"

"They just took her down there to talk to her."

"Why?"

"Barbara, I don't know. I don't know what happened." He looked dazed, bewildered, and sadder than she had ever seen.

Denise was so numb and silent that the others were sufficiently worried about her to call in one of the ambulance men. He checked her over, and finding nothing that his ministrations could make better, quietly left. She wept a little, but most of the time sat staring into space. Nobody knew what to say, or how to be of comfort. There was a lot of conjecture about how the fire could have started, Bill still blaming himself for not making a better job of the rewiring. Someone suggested that Olivia might be a secret smoker. Or that she had an accident with matches. None of the relatives had met her, which made it easier for them to imagine her as careless, rather than the conscientious young woman Bill and Denise believed they had hired. Arson had not yet entered their speculations.

When all the likely possibilities had been exhausted, the conversation lapsed into uneasy silence before returning to the nagging questions: Why didn't Olivia try to get the baby out of the house? What was she doing when the fire broke out? Wasn't it her job to take care of Kristie? Bill had no answers. "But she was always so good with the baby," he kept saying.

Friends and neighbors kept stopping by, many of them unknown to the Fischers. At first Denise kept busy making telephone calls, behaving with the unnatural composure which precedes breakdown. Not knowing any of her friends, Bill's relatives had no idea whether the people now streaming in and out of the Fries house had come to comfort or to satisfy their curiosity. Leah was incredulous to hear one visitor say, "Denise, I think you should have another baby. . . ."

For years to come members of the Fischer family would carry the memory of where they were and what they were doing when they heard about the fire. There was Leah, on the last lap of her drive home from White Plains, turning into Nannyhagen Road and being shocked by the sight of fire trucks tearing toward her down this quiet and twisting rural lane. She pulled over to let them through, but before reaching her, they swung left into West Lake Drive, sirens screaming, and the uneasy feeling inside her turned to horror as she followed them around the corner and saw them pulling into her own driveway.

There was Barbara, told on her doorstep when she was already preoccupied with the pain of Kimmy's anniversary. There was her brother Bob, arriving at his home in northern Westchester after picking up his infant son, Christopher, from day care, hearing his telephone ring as he let himself in and rushing to answer it. The caller, a friend of Bill's, had heard about the fire from a Thornwood neighbor. And there was Bob's wife, Betsy, alone in her apartment in Greenwich, Connecticut, because she had a presentiment that she needed to be there, even though Monday was the night when she usually went bowling with her girlfriends.

Although Bob and Betsy were separated, their relationship remained friendly, and Bob regularly looked after Christopher on his wife's bowling nights. Fearful that he might have missed her, he burst out in relief when she answered his phone call: "You have to help me. The house is on fire and the baby is dead!"

She thought of the old frame house next to Fischer's Garage where there had been a couple of fires over the years. And she assumed that the baby was Barbara and Jim's grandson, E.J.

"Is Dad okay?" she asked, referring to Willie.

"It's not that house. It's my brother's. What shall I do?"

She could hear the panic in his voice. "Put Christopher in the truck and take him to my mom's house. I'll call and tell her you're on the way. Then I'll meet you by Bill's place."

Betsy, a bright and pretty woman in her mid-thirties who worked as analyst in a petroleum company, had an uncanny sixth sense which experience had taught her to trust. Earlier this evening she had a strong intuition that she should not go bowling. "You deadbeat," one of her girlfriends had teased her when she excused herself. But for some reason she could not understand herself, Betsy knew she needed to remain at home by her telephone. It was as positive a feeling as she'd had a year ago when she reassured Leah about Kimmy being with God; in that instance, a certitude beyond faith, an instinctive understanding.

She stopped by her parents' house in North White Plains on her way to Thornwood. Bob had not yet arrived there. Despite the urgency, he was taking forty-five minutes to do a half-hour drive because he was nervous and knew it, and did not want to risk an accident which might harm Christopher. Rather than wait for him Betsy drove to the fire scene with her father, William Skelly. They left his car at the corner of West Lake Drive out of the way of the fire trucks, and started walking. It was still drizzling, and there was no wind to dissipate the smell of smoke which hung heavily over the area, filling their nostrils. Outside Bill's house a fireman stopped them.

"You can go home," he said. "There's nothing to see."

"It's my brother-in-law's house," Betsy explained.

"Oh, my God, I'm sorry," he told her.

"Did everyone get out?" she asked. She was hoping that Bob's informant had the story wrong, and that Kristie was safe.

His reply was evasive. "We don't have any information. The family is next door."

Betsy recalled: "I went to the back door of the Fries house, and introduced myself. Mrs. Fries told me I would find the others in the den. I walked in, and asked, 'Is everybody okay?'

"They all burst into tears. I sat down and hugged Leah. At that time John was outside, being questioned by the police. When he came back Bill asked him, 'What happened? What did you see?' He could not answer. He kept shaking his head and crying. He was trembling. We all knew that he had seen something so horrible that he could not put it into words."

Bob arrived next and asked the same question.

"John looked in shock. White as a ghost," Bob said. "He said that he was met at the door by Olivia with a fire extinguisher in her hand. That he ran down the hall, heard the smoke alarms going off, and kicked in the door to the baby's room. Then he could not talk about it anymore. It was weeks later before he told me the rest of the story."

Bill's son, Troy, was the last family member to join the group. He had a job as an industrial designer with a company in Mount Vernon, about halfway between Thornwood and his bachelor apartment in Manhattan. He often worked late, and was still at his office when his grandmother, Ann Scheller, Grada's mother, telephoned at about 6:30 P.M.

"There's been a fire at the house, and the baby is dead," she told him. She sounded very distressed.

"Where is everybody?" he asked.

"I don't know."

"I tried to make some phone calls," Troy related. "I called the house. The phone rang but there was no answer. I called Barbara. No answer. I called the garage. It was closed. So I sat down and waited, and at about seven P.M. Leah called. She was hysterical. She said she was at the Fries house, and asked: 'Can you come up?'

"I took the train there. Bob and Betsy met me at the station. I found everyone sitting around, and nobody talking. Denise kept going into the kitchen to make phone calls. We realized that it was her way of coping, and that she should be left alone. My father was in the group, and when

I came in I embraced him. He was sobbing, and that was a shock to me. I had only seen him cry once before.''

For Troy, his father's tears evoked the painful memory of his decision to leave the Thornwood house after Denise moved in. He had actually left twice, the first time a few weeks after her arrival. Several months later his funds ran out and he was obliged to return for the summer of 1991. By then his old bedroom had become a storage room for Denise's bicycles, and he was directed to sleep on the living-room convertible. During that summer his father told him about Denise being pregnant, and their plan to get married, covering his awkwardness by breaking the news in the kitchen while making himself a sandwich. Neither Troy nor Leah was invited to the wedding.

Shortly after that the bicycles were stored elsewhere, and Bill set about turning Troy's room into a nursery. Shelves where Troy had kept boyhood treasures were ripped out, and the mementos of his twenty-four years—books, art materials, bottles and paints, bits of leather and tree bark for the projects he was working on—put in boxes and stored in the basement of the old family house. Troy felt helplessly dispossessed.

He left angrily, a few weeks before Kristie was born. On returning to pick up his last few possessions he had a frank talk with his father, and to his surprise Bill became tearful.

"I didn't realize that his feelings ran that deep, that he cared that much," Troy said. "It was something I had never understood in this family, things not being talked about."

That was the beginning of a better relationship between father and son. Although Troy had many of the Fischer family's characteristics, particularly that of being a very private person, he and Bill shared few interests. Troy had no ambitions to go into the family business; like his maternal grandfather, Jan Menting, he was essentially an artist. He wore his hair long, liked music and painting, and had never felt the slightest empathy with the clique to which John Gallagher belonged when they were in the same high school: a group of teenage boys who hung around auto shops picking up spare parts, building engines, and eventually putting a little buggy together. John was far more suited to working with cars than he was.

Troy suspected that, thorough and conscientious as his father was at his work, he would not have chosen the automobile business he inherited. Maybe they weren't so different after all. There was a sensitivity in Bill which he had not appreciated until recently, a rediscovery of fatherhood which had unexpectedly improved their own relationship. Troy had visited White Plains Hospital a few hours after Kristie was born, late in the evening after Leah and John had left, and felt a stronger sense of family than he had known since before his parents' divorce. Kristie looked like all other babies to him, but it was a powerful thought that this new life contained his own bloodline. He was peering at her through the glass window of the hospital nursery when a stranger asked if he was the new baby's uncle. "No, I'm her brother," he said with pride. Tonight he felt in her loss the loss of part of his own identity: Suddenly he wasn't Kristie's brother anymore. Struggling with that thought gave him a glimpse of his father's grief and deprivation, and in an unexpected role reversal he put his arms around Bill, and tried to comfort him.

When the telephone became free, he called his mother in Manhattan. She had recently remarried, but remained in close touch with her children.

"Are you all right? Is Leah all right?" Grada asked anxiously.

"Yes," he said. "But the baby is dead."

Later she recalled: "My husband had to calm me down. It was such a shock. Troy's voice was different, not at all like his, and he sounded terribly sad."

She asked for details, and he told her what he knew. She had never seen the baby or Olivia, but she felt an involvement, having helped Leah shop for gifts of baby clothes. Her next question came out of her long memory of living in that house. "If Olivia couldn't open the door, why didn't she get the baby out through the window? That room is at the back of the house where the windows are only about eighteen inches from the ground, and you can see right in. Why didn't she go outside and smash the pane?"

During the evening Lieutenant Louis Alagno stopped by to tell the family: "There's a possibility that it was arson."

"Is that what you think?" Leah asked, surprised.

Alagno avoided a direct answer. "It's a possibility," he repeated.

After he left, they began to speculate. If there was an arsonist, John Gallagher felt it had to be Olivia because he had seen no one else around the house. Bill Fischer was reluctant to believe that this young girl might have set the place on fire, but he blamed her for failing to try to rescue Kristie. He and Denise had been assured that she knew emergency procedures.

"Why didn't she get the baby out?" Denise asked angrily. "That's the first thing you do in a fire emergency, get everyone out of the building."

Betsy's father, a lieutenant in the White Plains fire department until his recent retirement, ventured: "I have seen people do very strange things in fires. They panic. I have found children hiding in closets, and adults in shower stalls. Something like that might have happened to this girl. She just might have panicked."

Leah asked where Olivia was right now, and where she would stay tonight.

"I don't care," Bill replied. Naming the agency through which they had employed her, he added: "E. F. Au Pair can handle it from here."

He was assuming that the agency's local representative would pick her up from police headquarters. It had not occurred to him, or to any of the family, that she might spend the night in jail.

While they were talking, Kristie's body was quietly removed from the house next door, and the accelerant on her diaper discovered. None of this was told to the Fischers that night, and after the firemen had gone home and a police guard was left on their property, there seemed no more reason for them to wait next door. Although they were concerned about pipes freezing and rain getting into the building, there was nothing to be done about this until morning. At about 11:00 P.M. they drove to the old family house in North White Plains. "We have three spare bedrooms and you can stay as long as you need," Barbara told her brother.

Nobody felt like going to bed. Denise was still struggling with the denial stage of grief, unable to accept that she no longer had a baby. It was more than she could grasp, that she had said good-bye to a healthy daughter before going to work that morning and had returned to a total void. She kept saying that she wouldn't believe Kristie dead until she saw the body. The others exchanged glances, horrified at the thought.

John was in no state to drive home to Mahopac, and no one suggested it. The Fischers were all deeply touched that he had risked his life to try to save Kristie, and felt very protective toward him.

Jim was watching him carefully. "He was ashen in color, sitting there in a daze, with no expression on his face," he noted. "He said very little. It was as though he was trying to block something out, and couldn't."

At the Fries house, someone had offered John a drink of whisky. He gulped it down, and then another. "He had four straight shots, and never felt it," Jim said. "He was stone sober. When you get into severe shock like that you can drink all the drinks you want and it does not affect you."

More than anyone else in the group, Jim had a sense of what John had seen. Years earlier, when he was a volunteer fireman, he was called to a house where a man had been trapped above a blazing stairwell. "I remember almost stepping on his body like it was a piece of wood, not realizing it was human. I will never forget the sight. It made me feel sick to my stomach. John must have seen something like that. I didn't want to know the details."

There was one important detail that Betsy did feel able to question. "Maybe the heat expanded the nursery door," she suggested. "Maybe it wasn't actually locked."

"Yes, it was," John assured her. "That door was locked from the inside."

The entire episode defied logical explanation. They talked until past 3:00 A.M., trying to absorb the shock and to share the grief. Suddenly Jim remembered the one close relative who did not yet know about the fire. In a sad, tired voice he asked: "Who's going to tell Willie this time?"

"I'll tell him," Bill said. "She was my daughter. But let him sleep tonight. I'll tell him in the morning."

13

It was an unusual family. There were those who were born Fischers, and those who became Fischers by marriage and osmosis, and after a while it was hard to tell the difference. Jim Donnelly, a kindly and corpulent man who in good times was cheerful, extrovert, and gregarious, did not look or behave remotely like a Fischer. Yet he had been fully assimilated into the family, and felt more comfortable with his in-laws than with some of his own relatives. In his opinion: "You can ask anyone in this town about Willie Fischer, or about any of my in-law family, and you won't hear a bad word said of them. They never stole from anybody, never cheated anybody. They are good people, every one of them."

Willie's father, Jacob Philip Fischer, emigrated from Germany and settled in St. Louis, where Willie was born. After a few years he moved his family to Westchester and ran a small repair shop in North White Plains. In 1929 he extended the operation and opened Fischer's Garage by a main road that linked the city of White Plains with the developing villages to the north. Business grew as traffic became heavier, and as the automobile developed from a luxury to a way of life. Compared with the newer neon-lit service stations which had since sprung up along the same highway like clones of one another, Fischer's Garage now looked elderly and almost insignificant. But it was bigger and better equipped than it seemed from the outside, and its reputation for prompt, courteous, and reliable service was unparalleled in the area. The service stations did little more than pump gas, but Fischer's Garage specialized in repairing cars, and needed no advertisement. Like the present management, some of its customers were from the third generation of the same family. Two satisfied customers, Denise and Betsy, met and married the current owners as a consequence of bringing their cars to be serviced.

Jake Fischer, as he was locally known, bought the large frame house next to the garage when Willie (the first William Philip Fischer) was a child. From early on this boy loved repairing engines and became his father's natural successor. Even in his retirement nothing delighted him more than to have a customer bring in a piece of machinery that nobody else could mend, anything from a lamp to a lawn mower, but best of all a vintage car assembled by craftsmen of another era.

"Let's see if I can make it work," he would say, invigorated by the challenge. And if anyone could, it was Willie.

The house of his boyhood had been his home ever since. His wife, Ethel, of German and Irish stock, gave birth to their first child, William Philip Fischer, Jr. (Bill), in 1943. Barbara Ann followed in 1945, and Robert Carl (Bob) in 1951. Ethel died in 1972, and since then Willie had lived alone in one or other of the house's two apartments, closely surrounded by his children. He was too unassuming to be a patriarch, but everyone in the extended family loved him for his kind and gentle ways.

This family grew as the children married because every new in-law who joined the clan became so intensely part of it that even subsequent divorce did not sever the relationship. The names might change, but those who were once Fischers remained Fischers. It was typical that Bill stayed on excellent terms with his ex-in-laws after Grada had left him, and that all the other Fischers continued to think of her and her immediate relatives as essential parts of their family. "She will always be Aunt Grada to me," Debby remarked, intending no slight to Denise.

Even Grada's divorced parents and their second spouses were counted into the clan. It therefore seemed logical for Bill and Denise to invite Grada's mother, Ann Scheller, to fill the role of Kristie's grandmother because Ann was already grandmother to Troy and Leah, and both their own mothers were dead. Grada was delighted because this linked the children of Bill's two marriages.

"This is a very accepting family," Betsy commented. "Nobody ever points a finger." On the brink of a divorce herself, she still considered herself a Fischer, maintained a close friendship with Leah, and wanted Christopher to grow up among the Fischer relatives. Equally, they would have been hurt and amazed if she had assumed that separation from her husband meant separation from them.

110

The bonds went deeper than most of them realized because they were all so reserved. In the view of one in-law, family gatherings in normal times were rather tedious events, where people sat around observing the pleasantries while discreetly glancing at their watches. Or, in John Gallagher's description: "You can walk into a room full of five hundred people and pick out the Fischers because they are the ones with the least to say."

Yet in times of need they were all immediately supportive. Without hesitation, most of them took vacation time off from work to help Bill and Denise after the fire. Jim Donnelly, who at that time was managing a gas station, gave up the entire week to chauffeuring his brother-in-law on essential errands, from the police station to the funeral parlor to various cemeteries, knowing from his experience of a year earlier that a newly bereaved parent is in no shape to drive a car.

"That period of time flows into one big lump," Jim said. "It was hard to remember what day it was. At one time that week I was up for sixty hours."

Most of the relatives heard of Olivia's arrest for arson on Tuesday's early morning radio news, and gathered again at the Donnellys' home to offer sympathy and help. Barbara and Jim's daughter Debby was among the first to arrive, carrying two bags of clothes which Leah had recently passed on to her and was now glad to have back. Debby's husband, Rick, stayed at home for the day with E.J., knowing that it would be more than Denise and Bill could bear to have a baby around.

Soon after 9:00 A.M. Debby, Leah, and John Gallagher set off for the Fischer home in search of the cats. A policeman guarding the property wanted to know who they were, and barred them from the house until more investigating had been done. Leah was distressed to see some of her ruined bedroom furniture thrown out on the lawn, and even more anguished when someone in the neighborhood said there had been a report of a dead cat in the area.

"This on top of everything else was the last straw," Debby remarked.

For reasons of their own, the police were also interested in finding the cats. Back on the job after only a few hours rest, Police Chief Paul Oliva was developing a theory that Olivia Riner may have hated cats, and started the house fire by pouring flammable liquid on the animal sleeping on her bed. That could explain her obsessive talk about the cats rather than about the baby, as well as the small fire that penetrated her bed covers. Joe Butler, the arson investigator, stuck to his opinion that it was not a cat's body that had covered the protected patch in the middle of that blaze, but the infant seat with Kristie in it. The police chief did not agree. He continued to argue that if the baby had been doused on Olivia's bed, Olivia would have been burned as she carried the smoldering seat to the nursery. In any event, he needed to have the Fischers' four cats rounded up and examined for burns and accelerants.

Unaware of all this, Leah was walking around in the woods at the back of the property, holding out a can of tuna fish and calling the cats by name. There was a shed next to the Fischers' carport, raised from the ground on cinder blocks, and after a while O.J. came crawling out from beneath it, soaked and frightened. Peering under the shed, Leah, Debby, and John spotted Fleetwood and Kabuki huddled out of reach, still too scared to respond to a familiar voice and the smell of food. They wrapped O.J. in a towel, put him in Leah's car, and drove to the Donnellys' home, where they dried him off and left him in a box in the playroom.

They came straight back and after about forty-five minutes were able to coax Fleetwood and Kabuki out from under the shed. But there was no sign of Oliver, the black cat Denise brought with her when she moved into the household; the cat who, according to Olivia, was lying on her bed immediately before the fire in her room started, and who came running into the hallway "very angry" to warn her that something was wrong.

All three animals were checked by a police officer before Leah was allowed to take them away. Debby could not think why they were being sniffed over. "They just smelled like wet cat," she remarked.

But at police headquarters Paul Oliva was getting impatient. "We're short one cat," he muttered. "I want to know what was burning on that girl's bed. So you had better find the goddamn cat and see if she spread paint thinner on it."

In the meantime, Detective Bruce Johnson had been interviewing Bill and Denise. He was shocked by their changed appearances when they arrived at the police station.

"I could not recognize Denise Fischer from the lady I had seen the night before," he said. "She looked as though she had been crying until she could not cry anymore. Her eyes were black. I have never seen anyone look so bad. Bill looked terrible, too. They were both hysterical when they came in."

Johnson had to put aside his sympathy and get on with the investigation. One of the first clues had been the charred box of Diamond kitchen matches, found on the nursery floor near Kristie's body. It was important to know if they belonged in the house, or were brought in from outside. Almost casually, he asked Bill whether he kept stick matches around.

"Yes," Bill told him. "There were two boxes of Diamond matches and two boxes of long fireplace matches in the bookcase cabinet in the upstairs living room."

Johnson recounted: "When they had calmed down I took them up to the house, opened the door to the cabinet, and there was just one box of Diamond stick matches, with the same bar code as the box we found in the nursery." Both boxes of fireplace matches were still there.

In the downstairs work closet there was further evidence of the fire being an inside job. As a meticulous workman, Bill had a good memory for the quantities of liquid in the various containers, and knew instantly that a considerable amount of flammable fluid was missing. He told Johnson that the plastic container of paint thinner, found almost empty and lying on its side, had been full and standing upright. He remembered this well because he had used it recently to clean his brushes after painting the new door to the nursery. He said that the emptied can of Coleman appliance fluid had been about a quarter full and that the cap, now loose, had been firmly screwed in place. The one-gallon jug of charcoal lighter fuel, now virtually empty, had contained about three quarts.

Told of these findings, Chief Oliva observed: "It is possible that someone else came into the house and set one of those fires. But not all three. And someone else would have brought his own damn matches."

On that morning after the fire, Troy returned to the scene with his mother, Grada, and her father, Jan Menting, who had built this house thirty-six years earlier. Since all three of them lived in Manhattan, they drove out to Westchester together. Jan, a quiet and thoughtful man who had emigrated from Holland in the 1950s, had been unable to sleep after Grada telephoned him with the news. He was still fond of his ex-son-in-law, and although he had never seen Kristie, the loss of her life distressed him profoundly. He had given up his interest in this house when Grada was thirteen, at the time of his divorce from her mother, moving on to a second marriage and a new life in New York City. But although emotionally detached, he had never lost his personal involvement with the building. This was a house created out of his own dreams, planned on his own drawing board, built to a considerable extent with his own hands, and he knew every idiosyncrasy in the place. Now it had been violated, and he needed to understand how and why.

It was an easy house to break into, he had always known that, and yet its unusually open design was an effective deterrent. He thought it impossible for an intruder to move from room to room without being seen or heard by another person on the same floor. Even if a burglar had the place to himself, the plate-glass windows and skylights would make him vulnerable to observation from outside. Few would take the risk. While the three generations of the family lived here, there had been only one small robbery. When Troy was about sixteen a boy from his high school climbed in through his bedroom window and stole his guitar. It was the same low window about which Grada had wondered, why didn't Olivia break it to save the baby?

They found Bill and Denise at a neighbor's house, being soothed by coffee. It made Grada's heart ache to see Bill so distressed. She knew him as a man who had difficulty expressing his emotions; this rare acknowledgment of them indicated the depth of his pain. At this point Denise seemed to be holding herself together better than he was.

"We just let them talk," Grada remembered. "There was nothing we could say except to tell them they were not alone, and that we cared." She hugged them both, a spontaneous gesture which overcame any residual awkwardness between her and Denise.

By now it was almost noon, and the police were releasing her old home back to the family. Grada walked through it with her father, son, and daughter, their memories of having lived here harshly supplanted by the shambles around them. Grada had come for Leah, to comfort her and to help her sort through the wreckage of her bedroom.

"It had been completely torched," she related. "Leah was already traumatized by the loss of her little sister, and now she was seeing that she had lost everything else; all her clothes, and the personal things that meant a lot to her. It was the worst thing that had ever happened to her, far worse than our divorce, and yet so much else was going on that her grief had to be pushed aside.

"It did not make sense to me that her door was locked from the inside, or that someone could have come into that house without Olivia knowing. All the downstairs windows make a very gravelly sound as they move on their tracks."

Troy had the same vivid memory of those noisy windows from his teenage experience of trying to sneak in and out at night and always getting caught.

Jan went from room to room, assessing the damage. Although it was severe, he was relieved to see that the building could be restored. But that was of least importance to him. This was only a house, he told himself. It was the scene in the nursery which horrified and absorbed him.

The charred infant seat was still there, outlined by a circle of burned carpet like a deeply drawn scar. It seemed to him like the mark of a sinister cult, a circle of fire deliberately set around a human sacrifice.

"It looks almost like a ritual killing," he said to Grada.

When Betsy returned to help that morning, she too had a strong sense that something evil had happened. Debby took her aside to ask whether she thought Kristie had suffered. Everyone in the family desperately wanted to believe that this baby was already dead when the flames reached her.

"You're kind of weird," Debby said. "You can tell these things. Can you feel anything in the baby's room?"

Betsy shook her head. "No, because she's at peace."

"How do you know?"

"If she had suffered I would still hear her screams."

Later Leah asked Betsy the same question. They both thought it uncanny, her instinct for things unseen. Betsy was such an unlikely psychic, so warm and open, so insistent that there was nothing unusual about her own peculiar insights. Exactly a year ago she had known that Kimmy would die the next day, and she was right. "We all knew there was no hope for her, that it was only a matter of time," Betsy explained. "But one day I knew it would happen tomorrow, and it did. It was like I knew I shouldn't go bowling on the night of the fire, although I didn't know why. And when I walked into Kristie's room the next morning I knew she hadn't suffered, in spite of that circle of fire. I knew that she was being taken care of, that somewhere she was a child again, and happy. I think most people have this kind of power. They just don't realize it."

She joined the others in helping Leah to salvage some belongings, but almost everything was wrecked. Leah's room was the former master bedroom, which her father had given her only two months earlier when, as part of his renovation plan, he made a new bedroom for himself and Denise out of the upstairs den. Soon after Troy's old room became the nursery, Leah's became Olivia's. Leah had been delighted to inherit the larger room with its walk-in closet, and soon filled it with her own possessions and many of John's. He kept his dress clothes there because the only times he wore them were when they went out together, and he usually came here directly from work. These clothes of his were also destroyed, but what they would both miss the most were the keepsakes: old photographs, letters, Leah's high school yearbook signed by all her classmates, jewelry that John had given her, his high school ring, the two gold pins that had been awards to him from his employers. On a wicker table in Leah's room there had been a jewelry box next to a plastic radio. The box had melted into the radio, and the jewelry had melted into the plastic. Leah was sorting through the mess, trying to rescue a few pieces, when a lot of charred stuff fell down from behind her door.

"What's that?" Betsy asked.

"Those were your Christmas gifts," Leah replied. She shook her head, laughing. "It doesn't pay to shop early." But soon the laughter became hysterical, and she collapsed in tears.

The police had already been at work, cutting out the locks from Leah's door and Kristie's. They were hoping to find fingerprints, knowing that the last person who touched the doorknobs on the inside, activating the lock mechanism, had to be the arsonist. Subsequent laboratory tests would show nothing.

Bruce Johnson, meantime, had gone through Olivia's room, the least damaged of any of the bedrooms. Other than her burned bed everything was intact. In addition to her large but limited wardrobe of jeans and casual tops, he found several clues to her personality. There was the locked book in which she kept her diary, written in her neat print-like hand. Along with *The Silence of the Lambs* were several Western-style paperbacks, also in German, which seemed to constitute her entire reading material.

On a shelf in her closet he found a pile of baby clothes, neatly folded. Olivia had told the Fischers that since she had left Switzerland her cousin had had a baby, and she wanted to send a present. Denise had said that she would be glad to contribute some of Kristie's clothes as soon as they were outgrown. She was not yet ready to do this, and when Johnson showed her the items from Olivia's closet, Denise instantly recognized them as sweaters, overalls, and suits of Kristie's which had never been worn. She explained: "I had noticed that there were less clothes in the nursery drawer, but I didn't think much about it because I had such an enormous amount of baby clothing which relatives had given me."

In the top drawer of Olivia's dresser Johnson found a cache of junk food. Candy bars, potato chips, and a large quantity of marshmallows which had been transferred from their original packages into four Ziploc bags. Confronted by this evidence of an apparent eating disorder, he wondered whether it was triggered by homesickness, or by an older unhappiness which Olivia had tried to escape by coming to America.

He also confiscated her camera. When the film was developed, there was one surprise among the snapshots. The first few on the roll were family pictures, including some of herself, taken in Switzerland. Then came the American ones, probably intended to be sent home to her parents: the house on West Lake Drive, the baby, her new bedroom with its pretty chintz bedspread and matching curtains. What baffled Johnson was the close-up shot of the yellow and silver fire hydrant outside the Fischer house, squat and snub-nosed, poking up from among the fallen leaves. Olivia had focused directly on the hydrant, omitting the surrounding scenery. What was her interest in it? This was another piece of the puzzle which he would lie awake at nights worrying about.

When he reported these findings to his immediate superior, Louis Alagno, it set Alagno musing on a murder trial defense he had recently read about: junk food–induced homicide. In this case it was argued that as the result of an excess sugar intake the accused person became so crazed as to be out of control. From the snapshots in Olivia's camera, and from his view of her last night, Alagno estimated that she had gained close to twenty pounds in about six weeks. In the Swiss pictures she had the taut, slender body of a child, but now there was a puffiness about her face, and the beginnings of a double chin. He wondered what inner turmoil might have caused her to shut herself in her room, stuffing food.

———

Back at Barbara's home that Tuesday afternoon, there was a telephone call from the Medical Examiner's office. Bill took it on a downstairs phone, and listened in shock to the autopsy report. Kristie had died of massive burns and smoke inhalation. There were no signs of suffocation, contusion, or broken bones. She was not, as the police first assumed, the victim of a prior accident which someone attempted to cover by setting a fire. She was a victim of the fire itself, doused by a liquid accelerant apparently while she was still alive. There was a lethal level of carbon monoxide in her lungs, which she could not have ingested if she was already dead when the fire started. And since Olivia Riner already stood accused of arson, Bill drew the inescapable conclusion. He collapsed sobbing in Barbara's arms, the first time she had ever seen her older brother cry.

"She murdered my baby!"

14

Earlier the same day, Tuesday, December 3, an unusual phone call was received at the offices of the Swiss Consulate in New York City. The caller was Kurt Riner, chief of civil defense for the town of Wettingen, near Zurich. His was a job which involved training people to deal with major disasters, from fires and storms to a possible nuclear attack. It was not a sumptuously paid position but it commanded respect, on the likely assumption that anyone who chose this work was a responsible, public-spirited citizen.

This was the image Kurt Riner projected over the transatlantic telephone. His call was taken by Denis Charrière, deputy head of chancery, who was relieved that Riner spoke standard German rather than the colloquial Swiss-German which Charrière had to struggle with, his primary language being French. Since Switzerland is a nation of three languages and many dialects, there has to be a lot of linguistic interchange in its government offices.

Riner sounded agitated. He explained that his daughter was employed as an au pair in an American household where a baby had died in a fire the previous evening. She had been accused of arson, and was in police custody. He had heard this much from the Zurich office of E. F. Au Pair, the agency which had arranged her employment, but he did not know any details. Could the consulate help?

Charrière asked Riner if his daughter had any psychological problems, if she could possibly have caused the fire. No, the father replied adamantly.

"I told him I would try to contact his daughter, and asked him to call me back in half an hour," Charrière reported. "I telephoned the Mount

119

Pleasant police department, and said I was from the consulate. Olivia was brought to the phone. She talked so quietly I could hardly hear her, and I had to ask her to speak up. She explained very quickly that she had been alone in the house when she suddenly saw fire, and telephoned the fire department. I could tell from her voice that she had gone through a very difficult experience."

Charrière learned more about her when Riner called back.

"Her father told me that she was very shy and quiet. He said that if she was accused of a crime she would not have the courage to defend herself. He said that when she was afraid, she was likely to withdraw, to close herself off and not talk anymore, and that her silence might be taken for guilt. I realized that this was a family which was very close, with parents who knew their daughter well. I could feel the horrible situation they were in. He told me that he and his wife would be arriving in New York the next day, and would need help because they did not speak English. I promised that we would do what we could."

It was an unusual case, even for an overseas consulate. The Swiss have an international reputation as law-abiding citizens; every year only about four hundred of them are arrested outside their own country. Most of these arrests are for minor infringements of local statutes, the kind foreigners don't always know about, punishable by a small fine or a couple of days in jail. In Switzerland itself, a country to which women's liberation came late, it is rare for a woman to be involved in violent crime. The overwhelming majority of the Swiss prison population is male. Hence, to the consular officials in New York, a major arson charge against a young Swiss girl seemed preposterous. It was easier to believe that someone had made a mistake, that this was a classic case of an innocent abroad, trapped in every traveler's nightmare.

Kurt Riner (or possibly an English-speaking friend representing himself as Riner) also telephoned the Mount Pleasant police headquarters, and in accented but fluent English spoke to Bruce Johnson.

"He wanted to know what had happened, and I told him that his daughter had been charged with arson," Johnson said. "I asked him if she had any psychological difficulties, any history of lighting fires, any problems whatsoever. He was very defensive, and said no to all my questions."

Olivia was brought from her cell to take the call in Louis Alagno's office. Standing on guard by the doorway, Bruce Johnson was surprised to see her burst into floods of tears as she spoke to her father (and at this point the speaker evidently was Kurt Riner) in a language he wished he understood. All that came through to him were her sobbing protests: *"Nein . . . nein . . . nein."* It was an uninhibited display of emotion, the first he had seen from her.

A few hours later, at 4:00 P.M., Olivia was taken to Mount Pleasant's small courtroom, in the same building as the police station, to be arraigned for first-degree arson and second-degree murder. The murder charge had been added upon receipt of the medical examiner's report, shortly before it was telephoned to Bill Fischer. The Mount Pleasant police had been as shocked as Bill to learn that Kristie was still alive when the nursery fire was set. Every officer in the investigation, including the department's case-hardened chief, had been working on the assumption that the fire was a cover-up for an earlier, unintended death. But the autopsy finding drastically changed the nature of the crime. This baby did not die by accident, but by deliberate, evil intent. Whoever killed Kristie Fischer wanted her dead.

Olivia did not seem apprehensive as she was led into court. Her emotions were under control again, and she had withdrawn into herself in the way that her father understood, baffling to everyone else.

"I would have expected her to be tearful and frightened, surrounded by these strange people accusing her, not speaking her language," remarked Teresa Signorelli, clerk to the court. "I have seen girls her age on petty larceny or minor assault charges, shaking and scared. But there was no expression, no emotion on this girl's face. Her whole personality was blank. I had the feeling that she had removed herself from all that was going on around her, as though she was not part of it."

After the brief arraignment she was taken, unprotesting, to the county jail in nearby Valhalla, to be held without bail.

With the hindsight which he would like to have had at the time, Louis Alagno regretted not assigning a second detective to the investigation. "Bruce was overwhelmed," he said. But with only three detectives, one of them off sick, this small police department's resources were already strained, and the early evidence in this case seemed strong enough for a conviction. Police Chief Paul Oliva regarded Olivia's singed eyelashes as virtual proof that she had been very close to a source of combustion. There was also her admission of being alone in the house with the baby, her statement that no one else could have entered without her knowing, and the matches and accelerants missing from the Fischers' store cupboards consistent with the matches and accelerants which appeared to have been used for the fires. Even the locked nursery door seemed to fit this scenario: In Chief Oliva's opinion, "locking it was a psychological thing, like saying that she did not have to deal with what was happening on the other side." Both he and Johnson were reminded of the Hungarian roofer who sat in his kitchen calmly eating pigs' knuckles while his wife was bleeding to death upstairs. The evidence in that case was also circumstantial, but the Mount Pleasant police won a conviction. What was lacking with Olivia Riner was motive.

Paul Oliva was not seriously worried about this. "So far as I am concerned, we had sufficient evidence to charge her," he said. "The rest is up to the prosecution."

Although he saw the case as highly unusual, he did not envision the widespread publicity which it would generate on account of its strong emotional content, and its relevance to working mothers. At that time there were ten million women with children under the age of six in the United States work force, all dependent upon a patchwork of child-care arrangements which at some level or another most of them worried about. The murder of Kristie Fischer absorbed and appalled them, as a manifestation of their worst nightmares.

With even more thoroughness than most working mothers, Denise Fischer had researched all her affordable infant-care options. By nature and training she was the kind of person who investigated every aspect of a problem before arriving at a carefully considered solution.

"I read every magazine article I could find on the subject, every book in the library," she said. "We did not have a grandmother available, and I did not want day care because it would have meant taking the baby out of the house." That ruled out Barbara's offer to look after Kristie in her home, a decision both women would regret. "I looked into the possibility of hiring an American au pair, but from the experience of our friends, it seemed that Europeans were more conscientious."

Denise considered giving up work and taking care of the baby herself, but when she weighed the loss of income against the quality of life she wanted for her family, it made more sense to find reliable help. At thirty-nine she was well established in her career as a tax accountant, and Bill Fischer had learned from his first marriage the folly of expecting an intelligent, ambitious woman to be content as a traditional stay-at-home wife.

In her search for the perfect home help Denise contacted several private agencies, with disappointing results. Many of them failed to return her calls. Toward the end of her pregnancy she followed up on a magazine advertisement for E. F. Au Pair, one of eight agencies in the country designated by the Immigration and Naturalization Service to place young European women in American homes. She received a prompt and informative response from the agency's U.S. headquarters in Cambridge, Massachusetts, outlining a program which was officially described as a cultural exchange. In reality it was a government-approved source of supply for mothers' helpers: middle-class European girls who were willing to take care of children in exchange for the experience of living with an American family. This program had been designed a few years earlier as part of a campaign to control and legalize the flow of immigrants coming into the United States for domestic work. While it permitted several thousands of au pairs to enter the United States every year, it limited these young women to one-year cultural-exchange visas which could not be used as work permits for any other job. An au pair who became unhappy with her situation was not free to find other employment; she simply had to go back home.

Wages and working conditions were also regulated, although the Immigration and Naturalization Service and the Internal Revenue Service were in some conflict as to whether the $100 a week which a host family was required to pay its au pair was tax-free pocket money or taxable wages. Host families also had to pay their au pair's airfare and agency fees, bringing their average weekly expenditure up to $170 for the one-year contract. This was an affordable sum for many two-income middle-class families, and the demand for European girls usually exceeded the supply.

It was an illusion to describe them as nannies, although many mothers did. A certified, experienced nanny could command more than twice that money. What in fact E. F. Au Pair and competing agencies promised was a carefully evaluated English-speaking young woman between the ages of eighteen and twenty-five who had some practical experience in caring for children; essentially a competent baby-sitter who would live as a member of the family. An au pair could not be called upon to work more than forty-five hours a week, the work to be limited to child care. She must also be given the opportunity to attend an adult education course at a local school or college, theoretically to improve her knowledge of English. Some European girls pursued their study of the language diligently; others filled the educational requirement by developing a hobby like photography or calligraphy. All of them were supposed to be in regular contact with an agency counselor in the area.

The idea of another language being spoken in her home appealed to Denise. More important, she wanted to keep Kristie's upbringing under her personal control, and like every other eager new mother, she had positive ideas about this. Her practice of using the infant carrier rather than the crib for the baby's daytime naps was in line with her belief that the carrier gave a feeling of security, like the comforting enclosure of the womb. She had read a lot about infant care, and was anxious to do everything right.

It was typical of her relationship with Bill that she did the research and he went along with her decisions, opposing her only when he felt strongly about an issue. Employing an au pair was beyond his experience, indeed beyond that of most Fischer relatives, who wondered among themselves why Denise would trust a strange young girl, a foreigner at that, to look after her child. In their circle many mothers made informal cash arrangements with trusted neighbors who would baby-sit in their own homes; others gave up outside work, while their husbands took on two jobs. An au pair was, in the view of most of the Fischers, a dubious and exotic solution to the child-care problem.

"I didn't think it was a good idea," commented one of them. "Bringing a stranger in your home, you never know."

But he kept the thought to himself.

In line with its standard procedure, E. F. Au Pair asked Denise for information about her family, home, interests, and child-care needs. The agency claimed to have a "unique matching process" for its au pairs and host families.

"They said they would give us as many résumés as we wanted, but only one at a time," Denise recalled. "Olivia's were excellent, so we did not ask for more. She had worked for a pediatrician, and wanted a career working with children. We thought about it, talked about it, spoke to her on the telephone, and felt pleased with our choice."

They were assured that Olivia's references had been carefully checked, and that before leaving Switzerland she would be instructed in infant supervision, first aid, and emergency procedures. In the United States an agency counselor would introduce her to other au pair girls in her neighborhood, and be available to resolve any problems which she or the host family might have. E. F. Au Pair's glossy brochure intimated that such problems were rare. The booklet was liberally illustrated with photographs of fresh-faced young women joyously nurturing happy youngsters: reading to them, playing with them, showing them how to bake European delicacies.

Kristie was seven weeks old when Olivia arrived at New York's Kennedy Airport with a planeload of au pair girls from Europe. Bill and Denise instantly recognized her from her photograph, and felt reassured that she looked so friendly and sensible, so eager to hug the baby they had brought to meet her.

She was one of the last to come out of Customs to the barrier where they were waiting, moving toward them with painful deliberation. "She had four large suitcases, and could carry only two of them," Bill remembered. "So she would walk ten feet, go back for the other two, and then walk another ten feet, never letting any of the bags out of her sight. She was being very, very cautious. I wondered if she had been told that she could be ripped off in New York."

For the next four weeks Denise, continuing her maternity leave, was with Olivia every day, showing her how she wanted Kristie cared for, and introducing her to the neighborhood. In all this time she saw nothing to make her doubt the wisdom of her choice.

At the beginning of her fourth week Olivia attended one of the monthly E. F. Au Pair meetings for European girls in her area, and seemed gratified to discover that her job was easier than most. She reported to the Fischers that some of the other girls had to work very hard, looking after several preschool children. One au pair felt overburdened because the mother in her host family was out every evening, working.

"You must let us know if you are unhappy about anything in this household," Bill told her. Olivia shook her head and smiled, indicating there was nothing. The au pair meeting had been held at the home of an agency counselor, and she had been driven there by a German-speaking girl named Helga, who worked for a family in the nearby town of Greenburgh; Helga was charming and vivacious, and the Fischers hoped that this would be the beginning of a friendship.

Many months later they would see a copy of the report which E. F. Au Pair's local counselor asked Olivia to write at that meeting. Its sentiments were exactly what they might have wished for in a person entrusted with their baby.

Asked what issues or concerns had arisen for her since she arrived in Thornwood, she had written: "I have no problems with my family and when, then I can speak with they."

In answer to the question "What is it like to be an au pair?" she wrote this enthusiastic response: "For me it is an experience to see the babies first year. All the mistakes, the fun, how the baby learn, to understand what a baby think, see and talk. At the moment the baby look, eat, sleep, make a dirty diaper and eat more. But every day I can see something new or different. Only little things but they are important for the baby. The baby see another baby in the mirror and make funny little noises or want hold the bottle. The bottle is heavy and to big for the hands. And try to hold the bottle a second time. Maybe in some few weeks bottle is not to heavy and the baby can drink alone. Or it's an art to give a baby a bath. The first minute the baby cry and kick. When the bath is finished the baby cry more because the baby must out of the water. What she want now? But I enjoy every second they I can be with the baby and see what's happened, what's the baby do. It's simply the best thing on the world to look on a little child!"

The parental role of the agency which Denise had thought so reassuring would, at the time of crisis, become so defensive of Olivia as to work against the Fischers' interests. E. F. Au Pair was not merely an American employment agency with Swiss connections, but the offshoot of a large international organization, Educational Foundation (from which it took its initials) for Foreign Study, based in Stockholm, which ran student-exchange programs and language schools across Europe and the United States. The future of all this could be at stake if one of its au pair girls were to be convicted of murdering an infant in her charge. And so from the beginning of this case a decision seems to have been made to provide Olivia Riner with the best defense that money could afford, while offering the Fischers no more than the agency's condolences.

It was a decision which made a world of difference to Olivia. If she had come to the United States as European mother's helpers used to travel, privately sponsored by a host family or on her own resources, her defense would probably have depended upon a Legal Aid attorney with limited time and financing. Instead, E. F. Au Pair went to the prestigious Manhattan law firm of Morrison, Cohen, Singer and Weinstein, and hired Laura Brevetti, a skilled and aggressive defense attorney whose previous experience included nine years as the attorney in charge of the federal government's Organized Crime Strike Force for the state of New York. In this unusual job for a younger woman, she had developed toughness and insight. Now in private practice, she could apply her inside knowledge of prosecution strategy to build an unassailable defense. She had a reputation for total commitment to her job; never having married, she often stayed working in her office until late at night, functioning on adrenaline and concentrating on victory. In court her manner was eloquent, organized, and clearly focused. Faced with a devastating challenge to its future existence, E. F. Au Pair could scarcely have chosen a stronger advocate.

She appeared at the Mount Pleasant police station on the afternoon of Tuesday, December 3, the day after the fire, in time to see Olivia taken to the upstairs courtroom and formally charged. A tall, impeccably groomed forty-year-old with crisp, blonded hair, a flawless complexion, and an assertive manner, she made a sharp contrast to the waiflike creature in patched jeans, her face pale and strained, her expression disconsolate, who was led into court in handcuffs.

Laura Brevetti returned to Mount Pleasant three days later for a preliminary hearing. Bruce Johnson marveled at the careful coordination of her outfits. He noted that on the Tuesday her eyeglass frames were the same crimson as her faultlessly tailored suit; on Friday the frames and outfit were a matching bright blue. The effect was striking. Attorneys with such costly fashion sense were not normally seen in courthouses of the outer suburbs.

She had already worked out an agreement with the District Attorney's office for the hearing to be waived in favor of the case going straight to a grand jury. Her aim was to cut down on the time Olivia might have to spend in jail. If the grand jury failed to find a case against her, she would be released immediately. If it handed up an indictment, she might be freed on bail. The Friday court session was therefore a brief formality.

By this time Kurt and Marlise Riner had arrived. They were a quiet, unpretentious couple, jet-lagged and washed up by a tide of circumstance which seemed to overwhelm them. Kurt Riner had something of the look of Bill Fischer, except that the lines of his face were harsher, and his features pinched. It was the short golden-brown hair, the light mustache, and the well-proportioned, muscular body rather than any aspect of his personality which made the connection. Bruce Johnson tried to talk to him, assuming his knowledge of English to be as good as it had sounded on the telephone. But now Riner indicated that he did not speak the language. Johnson was puzzled. The man who had called from Switzerland three days earlier had said that he would like to have a personal meeting with Johnson soon after he arrived.

Marlise looked younger than her husband, in experience as well as age. She had been nineteen when she gave birth to Olivia; twenty years later she still had the gawky posture of a teenager. Their only child bore a strong resemblance to both parents, with her father's coloring and determined chin, her mother's short upper lip and long pointed nose. In repose, both of the women's faces had an expression of mild discontent.

The Riners sat near the front of Mount Pleasant's small courtroom, ill at ease but trying to project encouragement. Like their daughter, they kept their emotions hidden. But as Olivia was led back to jail Marlise smiled at her and gave a thumbs-up sign.

15

Having salvaged what they could from the fire, the Fischers reassembled at the family house. They would be there daily all week, bringing food, offering comfort, anxious to do something, anything, to help. Only Willie was absent. He had not been seen since Bill broke the news to him that morning, stricken by a grief too intense to be shared. Tomorrow would be Kimmy's anniversary, and the loss of another grandchild was more than he could face in public. He kept his feelings to himself until about six months later, when over a meal with Barbara and Jim he made an uncharacteristic remark, entirely out of the context of their conversation. "Two of my grandchildren dead . . . Why didn't God take me instead?" It was quoted around the family as evidence of his silent pain.

While he mourned in the solitude of his bedroom, his descendants sat around upstairs in Barbara and Jim's living room, going over the events of the past twenty-four hours and thinking of the practical things which needed to be done. It was late Tuesday afternoon, the day after the fire, and the medical examiner had just released Kristie's body. Denise was still insisting on seeing her baby before she would discuss funeral plans.

"She wanted to go that night, desperately," Betsy remembered. "Bill did not particularly want to view the body, but if it would help Denise to deal with Kristie's death he was willing to be there for her.

"We had all gone into Barbara's kitchen. Denise was standing there, rocking, like people do when they are nervous. She began to break down again. Then she and Bill went back into the living room to be by themselves.

"I said to Bob, 'She should not do this.'

"He said, 'If it's what she needs to do, we should let her.'

"I said, 'No way. Denise should remember that baby's smiling face, the last time she saw her alive. Otherwise the memory of that burned little body will be etched on her mind for an eternity.'

"Bob and I got into an argument about it. Jim was watching Barbara, and Barbara wasn't saying a word. I turned to Jim. He said, 'I agree with you.' Leah agreed the most. And John said, 'She should definitely not see that baby.' "

They were silent for a while. Jim was remembering his unforgettable sight of a man who had been burned to death. Kristie's body must look like that, he was thinking, and it should not be shown to Denise. John was still in yesterday's nightmare, trying to accept that what he had seen in the nursery was real. Barbara, knowing that she would have been traumatized by such a sight, was recalling her discomfort in the presence of her own dead child, painfully aware that tomorrow would be Kimmy's anniversary, and that with the family in mourning again, only she and Jim were likely to remember it. She was feeling very depressed.

Earlier in the day she had not gone with the others to sort through the wreckage at Bill's home. Her avoidance of the house last night had been very deliberate, and she would go on avoiding it for months to come until it was completely rebuilt. She shrank from being anywhere near a place where a child had died. When told about the charred infant seat partially melted into the nursery carpet, she knew she had been right to stay away. "I would have pictured Kristie dying in it, and that would have made me feel even worse."

Jim had been trying to cheer himself with the thought that it had been easier for him and Barbara to deal with their loss. "We got to say good-bye to Kimmy," he reminisced. "And we were prepared, even though when the time came we were not ready. But to have a healthy child die instantly, that's different."

He was grateful for the memory of how peaceful Kimmy had looked before she was buried, emaciated yet unblemished in her white Communion dress. But the image of a badly burned baby on a mortuary slab was nothing he wanted to contemplate. Quietly he left the room to make a telephone call.

Shortly afterward he announced to the others: "Don't worry. Bill and Denise will not be viewing the body."

They understood. Jim had fixed it. He was sufficiently well known in the community—at his church, as the chairman of his parish social concerns committee, as a Republican party committeeman, and as the popular umpire of college and high school baseball games—to have useful contacts in the right places. Evidently there was one in the Medical Examiner's office. Or else at the funeral parlor. The Fischers knew better than to inquire.

One of them raised the question: "If the baby's remains aren't properly identified, how can we be sure it was Kristie?"

This doubt allowed a shred of hope which Bill and Barbara and Betsy immediately seized on. Suppose, Barbara ventured, just suppose there was a mother out there with a sickly baby about to die. Maybe she paid Olivia to trade her infant for Kristie, and to burn the evidence. Some women were that desperate to have a healthy baby. Maybe Kristie was alive somewhere . . .

It was an unlikely theory, but persuasive enough for Bill to ask the Medical Examiner's office to do a genetic test. In the meantime the Fischers began to weave their own tale around Olivia, filling the gaps in their knowledge with supposition. As they went over the story of her last few days in the household, there was one piece of unexplained time that gave rise to a variety of speculations.

Denise had gone back to work the previous Monday, exactly a week before the fire. She was at home that Thursday for Thanksgiving, and Friday was another holiday. In an effort to make the celebration pleasant for Olivia, she had responded to a local newspaper advertisement by inviting a German-speaking student to the Thanksgiving meal. Coincidentally, the advertisement was placed by an affiliate of the au pair agency, the E. F. Language School, which operated out of Marymount College in Tarrytown, eleven miles from Thornwood. The school wanted to expand the American experience of its European students by having them invited into local homes, and in response to Denise's Thanksgiving invitation it selected an East German student named Iris. Bill drove to the college to pick her up.

Iris turned out to be a cheerful, friendly girl with limited English. Olivia chatted freely with her in German, and seemed so comfortable in her company that by the end of the day she had visibly gained self-confidence. Denise prepared the meal and took care of Kristie, it being understood that this was Olivia's day off. Normally Olivia would have been off again on Saturday, but that was a day when Bill and Denise wanted to go hiking with friends, so they had asked her to take Friday instead. During the Thanksgiving celebration Olivia and Iris planned to spend this next day together. In the hope that it would be the beginning of some social life for Olivia, Denise offered the use of her car.

There was an unusual guest list at that Thanksgiving meal, one that spanned four generations and almost a century. Leah was absent, celebrating the holiday in New York with her mother, Grada. But Grada's mother, Ann Scheller, came to dinner at this house which had been hers before it was passed down to Bill and Grada, and later to Bill and Denise. She was accompanied by her second husband, George, and George's ninety-six-year-old mother. The interweavings of the extended Fischer family were so seamless that there was no tension, nor did it occur to anyone that there might be.

Nanna Ann, as Denise had fondly named her, sat with Kristie on her lap as though it was the most natural thing in the world for a man's ex-mother-in-law to become the adopted grandmother of the child he had fathered by his new wife.

Bill explained: "My ex-wife, her new husband, my ex-mother-in-law, her new husband, my ex-father-in-law and his second wife—all of us get along. We have seen too many bitter divorces in other families."

Ann was just as pragmatic. "Billy will always be my son-in-law," she explained. "I like him a lot. The fact that he and my daughter did not make it is no reason for me not to stay friendly with him."

She was a slender, attractive woman who, like Grada's father, her ex-husband Jan Menting, had been born and raised in the Netherlands. Geographically this may have given her an advantage in assessing Olivia, and what she observed left her with a feeling of disquiet.

"There was something strange about her, a look in her eyes," she said later. "She was not like any young girl I had ever met. Something was wrong, but I still don't know what it was. My husband had the same feeling; so did his mother. We talked about it when we got home. George said, 'I like the other one a lot better,' meaning Iris. But I did not say anything to Denise or Billy because they seemed to be so happy with Olivia."

They were the only Fischer relatives to meet her until they all saw her in court the following summer, on trial for the murder of Kristie.

At about 11:00 A.M. on the day after Thanksgiving, Olivia set off in Denise's car to pick up Iris. Two hours later there was an anxious telephone call from Marymount College: Iris had been waiting all this time but there was no sign of Olivia.

She should have reached the college before 11:30. Bill had taken her to Marymount with him the previous day to show her the route, and had loaned her a map. But this was the first time she had driven alone since she came to live with the Fischers. Deeply concerned, Denise telephoned the Tarrytown police and the parkway police to inquire whether a white Honda Civic had broken down or been involved in an accident anywhere between Thornwood and Marymount College. She was told no. Bill then drove to the college himself, vainly searching for her.

Olivia arrived home at 3:30 P.M., unconcerned.

"Where were you?" Denise asked her.

She looked surprised. "What do you mean?"

"The school called and said you did not show up."

"I was there," she insisted. She told them that she had gone straight to the college but could not find her new acquaintance. She said she inquired at the reception desk and among students in the hallway, but no one seemed to know where Iris was. So she drove into White Plains, parked the car, and strolled around. On Mamaroneck Avenue, the town's main shopping street, she bumped into Helga, the girl who had taken her to the au pair gathering three days earlier. Olivia related that Helga had the children from her host family with her, and that they chatted for a while. Then she came home. Being uncertain of the route, she became slightly lost, and had to use the map.

Denise thought this an odd story, but did not question it. Her overwhelming feeling was of annoyance at having her own day spoiled by needless anxiety.

"I thought it inconsiderate of Olivia to disappear for so long," she said. "She could have telephoned."

Four days later, with a fire and a dead baby in the interim, some of the Fischers began to raise doubts which had not occurred to Denise. They wondered if Olivia had actually gone to Marymount. And what she did in White Plains other than encounter Helga. Several hours were unaccounted for. It was tempting to imagine a sinister explanation, given the enormity of the crime with which she was charged. They were still conjecturing about kidnapped babies and money changing hands when the test results came back from the Medical Examiner's office, leaving no doubt that the dead baby was Kristie Fischer.

Only then could Denise be persuaded to discuss funeral plans. She and Bill were still so deeply in shock that Jim had to keep reminding them of what needed to be done, like selecting a burial plot and giving instructions to the funeral parlor. Being useful in this way helped him to get through Kimmy's anniversary. While Barbara needed solitude to grieve alone, he was restored by meaningful activity. And better than anyone in the family, he knew how to handle the practicalities of burying a child.

One priority was to plan the funeral service. Denise no longer regarded herself as Roman Catholic, Bill had been brought up as a Methodist, and neither of them had been to church in years. They wanted a Christian burial but did not know anyone they could ask to officiate.

Betsy volunteered: "If you don't mind what denomination, let me make that my job."

She had in mind the rector at her sister's Episcopal church, who baptized Christopher after there had been some difficulty about arranging the service at her own church. She remembered this priest as a caring and sensitive man, the father of small children. And she knew that the Fischers did not simply need an ordained minister to read the funeral rite. They needed one who would speak to their pain.

Early on the morning of Wednesday, December 4, one of the nurses from St. Agnes Hospital called at the Donnellys' home. She had helped to care for Kimmy toward the end of her life, and stopped by to express sympathy on this first anniversary of her death. She had no idea that she was walking into a household mourning the death of yet another child, although like everyone else in the area she knew about the fire in Thornwood and the au pair charged with murder. But she did not know of the connection with the Donnelly family. Shocked, she gave Barbara a tearful embrace and quickly left.

Kimmy's godmother also stopped by on her way to work, bringing flowers. Barbara was touched by these two women's kindness, and by the fact that Bill was not too preoccupied with his own tragedy to say a few words of comfort to her. Otherwise the pain was entirely hers and Jim's and their children's. They went through the day acutely aware of the anniversary, yet feeling constrained from talking about it. The family had so much else to mourn. Denise was in a terrible state, crying most of the time. Barbara was glad that her sister-in-law was still upstairs when those two early callers came with their reminders of Kimmy, and that the others had their own concerns to fill the day. John and Leah were anxious to visit John's mother, who had been unable to speak to them on the telephone since yesterday's throat surgery. Troy, who had returned to spend the whole of yesterday with the family, had to return to his job.

All this made it easy for Barbara and Jim to slip out of the house without telling anyone where they were going, and make the short drive to Gate of Heaven to put flowers on Kimmy's grave. They had not yet put up a headstone, but in that huge cemetery they could always go directly to the place: a left turn after the wrought-iron entrance gates, past St. Francis Mausoleum, then almost a mile along tree-lined avenues of the dead to a row of graves near a stand of weeping willows. Although most other grave sites in that area had been filled, there was a vacant plot next to Kimmy's; they thought how appropriate and special it would be for Kristie to be buried there, so that these cousins who had never met in life might be united in death.

Barbara reflected: "Kimmy never knew Kristie, but I feel she would want her with her."

Back at the house Jim expressed something of this thought to Denise, hoping it would comfort her.

"Now that Kristie is in heaven she has Kimmy and Grandma Fischer to look after her," he said.

"I don't believe in any of that," Denise retorted.

Surprised by the anger in her voice, Jim made no comment. She was so new to the family that he did not know where her sensibilities lay, and he badly wanted to say the right thing. He thought of Kristie's baptism with renewed guilt, glad that it was done but wondering if he would ever feel able to tell her about it.

There were long periods that day when the family simply sat around, mutually supportive but barely communicating. The normal Fischer silences had intensified since that telephone call from the Medical Examiner's office.

"After Bill and Denise learned that it was murder it was very quiet here," Barbara remarked. "What could we say to them? We were all numb. We could deal with Kristie's death up to that point, thinking it was an accident. But to find out that this innocent little baby was murdered . . . What goes through a person's mind to do a thing like that? We just kept asking why. Why?"

Even Jim with his un-Fischerlike need to talk was at a loss for words. "There was nothing you could think of to say," he recalled. "You just sat there. There is no defense against a thing like that."

They worried about Willie, still in his room, barely touching the food that Barbara took to him. A man of seventy-eight could have a heart attack in such a state of shock.

"We would not have dared bring in a doctor, God forbid," Jim related. Instead he asked a paramedic from the ambulance corps, another of his connections, to stop by on the pretext of offering condolences. "I left her alone with him. She held his hand, took his wrist, felt his pulse, and talked to him for ten or fifteen minutes. She told us that he was all right, that he was dealing with it as he knew best. And after a few days he was ready to do what we asked, to get dressed and go to the funeral home, just as he did for Kimmy. He did not break down. Like Bill he is a very private person. The Fischers do their own mourning in their own time and their own way."

That was Barbara's problem. She needed space and quiet to be alone with her anniversary memories of Kimmy, but there was no privacy to be had. Normally abstemious, she sat silently drinking wine one evening, several glasses of it. Watching her solicitously, Jim remarked: "Maybe she'll sleep tonight." Only he knew how little she had been sleeping.

"All that week our house was wall-to-wall people," he said. "Bill's friends, Denise's friends, the Fischer relatives, my sister and her two adult children, lots of neighbors. There were people bringing food, people until one-thirty, two in the morning. Bill said they didn't want a wake, but every night there was a wake in our living room."

And there were the cats. Barbara detested cats, wanted nothing to do with them, felt uncomfortable if cats were anywhere near her, and now there were four in the house. Denise's longtime pet, Oliver, had finally been found, terrified, sodden, and famished under the shed where the others had hidden. The blackness of his fur had so effectively merged into the surrounding gloom that he had not been visible when they were discovered. Hours later someone looked again, and a pair of cat eyes were seen glinting in the dark. Still Oliver refused to come out until Denise was fetched; then, warily, he responded to her voice. A police officer looked him over but found no trace of accelerants. That dispelled the chief's theory about a cat being doused with paint thinner on Olivia's bed. It also added credence to her story about Oliver being frightened by a mysterious source of fire. If only that cat could talk . . .

But taken to the Donnellys' home he cried instead, the others joined in, and the sound of those cats crying was like the wailing of babies in distress.

In Barbara and Jim's section of the old house, the master bedroom was on the main floor. There were three more bedrooms and a bathroom upstairs, which became home for Bill, Denise, and Leah through most of December. John Gallagher remained with them, more deeply attached to the Fischer family than he had been before. Leah needed his support, and he needed hers as badly. He slept in the guest room; Bill and Denise had the room which formerly belonged to Debora and Kimmy. In deference to Barbara the cats were shut in young Jimmy's old room, now occupied by Leah. She was happy to care for them—indeed, accepted it as her responsibility—but being unaccustomed to this strange, confined space, they continued to cry night after night. Sleeping downstairs, Barbara was spared the noise, but Leah had to borrow the earmuffs her uncle Jim wore for target shooting in order to get some sleep.

"It was hard on all of us," Leah said. "We were crowded into that house, we had none of our own belongings, and we felt helpless."

Betsy commented: "Leah was still trying to realize that it was not a bad dream. She had lived in that Thornwood house all her life, and loved it. Now she had nothing left, and nowhere to run and hide. At her aunt's house they were all like displaced people, refugees. And whenever anyone turned on the news, there was their story. It was impossible to get away from it."

Fascinated against their will, they kept tuning in to find out whether the network reporters knew more than they did. It was an odd experience for them, sitting in front of a television set presided over by a portrait of Kimmy on this first anniversary of her death; seeing the wreckage of their home and of their lives exposed to curious strangers, detesting the intrusion yet ineluctably drawn to being spectators too.

Their story had made prominent headlines in the morning newspapers. BABY'S DEATH IN FIRE CHARGED TO AU PAIR. FIRE KILLS TOT; BABY-SITTER CHARGED WITH ARSON. BABY'S NANNY SET FATAL FIRE, POLICE CHARGE. And that was only the beginning.

Questioned by the media, Police Chief Paul Oliva was being defensively canny. He didn't trust reporters; never had. His instinct, which he did trust, was to tell them as little as possible. He made a brief announcement that the police had evidence that tied Olivia Riner directly to the fire's ignition, but he declined to say what it was. Asked if there were any witnesses, he acknowledged that shortly after the fire broke out a boyfriend of the baby's twenty-two-year-old half sister had arrived at the Fischers' house. He refused to name the man, but insisted he was not a suspect. Beyond that the chief had no comment.

His reticence was a relief to Bill's relatives, who were beginning to feel under siege. Earlier in the day reporters had approached some of them outside the burned-out house; now other reporters were calling at Fischer's Garage, trying to question the staff. They wanted to know the whereabouts of Bill and Denise, but nobody was talking. None of the media people made the connection between the garage in North White Plains and the house next door, there being no listing under the name of Fischer at the house. Willie did not see the need for a telephone. All this made it possible for Bill, Denise, Leah, and John to slip in and out of the Donnellys' rear entrance and cross to the back of the garage where their cars were parked, unseen by those who hung around in wait for them only a few yards away.

16

The Reverend Steven Jay Yagerman was driving his three small daughters to school with his car radio tuned in to the local news. He heard the beginning of an item about a baby-sitter accused of setting fire to a house with an infant in it, and instantly switched stations. This was nothing he wanted his children to hear. At the ages of five, seven, and ten, they all had personal acquaintance with baby-sitters.

After dropping them off he went to work out at a neighborhood health club before starting his day as rector of All Saints Church in the Westchester village of Briarcliff Manor. At about 8:50 A.M., in the hallway of Club Fit, he encountered a parishioner, Pamela Knoll. She was surprised and relieved to see him there because she had been trying to reach him by telephone. She had called on behalf of her sister, Betsy Fischer, and tearfully she began to tell him about the very incident which he had partially heard on the radio. Betsy, she explained, was the dead baby's aunt, whom he would remember from Christopher's baptism. It was a slender connection to his parish which was four miles north of Thornwood.

"The Fischer family does not have a priest. Can you help them?" Pam asked. She knew he would not refuse.

"I'll do as much or as little as they want," he assured her.

Later in the day Betsy telephoned. She told him the larger story, about this being the first anniversary of another child's death in the family.

"You will be walking into a house full of people who need a lot of help," she warned him.

He promised to be there that evening.

During the next few hours he worried and prayed about the meeting.

He had ministered to many bereaved families, but never to one who had lost a small child. He was very close to his own children, and saw more of them than most fathers because he was in the neighborhood all day, and his wife worked in town. The pressures and problems of a two-income family were all too familiar to him, and it was not difficult to imagine himself in the Fischers' place; yet he shrank from the thought.

During the day he telephoned a priest from a neighboring parish who had recently conducted a funeral service for a two-year-old. "I asked his advice. I told him that I wasn't sure how to handle this, that I wanted to be helpful and pastoral but I was afraid of making a mistake.

" 'We all make mistakes,' he said, 'and that's all right because nobody else knows what to do either. The important thing is that you go, and that you listen. If you find yourself talking too much you are probably doing something wrong. But there are no rules. Just follow your instinct.'

"He said he would pray for me."

When he called at the Donnellys' home a few hours later he found the living room crowded with people. He was shown to an upstairs bedroom, Kimmy's old room, for a private conversation with Bill, Denise, Leah, and John.

"I didn't know what to say, so I decided to make myself vulnerable. I told them that this experience was new for me, and that I would be struggling with it along with them."

It took him a while to figure how John fitted into this family, and he was hesitant to ask because this young man looked so withdrawn and downcast. He would start to talk, stop in midsentence, and bury his face in his hands. Finally he managed to say enough for Father Steve, as he was known to his parishioners, to realize with horror that John had actually seen the baby in flames.

"They all told their stories," he related. "Where they were, and how it was for each of them. Although I did not know them they spoke about their feelings so honestly. I felt so hurt for Bill, blaming himself for going back to work after lunch. They were all totally bewildered. And as their stories were told, one after another, it was like the Berlin Wall falling. The room was thick with emotion, and I was conscious of being in the presence of something very unusual, very special, because it takes something like this for people to share themselves so deeply. I felt like they were ministering to me."

After listening to them for more than an hour he offered a prayer, tentatively at first, fearing they might resist the suggestion. But they seemed to welcome it. It was evident that they wanted him to conduct the funeral service, and he promised to return the following evening to discuss details. He now knew what form it should take. Denise made it very clear that she did not want it said that Kristie's death was God's will, or that her baby had gone to a happier place. She was offended by such platitudes. Rather did she need to express her rage and grief and pain.

He assured all four of them that it was all right for them to be angry, and sensed that this was something they needed to hear.

Before there could be a funeral Bill and Denise had to purchase a cemetery plot, and as Jim drove them around the Westchester cemeteries he was careful not to influence their choice. He had stated his feelings only once, in the matter of Denise seeing Kristie's body. Beyond that he resolved to keep his opinions to himself. He well remembered how he and Barbara felt when they went to choose Kimmy's last resting place, a few days before she died.

"You need to go to the cemetery and look around. When you find the right spot you know it," he said. He would not have wanted another person's preferences confusing their choice.

He drove them to Gate of Heaven where they looked at the plot next to Kimmy's. Bill was privately thinking how dearly he would like to have Kristie buried there, but hesitated to say so, uncertain of how Barbara and Jim would feel. Perhaps they would prefer this to remain Kimmy's special place; having the children's graves side by side might be too distressing to them. It wasn't a question which a man of Bill's reticence could comfortably ask. Jim was wrestling with similar doubts about his brother-in-law's feelings when the three of them walked into the cemetery office.

There was a long table in the room. Bill, Denise, and the office manager sat at one end of it. Jim settled down at the far end, out of the conversation.

"Was the baby baptized?" the manager inquired.

"No," Denise replied promptly.

As a Catholic in a Catholic cemetery, Jim had a shrewd idea where this discussion was leading. He tried to catch the manager's eye. But the manager did not look his way, and this was not the moment for Jim to tell his secret. Bill was trying to explain that the two families were related, and was picking up the impression that, for reasons he did not understand, he and Denise were somehow unacceptable. They left without making a decision, and went on to look at the nonsectarian Mount Pleasant Cemetery on the other side of the Bronx River Parkway. It was smaller, pleasantly landscaped, and a little closer to their home. They were shown a plot near the crest of a hill, and Denise liked the fact that, standing there, it was possible to look out across acres of countryside to a forested horizon. Just as the Donnellys were taken with the idea of Kimmy's being buried in a tree-lined valley, the Fischers were comforted to think of Kristie's grave having a fine view.

As soon as he returned from the cemetery tour Jim contacted his priest at Holy Name, Father Al, to share his concern about the misunderstanding at Gate of Heaven. Father Al telephoned the cemetery's manager, and the manager telephoned Bill to say that he would be happy to sell him the plot next to the Donnellys'.

"By then we did not feel wanted there," Bill said, months later. Jim, however, had the impression that it was the painful proximity of Kimmy's grave which caused his in-laws to decide on the plot at Mount Pleasant Cemetery. He did not want to make it more difficult for them by asking. He felt sad, but he understood.

"Whatever they wanted was fine with me," he said.

Denise favored cremation before burial, and Bill agreed. He would have gone along with anything she wished that week.

"Why cremation?" Leah asked him, doubtfully.

"What does it matter?" her father replied. "Leah, what was left of her was only half a person. She was burned to a crisp already."

He felt he would never be able to forgive himself for going back to work on the afternoon of the fire, leaving Kristie alone with Olivia. The memory which now haunted him, and would probably haunt him for the rest of his life, was of holding his baby in his arms and tenderly whispering the promise that he would never, ever let anything happen to her.

The funeral was arranged for Friday morning, at the same time as Olivia's second court appearance in the presence of her parents and Laura Brevetti. Jim had arranged that too, synchronizing the times so that

Kristie's burial would escape the attention of the media. He assumed, correctly, that reporters working on what was becoming known as "the nanny story" would be more attracted to the hearing in court. By intention, there was no obituary notice in *The Reporter Dispatch,* Westchester's daily newspaper.

On Thursday evening Steven Yagerman returned to the Donnellys' home as promised, and enlisted Denise's help in planning the funeral. He did not know it, but this was the week of her fortieth birthday, an anniversary she did not want to have remembered, or would ever be able to forget. What he did observe was that giving her some control over the arrangements absorbed and calmed her, helping to mitigate the fact that everything else in her life had been cruelly wrenched out of control. Noting her response, Bill withdrew and left them to go over the service together. Addressing the priest as Steve (the word *Father* seemed to cause her difficulty), she made it clear to him that the prescribed readings of the Episcopalian rite offered her no comfort. She did not want to hear about the souls of the righteous being in the hand of God, or about death being swallowed up in victory. With an open Bible between them they searched the Scriptures for passages more meaningful to her.

Eventually she settled on a particularly stark translation of Psalm 55, expressing the bitterness of a man betrayed by a friend he trusted. It ended with a blistering cry for retribution: "But you, O God, will bring these murderers and liars to their graves before half their life is over."

Steven Yagerman commented: "Denise was comparing translations with the attention of a biblical scholar, favoring the one which was most graphic and earthy because it spoke to her pain and desolation. I was impressed by her reading of the various passages."

He offered to substitute the verses of her choice for one of the standard readings. "It's unusual," he conceded. "But it's unusual to have a mother whose baby has been murdered."

Later that evening, sitting at his word processor in a rectory made homey by the ingenuous drawings of his children, he agonized over a funeral address. He was trying to give expression to the emotions Denise had conveyed to him, and at the same time to offer hope. He was tempted to think, as he had done twenty-four hours earlier when he set off for his first visit to the Fischers: "I am not really up to this." But he was committed now, and would not have withdrawn if given a choice.

He felt overwhelmed by the depth of suffering which the entire

Fischer family had undergone in the space of a year. It struck him that there was a curious continuity to it. Kristie, he realized, must have been conceived at about the time of Kim Marie's death. His mind played with their names, and added another—Kimmy, Kristie, Christos—like declensions of a single noun. The thought led him to a further simile, the sacrifice of innocence: Kristie in the fire, Christ on the cross. And thus he began to compose his funeral sermon.

The following morning he delivered it before about two hundred people, overflowing two large adjoining rooms at the Ballard-Durand Funeral Home in White Plains. Some had to stand outside the building. They were friends, neighbors, business associates, and acquaintances who had learned about the service by word of mouth. Many arrived early and sat waiting in respectful silence, their attention focused on a happy photograph of Kristie beside a marbleized funeral urn containing her ashes. The family had searched the rubble of her nursery for the much cuddled white teddy bear given to her by Leah, intending to have it placed in her casket before the cremation. But it had been reduced to ashes already. There were so few remembrances of this baby left.

"Oh, if only words could heal . . ." Steven Yagerman began his homily, wishing it were so. He developed the thoughts which came to him last night, about the willful destruction of innocent life, and he tried to make sense of this by pointing out that from such tragedy can come strength and grace and healing. He spoke of the new understanding of God's humanity which followed the Crucifixion, and the closer relationship between Christians and Jews which came out of the Holocaust. And he put the murder of Kristie Fischer in a category with these outrages "because, after all, a baby is God's message of hope that the world should continue."

His mention of the Holocaust struck a deep chord in a slender white-haired man seated among the mourners, Jan Menting, the architect and builder of the house where Kristie died. Half a century ago he had been a student in The Hague when it was under Nazi occupation, living on the edge of a Jewish neighborhood, powerless to prevent the unexplained disappearance of his friends and neighbors, one by one. That experience had left him with a lasting determination to take positive action whenever he saw truth or justice perverted. The cruel death of Kristie Fischer, his sense of an evil presence in the ruins of her nursery, and the priest's unexpected reference to the Holocaust combined to have a powerful effect on him. As an intellectual who thought of himself as an atheist, he could not relate to the rest of the funeral service. But that comparison with a horror he had personally known, made by a priest who was not even born when it happened, was the beginning of his intense involvement in a search for the truth about Kristie's death.

"When we come through this deep disillusionment we reach a new wisdom which places an obligation upon us," Steven Yagerman was concluding. "An obligation to share how it was that we made it through this, and what we learned along the way. I guarantee you that others in future will need to know how you did it. And part of your healing will be in helping those others to face the unfaceable. . . ."

Some of the Fischers mentally filed his remarks as a future source of comfort. Right now it was as much as they could manage to get through today. After the brief service a small procession of them drove to the cemetery, led by the funeral director, Carlton Odell, in his station wagon.

"They did not want a great big hearse for such a little casket," he explained. There were few flowers; instead Denise had asked for contributions to be sent to a local fund for abused children. Outwardly this barely resembled a funeral procession.

On the journey Odell remarked to his only passenger, the priest: "I think I'm getting too old for this."

It was the emotional impact of this particular funeral, rather than his sixty-two years, which was depressing him. He had known the Fischers for most of his life. Fischer's Garage had serviced his company's funeral cars for decades. He remembered Bill and Bob as little boys playing around their father's shop, and nineteen years ago he had assisted at their mother's funeral. It was against nature for him to be burying Bill's child.

It was a bright, cold day, flaking with snow, and the wind which blew across that high ridge of Mount Pleasant Cemetery was bitter. They all had a feeling of having been here before. It was Kimmy's funeral all over again. Only the place was different.

Betsy sensed the struggle which some of her unchurched relatives were having.

"They had a year to think about death," she said. "When it struck again, only harder, they desperately wanted to believe that there was something beyond it."

Leah conceded: "It was a comfort, the things Steve said, the ideas he shared. We are not a religious family but it helped to be told that wherever Kristie had gone, she was being taken care of."

The funeral urn had been placed in a small white casket for burial. Everyone was tearful as Father Steve said the words of committal. Denise sobbed inconsolably. Leah clung to John for physical support. And again Troy held Bill in an emotional embrace.

Moved by this tender reunion of father and son, one relative whispered, "To think it took a baby's death for this to happen . . ."

They hurried back to their cars. "We just wanted to get it over with," said Bill's brother, Bob. As a young father, he had been devastated by the events of this week. He had thought himself tough and resilient, and it was a shock to realize how vulnerable he could be.

Afterward, back at the Donnellys' home, the atmosphere was very different from the day of Kimmy's funeral. Then it was sad and accepting; now it was angry and bewildered. This was a large gathering of people who did not normally come together in the same place, in-laws and ex-in-laws spanning three generations. A few of them had never met before; others had the inborn Fischer reluctance to share themselves. But there was no hint of any of this today. A stranger walking into Barbara and Jim's living room would have seen an unusually united family reaching out to one another in a very caring and supportive way. Nothing epitomized this more than the sight of Bill, Denise, and Grada sitting together on the stairs, talking as intimately as if the three of them had been close friends for years.

17

Detective Bruce Johnson was trying to find out what Olivia did and who she saw in the days before the fire. Even the most trivial information could be important. At his request Iris came to the Mount Pleasant police station to be interviewed, accompanied by the E. F. Language School's director of student activities, a young Englishman named Richard Polley. She was too insecure about her English to come alone, and Polley spoke fluent German.

With his help as translator she told Johnson of her certainty that Olivia did not show up for their planned meeting the previous Friday. The language school was in one of the college's smaller buildings, with an obvious place for people to meet at its entrance. Iris had waited there for some time, but saw no sign of Olivia. Polley, whose office was nearby on the main floor, confirmed her story.

Finding him receptive, Johnson asked him a favor. Would he translate the recent entries in Olivia's diary? The detective handed him the book, open to a page of her precise handwriting. Johnson already knew that its contents were innocuous because Mount Pleasant's only German-speaking police officer, Claudia Bolwell, had read off a translation to him. She was now back from vacation and her fluency in German caused Johnson to wish all over again that she had been near enough to be called in on the night of the fire.

"Maybe talking woman to woman, in her own language, Olivia might have opened up to her," he mused. But he thought it unlikely. After his chief had failed to win her confidence he doubted if anyone could.

He showed Richard Polley the diary to make certain that there was no nuance of phraseology which his colleague might have missed. Apparently there was not. The last month of almost daily entries, covering Olivia's time with the Fischers, told the expected story of a young woman who had looked forward to a year in the United States but was having a hard time settling in.

"That period started with her being extremely homesick over several days," Johnson summed up. "She wrote that she wished to go home but couldn't because her father would not accept her failure to fulfill her obligation to stay for a year. She would cry at night, but did not want anyone to see. All her emotions were kept inside.

"Her grandfather had just died; she wanted to talk to her grandmother on the phone, and finally did. Her feelings started to get better after that. Soon after she arrived she had a birthday, her twentieth. As time went on she was wishing that Denise would go back to work so that she could be alone with the baby to raise it the way she wanted. She seemed to have strong opinions about infant care. One day she wrote about the baby being taken to the pediatrician to get two shots, and Denise and Bill having her in their room that night because she was fretful. Olivia was critical of this, commenting that these parents behaved as if theirs was the only child who had ever had an injection. Reading the diary, you got a feeling that she wanted to take over this baby, and regretted not having the opportunity.

"She seemed to be more content as time went on. She wrote that she loved the baby, and that the baby was beginning to recognize her. And toward the end she was feeling that this year would not be as bad as she had feared."

Continuing his check into her activities, Johnson located Helga, living with a family in the small Westchester town of Greenburgh. He found her to be, like Iris, friendly and eager to help. She was astonished at Olivia's story about the two of them meeting on the street in White Plains, and denied it vehemently. She said she had not been anywhere near White Plains on that previous Friday, but had remained in Greenburgh for the entire day, which was confirmed to Johnson by the mother of the family.

He wondered why Olivia had lied so elaborately. She might have lost her way to Marymount and been embarrassed to admit it, or she might not have wanted to spend her day off with a girl she barely knew. With Denise's car to herself for a few hours, she might have preferred to enjoy her freedom alone. Her tale about missing Iris could have been an easy lie to cover a truth she did not want to tell. All that he could understand. What puzzled him was her invention of a chance meeting with Helga. It was an unlikely encounter in a busy town of fifty thousand people. Why pretend that it happened?

In the days immediately following the fire Bruce Johnson made several return visits to the house on West Lake Drive. It was a building which appeared larger on the outside than it was within, and the more he paced around the downstairs area, the less likely it seemed to him that an intruder could have moved from room to room unobserved. The hallway leading to the three bedrooms, bathroom, and laundry room was only nineteen feet long, and so narrow that a person standing in the middle of it could touch both walls with his hands. Footsteps echoed on those vinyl tiles. The sliding windows slid noisily. And he had detected nothing wrong with Olivia's hearing.

"There is no doubt in my mind that she knew exactly what happened to that baby," he concluded.

He retraced her account of the fire, even taking a new light bulb to the house and screwing it into her bedroom lamp socket to confirm that the old one had indeed blown when she tried to turn on her desk light to read the fire service's telephone number. He found Denise's handwritten list of emergency numbers exactly where Olivia had dropped it in her panic, on the floor by the family-room phone where she made her emergency calls. He also inspected the burn patterns on beds and carpets, and estimated that "an incredible amount of accelerant" was used, probably close to two gallons, with about two quarts of it poured around the baby. Joe Butler had judged that three pints of flammable liquid would have been sufficient to set the three fires, but that was before anyone realized how much was missing from Bill's store cupboard. Now it was impossible to know whose was the best estimate because all the accelerants burned off.

"I think she poured solvent in Leah's room first because of the extent of the damage," Johnson said. He was struck by the horseshoe-shaped burn pattern around the queen-sized platform bed. "One of the things the textbooks tell you is that burning somebody's bed is a sign of jealousy. And I think this girl was mad as hell at Leah. According to her diary, she thought of her as a typically spoiled young American.

"After Leah's room I think she went to the baby's room, using a lot more fluid, then to her own room, where I think she ran out of solvent.

The burn configuration on her bed was like a half circle, as though there wasn't enough liquid to finish the job. Then I think she put the cans back in the closet where Bill kept them, ignited the fires in the order they were set, and locked the doors behind her. The only door that wasn't locked was the one to her own room, and that was the only fire she put out.''

Like his chief, Johnson argued against Butler's theory about the infant carrier being on Olivia's bed when that fire was started. He could find no corresponding depression on the covers, and concluded that the unburned area had been protected by a light weight object like a towel or piece of clothing. But he could find no trace of what it might have been.

He looked around the laundry room and noted that, as in the bathroom, the windows opened outward on a crank, making it virtually impossible for anyone to break in without smashing the panes. The firemen had told him that they found these windows intact and closed, which left the sliding windows in the three bedrooms as the only likely source of forced entry, and he felt he had already eliminated those.

It was hard to think of everything, but later he would blame himself for failing to disconnect the pipe beneath the laundry sink and check the liquid in the trap. Assuming that the damaged soda bottle on the nursery floor came from the laundry room's recycling bin, and that it had been filled with a solvent from Bill's work closet, the logical place for an arsonist to make the transfer would have been over that sink. Traces of solvent in the trap would have been one more indication of an inside job.

Hindsight also led him to wish that he had taken many more samples of burned carpet and bedding from Leah's room. Forensic tests would confirm that it was indeed paint thinner which soaked Kristie's diaper, and that to a 99 percent certainty it was the same paint thinner as the residue in one of the cans in Bill Fischer's store.

"But you can't say that in court," Johnson explained. "Legally ninety-nine percent isn't good enough. It has to be a hundred. If we had tied another accelerant, like the charcoal lighter fuel or the Coleman appliance fluid, to the fire in Leah's room or to the one on Olivia's bed, it would have been important evidence. But we could not make that connection. And there was not much more we could have done. There was enough soot and water in that house to destroy most of the evidence.''

Johnson regretted that Kristie's infant carrier was not removed on the night of the fire, if only to spare Bill and Denise the pain of seeing it. He doubted if it had much evidential value, other than its emotional impact upon a jury. But he felt compassion for the Fischers, and a strong empathy with Bill. In time to come he would realize that an unspoken friendship between the two of them began at about 7:45 P.M. on Monday, December 2, at the moment when Bill and Denise were ushered into the back door of the Fries house, and he hurried Olivia out at the front. This wasn't just expedient police work on his part. It was his instinct about the kind of people the Fischers were, and the depth of their pain. He and Bill were of the same generation, born into the same community, shaped by the same work ethic and family loyalties. He could identify with this man and his wife even before exchanging a word with them. They were out of the same mold as Paula and himself. From now on his desire to see justice done in this case would come not only, as it always did, from pride in his job but also from his personal desire to help this couple to recover and get on with their lives.

He was back at the ruined house with them on the Thursday after the fire, the day before Kristie's funeral, taking video pictures of the scene. It was his third photographic session. He took some pictures while the firemen were still there on Monday evening, a few more on Tuesday showing the rooms being cleaned of debris, and the rest on this Thursday when Bill, Denise, Leah, John, Jim, Bob, and Betsy were all at the house helping to salvage belongings.

At the Monday-evening taping he managed to record one scene only seconds before the firemen demolished it. They were about to smash Olivia's window out, removing all traces of its position at the time of the fire, when Johnson captured the scene on video, including the sound of splintering glass. Other clues were irrevocably lost before he could record them.

He was alone at the house for most of the Tuesday taping, and did little more than Leah's room before his camera battery gave out. Returning at about 11:30 A.M. on Thursday he worked around the family as they searched the debris for personal treasures, including the white teddy bear which they hoped to put in Kristie's casket. As he moved around the house his microphone picked up snatches of their conversation, including a comment from Leah, "This is my room, and it's the worst of all," as she ducked past him in the hallway.

"She was shell-shocked," her uncle Jim recalled.

After he had finished photographing the house, Johnson took a shot of Leah and John outdoors, sorting among the rubble of furnishings which the firemen had jettisoned out of windows, Leah hunting for some earrings which were precious to her because they had been a present from John.

These details seemed inconsequential at the time. A more memorable incident to the Fischer relatives working among the ruins was the arrival of a Federal Express messenger with a letter from a syndicated talk program, *The Maury Povich Show*, offering Bill and Denise the opportunity to tell their story on national television. Sickened by the intrusion, Bill flung the letter aside. And that, he assumed, was the end of his contact with the TV media.

He would soon be proved horribly wrong. Less than six weeks hence, a television version of the Fischers' story would be aired across the nation, without the family's approval and with little relation to the truth as they saw it. This show would be based on the police videotapes Bruce Johnson had just made, tapes never intended for public exposure, with their background comments misinterpreted to give a very different perception of why Kristie Fischer was murdered and who might have been responsible.

18

It was a little more than half a mile from the Fischers' home to the nearest shops, but not a journey to be done on foot. Most of it was on Nannyhagen Road, a two-lane highway without a sidewalk, which twisted down a steep hill. Trees, hedges, and bends in the road could conceal oncoming traffic until it was dangerously close. And yet for a girl in Olivia's position, lonely and in need of human contact, this was the obvious walk to take. Most roads in the immediate vicinity were like West Lake Drive, semi-rural with detached houses well spaced, lacking pedestrian pathways because in the exurbs of Westchester almost everyone goes everywhere by automobile.

It is a paradox of the American landscape, and a revelation to visiting Europeans, that although a great deal of countryside exists, very little of it can be comfortably traversed on foot. When Denise warned her new au pair that she would be coming to a rural neighborhood, Olivia probably equated Thornwood with the picturesque Swiss villages she knew: communities with a visible heart, enticing places to stroll, and shopkeepers with time for friendly conversation. What she found instead at the bottom of Nannyhagen Road was the Rose Hill Shopping Center, a functional strip of shops behind a large parking lot. It was not a place where people were tempted to linger.

In Switzerland she loved to go horseback riding, and one of her first questions on the day after her arrival was about riding facilities in the Thornwood area. Denise was not encouraging. She warned that it was a very expensive sport. "I don't know, however, what she means by expensive," Olivia wrote in her diary.

Ten days later, on November 12, she made this entry: "Today I was alone the whole afternoon with Kristie and it was simply wonderful. We understood each other really well.

"However, slowly but surely I want to get away from here and see something of the United States. I know all about the house, but I am lacking the rest of the United States. I want to explore it on my own and find out what is where and what goes on here. Most of all I am trying to find a place where I can ride. I am missing it a lot, even if during the last lesson Ganges deposited me roughly on the ground i.e. the floor of the riding school. The pain has disappeared a long time ago and I am anxious to ride again."

She never did have the opportunity. In her first three weeks at the Fischers' home, before Denise went back to work, Olivia was given several hours of free time every day. But she could not go far without transport, and there was only the Rose Hill Shopping Center to which she could comfortably walk. After her arrest, when her photograph had appeared in the newspapers, the proprietor of Rose Hill's cigarette and candy store identified her as someone she had twice seen at the shopping center and remembered clearly because of her unusual behavior.

The first occasion was late one morning when the young woman, who she felt sure was Olivia, came into her shop alone. She hung back by the entrance for several minutes, as though undecided about what to buy. Then nervously she picked up a pack of cigarettes from a display stand where the price was marked on a handwritten sign. Without a word she put the exact money on the counter and left. Olivia would have been self-conscious about her limited English, but there was also something strange about her which the storekeeper could not forget. Later she asked her assistant: "Is it my imagination, or is there something wrong with that girl?"

"It isn't your imagination," the assistant replied. "She looked really out of it."

Initially Bruce Johnson might have discounted the incident as one of mistaken identity. Olivia said she did not smoke, and there were no cigarettes among her belongings. However, the storekeeper had an additional recollection which confirmed his impression that her silent customer was indeed Olivia Riner.

She told Bruce Johnson that she saw this same girl a second time, on Saturday, November 30, two days before the fire. This was the day after Olivia's unexplained outing in Denise's car; the day that she was left alone with Kristie while Bill and Denise went hiking. That morning as

the storekeeper was driving into the parking lot she passed Olivia walking along the road toward the shopping center carrying a baby. It was
a troubling sight. No woman in her experience would walk on a traf-
ficked street with an infant in her arms. It was far too dangerous. Also
this baby was wrapped only in a light blanket with no head covering.

"It was bitter cold, and the wind was unbelievable," the storekeeper
recalled. This girl was as poorly clad as the baby, wearing only a jacket
with her jeans. And thus Olivia must have carried Kristie down the
treacherous hill of Nannyhagen Road.

Minutes later a girl and baby fitting the same description were seen
in the A & P Sav-A-Center, the supermarket dominating Rose Hill's
shopping strip. A woman who worked there, assuming her to be a poor
young mother, was tempted to say to her: "I have a warm baby blanket
and a stroller at home which I would be happy to give you." But the
girl's withdrawn demeanor discouraged her.

"I didn't like to interfere," the woman said later. "It's hard to know
whether you are doing the right thing."

After about half an hour the cigarette-store owner was looking out
through her shop window when she saw Olivia leave the shopping center, carrying the baby across the parking lot in the direction of Nannyhagen Road. She, too, wished there was something she could do about
it, but didn't know what.

"Such a cold day!" she remarked to her husband. "Why doesn't that
baby have something on its head?"

For Bill and Denise that Saturday was a happy day out, with no inkling
that their infant daughter was being neglected. Soon the weather would
be right for cross-country skiing; then they would take Kristie with them.
They had it all planned. They would bundle her up in one of the several
snug outfits which (along with a baby carriage) had been available to
Olivia that day, and Bill would strap her to his back. On this weekend
before the fire they went shopping for a backpack carrier for Kristie,
found one they liked, but decided to defer the purchase until the following week when the price would be reduced in a winter sale.

Olivia's entry in her diary for this Saturday made no mention of her
walk to the shopping center. "Today was what I would call a horribly
normal working day. I was watching the little girl," she wrote.

"Every day I am taking care of her I feel closer and closer to her. As if she were my sister or my baby. I really do love her. I also understand her gestures and noises better every day. When she is hungry, her diaper is dirty or she feels like playing. If one considers how we are created and how fast we develop in the first years of our life. Life is the most beautiful thing this world has ever brought forward. It is something every human receives and which he should protect as well as possible."

She continued in this philosophical vein on the following day, the day before Kristie's death. "Now I have been here one month! How fast the time passes when you feel really well at a place and have something to do. The way I feel now, the remaining eleven 'working months' will pass even faster and then I must or can go home again. I made a firm resolution to enjoy everything here fully because it is only once in your lifetime that you get such an opportunity and you have to grasp this opportunity, because otherwise it is gone and you will be sorry about it for the rest of your life. I have grasped the opportunity and do not regret for one second that I am here!"

Bruce Johnson was trying to make sense of these contradictions when another ingredient was added to the mystery. It came in a telephone call to the Mount Pleasant police department from Lisa Foderaro, the *New York Times* reporter who was covering the arson story. She stated that in reaction to her published account of Olivia's arrest a New Jersey reader had telephoned her to point out a striking similarity between the circumstances of the Thornwood fire and a short story, "The Heroine," written by the American author Patricia Highsmith more than twenty years earlier.

According to the New Jersey informant, a Highsmith book titled *Eleven,* made up of a collection of her short stories including "The Heroine," was currently being sold in Switzerland. He had purchased a copy when recently traveling there. Published in Paris, this edition had English text on one side of the page faced by a German translation, intended for people trying to perfect a second language.

Johnson obtained a copy of "The Heroine" and read it several times, with mounting astonishment. It was a haunting and eerie tale whose plot came uncannily close to the case he was working on. So close, in fact, that he felt himself to be in a kind of time warp, as though this author's imagining of a generation ago had suddenly become reality, and he had been thrust into the middle of it. It was like the inexplicable human experience of sensing that one has been in an unknown place before, except that this earlier incarnation was fiction, and with a few changes in detail it now seemed to have become fact. Forever after he would be nagged by the thought that Olivia could have read the story and, consciously or otherwise, acted it out.

"The Heroine" opens with a twenty-one-year-old young woman named Lucille Smith being hired as nanny to a family in Westchester. The two small children in her charge, Nicky and Heloise Christiansen, quickly become fond of her, and the children's mother thinks she has found a treasure. The reader of the story is, however, let into a secret of which the Christiansens are unaware. Lucille's mother has recently died in a mental institution. And Lucille may have inherited some of her instability.

Desperately needing to feel loved and appreciated, she works unusually hard to give the impression of being the perfect nanny. But nothing she does is sufficient to satisfy her own need for approval.

While playing an adventure game with the children she imagines herself in the role of their rescuer, and begins to wish for some real catastrophe, so that she can prove her great courage and devotion.

Alone in her room one evening she dwells on the fantasy. Although she has told Mrs. Christiansen that she is not a smoker, she smokes three cigarettes from a secret hoard, and they have an exciting effect upon her. Idly, she sets a small fire in her ashtray, and this gives her an idea; that there might be a fire in the house to endanger the children.

By now the house is in darkness. She goes down to the garage, rolls out the heavy gas tank, and splashes its contents around the exterior walls.

"Then," the author relates, "she struck her match and walked back the way she had come, touching off the wet places. Without a backward glance she went to stand at the door of the servants' house and watch." She waited there, intending to let the flames leap up to the nursery window, before rushing in on her rescue mission.

"She had lit the fire at five places, and these now crept up the house like the fingers of a hand, warm and flickering, gentle and caressing. Lucille smiled and held herself in check. Then suddenly the gasoline tank, having grown too warm, exploded with a sound like a cannon and lighted the scene for an instant.

"As though this had been the signal for which she waited, Lucille went confidently forward."

Thus the story ends. The rest is left to the reader's imagination.

Police Chief Paul Oliva was so fascinated with this tale that he wrote a book report on it, the way he learned to do in high school. With his notes on "The Heroine" spread out before him, he tried to determine whether Olivia might have tried to live out a fictitious fantasy.

"The principal character is a governess who comes to Westchester," he wrote. "Has disappointing previous employment and suffers the experience of mother's expiration." Here he made a note of the fact that Olivia had been distressed by the recent death of her grandfather.

"Psychological problem translates to a subconscious shortcoming based upon a suspected negative hereditary factor from the mother. . . . In her solitude she fantasizes a variety of heroics. . . . She set five fires with gasoline on the master house and delayed heroics until she was sure that the danger had peaked."

He wasn't sure what to make of it. It was not admissible as evidence, and not all of the details fitted, but those which did appeared to go well beyond coincidence. He was particularly struck by the multiple fires lit with a flammable solvent—whether gasoline or paint thinner—which was poured from a can in a circular movement, around the outside of a building in one instance, on the inside in the other; both of them directed at an occupied nursery. Some similarities were glaring: girls of much the same age, newly employed in Westchester households where they were trusted, appearing to love the children in their care, yet uncomfortable within themselves and essentially lonely.

There was even the tantalizing detail about the cigarette smoking. At first Bruce Johnson had some doubt about this. He wondered whether the Rose Hill storekeeper had misremembered what she sold Olivia. From his knowledge of this girl, candy was a more likely purchase. And yet . . . Was it too farfetched to suppose that before leaving Switzerland, Olivia bought this collection of short stories and was drawn to the one about a girl close to her age taking the same kind of job in the same American county? And that subsequently she copied Lucille in having an occasional cigarette, lighting one or two as a stimulant and an adventure, and then a larger fire to prove herself a heroine . . . ? Now that his preliminary conclusion—of the fire being set to cover the fact that the baby was already dead—had been disproved, Johnson found the heroine theory persuasive. He still did not want to believe that Olivia had deliberately set fire to a living baby.

He thought this short story was the kind of fiction which would appeal to her taste for the macabre. Her recent reading matter, Thomas Harris's best-seller, *The Silence of the Lambs,* was a study of a serial killer who cannibalized his victims. Patricia Highsmith, author of "The Heroine," was a spinner of eerie and obsessive tales, many of them as gruesome. From Highsmith to Harris seemed a logical step. But had Olivia read "The Heroine"?

Johnson searched through her possessions but could find no trace of it. And he could not question Olivia about the book because she was now in the county jail, represented by an attorney, irrevocably beyond the reach of police interrogation.

He telephoned the police department in Wettingen, her hometown, with Officer Claudia Bolwell on an extension phone in case she was needed as translator. Over the next few days there were several of these conversations. Initially he spoke to a police officer surnamed Suter, who was very cooperative. Johnson asked him whether the Patricia Highsmith book was currently available in Wettingen. Suter told him that very close to Olivia's home there was a kiosk which sold popular fiction, and he offered to call the woman who managed it. While Johnson held on, Claudia Bolwell was able to hear Suter conversing with her on another telephone. He came back with the response that there had been two copies of the Patricia Highsmith book in her inventory, one of which was sold in October. The second copy was still in stock.

"Does she know who bought it?" Johnson asked. He felt the excitement of being on the edge of a discovery. October would have been a likely time for Olivia to stock up on German-language reading matter before leaving for the United States on November 1.

The bookseller did not have an immediate answer to his question. But she would try to recall.

Johnson asked Suter for the second copy of the Highsmith book to be sent to him. "Mail it to me, overnight express, and I will reimburse you," he promised. But the package never came. And the next time he telephoned he was referred to a different Officer Suter who appeared to know nothing of the investigation.

"It was like they were all related but didn't talk to one another,"

Johnson muttered, unaware that Suter was a common surname in the German-speaking section of Switzerland.

"I asked the Wettingen police if they would find out some background on Olivia Riner, talk to people who knew her. They said they would get back to me, but didn't. I called several times. One time I was given the name of a man to speak to, but whenever I asked for him he was out in the field. I also got through to the doctor's office where Olivia worked, but he never returned my calls. As soon as these people understood what was at stake they clammed up."

On his final call to the Wettingen police station he was put through to the commandant who told him that if the Mount Pleasant police wanted any further assistance they would have to get it through Interpol.

Johnson called Interpol's Washington office and asked for a background check on Olivia Riner. He received a Teletype response, "No previous arrests," and the suggestion that he should contact the U.S. Federal Bureau of Investigation station in Berne.

"I really hoped that someone from that F.B.I. office would help," he said. "I called Berne, and at first the man there sounded excited about doing something a little different. This guy said he would check into how many Highsmith books sold in Switzerland, but he never did. I asked if he could interview the lady at the kiosk but I never got an answer to that either, although I spoke with him several times. I had my superior speak with him. I had the D.A.'s office speak with him. Finally the F.B.I. people said there was nothing they could do. Apparently someone got to the woman in the kiosk and told her not to talk to anyone. And by this time nobody at the police station would talk either."

A few days later Johnson checked into his office and was told that a woman had called him from Switzerland, leaving her home telephone number. He couldn't believe his luck. It had to be the bookseller from the kiosk with some information she didn't want to send through the Swiss authorities; anybody else would have left a business number.

He tried to return the call and got a wrong number. Then he realized: "Whoever took the message at our front desk got one of the digits wrong. I didn't know the woman's name or the name of the kiosk. And she never called again."

There was almost nothing to be learned about Olivia in the United States. Johnson telephoned the office of E. F. Au Pair in Boston and spoke with the agency's director, Louise Jakobsson. She had already told *The New York Times* that Olivia Riner had "an impeccable record and lovely recommendations saying that children loved her, and she was so nice and mature." She had nothing to add, except to refer Johnson to her agency's legal department. He was not given access to Olivia's references, or told who supplied them.

On December 5, three days after the fire, Louise Jakobsson sent a reassuring letter to twelve hundred American host families who had contracted for au pair girls through her agency. "We would like to assure you that our screening and training process is thorough and comprehensive," she wrote. "E. F. Au Pair is making every effort to provide adequate support and assistance to all our program participants."

After that she became unreachable by telephone. All press queries to E. F. Au Pair were referred to a New York public-relations agency whose representative declined to comment on the case.

Johnson badly wanted to go to Switzerland. It was a bold proposal to put to a small-town police department whose budget was already trimmed to the bone.

"I thought it was extremely important," he said. "When you are investigating a homicide you always research your background first. It pays off. Here we didn't have much to begin with, but in this girl's hometown I think we would have got a whole lot more. An investigator should have gone there early on, before the Swiss authorities clammed up. We could have talked to neighbors, people who knew her in school, people she worked with. It would have meant bedding down there for quite a few days, but what would that have cost? A couple of thousand dollars? That's nothing in an investigation like this."

It was Paul Oliva's view that if anyone went to Switzerland it should be from the Westchester County District Attorney's office. But he wasn't pressing for it.

"Based on the evidence we already had, I felt we were in pretty good shape for trial," he said. "And I don't know how well Bruce could have communicated with the Swiss. He didn't speak the language, and they were stonewalling him already."

But he conceded: "Ordinarily you would expect someone charged with a crime like this to have a history. But categorically you can't say that. Maybe she was just too young and innocent to understand what the hell she was doing.''

There was another unmentioned factor. If the police chief approved a trip to Switzerland, it was likely to precipitate a bitter public argument at the next monthly meeting of the Mount Pleasant Town Board. The animosity between Paul Oliva and the town supervisor, Robert Meehan, was always simmering below a thin layer of civility, easily ruptured. The two of them were still at odds about Meehan's controversial plan to reorganize the auxiliary police over Oliva's protests. Meehan had won that round, and was likely to win again if public funding was involved. In this contentiously governed community, Paul Oliva was not always free to run his department as he deemed best. Earlier administrations had trusted his professional judgments, but not the current regime. Meehan's was a divided government in which some of the infighting at town board meetings had become embarrassing in its pettiness. At times the quality of repartee transformed these public sessions from civic enlightenment to low comedy. Oliva could write the script for the predictable argument about his use of tax revenue to send a detective to Switzerland (in the skiing season, no less!).

Since he didn't feel strongly about it himself, it was politic to let the D.A's office make that decision.

District Attorney Carl Vergari had assigned his senior trial lawyer, George Bolen, to this case, and Bolen had begun to spend several hours a day working with the Mount Pleasant police. Out of the thirty assistant district attorneys, he was widely regarded as the best prosecutor, with a reputation for being diligent, dedicated, and legally correct. His most famous case, one that had become permanently linked with his name, was his successful prosecution of Jean Harris, headmistress of an elite girls' boarding school in Virginia, for the murder of her lover, Dr. Herman Tarnower, at his Westchester home. After that highly publicized victory of ten years ago, Bolen had been tempted by an offer to work for a private law firm, but, a prosecutor at heart, he was soon back in the D.A.'s office, doing the job which seemed as well tailored to him as the conservative gray suits he habitually wore in court. He sincerely believed that the aggressive pursuit of justice was a high form of public service.

Vergari, operating his department under severe new budgetary restrictions (the same economies which had delayed his arson expert's arrival at the fire scene), was as reluctant as Paul Oliva to send an investigator to Switzerland.

"It won't achieve anything," he argued. "The Swiss authorities are being far too protective."

The country's newspapers were taking the same kind of editorial stance. From the beginning, the Swiss press assumed Olivia's innocence. The German-language tabloid *Blick* published an interview with the administrator of the trade school where Olivia had trained as a medical assistant. This woman remembered her as an excellent student, and refused to believe her capable of murder. The same newspaper quoted an unnamed neighbor of the Riners as saying: "The family is without blemish and works hard. Olivia was always friendly and caring. It is simply impossible that this girl did such an atrocity." And the pediatrician who had not returned Johnson's call told Swiss reporters that it was outrageous to suggest that she could have harmed a baby.

Bruce Johnson continued to believe that elsewhere in Wettingen might be people who knew a darker side of her. He was angry and frustrated about being denied the chance to search for them.

"It was another stonewall," he complained. "I was very upset about it, and always will be. If I couldn't go, I would certainly have expected the D.A.'s office to have the resources to send someone to Switzerland."

19

Linda Sawyer, free-lance television reporter and producer, was one of the first mass-media journalists to take up the story. Young, vivacious, and hardworking, she was the physical embodiment of what the readers of popular fiction, and the watchers of TV dramas, expect women reporters to be. The fact that she was very tall, very blond and attractive, with a penchant for wearing clear, bright colors, made her appear a little larger than life. She was hard to miss in a crowded room, and what remained of her after she had left was an impression of caring enthusiasm; a trusting look in her clear blue eyes which seemed to compel people to reveal themselves to her—and by extension to millions of TV viewers across America. She was skilled at quickly getting the story, presenting it, and going on to the next.

The life-style which went with her job was a demanding schedule of catching planes and taxis, living out of suitcases, staying in cities she barely got to see, and skillfully covering the signs of exhaustion so that on camera she always managed to look bright, intense, and involved. At the beginning of December 1991 she was completing a six-part television series about Aileen Wuornos, a Florida prostitute who had admitted to the murder of seven of her male clients—"America's first woman serial killer," in the phrase Linda used on the air. Hyperbole was an essential ingredient of her occupation.

At this time she was working for a nationally syndicated program, *Now It Can Be Told,* presented by the popular talk show host Geraldo Rivera. This nightly series was aimed at revealing new information about a variety of emotionally appealing news stories, essentially a mixture of straight reporting, speculation, and voyeurism. In the New York area it was aired in midevening, appropriately bridging a gap between the six o'clock news and the entertainment shows.

On the morning after Olivia Riner's arraignment, Linda Sawyer was flying from New York to Florida to finish working on the Wuornos case. On her customary dash through La Guardia Airport, she stopped to buy a couple of newspapers, and in the compulsive way that journalists do she unfolded them on the plane and began to read while still catching her breath.

The account of Kristie Fischer's terrible death, and Olivia's alleged involvement, grabbed her attention—not only as the kind of story which might provide material for her program, but because it spoke to her personally. The other side of Linda Sawyer's life was less glamorous but more important to her than the image she projected on-screen. She was a single mother with sixteen-month-old twin daughters whom she adored, and saw too rarely. As the family's only breadwinner, she was caught in the necessary cycle of having to earn enough money to pay the help who made it possible for her to earn enough to support the twins, the help, and herself.

The help in this case was Annie McKee, an impeccably trained young woman from a prestigious nanny school. Linda had taken enormous care in selecting her, knowing that whenever she was out of town on assignments her precious baby daughters would be entirely dependent upon their nanny. She had hired her when the twins were eleven weeks old, paying a heavy finder's fee to an agency, and a generous salary. As her children grew—happy, nurtured, and well adjusted—she knew that the investment had been infinitely worthwhile.

"I needed the best, and refused to settle for less," she explained. "I needed Mary Poppins to raise my children, and I found her. Annie is twenty-one going on forty-one. She is wonderful, loving, and very responsible. She has known since she was ten that she wanted to be a child-care giver, and she trained very carefully for the job. I do not have a traditional family, but the unconventional way in which I built a traditional home was to find another parent who would cherish my daughters as I do. Can you imagine how I would feel if I were out in Texas or California, worrying if they were properly cared for?"

With steadfast faith in her beloved Annie, that concern had not crossed her mind until now. But there in the cramped space of her aircraft seat, pushed into her face by the proximity of the passenger in front, was a newspaper photograph of a young woman close to Annie's

165

age, charged with murdering a baby while the infant's mother was at work. Oh, my God, she thought, could I ever be in that mother's place? Still breathless from her dash to the plane, she felt a wave of panic.

"That story horrified me, and rocked me to the core because of my personal situation," she said. "Although I was certain that I had found my Mary Poppins, the thought suddenly crossed my mind: How well does any mother truly know her nanny?"

As soon as she was allowed to unhook her seat belt, Linda rushed to the front of the plane to use the air phone. "I put my Visa card into the machine, called home, and waited anxiously. Annie picked up and I could hear my little girls. I asked her if they were all right, and she assured me that they were, sounding surprised that I had called from the plane. But for that brief moment before she answered I was in terror. Reading about what happened to Kristie Fischer made me realize how vulnerable working mothers can be. We bring strangers into our homes to care for our children, and no matter how thoroughly we do the research we never really know. Yet what choices do we have? A woman in my kind of work cannot rely on day care; the hours are ridiculous."

While doing her Florida interviews, Linda kept thinking of the baby who died in Thornwood, only half an hour's drive from her own Connecticut home. She dwelt on this so obsessively that a kind of identity transference took place, and the image of the accused au pair girl began to merge with Annie's. Later she would acknowledge that her anxieties as a working mother overwhelmed her objectivity as a journalist. She imagined how outraged she would feel if Annie were accused of harming a child, and how dedicated she would be to proving her nanny's innocence. Guilt was not possible to contemplate because it would call into question her own judgments and sense of responsibility. It therefore became imperative to her to discover exactly what happened to Kristie Fischer, even though at some subconscious level she knew how she wanted the story to turn out. She wanted a different explanation for this baby's death than the one suggested in her newspaper. She wanted Olivia to be innocent.

She even began to need Olivia's innocence to validate the decisions she had made as a working mother. And she saw herself breaking the story which would liberate this young Swiss girl from an unjust accusation. At the same time it would give her lasting peace of mind about the child-care arrangement she had made for her twins.

"I knew that as soon as I got back to New York I would walk into my editor's office and say, 'I have to do this story,' " she recounted. " 'This one's mine, whatever else you may have lined up for me.' "

She was given the assignment, and began making phone calls.

She found, as all the other reporters did, that no one in the District Attorney's office was talking, and that Police Chief Oliva would add nothing to his original statement. He insisted that the police had positive evidence of Olivia's guilt, but would not disclose what it was. He also refused to identify the young man who called at the Fischer house shortly after the fire started, other than to say he was a friend of Bill Fischer's elder daughter, and not a suspect.

Laura Brevetti was not talking either. Telephone calls to her Manhattan office were taken by a secretary, with no promise that they would be returned. But Linda Sawyer was more persistent than most.

"I did some checking," she said. "Everything that I could find out about Laura Brevetti pointed to her being a workaholic. So I called her office at seven o'clock one evening when all the secretaries would have gone home. As I hoped, she picked up her own phone, and I knew that this was my chance.

"It was obvious why she had not been responding to the media. There was a police chief saying that he had a clear-cut case against Olivia Riner, and she was still figuring out how to defend it. She knew she had to wait, perhaps for just the right journalist to walk into her office. And I was the one. I was ripe for the picking. Nobody had the background I had. Nobody had the reasons I had.

"I told her why it was so necessary for me to know that Olivia did not kill that baby. I was quite convincing. She told me to come to her office the following day, and gave me an appointment for two P.M."

Their meeting took up the afternoon, and continued beyond dinner. "We went to a late café with a group of Laura's friends who were quite fascinating. One of them was a television producer whom she introduced as her boyfriend. She connected with me, and I connected with her. We sat talking until the small hours of the morning."

Linda went home believing herself to be the journalist Laura Brevetti had chosen to tell Olivia's story; also believing this to be the most important assignment she had ever undertaken. Every investigative reporter hopes to uncover hidden truths, and by exposing them to make a difference. Linda assumed she knew the truth before the uncovering began.

Her emotional involvement was as deep as it was immediate. She believed that in Laura Brevetti, ten years her senior, she had made a friend. More important, that Laura (as she immediately called her) had made a friend of her. It was Linda's perception that behind the self-assurance of the successful attorney was a lonely woman who had missed out on marriage and motherhood, and who consequently felt alienated from her own background. She had grown up in Brooklyn, in a large Italian-American family where women were expected to fill traditional domestic roles. Having chosen a career instead, and reached a point of no turning back, she seemed to Linda to be in need of reassurance and understanding. And there was Linda, another career woman toughing it out in another male-dominated profession, eager to reassure and understand.

Over the ensuing weeks, Linda was given a rare insight into how a skilled defense lawyer prepares for a major trial. At first all the legal maneuvers were concentrated on getting Olivia out of jail, a task which seemed overwhelming in light of the $500,000 bail figure set by Westchester County Court Judge Donald Silverman. This high figure was thought necessary to deter Olivia from attempting to leave the country. There was a great deal of concern that she might, especially since the Swiss did not have an extradition treaty with the United States—an unusual factor which, in Laura Brevetti's words, "made her a victim of her own country's benevolence." Like the Mount Pleasant police, the D.A.'s office was fearful that Olivia might seek refuge in a Swiss Consulate, and be spirited back to Wettingen. This suggestion outraged Swiss consular officials in New York, who insisted that they had no intention of dishonoring their commitment to respect the laws of their host country. But the fact that they were actively assisting Kurt and Marlise Riner made for a delicate situation which thrust this small-town murder case into the arena of international diplomacy.

If the bail money could not be raised, Olivia would have to remain in prison until her trial, several months hence. Her plight was sympathetically reported in the Swiss-German newspapers, and soon promises of loans for bail money started pouring in from concerned Swiss citizens. Initially the issue was presented to them as one of simple justice, regardless of what might have happened on the afternoon of the fire. But before long, the legal presumption of her innocence became, for most of her fellow countrymen, a fact.

The Riners were portrayed as a decent, law-abiding couple with no significant savings. His salary as a small-town public official, coupled with hers as a clerk in a garage, gave them a modest standard of life in a rented apartment. On the face of it, they were the epitome of the middle-class German Swiss, shaped by the national virtues of honesty and hard work, with a daughter whose school and work record seemed to be impeccable. In the German sector of Switzerland, there was a collective sense of outrage about the unlikely charge against her.

In this gathering sympathy for Olivia, her status subtly changed. Describing her, newspapers on both sides of the Atlantic elevated her from au pair to nanny. And nanny stuck. The word was more familiar, easier to fit into a headline, and unintentionally helped her image. There is a mystique about a Swiss nanny. The phrase conjures a vision of a starched and smiling children's nurse, ever attentive to the infants in her care. The reality in this case was a girl of barely twenty, more child than woman, who was trained as a medical assistant in a vocational school, and had a little practical experience. Her uniform was the teenage dress of her generation, jeans and a sweatshirt. It was not quite the same thing.

To Linda Sawyer, however, Olivia was as much a nanny as her own. And she was totally committed to her defense.

On Christmas Eve Laura Brevetti announced an agreement she had worked out through the legal system and diplomatic channels. Bail was reduced to the $350,000 covered by the private loans which had been pledged by Swiss donors, and conditions were set to ensure that while Olivia was technically free she would remain under surveillance.

Her mother would have to remain in the United States as her guardian and companion. Both their passports would be impounded until the trial was over. Olivia was required to sign an extradition waiver, and the Swiss authorities promised to turn her over to U.S. law enforcement officials should she seek refuge at their embassy or at one of their consulates. While awaiting trial she was restricted to living within the Westchester–New York City area and obliged to wear an electronic device which would sound an alarm at the office of the monitoring company if she should attempt to go outside her prescribed boundaries. This monitor, suggested by Laura Brevetti, was a new and unusual condition which clinched the deal.

Olivia's release was delayed for several days while the United Bank of

Switzerland's "irrevocable letter of credit," which Brevetti had offered as security, was converted into U.S. currency at Judge Silverman's insistence. The New Year's Eve newspapers carried a smiling photograph of her walking away from the jail building, accompanied by her parents.

For the next six months she and her mother lived anonymously above the New York City headquarters of the Swiss Benevolent Society. This charitable organization occupied an old brownstone house on a quiet street to the west of Central Park. Occasionally its upstairs rooms were rented to students, but this was no longer a paying proposition, and when Olivia and Marlise arrived, most of the student accommodation had been unused for some time. They were directed to a shabbily furnished twin-bedded room which had clearly seen better days, and to a makeshift sitting room on the same floor. After the office staff downstairs had gone home, the two of them were usually alone in this gloomy Victorian building. A forbidding security system on the front door protected them from any possibility of intruders.

Reporters assumed that Olivia was still in Westchester, and after checking the local motels gave up trying to locate her. As it turned out, the least conspicuous place for her to stay was in the heart of America's largest city. In her daily casual attire, with the electronic monitoring anklet concealed by her jeans, she looked like a student or an out-of-town visitor, and there were tens of thousands of them milling around New York.

Only Linda Sawyer was let into the secret and allowed past that firmly locked door. Through Laura Brevetti she was given frequent access to Olivia, and to information being gathered for her defense. During the next few weeks she came to know her well, and to feel very protective toward her. She took her out to New York restaurants, and over various meals learned about Olivia's lonely childhood, her rigid perfectionism, her earnest desire to please, and her propensity to criticize others as well as herself. The topic they both studiously avoided was the fire at the Fischers' home and the manner of Kristie's death. There were questions Linda was longing to ask but knew she must postpone until after the trial. Then what a story she would have!

She observed that Olivia and Marlise seemed to have an unusual relationship. She sensed neither a deep emotional bond nor an antipathy between them; they were more like acquaintances than mother and daughter. Marlise was at a disadvantage, unable to converse in English and lacking the educational background which allowed Olivia to improve her knowledge of the language, and to speak for the two of them, as they moved around New York. This led to a kind of role reversal. Sometimes Olivia would chide her mother for smoking cigarettes, and Marlise would giggle like a mischievous child and defiantly puff away. Watching these lighthearted interchanges, Linda thought it outrageous that Olivia could be suspected of arson and murder. She seemed to be so trusting about the outcome of her trial. It was as though she knew herself to be protected by her own aura of innocence.

"I believed in her so much I would have hired her to look after my children," Linda recalled, months later. "I wanted to believe in her, I truly did. I wanted to rescue her so badly I would have given her my blood. This was much more than a story to me. It was the one case where I could make a difference. I felt she was wrongly accused, and that if I worked hard enough on the story I could put it right. And I was so affected by what had happened, thinking that Denise Fischer could have been me."

With little to do but wait for the trial, Olivia and her mother spent their days sightseeing around New York. They lived like tourists on an extended visit, eking out a budget in cheap lodgings. Kurt Riner had returned to his job in Switzerland, but kept in touch by telephone. From time to time Olivia would be summoned to confer with Laura Brevetti in the elegant skyscraper office of her law firm, just the other side of Central Park. After answering the necessary questions she would be dismissed, while Brevetti continued to work late into the evenings, night after night.

Linda Sawyer, meantime, was doing her own investigation in the Thornwood area, gathering material for a television program which she believed would clear Olivia's name and uncover a very different explanation of how and why Kristie Fischer was murdered.

20

There was little joy to the Fischers' Christmas. Barbara made a brave effort to be festive for the sake of the children: her grandson, E.J., who was fifteen months old, and Bob and Betsy's son, Christopher, who was two.

It was a holiday that could have passed uncelebrated since both infants were too small to carry a memory of it into future years. But in this aftershock of Kristie's funeral the adults needed a customary reason to come together again, to have the stability of holding on to a tradition deeply rooted in their own past. There had always been Christmas for Fischer children at the old house. To deny it would be like saying that the family was crumbling apart.

While E.J. and Christopher played in innocent oblivion, the adults were deeply conscious of other children who should have been there. Ornaments bearing photographs of Kimmy hung from the Christmas tree. And Kristie's terrible death, only a little over three weeks earlier, was on everyone's mind.

"It was hard to put Christmas back," Betsy said. "But we got through it quite well because it was important for the children. They were having fun, playing on their new rocking horse. Watching them, Denise got very misty-eyed. She sat in the corner of Barbara's living room, on the couch with Bill, and did not move. Barbara hugged E.J. a lot. Although it was hard for her, she said she wanted to do Christmas because it would help her try to forget. And it was worth the effort to see the children's eyes light up.

"We all took gifts. Troy gave picture frames that he had designed himself, all of them different. Some were chrome, others were silver or wood. Everyone was going out of the way to comment on the gifts.

172

And everyone in the immediate family was there—the two children, Barbara and Jim, Bill and Denise, Bob and I, Debby and her husband, Rick, my father-in-law, Willie, Troy, Leah and John. We needed to be together.''

Only one person on that guest list was not a Fischer: John Gallagher. Without a word being said, the family was acknowledging that he had become one, on account of his heroic attempt to save Kristie.

Bill's reconstituted family—Denise, Leah, John, and himself—had moved out of the Donnellys' home a few days before Christmas. Through a real-estate agent friend they were offered a three-bedroom condominium which would be available until April. It was next to the Rose Hill Shopping Center, conveniently close to the house on West Lake Drive for Bill to oversee its cleanup and rebuilding. But emotionally it was a long way from home.

Bill and Leah had such fond memories of that house, with its unusual sense of light and space. The inverted arrangement of downstairs bedrooms allowed for a large second-story living room which seemed to be poised among the trees, open to the sky yet wonderfully secluded. This was the time of year when there would be a Christmas tree reaching up to its cathedral ceiling, looking as though part of the surrounding woodlands had been brought indoors and made to sparkle. They might never again live in a house as special. Leah could not imagine another family home; it was the only one she had ever known. Her parents had moved into it the year she was born. Both she and her father missed it constantly. But Denise, who had none of their emotional investment in the place, knew that she couldn't go back.

The fact that the condominium was only a temporary refuge added to their rootlessness. The place was pleasant enough, but Leah felt ill at ease there. Still deeply traumatized, she would have been uncomfortable anywhere.

"I was shattered," she said. "I was afraid of everything. All houses have their noises, and you get used to them. But these were creaks and clicks I did not know. I would turn the television on so I did not have to hear them."

It would have been a comfort to have her beloved cats with her, but they had to be kept in the garage out of respect for the homeowner's concern that they might cause damage.

"They would scratch and cry and try to get out," Leah recalled. "It was awful. Just awful."

The bedroom where she slept had a door leading onto a deck, and that too made her fearful. She imagined someone crouched outside there, waiting to steal into her room and hide in her closet, waiting to attack her. Or perhaps to set fire to her bed.

The parking space for her car was some distance from the condominium, and she dreaded that lone walk, especially after dark. Her sense of security, her faith in the established order of life, had been so horribly violated that it would be a long time before she could feel safe again.

Her father and Denise were preoccupied with their own tragedy. John was a comfort, but he too was still in shock. The two of them found security of a sort in the familiar but crowded space of the Gallagher home in Mahopac and, increasingly, drove the fifty-mile round trip to stay there overnight. It meant seven adults in a small house with only one bathroom, but to Leah it was a haven. Surrounded by John's family, she felt protected.

Her overnight visits there had become more frequent even before the fire, with the arrival of Olivia. For many months John had been in the habit of spending weeknights at the Fischer home, which was closer to his work. But with the advent of an au pair, Bill and Denise made it clear that they did not want him to continue sleeping on their family-room sofa. It was the area Olivia would use as a sitting room, and they felt she would be uncomfortable to have a man staying there.

Leah commented: "I understood the reason for that request. So did John. He is very sweet and considerate, and he would never get into an argument with my father or Denise. But we spent more time at his house after that."

Early one morning in January, after an overnight visit in Mahopac, Leah and all the Gallaghers were preparing to go to their various jobs. It was barely 6:45 A.M., still dark outside, and as usual cars had to be shifted around in the broad driveway so that those who needed to leave first could get out. A car John had been repairing was blocking his mother's; he went to move it, found the door lock frozen, and was struggling to open it when he heard several other automobiles skidding around on the sand at the entrance to the driveway. It was an unexpected, jarring sound on this quiet rural road at such an early hour. He looked up, and in the dim predawn light saw the shapes of several strangers piling out of their cars and advancing toward him.

John ran up onto the wooden deck to the back door of his home, aiming to get inside before the intruders caught up with him. Leah, who had watched the scene from behind the wheel of her parked Toyota, got out of her car and also hurried toward the house. One man in the group, who was holding a microphone, ran after John, breathlessly shouting: "I have a question for you concerning the Fischers' baby. Just a couple of questions, man. I mean, you're a hero, you were there. I just want to ask you one quick question. A question, man. You went into the room, right? What did you see when you went into the room?"

John had been warned by the District Attorney's office that reporters might ferret out his identity and try to interview him. He had also been instructed not to discuss the case with the media. But he was unprepared for an onslaught like this. Certainly not on his own home territory, when it was barely light and he was barely awake.

"I have no comment," he replied, anxiously tapping on a glass panel of the back door, hoping that someone would open it quickly.

The reporter persisted: "You say you went in. Did the baby—could you see the baby in the room? How come your name has not been heard? What you did was a real heroic thing. How come nobody's heard from you, John, when you're a hero?"

At that moment Carol Gallagher opened the door for her son. Leah was running up the wooden steps of the deck to join him.

"Excuse me, excuse me, please," she said to a reporter who was blocking her way. Afterward she wondered why she had been so polite. Her heart was pounding as she and John piled into the kitchen.

"John, you're the hero," the reporter called after him. "You're the hero, man."

On his dash to the house John caught an unforgettable glimpse of his father, peering through his bedroom window while rubbing the sleep from his eyes, with the bewildered expression of one trying to determine whether he was actually seeing this invasion of his property, or merely dreaming it.

Carol Gallagher recalled: "There were two cameramen, a black fellow and a white woman, and they all left their cars blocking our driveway. Michael and Renee and John and Leah and I had to get to work, but none of us could leave the house because our cars were blocked. We asked the reporters to go away but they kept saying, 'Don't you have a comment?' We told them no, but they continued to sit out there. One of them ran up onto the deck to try and get photographs of John and Leah through the window, as they sat in the living room."

The woman in the group outside was Linda Sawyer, and she had a very different perception of the confusion around her—one which in part was colored by hearing someone in the Gallagher family ask rhetorically: "How the fuck did they find out where we live?"

Carol related: "Eventually we called the Commack police. They asked if John was under subpoena, and when we told them yes, two patrol cars showed up within five minutes. By then it was 8:40 A.M. and we were all late and upset."

They thought that was the end of it. They reasoned that the camera crew had left empty-handed, and the police intervention made this intrusion unlikely to recur. But they were badly shaken by the experience, and once again Leah's faltering sense of security was utterly destroyed.

21

Assistant District Attorney George Bolen had feared something like this. He saw himself as an old-fashioned prosecutor who played by the rules; using the media to influence public opinion was not one of them. He had explained to the Fischers, and to John Gallagher, why he did not want them talking to reporters. From his prosecution of Jean Harris, and from his wider experience around the Westchester County Courthouse, he knew what could happen to people who were caught up in a sensational murder trial; how an off-the-cuff comment could come back to haunt them as a headline. How it might be perverted or misquoted to make an innocent person look guilty.

The media in general, and television in particular, had become more intrusive in the ten years since the Harris trial; also in these early weeks of 1992 murderous nannies were in the news. In January a sensational new movie, *The Hand That Rocks the Cradle,* had its premiere, and almost immediately was drawing packed audiences across America. It would remain a box-office hit for many weeks, not because it was great art but because it struck a sensitive nerve in every parent who had ever left a child with a baby-sitter.

The film told the bizarre tale of a nanny who wreaked havoc in a household as her way of settling a personal vendetta. After endearing herself to the mother and children, she suddenly attempted to destroy their house and to kill them. The story was a variation on the theme of "The Heroine," and the movie's instant success sparked a rash of newspaper and magazine articles about the risks and problems of leaving one's children with hired help. There were letters to editors citing nanny horror stories, and advice columns suggesting precautions for parents to take—from carefully checking references to installing closed-circuit television devices so that nannies could be monitored at long distance.

America's working mothers reacted to the film in much the same way as Linda Sawyer responded to the Fischers' tragedy. They did not want to believe that it could happen to them. But inevitably the movie recalled last month's headlines about Olivia's arrest, bringing that story—and all the anxious questions it raised—back into public consciousness. Wherever *The Hand That Rocks the Cradle* was shown, there was talk of "the Swiss nanny case," and Americans who had not previously heard of the events in Thornwood heard about them now.

Making a direct link between the known facts of Kristie's death and the fiction of the movie, the national magazine *People* commented: "Until the trial later this year the Fischers must live with the agony of their loss and the wrenching possibility that, if Riner is indeed guilty, they delivered their daughter into the hands of a killer."

This was nothing young parents and grandparents wanted to contemplate for themselves. The movie, after all, was fiction. It would be a comfort and a relief to learn that the charges against Olivia Riner came into the same category, and that murderous nannies belonged with ogres in fairy stories.

In this climate of public opinion, on February 14, 1992, Valentine's Day, Geraldo Rivera devoted half of his *Now It Can Be Told* program to the Kristie Fischer case.

Rivera, whose name first came to public attention as a hard-hitting investigative reporter, was better known as the instigator and star of *The Geraldo Show,* a daytime television interview program widely regarded as the most sensational of the network talk shows. There seemed no limit to Rivera's daily ability to bring into the living rooms of America an extraordinary array of unlikely people: transsexuals, incest victims, surrogate mothers, children of artificial insemination, women seduced by their mothers' boyfriends, women whose mothers had seduced their own boyfriends—all of them willing to publicly share intimate experiences which most people would hesitate to tell their best friends. It was like mass therapy, without the healing. Instead there were breaks for commercials, and the promise of more tomorrow.

Rivera brought the same approach to his new program, *Now It Can*

Be Told, which promised exclusive insights into current news stories. His output was such that it took a team of others to do the legwork. His presentation of "the Swiss nanny case" was produced by Linda Sawyer, and was largely the result of her research.

George Bolen obtained a copy of the transcript from a reporter in the courthouse press room a day or two before the show was aired. He alerted the Fischers to watch the program, and warned them that they would find it offensive. Earlier, someone in Rivera's office had approached him for an interview, and he had declined. The request irked him because of its clear indication that "the sleaze merchants," as he called them, were onto the story. But what came on the screen that Valentine's night was far more damaging than Bolen had feared.

The program opened with the stark announcement by Geraldo Rivera: "Today, exclusive, we find a key suspect in a horrifying crime that mirrors the terror of one of the country's hottest movies."

The camera closed in on his lean and swarthy face, crossed by an expression of concern.

"It's one of our worst nightmares, leaving our child in the care of a nanny or a baby-sitter who ends up neglecting, abusing or even, God forbid, murdering the kid," he confided to his viewing public. "That certainly was our impression in the case of a horrifying incident which took place in an affluent New York suburb this past December. But our Alexander Johnson has uncovered new evidence that the authorities apparently chose to ignore."

Appearing on screen, Alexander Johnson was immediately recognized by the Gallagher family as the reporter who chased John up to the back door of his home, repeating, "You are a hero, man. . . . How come nobody's heard from you when you're a hero?" But tonight he was telling viewers a different story.

He claimed to have obtained exclusive information that, having swiftly arrested Olivia, the Mount Pleasant police deliberately ignored a possibility that John Gallagher could have been the arsonist. "Sources tell us that Chief Oliva has a long-standing friendship with the Gallagher family," Alexander Johnson observed, meaningfully.

This unverified (and untrue) statement was juxtaposed with clips from the film *The Hand That Rocks the Cradle,* and with the police recording of Olivia's emergency call for help. Her voice, calm at the beginning, was heard rising to hysteria as the desk sergeant argued back to her that 5 West Lake Drive did not exist.

This impression of police ineptitude was followed by a comment from Laura Brevetti, looking confident and efficient in her book-lined office: "You can hear her voice in absolute panic when he said 'There's no such address.' Total frustration, total fear that no one would arrive to put out the fire."

She went on to describe the arrest of her client as "a rush to judgment for no apparent reason other than she was the convenient suspect."

Rivera interpolated: "The nanny Olivia Riner really thought that she was alone with three-month-old Kristie Fischer when that fatal fire broke out. Until now so did everyone else, including the cops. But we've uncovered a shocking possibility. Someone else may have been there."

The scene shifted to the exterior of the Gallagher family home at the time of the early morning invasion by the television team. John Gallagher was photographed averting his face from the camera as Alexander Johnson asked him: "You went into the room, right?"

From his studio Rivera posed the rhetorical question: "Who is this mystery man and why won't he talk?"

The camera focused back to Johnson asking John what he saw in the baby's room, and John (his back still turned to the camera) muttering that he had no comment.

After a station break, Johnson returned to identify this "mystery man" in the preceding pictures.

"His name is John Gallagher, and though he lives some twenty-five miles away from the scene of the crime, he frequently visited the Fischer house to see his girlfriend. *Now It Can Be Told* has exclusively obtained the police report that contained Olivia Riner's statement to law enforcement on the night of the fire. She told officers that when she ran outside to get help to save the baby, John Gallagher was standing right in front of the Fischer house. She also reported that Gallagher ran back inside and tried to rescue the infant. Though he was unsuccessful, he acted very much like a hero that night. But oddly his name has never come up in any newspaper account of the case. Two months after the fire we located John Gallagher at his home."

This was the first time that John had been publicly identified as the young man who was first on the scene at the Fischer home. But now, without being told of his attempt to save Kristie's life, millions of viewers were hearing that, as the boyfriend of Kristie's half sister, he may have had a motive to cause the fire.

Before the cameras shifted back to the early morning scene outside the Gallagher house, a copy of a document was flashed on the screen. It was not explained, but from a quick glance it could be seen as John Gallagher's application for a pistol permit. Juxtaposed with photographs of the fire raging at the Fischer house, the implication was obvious: This young man could be a killer.

In that context, it seemed appropriate for the reporter to be pestering John. Still unable to photograph his face, the cameraman had caught a final shot of him retreating to the house—the back view of a young man with short reddish hair, wearing a ski jacket. The video picked up the sound of his voice, riding on the steam of his breath in the early morning cold: "I have no comment." The next shot showed Leah, hurrying with him to the back door. As it was presented, their behavior began to look like guilty avoidance.

Alexander Johnson observed: "Gallagher turned out to be a very reluctant hero. The woman with him is Leah Fischer, baby Kristie's stepsister. The same two were captured on this police video, shot the morning after the tragic fire. Their voices indicate a mood anything but tragic."

The next segment of the program was devastating.

Parts of Bruce Johnson's police film were shown, with some of the voices his soundtrack had picked up. There was his shot of Leah and John outside the house, searching among the wreckage, and one of Leah's burned-out bedroom, empty, with the sound of people talking off camera. Their conversation was so muffled that what one of them was thought to have said, and whose voice it was thought to be, was spelled out in a caption:

"John Gallagher: 'You and I will stay at my house for a while, and we'll have barbecues.' "

Then the sound of a woman's laughter. The way this was presented, it seemed as though John and Leah were making jokes—gloating, or worse—over the burned-out house and the dead baby.

The Gallaghers and the Fischers watched the program in horror, gathered in their respective living rooms.

"Mom, how can they do this?" Renee Gallagher asked her mother, tearfully.

"They can do whatever they want" was Carol's bitter response. "It's called freedom of the press."

John was thirty miles away in Hawthorne, watching the program with a group of men friends. One of them, a police patrolman who had not been involved in the case, was as shocked as the rest of them. "I can't believe this," he said.

"I can't believe it either," John responded, shaking his head.

"You might want to talk to a lawyer about it," his friend suggested.

"Yeah, I think I gotta."

But he never did. Like his mother he felt helplessly overwhelmed. Hiring a lawyer to prosecute was beyond the Gallaghers' life-style or understanding. Also, whatever action they might try to take was too late. The damage was done.

Leah saw the show with her father and Denise, in the living room of their rented condominium. "I felt sick to my stomach," she said.

Her mother, Grada, had the same reaction. Watching in her Manhattan apartment, she felt helplessly enraged about the slur on her daughter, and she taped the program for Troy. But he refused to replay it.

"I don't want to see it, ever," he told her. "It's an outrage. Some of these newscasters act so concerned, but all they're doing is feeding people dirt."

The program ended with a dialogue between Alexander Johnson and Geraldo Rivera, one that sounded solicitous but rehearsed, with Rivera adding his own innuendos.

"Though Olivia's clothing showed no trace of hydrocarbons in police tests, we will never know about John Gallagher's clothes," Johnson stated. "They were never tested. And what about the motive for this horrible crime? Police say she had one: homesickness for her native Switzerland."

Rivera asked: "You mean the official motive that they attribute to the nanny is that she was homesick?"

"Homesick," Johnson repeated.

"That's the best they could do?"

"So far."

"No money? No affair with the father of the family? Just homesickness?"

"That's the official record, exactly." (In fact, there was no "official record" of an alleged motive. And no one had remotely suspected a liaison between Olivia and Bill; that suggestion was entirely Rivera's.)

"Now we're not indicting this guy Gallagher," Rivera summed up. "The fact that he runs away from the camera or the fact that he's sifting through the wreckage and laughing the next morning—we don't mean

to attribute guilt to him. However, the fact that he was not questioned—
has he been questioned to this date?"

"As far as we know, no," Alexander Johnson replied. "When we tried
to get comments from him as to whether or not he had been questioned, we got nothing. When we went to the police chief, again, he
wouldn't speak to us. . . . Sources tell us no, he has not been treated as
a suspect or brought in for questioning."

Again there was no hint of who the sources might be. In any event
they were wrong. On the night of the fire John Gallagher was indeed
questioned by the police.

"Stay on this one," Rivera urged his reporter. And he concluded:
"We alert all the other journalists in the New York City area to take
another look at this case. I smell a rat."

This comment so enraged Jim Donnelly, watching the program in his
living room, that he might have flung something hard at his twenty-six-
inch screen if Kimmy's portrait had not been in its customary place.
Instead he limited himself to arguing back at the smoothly groomed
image of Geraldo Rivera.

"So do I," he yelled. "And it's you."

Most of the material in that program was privileged information. Bruce
Johnson's videos of the fire scene had been turned in to the District
Attorney's office, and under the evidential rules of discovery, the District
Attorney had sent copies to Laura Brevetti. These rules were rigorously
enforced in New York State. If a prosecuting counsel failed to make the
defense aware of every scrap of physical evidence, one small omission
could be grounds for a mistrial.

It would also have been a serious breach of legal ethics for either side
to publicize evidence prior to criminal proceedings, especially in ways
that could influence the outcome of a trial. Yet somehow, someone had
made available to Geraldo Rivera two of the videos taken by Bruce Johnson, his taped interview with Olivia immediately after her arrest, the
tape recording of Olivia's frantic telephone call to the Mount Pleasant
police, and John Gallagher's application for a pistol permit (which he
had filed months earlier when he wanted to go hunting). The gun-
license request, which was not considered at all relevant to the murder
of Kristie Fischer, had been denied, apparently because state computer
records showed that John had amassed a number of speeding tickets.

When these items were presented together, linked by photographs of John evading reporters, and with that comment from the fire scene about making a barbecue ascribed to him, the effect was damning.

Overnight there was a perceptible shift in public opinion. Those who had watched the show spread the word to those who hadn't: "It was the boyfriend who did it." And by implication, it was Leah who helped him. From that supposition, a scenario was invented: one in which the daughter of this house and her boyfriend were so resentful of the new wife, and so jealous of the new baby, that they conspired to ruin the life of the mother by eliminating the child.

There were obvious flaws to this theory. Why would Leah condone the destruction of the home she loved, and of everything she possessed? How could she suppose that her relationship with her father could improve after such a horrible tragedy? But it was easier to ignore these questions than to acknowledge the possibility of Olivia's guilt. The Rivera program confirmed what most parents wanted to think, that she was innocent, and the expression of this opinion on national television gave it authenticity. Immediately after Valentine's Day the tone of gossip around Thornwood changed.

People who did not want to be named were more than ready to offer their own ideas.

"A lot of my customers think Olivia Riner is innocent," a local hairdresser commented. "They didn't think that at first, but now they are wondering why, if she started the fires, would she stay in the house to call the police? One woman said that arson is an American crime, and that a European girl would not think of it."

"People who come into my store are a hundred percent in her favor," said the owner of a small grocery shop. "They don't see how or why she would have committed this crime. This is just a simple little girl of twenty who came from another country to do a job here."

There was widespread empathy with these sentiments. Many families in the Thornwood area were of German-speaking immigrant stock, and Olivia Riner seemed to personify their own hardworking, sometimes misjudged ancestors.

One such resident, a woman active in local affairs, came up with a detailed hypothesis which she discussed widely among friends and neighbors: "It just doesn't make sense to say that the girl did it. If she had a criminal record in Switzerland, the Swiss wouldn't have been behind her. So if she didn't do anything over there, why would she come here and set those fires? And why was Gallagher on the scene so fast? I don't believe his story. I think he and Leah were upset because of Denise.

"I think the liquid was poured through the window from outside. Bill knows in his heart that the nanny didn't kill his baby. Bill only has to go into the local deli and hear the comments. We had fires in this neighborhood before this girl ever came to the country. After that Geraldo film the beauty parlor was abuzz. Everyone was saying the same thing, that *she did not do it.*"

22

It was not only what the Geraldo Rivera film said about John Gallagher, but what it left unsaid—the insight it gave into how Olivia's defense would be conducted—which troubled George Bolen.

He knew that Bruce Johnson was the only one who had the videotape before passing it to him, and he was positive that it was not leaked from the District Attorney's office. He was meticulous about protecting evidence.

"Bruce gave the tape to me personally," he recalled. "By law I was required to give a copy to the defense and I had that copy made in-house. I gave it directly to Brevetti on January ninth, 1992, and she signed for it. Five weeks later I was shocked to see it played on the Geraldo Rivera program, artfully spliced and with the speakers wrongly identified. That tape did not come from me, or from anyone in my office. Nor, I am sure, did it come from any of the police officers involved in this case."

If Bolen was right, the tape had to have come from Laura Brevetti's law firm, with or without her knowledge. The fact that she allowed herself to be interviewed for the Rivera program, and was presented sympathetically, suggested—but did not prove—that she knew. It also gave George Bolen an insight into her likely strategy in this case.

He had already speculated that she might imply that John Gallagher was the culprit. "It's a typical defense tactic, to try and remove suspicion from the accused person by pointing a finger at someone else," Bolen said. "I had warned John and Leah that he might be accused of this crime, and she might be considered an accessory. I don't think they believed me, but I have been around courthouses long enough to know that it happens." But even he had not expected the accusing to be done on national television.

It was not his style to let personal feelings color his conversations with witnesses. He felt for the Fischer family deeply, but seemed to be at pains not to let this show. He came across to them as dedicated and concerned, but uncommunicative. They called him George but did not feel they knew him, or ever would, not in the comfortable, neighborly way they were coming to know Bruce Johnson. They had no sense of how he was agonizing about that TV program, on their behalf as much as for the damage done to his case.

"What upset and disturbed me," Bolen later admitted, "was all the additional suffering this would bring to the family and to John Gallagher. Imagine Bill and Denise being put in the position of having everyone around them suspecting Leah and John."

He was concerned that this suspicion might cause a rift in the family, unaware of the lasting loyalties which bound the Fischer clan. Denise, who had previously seemed uncertain of her place in the family, had become truly part of it since Kristie's death, and spoke for them all when she said: "If I thought for one moment that John was guilty, I too would be on trial for trying to murder him with my bare hands."

The morning after *Now It Can Be Told* was aired, Bolen received a telephone call from Linda Sawyer, asking if he would participate in a follow-up report. "The nanny case" was a hot topic, and she was eager for more. He responded by asking where she got the videotape.

"Please, you have to be kidding me," she said. "I can't reveal my sources."

"You should know that you misidentified the voices," he told her. "That was not John Gallagher, or Leah Fischer."

"Then whose voices were they?" she asked.

She recalled: "If he had given me the information, I could have made a retraction. It was a five-night-a-week show, and I could have done it that evening. But he refused to tell me who it was. He said he would not give the question the dignity of a response. And hung up.

"I thought he was bullshitting me. I called my source and repeated what he had said. And the source said that the information I had presented was absolutely correct."

She said that this unnamed source had given her a copy of the tape with the comment: "Can you believe it? That's Gallagher and Leah Fischer walking around the ruins and laughing about having a barbecue."

Linda added: "I too identified the voices as John's and Leah's after comparing them with other parts of the tape. I must have listened to it a hundred times. The voices were muffled, but if you raised the volume you could hear what they said quite clearly."

Her assumption about John and Leah's involvement seemed to confirm gossip that she had been picking up around Thornwood: gossip about some of John's male contemporaries being involved in petty crime, almost as a way of life. One of them was widely suspected of some of the arson attempts which had plagued the neighborhood for months. There had been a rash of nuisance fires, none of them life-threatening, in trash cans and garbage piles and in an old barn near the Fischers' home. The Mount Pleasant police believed all of them to be the handiwork of this same young man, a known troublemaker, so carelessly inept that on one occasion they found a trail of footprints in the snow from a newly burned barn to the door of his home.

They were equally sure that he was not responsible for the fire at the Fischer house.

Bruce Johnson commented: "Forget that fellow as a suspect. He's just a pain in the ass. Been in trouble ever since he was a little boy—arrested for burglary, criminal mischief, possession of stolen property. I think he did some of the small fires, but this one was not his mentality. He's a sick kid, not a murderer. And he's not smart enough to carry through anything as premeditated as this. You should see the kids he hangs out with—talk about unintelligent people. If we had thought for one moment that any of that crowd was involved in the death of Kristie Fischer, don't you think we'd love to have arrested them?"

Linda Sawyer, however, had been picking up threads of disparate tales around Thornwood, mostly late at night in the kind of bars that she would never have visited alone but for the importance of this story, and weaving those threads into a narrative which seemed so logical that she could see no other explanation for the fire which killed Kristie. She learned that John and this suspected arsonist had been in high school together and shared an enthusiasm for car racing, which could have made them friends; there was also barroom talk about outstanding favors which this young man was said to have owed to John. None of it could be proved, but the pieces could easily fit into a plot based upon the settling of old debts; a plot compounded by jealousies over a new wife and baby displacing the daughter of a family, and her boyfriend with her.

Linda rationalized that such a plot could have been carried out without much risk, given the facts that John was friendly with the police patrol officer who questioned him on the night of the fire, and also known to the lieutenant in charge of the investigation, and that neither of these officers saw fit to take him to police headquarters before he left the fire scene, to have his hands and clothing examined for traces of flammable liquid.

(Later the police acknowledged that they should have done this, if only for their own and Gallagher's protection. "But d'you know what we'd have found?" a senior officer remarked. "Gasoline, engine oil, all kinds of accelerants. The guy had just finished a day's work in an auto-repair shop.")

Direct involvement by John Gallagher, possibly with an accomplice, seemed much more plausible to Linda Sawyer than criminal action by Olivia. There could be a motive for him, but none for her. He fitted the contemporary profile of an arsonist, a male between the ages of sixteen and thirty who had not made much of a mark in the world. And it was easy to imagine village police officers seizing upon a foreigner just because she was a foreigner, while protecting one of their own.

Digging deeper, Linda found that John had left Westlake High School before the end of his senior year, without graduating. He was no scholar, and had a reputation for a hasty temper which had involved him in teenage fistfights. She assumed (wrongly) that he had been expelled. As Linda saw it, everything pointed to his having guilty knowledge of the fire at the Fischers' house. Why else would he have his truck parked in their driveway, and be sitting in the driver's seat, waiting, while Kristie was burning to death? And while Olivia was making her hysterical telephone call to the police, pleading for help. It seemed outrageous to charge her with murder, and to cast him in the hero's role. Surely it had happened the other way round.

From this perspective, Linda Sawyer convinced herself that in pointing to John Gallagher she was serving the cause of justice. She saw herself as the lone investigative reporter, putting more time and energy into researching this story than anyone else, and she was right about that. After the Fischer family refused to talk, and the police had said what little they intended to say, most journalists gave up for a time, knowing that more details would emerge when the case came to court.

189

But immediately after Linda revealed John Gallagher's identity, there was a rush to follow her lead. And so it was not just the Geraldo Rivera program that benefited from her reporting, but all the television and newspaper journalists from New York to Switzerland who took up her story, assuming it to be true. And that assumption created a lasting public image of Olivia Riner's innocence.

"After the show, Laura called me that night," Linda said. "She told me that I had done even more than I had promised, and that she would be forever grateful to me. She knew I would break the case, and give her enough to win."

A few days later George Bolen met with Bill and Denise, Leah and John, and Jim Donnelly at the Mount Pleasant police headquarters. Bruce Johnson was also there. Bolen wanted to know who made the taped remark about a barbecue.

"That's easy," Jim told him. "It was me. I said something about there being enough charcoal in Leah's room for us to take some of it home and start a barbecue. I made that remark as a tension breaker. I was trying to make Denise laugh. She had done nothing but cry for two days."

It was a plausible explanation. Of those who were looking over the ruins that day, searching for a lost toy to bury with Kristie, Jim was the only one who had already lived Denise's pain. If he had not tried to coax a smile from her, he too might have been in tears. Now in his impetuous way he was telling Bolen that he wanted to call all the newspapers and television stations and publicly take responsibility for his disastrous attempt at a joke, explaining the woman's nervous laughter as Denise's hysterical reaction to it. He was eager to do whatever it might take to lift the suspicion from John Gallagher.

Bolen saw only a risk of spreading the damage. By speaking out, Jim would be making himself vulnerable, too. And it would be even worse to admit that it was the *mother* of the dead baby who was laughing. How would *that* be understood by the public? Better to leave things as they were, and hope that the damning TV show would be forgotten before the trial began. Which is why Bolen hung up his telephone after Linda Sawyer asked him: "Then whose voices were they?" And why he argued that, hard as it might be for them to keep silent, the Fischers should continue to avoid speaking to the press.

Most of them trusted his judgment. Jim still wanted to issue a public denial, but deferred to Bolen. He didn't feel right about keeping quiet, and, blaming himself, anguished over what had happened to John. He developed a hearty mistrust of the media, stopped watching television news programs, and disbelieved the newspapers. Months elapsed before he felt free to express his outrage. Finally he could contain it no longer. One day he read a report in a tabloid newspaper describing Kristie as Baby Fischer in one place and Karen in another. Angrily, he telephoned the newspaper and bellowed into the phone: "I am a member of the Fischer family, and that baby who died was not Baby Fischer or Karen Fischer. Her name was Kristie, and please get it right. Kristie Fischer was a person, a living person, and don't you guys ever forget it."

There was no peace for the Gallaghers or the Fischers after the Geraldo Rivera show. Reporters and photographers hung around Fischer's Garage, around the Gallaghers' home in Mahopac, and outside the house owned by the only John Gallagher in the Mount Pleasant township. He was John's grandfather, the retired custodian of Westlake High School.

"He's the only Gallagher I know," commented Police Chief Oliva, responding to Linda Sawyer's assertion that he himself had a close relationship with John's family. "And if I saw him ten times in forty years, it's a lot."

The two other John Gallaghers—this elderly man's son and grandson—were telephoned, followed, and pestered for months.

"It was a horrible, horrible time," Carol Gallagher related. "We had hang-up calls, abusive calls. Somebody burned our mailbox. When the warm weather came we couldn't have a cookout because we couldn't use our own backyard. We had to sit behind closed doors, afraid to go out."

In her work as a payroll supervisor she encountered skeptical comments, and a lot of avoidance. Colleagues she had known and liked for years were suspecting her son of murder, "and it was difficult for me to deal with on a day-to-day basis." She had hoped for a very different outcome from that television program. "Deep down I wanted Geraldo to say, 'This is the boy who tried to save the baby.' "

Instead, John was greeted at his work the following morning by sidelong glances, and the meaningful remark: "Saw you on TV last night. It doesn't look good."

From then on he was pursued by every journalist on the story, and seen as fair game by news photographers because he had turned his face from Rivera's camera crew. Day after day they were waiting outside the Jaguar service department before he clocked in at 8:30 A.M., and again when he was due to leave. This repair plant was down a dead-end lane off a rural road outside the town of White Plains, with only one way in or out. Eluding someone at that entrance was virtually impossible, even when he hurried in from the back parking lot, with his head down, wearing sunglasses.

"After that Geraldo show it was nonstop, at work, at home, wherever I went," John said. "One day Channel Four news came looking for me on my job and asked people who knew me, 'Do you think John Gallagher could have done it?' Another day a woman from Channel Five told the foreman she had an interview set up with me. I walked up to the front with him to see who it was, and he asked me if I knew her. When I said no and started to go back in, they photographed me walking away and showed the picture on TV. Sometimes I could see the reporters and camera people outside and I would tell my boss, Jim Westbrook, and he would have them removed. He was behind me one hundred percent. He knew I couldn't stop them harassing me. It was absolutely out of my hands."

On one occasion John was driven out of the Jaguar plant by a colleague who was road-testing a black car with black-painted windows. He recounted with some amusement: "There was Channel Four outside the building, Channel Seven at the top of the street. We drove right by them, and they didn't know."

This was a rare moment of one-upmanship in a losing game. He didn't want to be acclaimed as a hero, but he hadn't anticipated being pursued and scorned. Sometimes he wished he had been nowhere near the Fischer house on the night of the fire. He wanted to put the experience behind him, but the searing memory kept returning, usually when he was out driving alone, thinking of something else. When it didn't come back in that unexpected and unwelcome way, there were the journalists and photographers, hovering around to remind him. And not only him, but members of the Fischer family.

At his garage Bill was besieged by requests for interviews, comments, opinions, and photographs of Kristie. He said no to them all, and would have given up answering his business phone except that this was his livelihood.

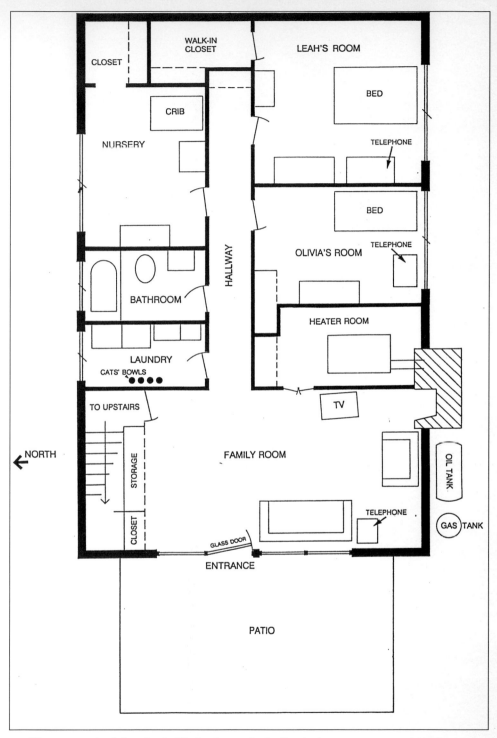

The entrance-level floor in the Fischer house. Scale: One inch represents approximately seven feet. (DRAWING BY JAN MENTING)

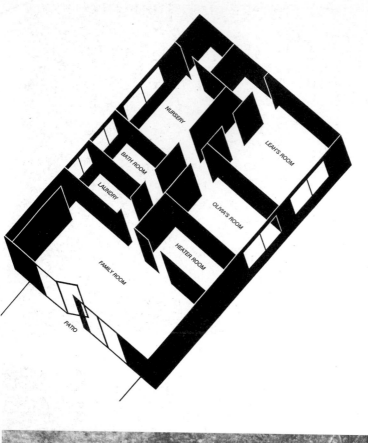

Three-dimensional plan of the same area, giving a sense of the proximity of the bedrooms and the narrowness of the hallway between them (DRAWING BY JAN MENTING)

Labels in drawing: NURSERY, BATH ROOM, LAUNDRY, LEAH'S ROOM, OLIVIA'S ROOM, HEATER ROOM, FAMILY ROOM, PATIO

The Fischer house at 5 West Lake Drive, Thornwood (JAN MENTING)

Side view of the house, showing the nursery window on the ground floor. The two other bedroom windows, Leah's and Olivia's, were identical, with one fixed frame and one that slid open horizontally. (Jan Menting)

Flames bursting out of the side of the house from the explosive blaze in Leah's bedroom
(Gannett Suburban Newpapers file photo)

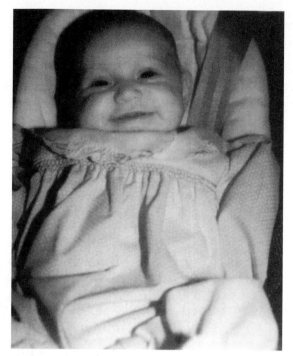

Kristie Rebecca Fischer, photographed in her infant carrier (FAMILY PHOTO)

Olivia Riner leaving Mount Pleasant Justice Court, following her arraignment for arson and murder. Police Lieutenant Louis Alagno in the background. (GANNETT SUBURBAN NEWSPAPERS FILE PHOTO)

Olivia's parents, Marlise and Kurt Riner, at Mount Pleasant police headquarters shortly after their arrival from Switzerland (GANNETT SUBURBAN NEWSPAPERS FILE PHOTO)

Olivia and her mother, Marlise, at Westchester County Courthouse on the first day of the trial. Linda Sawyer in the background. (GANNETT SUBURBAN NEWSPAPERS FILE PHOTO)

Laura Brevetti being interviewed on the day of the jury deliberations, with her private investigator, Christopher Rush (GANNETT SUBURBAN NEWSPAPERS FILE PHOTO)

Judge Donald N. Silverman (MARY MEENAN)

Assistant District Attorney
George Bolen (MARY MEENAN)

Detective Bruce Johnson
(STEPHEN LONGMIRE)

The defense team's triumphant press conference on the night of the verdict. Olivia, wearing her pale cream outfit, is in the center, with her father, Kurt Riner, immediately behind her. At left, Laura Brevetti. At right, Patricia Meier, a friend of the Riner family, acting as interpreter. Others in the picture are members of the Brevetti entourage.
(Gannett Suburban Newspapers file photo)

Jan Menting, designer and builder of the house at 5 West Lake Drive
(Stephen Longmire)

John Gallagher and Leah Fischer
(FAMILY PHOTO)

Denise and William Fischer leaving court on the day before the verdict (GANNETT SUBURBAN NEWSPAPERS FILE PHOTO)

"Is that Bill Fischer?" one anonymous call began. "Don't hang up. I want to tell you about John Gallagher. Did you know that years ago he burned his brothers and sister?"

There were other sick messages of this kind. As their recipients, the Fischers saw yet another dark side of human nature. But they soon learned the futility of arguing back.

At his workplace, Troy was asked: "What do you think about your sister's boyfriend?"

"Listen, none of that stuff you have been watching on TV is true," he snapped. "And I don't want to talk about it."

As he saw it, "They just wanted to hear all the dirt from an inside source."

At the White Plains auto dealership where she worked as assistant to the president, most of Leah's colleagues were ominously silent. "They avoided the subject, and that was hard for me," she said. "They didn't know how to handle it or what to say, so they didn't say anything."

She wished they would ask her about John, so she could tell them what really happened. She was getting such mixed reactions from friends. A few were supportive, but most of them excused their awkwardness with a hasty remark like "I know you don't want to discuss it."

"But they didn't know," Leah said. "They had no idea. And there were other friends, close girlfriends, who I expected to hear from, and didn't. And that hurt."

She was aware that these young women were wondering why she had not broken off her relationship with John, and since she had not, whether she might have joined him in a plot to kill Kristie. It was useless to try to convince them there was no such plot, and it compounded her sense of loss to realize that friendships she had valued had so little substance.

All this drew her closer to John, and to everyone else in the larger Fischer family. They had begun to feel like shipwreck survivors, alone against a hostile world, clinging to one another and to the wreckage of their lives. A single hope remained, and it helped to keep them going. In a few months' time Olivia would be tried for murder; then they believed the truth would be told, and justice done.

PART THREE

THE TRIAL

23

"Of course we saw *Now It Can Be Told*. We're not stupid."

Eric Dardenne, the Swiss deputy consul general in New York, considered its revelations "very important." As a lawyer and diplomat he had been following the case in detail, and reporting on it to his government. He was cautious about offering an opinion on the merits of Olivia's story, explaining that he wanted "to be very careful about this from an ethical point of view." But it was evident where his sympathies lay.

He had been impressed by a follow-up to the Rivera program in the form of a news item in the Gannett Suburban Newspapers, which covered the Westchester area, confirming that there had been an unusual number of "nuisance" fires in the Mount Pleasant police district. It listed eleven in the previous five months, all in the Nannyhagen Road area, close to the Fischers' house. Close also (which was not stated) to the home of the young man suspected to be Thornwood's amateur arsonist.

"Authorities have proved that an accelerant was used," the newspaper report stated, implying a link between the various blazing trash piles and the fire which killed Kristie. Eric Dardenne thought it significant that this arson epidemic began two months before Olivia arrived in the country, and continued after her arrest. Going back further, he learned of twenty-six fires in the Mount Pleasant area during the past two years. At least two were serious. One gutted a restaurant, and seemed to have been accidental. Another damaged the headquarters of the local ambulance corps, and had a striking similarity to the arson at the Fischers' house in that flammable liquid was used to set fire to a bed. Otherwise the methodology was so different that police discounted any possibility of the two crimes being connected, having already concluded that the damage to the ambulance building was the work of a disenchanted volunteer. Of the various burned buildings, only the Fischers' house was occupied when the fires were set.

The Gannett report lumped all the fires together, as though they were part of the same plan, and Dardenne found this persuasive. To him, twenty-six was "an incredible number of fires" for a semi-rural area, compared with the Swiss experience, where arson was rare. In his opinion the police should be investigating the Fischers' fire in relation to all the other arson in the neighborhood, rather than as an isolated incident with Olivia as the only suspect.

Dardenne was a very correct and conscientious European diplomat, always immaculately dressed, most often in a conservative gray suit which blended with his prematurely graying hair and neatly clipped beard. He came out of a more cultivated mold than Olivia but felt he understood her, and was protective toward her in an abstract way. He suspected that the Mount Pleasant police had judged her too hastily, on account of her behavior being foreign to them. It distressed him that on the night of her arrest her unemotional reaction was seen as indifference to Kristie's death, whereas he knew it as an indigenous stoicism.

"German Swiss people do not express themselves," he explained. "There is a coldness which comes from their climate—all those mountains. It is not strange for people living close to the snow to be like that. It is normal." He himself was from the French sector.

He argued in her favor: "When she was questioned by the police she was cooperative, her answers were coherent and logical, and her account of what happened was always the same. In my experience as a lawyer, if you are telling the truth the story will keep coming out the same because you have lived it. But if you are making it up, the details will keep changing, unless you have the memory of an elephant."

It was unthinkable to him that she could have committed arson, and then have immediately called the police. Everything about her demeanor spoke innocence to him. He could even empathize with her unlikely behavior on the night of the fire. Recently a car he had been driving was involved in an accident: "It was only a small accident, but I was in shock for one or two hours afterward. I was not myself. Here a baby is dead. You have a young girl who is new to the country, who cannot speak the language well, and the police are asking questions. At such a time, you want that she should behave normally?"

Over the next few months Dardenne spent a lot of time on Olivia's case, alternately fascinated and frustrated by the contradictions of the American legal system. He had helped to work out a bail agreement which he assumed to be watertight, but days later it fell apart. Marlise Riner had come to the United States on a sixty-day permit; he and his colleagues assumed that this was supplanted by Judge Silverman's requirement for her to remain in the country as a condition of her daughter's bail agreement. But when the permit expired, the U.S. Immigration Service threatened to deport her. Deportation for Marlise could have meant Olivia going back to jail, and Dardenne felt this was to be avoided at all costs. It was utterly bewildering to him that these various arms of American government should be in such contradiction with one another.

Working with Laura Brevetti, the Swiss authorities applied for an extension for Marlise. Although her daughter's trial was still months away she was granted only thirty more days. That period expired in March of 1992, and the U.S. Immigration Service promptly issued a deportation order.

"It was horrible," Dardenne recalled. "We did not get notice of the intention to deport Mrs. Riner until the order was already in place."

An appeal was made to Judge Donald Silverman, who explained that as a county court judge he had no authority over a federal government department. He was sympathetic to the plight of Marlise and her daughter, but could not help them. Finally it took top-level international diplomacy to get Immigration's ruling reversed.

"Our ambassador in Washington intervened," Dardenne related. "He brought it to the attention of the highest authority that the deportation order was unfair."

Only then was Marlise formally given permission to extend her stay until Olivia's trial was over, but in order to make this official she had to leave the country and reenter on a new permit. She chose to return to Switzerland for three days, on an understanding from the judge that her brief absence would not put her daughter's liberty at risk. The time consumed in arguing and arranging all this was an irritant to Swiss consular officials, who, in turn, had difficulty appreciating why their own system of government was so frustrating to the Americans prosecuting this case.

It made perfect sense to Eric Dardenne that the Swiss authorities were unable to supply the Mount Pleasant police with personal information about Olivia Riner.

"There is more privacy of the individual in Switzerland," he explained. "Here in New York a lot can be found out about a person by putting his American Express card into a computer. That would be a scandal in Switzerland. If you were to try to find that kind of personal information about five million Swiss people, you would get five million blank pages."

Olivia's blank page was, in his view, further evidence of her innocence. "My feeling from the beginning was that this case was nonsense, or else she was mentally ill," he said. "If she had a mental illness you could find that out." Presumably Swiss authorities had looked and drawn another blank.

The Mount Pleasant police had hoped, even expected, that their Wettingen counterparts would investigate Olivia's background for them by talking to people who knew her: former schoolmates, neighbors, and work colleagues. They wanted personal information in a hurry, unaware that such snooping was abhorrent to the Swiss, especially when the honor of one of their citizens was at stake. The Wettingen police might have responded to a formal request, transmitted through the Justice Departments of both countries and filtered down to them through layers of bureaucracy, an exercise which could take weeks. What they got instead was Bruce Johnson on the telephone. That unconventionally direct approach, followed by the revelations of Linda Sawyer's television report, added to the Swiss impression that the Mount Pleasant police, and the Westchester District Attorney's office did not have much of a case.

Olivia had been indicted on four counts of second-degree murder, and one count of first-degree arson, and Laura Brevetti had entered a plea of not guilty on all five. The murder charges presented alternatives for a jury to determine whether, if found guilty, Olivia killed Kristie intentionally, or as the result of a careless or malicious action which knowingly put the infant's life at risk. George Bolen had his doubts about winning one of these murder convictions. Without direct evidence, most jurors would not want to accept that a young, unsophisticated girl could have killed deliberately. Most jurors try to be objective, but they also want to sleep at night. So they would look for another explanation. Bolen judged that they would probably agree to this being a case of arson, but would want to believe that Kristie's death was somehow accidental.

Of the five charges, he thought that felony murder or first-degree arson held the best possibility of a conviction. He would be happy to win either of these. In both charges the primary crime is arson, committed in such a way as to deliberately endanger another person's life. Both carry the same penalty, twenty-five years to life, as second-degree murder. "Only most jurors don't know that," he remarked. Sentencing is not their business.

There was no doubt in Bolen's mind that Olivia deliberately set the fires, knowing exactly what she was doing and the risks she was taking. What he lacked, and might never be able to find, was motive. Preparing for trial, he examined several possibilities, but in every case a piece of the puzzle was missing. The most persuasive theory, certainly to a jury, was that Olivia started a fire intending to rescue Kristie but, finding the baby already dead from smoke inhalation, lit the other fires to cover up. She was not to know that her emergency call to the fire department would be delayed by a police sergeant arguing about her address.

Bolen was impressed by the correlation between Patricia Highsmith's story "The Heroine" and the known facts of this case. That short story might provide jurors with an acceptable scenario. He could see them rationalizing that, influenced by that tale, a lonely and homesick girl might try to win the Fischers' lasting gratitude by saving their child from a fire which she herself had set. But he could not introduce the Highsmith book into evidence unless he could prove it had been in Olivia's possession.

"That would have been enough to argue, circumstantially, that she had read the story," he said later. "But I would have had to know from the kiosk operator that the book was in her hands."

He felt more than usually frustrated by the inhibitions on a prosecutor: the telling details which a jury could not be told, and the latitude allowed to a defense counsel to discuss the case publicly, which professional ethics denied him.

Other prosecutors sometimes bent this rule, but Bolen always adhered to it—too rigidly, some of his colleagues thought, for his own good. He rarely gave interviews to journalists, and never while a case was in progress. He had learned the wisdom of occasionally stopping by the courthouse press room, but he went there to find out what was going on, rather than to share information.

It angered and offended him that in advance of Olivia's trial Laura

Brevetti had expressed her opinions on a national television program, implying that John Gallagher could have been the murderer. Although Brevetti must have concluded otherwise, Bolen saw this as a flagrant violation of the American Bar Association's Code of Professional Responsibility:

> A lawyer participating in or associated with a criminal or civil matter shall not make an extrajudicial statement that a reasonable person would expect to be disseminated by means of public communication if the lawyer knows or reasonably should know that it will have a substantial likelihood of materially prejudicing an adjudicative proceeding.

There was also the matter of John Gallagher's application for a pistol permit, flashed onto the screen during the Rivera program. This was classified information, never given out to journalists, available only to law enforcement officials with access to the state's computerized police statistics. Someone must have punched into the system and run a criminal-history check on John Gallagher, turning up his gun-license request and the accumulation of speeding tickets which caused it to be denied. To have made this public on the Geraldo Rivera show was a serious offense.

Bolen refrained from public comment about this violation of John Gallagher's civil rights. He did not want to draw any more attention to this young man. What irked him was how easy it was for the theory about Gallagher's involvement to be believed, and how hard it would be to select a jury who had not heard it.

In the weeks before the trial, there were the usual informal discussions between lawyers as to how the proceedings would be conducted. In a significant conversation with Laura Brevetti, Judge Silverman suggested that she might consider an insanity plea.

He had been studying the police evidence, along with a scale diagram of the ground floor of the Fischer house. From the close proximity of the rooms and the smallness of their size, he was finding Olivia's story hard to credit and thinking that a jury would have the same problem. If there really was an intruder on the same floor as she was, surely she would have been aware of doors being closed and fires being lit. Remembering the smell of having his own house decorated, he also wondered how she failed to notice the powerful odor of paint thinner as it was trailed from room to room.

He wanted to schedule the trial within a few weeks, and Laura Brevetti was pleading for more time to prepare her defense. He was used to attorneys complaining about feeling pressured, but guessed there was a stronger reason than usual for her panicky response.

"I had a feeling that she was alone in the case, that there was no one she could talk to about trial strategy," he commented. "I called her into my chambers because I wanted to have a conference with her that she could not have with anyone else."

In the privacy of his comfortable office at the courthouse, he told her: "I would like us to look at the facts of this case. Let us assume that the prosecution can establish a credible alibi for John Gallagher. If you take him out of your defense, what are you left with? It is a circumstantial case, but it might be a very persuasive circumstantial case. And let's face it, whoever committed this crime had to be very sick. If it was your client, it would be tragic for her to spend twenty-five years in prison.

"It may be that a psychiatric defense is available to you. You won't be able to argue manslaughter instead of murder, and you will have to admit that she did the crime. But instead of it being all or nothing, twenty-five years or acquittal, you will be giving her a chance of a much shorter sentence, possibly a mental health institution rather than prison, and perhaps for only a few years. If you go for that alternative it would be relatively easy to sell."

He ended the talk by promising her: "If you choose a psychiatric defense, I'll give you all the time you need to develop it, and reschedule the trial."

He had spoken to her almost like a father, although he was close to being her contemporary; a small dark-haired man, almost a head shorter than she was, disarmingly informal and almost boyish in manner. He had been a judge for only three years. Before that he too was a criminal defense attorney, and he had not forgotten the excitement of beating the establishment and winning a difficult case. Over time he came to realize that some of these were Pyrrhic victories, at odds with his own innate sense of justice. And eventually he acknowledged "that it is rare to have a completely innocent client, that it was no longer necessary to my ego to win, that I got no satisfaction out of helping guilty people go free, and that I did not want to spend the rest of my life doing this."

At the age of forty-one he took the risk of staking his future in an unpredictable election—a liberal Democrat running for a county-court judgeship in a heavily Republican area. At first he was thought to have lost, but a recount gave him a margin of one third of 1 percent of the votes. Although the job could be his for another seven years, he was already considering running for higher office in the judicial system. For reasons as altruistic as they were ambitious, he enjoyed being a judge. It allowed him direct and unprejudiced influence in seeing justice done, and gave him command of his own little world. The forthcoming trial of *The People of the State of New York* v. *Olivia Riner* fascinated him at several levels: as the arbiter in a sensational murder case, as a former defense lawyer trying to fathom an enigmatic defendant, and (a fact he refrained from mentioning) as the father of Miranda, born five months earlier than Kristie Fischer, whom he and his wife entrusted to the care of a South American nanny. The nanny was above reproach. "But when she first came to us, how did we know?"

All these factors motivated his offer to help Laura Brevetti think through her defense. He recounted: "She left that day saying she would speak to her client, and seriously consider my suggestion. She did not reject it out of hand. She asked for time to think about it. My feeling was that she got a little shook up at that conference. I laid the option of a psychiatric defense on her for two reasons. I wanted to get an impression of how sure she felt that her client was innocent. And I wanted to draw from her anything that might indicate that her client was guilty. I did not presume to ask what Olivia Riner was telling her about whether she was guilty or not.

"We set up a schedule for her to come back to me if she wanted to change her plea. She tried to stall on having to file an insanity notice. It would not have tied her to that defense, but it would have given the prosecution the right to examine her client. So for a while this remained an open issue, and she was begging for more time. Ultimately she decided not to file the notice.

"I was putting her to the test to see how she would react, and hoping it would tell me something, personally. The way it unfolded, it told me that her client might not be guilty. Because if I were representing a person who had admitted to me that she committed this crime, I would go for a psychiatric defense. After this I felt pretty confident that Olivia Riner was telling her attorney that she was innocent. Otherwise Laura Brevetti was taking a terrible risk."

24

Preparing her defense, Laura Brevetti made formal motions to have as much damaging evidence excluded from the trial as possible. Because this was a circumstantial case, Judge Silverman had promised that he would consider all her objections, and he scheduled a pretrial hearing for mid-May 1992. A few weeks earlier he shared some thoughts on the unusual nature of the case, contrasting it with one of his recent murder trials.

"This was a young man who had overcome all the disadvantages of growing up in the ghetto. He was an honor student, academically and athletically. Walking on a street one night he was accosted by a stranger, for no good reason, and killed. That, to me, is a story. It tells us a lot about the society in which we live.

"This"—referring to the pending trial of Olivia Riner—"does not relate to most people's lives, or say anything about the conditions of our time. It is what people want to read, but it is a bizarre aberration. Most people do not have a fear of another person harming their baby."

He was wrong about that, as time would tell. This case was fascinating to the public, women in particular, not just for its sensationalism but because it addressed the guilt and anxieties of working mothers. The judge was thinking on another level, about crimes of political and social significance, the kind that used to come his way when he started his career as a public-interest attorney. Even as a parent himself, married to a career woman, the broad import of this case at first eluded him. It became clear only later when women filled the public section of his courthouse, and during the course of the trial bonded together in an unusual way, not so much out of curiosity but because, like Linda Sawyer, they wanted to believe Olivia innocent, in order to validate career and child-care choices which they themselves had anguished over.

The main contention of Laura Brevetti's pretrial motions was that Olivia was unlawfully arrested and had not understood the Miranda warning, with the result that she responded to Bruce Johnson's lengthy interrogation without knowing that she had the right to remain silent. In a written statement to the court, Brevetti pointed out that her client came from a society where the police are obeyed, and an accused person has no right to legal representation during police questioning. Olivia "had never been in trouble before," and had "little or no linguistic or conceptual understanding of the rights read to her or the predicament she confronted."

Brevetti argued that her client was not offered the services of an interpreter and, after being charged with the crime, was "shuttled back and forth from a cell" between midnight and 3:00 A.M., "whenever police had additional questions or a new police officer came on the scene, on just the chance that she would break down and confess to arson and murder."

She alleged that the Mount Pleasant police did not seal off the crime scene until the defense's investigators were given an opportunity to examine it. Referring to Bruce Johnson's video, she charged that Leah and John were permitted to "rummage through the fire scene without supervision" on the day after the tragedy. She stated: "It is near to gospel that the first twenty-four to seventy-two hours after an arson or homicide are crucial, providing the opportunity to gather clues existing then but not later. Human carelessness by professionals reduces the chances; civilian interference destroys them."

The wording of this charge perpetuated one of the errors of the Geraldo Rivera program. The filmed shots of Leah and John searching through the wreckage were not taken the day after the fire, as Brevetti charged, but three days later, when (as the video showed) there was snow on the ground which had only just fallen.

Brevetti maintained that there was no physical evidence linking Olivia to the crime—no fingerprints, no trace of flammable liquid on her clothing—and "the autopsy report establishes that the infant died from the smoke, and burns. There is no evidence that she had been injured, poisoned, abused, or otherwise harmed."

She criticized the fact that "for reasons yet unexplained" the police eliminated John Gallagher as a suspect and "seized no evidence known to the defense from him although he was present during the fire." This was clear warning that she intended to cast suspicion on him at the forthcoming trial.

What the police regarded as the one piece of direct evidence in this case, Olivia's singed eyelashes, was ridiculed in Brevetti's statement: "It defies credulity that eyelashes would be singed while her full eyebrows, long hair (with bangs), hands and clothing would be totally undamaged."

This argument might well convince a jury. It took a knowledge of the dynamics of combustion to appreciate the significance of Olivia's eyelashes being singed while her eyebrows, hair, and clothing were unaffected. After reading Brevetti's statement, Paul Oliva gave his detective a final piece of advice before he retired as police chief: "Bruce, those eyelashes are a very important factor in this case. It was why we made the arrest. We had all that circumstantial evidence, but her eyelashes were the clincher. And before this comes to trial I want you to talk it over with George Bolen, and see that evidence comes out the way it is meant to come out. This whole case hangs on those eyelashes."

They were not an issue at the pretrial hearing, which concentrated on the admissibility of other evidence. Hearings of this kind are common procedure before a major trial: the defense's attempt to chip away at the prosecution's case before it goes to a jury. They provide a small preview of the trial itself, giving both attorneys a sense of how convincing some witnesses will be later on. At the end of a hearing the judge gives his ruling, determining how much of the known evidence will be allowed at the trial. Laura Brevetti petitioned to have all the charges against her client dismissed, not expecting to get everything she asked but hoping for some of it.

She gained almost nothing. George Bolen agreed that Olivia's diary and personal photographs would not be presented as evidence, but Brevetti lost all her other arguments, including her contention that the taped interview with Bruce Johnson was invalid on grounds that her client did not understand the Miranda warning.

Olivia sat demurely through the hearings, dressed in a plain white blouse, navy blue tailored jacket, and a matching pleated skirt. Her long hair hung straight down her back, the bangs almost covering her thick, dark eyebrows. The strange boxlike shape of the electronic monitor strapped to her left ankle protruded through her opaque navy stockings, an incongruous reminder that she was not the convent schoolgirl she appeared to be. Marlise Riner sat near the front of the courtroom's public section, watching tensely, wishing she understood better. She favored the same style of short pleated skirts and flat pumps as her daughter, and did not look much older.

The only witnesses to be called at this stage were police officers who had been at the fire scene. The first was Scott Carpenter, the young patrolman who reached there before any of his colleagues, and who stumbled into the smoke-filled nursery alone before Officer Miliambro arrived and they went back in together. Carpenter had been a policeman for only two years; this was his first encounter with murder, and the first time he had given evidence in court. He was uncomfortable with both experiences, and it showed. He had yet to acquire the easy confidence of the more senior officers who testified after him: Lieutenant Louis Alagno, Sergeant Brian Dwyer, and Detective Bruce Johnson. Hesitantly, Carpenter described seeing "a severely charred object which appeared to be a doll" on the nursery floor. "Then I saw it was a baby." Even now he had difficulty talking about it, and was easily shaken by the sharp cross-examination of Laura Brevetti.

"Did you close the door to the baby's room?" she asked.

"I don't know. I just wanted to get out of the house. I don't think I did. . . . I was choked up, and my eyes were burning as I came out."

He told about seeing Olivia outside the house, at first crying loudly and saying something about cats in a language which was strange to him; then responding to him in English.

"When you questioned Olivia, did you notice her clothing?"

"No."

"Of the rest of her appearance, nothing sticks in your mind?"

"No."

He was shifting on his seat in the witness box, wishing himself somewhere else. He was slim and pale, and the muscles of his jaw were tensing visibly. In contrast, Laura Brevetti seemed entirely at ease, elegantly attired in a softly draped beige dress and jacket, with pearl-stud earrings and a gold choker necklace. She had a way of thoughtfully pacing the courtroom floor before moving from one line of questioning to the next, adding to a witness's apprehension. It was one of her most effective tactics.

After such a pause she returned to the traumatic moment when he saw the dead baby.

"Did you notice a burn area on the floor?"

"Yes."

"Did you notice more than one?"

"I can't be sure if there was more than one. There was quite a large area around the baby."

"Would it refresh your recollection to look at the report?"

"I guess it would."

She handed him a piece a paper. There was a puzzled expression on his face as he read it, then he said: "There was an area around the carrier and another slightly to my left, but it seemed to be all one to me. . . . I just noticed the area around the baby." He looked pained as he remembered it.

Again she paced the floor, and the tone of her voice changed a little as she tried to stir another recollection.

"Did you observe the window when you were in that room?"

"No."

"Did you notice the flow of smoke in that room?"

"No."

"And there is only one wall where the window is, correct?"

"Yes."

"And you did not examine it?"

"No."

She was building up the case that an intruder could have entered the nursery through the low window, and that the first police officer on the scene failed to look for clues which could have been obliterated by the time Dwyer and Johnson arrived and noticed the heat break in the glass.

Pressing on with her questions, she managed to get Carpenter so rattled that at one point he blurted: "Look, you are told there is a fire and there is a dead baby in there. This a crime scene and it's complete chaos. I'm not looking here and there to see which officer is doing what."

Ignoring his indignation, she led him into his interview with John Gallagher in the police car while the Fischers' house was still smoldering. Carpenter's responses indicated that he never doubted the story his brother's friend told him. From the prosecution's viewpoint, it was becoming evident that the police erred in accepting Gallagher's account at face value, and should have covered themselves (and him) by having his clothes and hands tested before letting him go.

"Did you take anything from John Gallagher?" Brevetti asked.

"Only a cigarette." Sensing there was something wrong with this answer, he added hastily: "I didn't steal it."

She repressed a smile, and concluded by having him tell how he went back into the house later that evening and walked around. By then Kristie's body had been removed, and the fire fully extinguished. Brevetti asked him why he did this, and he admitted that he had no reason other than curiosity.

"You stepped on things?" she inquired, implying that on this unnecessary return visit he may have destroyed evidence. Her tone was coolly polite.

He paused, trying to remember. "I stepped where I stepped," he replied belligerently.

That was the moment when George Bolen must have decided not to call Scott Carpenter as a witness at the forthcoming trial.

Detective Bruce Johnson was much more experienced at giving evidence. His bland expression through an entire day on the witness stand gave no hint of his emotions, and he did not permit himself to be ruffled by questions implying that he deliberately intimidated Olivia. He described in detail his experiences at the fire scene, his conversation with her in the Fries house, and his long interrogation of her at the police station.

Brevetti elicited that he was six two and weighed two hundred and twenty-five pounds while Olivia was eleven inches shorter and about a hundred pounds lighter. Yes, he conceded, he may have put his hand on her arm to lead her to his car when he took her to police headquarters. And yes, when he was interviewing her in his office he did reach across his desk and raise her head by touching her under the chin, several times, because she was looking down and he could barely hear her. But he did not accuse her of killing the baby until after he had arrested her. He was adamant about that.

His answers gave a fair image of himself: a senior officer observing police regulations governing the treatment of a suspect, always keeping his feelings in check, never allowing her an insight into what he was thinking. Like Scott Carpenter he had been badly shaken, even enraged, by the sight of a baby deliberately burned beyond recognition. But he hid this reaction from Olivia. Only late in the evening, after he had formally charged her with arson, did the tone of his interrogation change: As he had privately admitted, for the first four hours he was gentle with her, "and for two I acted like a bastard."

Brevetti prodded him about those last two hours.

"Did you tell her she might as well admit to killing the baby because the next day there would be an autopsy? You went through a whole list of ways a baby could die?"

"Yes."

"She denied it?"

"Yes."

"Each and every one of them?"

"Yes."

"Did you tell her there would be fingerprints at the scene that would show she had committed the crime?"

Johnson paused. "It is possible," he conceded.

"Inspector Johnson, you should use your best recollection," she scolded. "Is it not a fact that you told my client that there were fingerprints which would show that she committed the crime?"

"I do not recall."

"And all these things—your telling about the fingerprints, your describing the ways in which a baby could die—you asked for one purpose?"

"Yes."

"You wanted her to confess?"

"Correct."

"And she did not confess?"

"Correct."

The most dramatic part of this pretrial hearing, which lasted almost two weeks, was when Johnson's taped interview was replayed for the judge's benefit. On the night of the fire Olivia had been sitting by the detective's desk, staring into her lap and twisting a sodden tissue. Now she was at the defense attorney's table, looking secure and alert, listening through headphones to her own small voice responding to Johnson's questions—and this time he was the witness being interrogated. Neither gave the other any sign of recognition.

Because Johnson had positioned the tape machine behind his desk when he made the recording, some of her answers replayed so faintly that the judge called for a transcript and adjourned the hearing until the forty-two-page document was produced.

Although Laura Brevetti argued, "My client did not always understand his [Johnson's] questions," the judge was more impressed by Olivia's reactions when she didn't. After studying the transcript, he ruled against all the defense motions, explaining that in his opinion Olivia fully understood the Miranda warning, demonstrated by the fact that she was not too shy or intimidated to interrupt the interrogation with questions of her own: "What's remain? . . . What's court of law? . . . The lawyer? . . . What's afford to hire? . . . Decide?"

Judge Silverman commented: "While her English is not perfect her language skills are functional. She has a fairly good vocabulary, and speaks in full sentences. I am struck by the fact that she appears to understand everything that is said, and that when she comes on a word which is not understandable to her she asks for an explanation."

He determined that she was not coerced or intentionally intimidated by Detective Johnson during their long interview. "It is my feeling that whether she was not guilty, or guilty, she wanted to leave the impression that she was willing to cooperate with the police. At no time did she indicate that she did not want to remain or to answer questions."

Although Laura Brevetti had lost every point, she made a brave attempt to turn the judge's ruling to advantage. After the hearing she gave one of the first of many informal press conferences in the large square lobby of the courthouse. Briskly she told reporters: "We must move on; we cannot look backward. While a defense attorney is disappointed when a motion is denied, I get a great deal of satisfaction from the judge's comments—his saying that through many hours of questioning this girl was fully cooperative. This behavior is totally consistent with innocence."

A week later there was a surprise item on *Fox TV News* on New York City's Channel 5. It concerned the high incidence of fires in the Thornwood area, and named the Mount Pleasant police department's suspect as Eric Trimpe, a man in his twenties who lived with his parents on Nannyhagen Road. By itself, this was not newsworthy enough for a prime-time bulletin. But the television reporter, Rosanna Scotto, made a direct link between these minor cases of arson and the fire at the Fischer house, a possibility the police had already discounted.

She described Trimpe as "a friend of John Gallagher," and emphasized that the outbreak of Thornwood fires began before Olivia came to the neighborhood and that no traces of flammable liquid were found on her. Anthony Provenzano, the new acting police chief, was quoted as saying, "If it's in regard to the arson investigation, there's no comment," which, in this context, might be interpreted as a police cover-up.

The implications of this report did not need to be spelled out, and would form a renewed basis for local gossip: Maybe John Gallagher hired Trimpe to set fire to the Fischer house. Maybe they did it together. Maybe John stationed his truck in the Fischers' driveway that evening so he could act as a lookout. It would not seem suspicious because the neighbors were used to seeing it there. Maybe John did it for Leah because she was jealous of Denise and the baby. At least there was material for a motive here, which did not exist anywhere else.

The timing of this TV report was a gift to the defense. It was a Thursday evening, and Olivia's trial was scheduled to begin the following Tuesday. Jury selection had just concluded, and the twelve prospective jurors and four alternates were enjoying their last few days of freedom before accepting the discipline of a major trial. The judge had yet to instruct them not to read or listen to anything touching this case. They were free to watch that news program, or to hear about it from others, just as they had been free to learn what was said on *Now It Can Be Told* three and a half months earlier. They would, of course, undertake to go into this trial with open minds. But suspicions had now been planted which might subliminally influence their thinking.

At the Mount Pleasant police department there was concern as to how the undercover investigation of Eric Trimpe was leaked. Some officers had their suspicions. There had been a jostling for power in the department, still unresolved, on account of Paul Oliva's retirement. In this atmosphere of uncertainty Laura Brevetti's private investigator, Christopher Rush, had been snooping around, talking to current and former members of the police department. What they told him was anybody's guess; it was what happened to this inside information that was most troubling. Evidently some powerful links had been forged between the media and the defense.

25

There were problems, which at first seemed insurmountable, about hiring an interpreter for the trial. Legally, it was essential for Olivia to understand everything that was said, which meant finding an expert in Swiss German capable of doing simultaneous translation. The court's budget for this job was a meager eighty dollars a day, absurdly low for the skills required. It takes one degree of linguistic ability to translate a manuscript, pausing now and then to ponder the nuances of a phrase or to use a dictionary; quite another to give a rapid verbal interpretation of what a speaker has just said, at the same time listening acutely to what he is continuing to say, without losing any of it. Few translators can work that fast or concentrate so intently.

One of the court's early efforts to find an interpreter produced an elderly woman who, although fluent in German, did not speak the Swiss dialect, could not do simultaneous translation, did not see the need for it, and wasn't sure she wanted the job anyway. She looked askance when told by the judge: "You cannot paraphrase what I am saying. Every word that comes out of my mouth has to be spoken to the defendant." Clearly this was beyond her competence.

Laura Brevetti offered to find a more qualified interpreter if the court would substantially increase its fee. The judge agreed, and in doing so gave her a psychological advantage. Whoever she found would have a sense of loyalty to the defense, even though the paycheck came from the court. And thus Maya Hess was hired.

She was a thirty-five-year-old Swiss who had settled in New York eleven years earlier, bringing with her two suitcases full of German textbooks and the confidence that she could earn a living as a translator. She did so well that she had recently opened her own agency, working out of her apartment in the Greenwich Village neighborhood of Manhattan. One afternoon in early May of 1992 she was busy at her word processor, dressed for comfort in sweatpants and pullover, when Laura Brevetti telephoned to ask if she could come for an interview—right now.

"I'm not dressed for the occasion," Maya protested.

"That doesn't matter. Come as you are," she was told.

She put her work aside and hurried uptown. Even the court's enhanced fee fell far short of her regular earnings, and it made no sense for her to accept a job which would take her away from her desk for several weeks, just when she was getting Hess Translations established. But the assignment intrigued her. Five months earlier she had read of Olivia's arrest with rather more interest than most because she herself was from Zurich, only a short train ride from Olivia's hometown of Wettingen. Maya had heard nothing more about the case until a few days ago when she was told that Olivia's trial would soon take place, and that her attorney was looking for an interpreter. She faxed her résumé, and this peremptory telephone call was the response to it.

The law firm of Morrison, Cohen, Singer and Weinstein was lavishly spread over three floors of a contemporary skyscraper in the most expensive section of Manhattan's East Side. Laura Brevetti's private office was similar to that of all the other partners, quite small and furnished in anonymous good taste. She was wearing a tailored linen pants suit in a shade of mustard which suited her, and her commanding presence dominated the room.

Maya was self-confident enough not to be intimidated. She didn't need the job. If she didn't get it she would write this off as an interesting afternoon. She had plenty of other work to do. But after a brief interview which she sensed went well, Laura Brevetti telephoned her client.

"Olivia must have been standing by because she arrived only fifteen minutes later," Maya recalled. "She bounded into Laura's office, smiling, casually dressed in jeans and sneakers. I spoke to her in Swiss German, and asked some questions about where she was from. After a few minutes Laura said okay, and that was it. I was hired."

Maya assumed Olivia's innocence. "The thought that she could be guilty never entered my head. When a person comes into a room looking as carefree and childlike as she did, it's hard to imagine her doing anything seriously wrong, let alone burning a baby alive. Sure, as I learned more about the case, some questions about her story came up in my mind, but I had great difficulty reconciling the charges with the girl before me."

Her assumption was reinforced as she came to know Olivia better, and was reminded of the lonely young girl she herself had been when she first settled in New York. She had kept a snapshot taken at that time, when her hair was fairer and longer and straighter, and her face more childlike; the girl in this photograph could have been another Olivia. Since then she had married, had a child, and divorced. Now, confidently supporting herself and a six-year-old daughter, she had a full and demanding work life, balanced by a circle of interesting friends. She was more educated and personable than Olivia was ever likely to be, with a warmth and vivacity which lit up her face. Olivia had disciplined herself to hide her feelings; in contrast, Maya had a straightforwardness and an independence which was immediately appealing.

Without realizing it, she was identified from the beginning as a member of Laura Brevetti's team. Not that she was asked or chose to be; it was simply assumed. She slipped easily into the role, out of a natural empathy for this vulnerable young girl who reminded her of her own past. Although they had not previously met, they knew the same places, and a few of the same people: Olivia had even attended the school in Zurich where Maya briefly taught. It therefore seemed natural for Maya to ask, before the trial began, if she might travel with Olivia and her mother to the Westchester County Courthouse every day, and for the two of them to welcome her company. It was about an hour's drive by car, a reverse commute from the inner city to beyond the outer suburbs, and Laura Brevetti's office had hired a limousine for the regular round trip. Even with the additional subway ride from her home to the Riners' lodgings, more than sixty blocks uptown, it was easier for Maya than battling public transportation all the way. She always sat next to the chauffeur, avoiding discussion of the trial. But in making light conversation to overcome the awkwardness, she came to know the Riners quite well.

Early on, she noticed that Olivia did not regard her mother as an authority figure, or feel the need to defer to her. Marlise was simply there, trying to be supportive to a daughter who seemed content with her own company. Both women concealed their emotions, but the mother showed most apprehension about the outcome of the trial. Olivia behaved with what her lawyer described as the confidence of innocence, yet this confidence was strange in light of her experience of American law enforcement and the gravity of the charges she faced.

After a pounding interrogation at the Mount Pleasant police station and almost a month in jail, how could she have such faith that the judicial system of this alien land would soon set her free?

In the clothes she wore for court, Olivia looked very different from the girl Maya had met in Laura Brevetti's office, and that was intentional. Linda Sawyer had taken her shopping. Combing through Blooming-dale's department store, across the street from the law office, Linda had picked out three basic outfits which created the image Laura Brevetti wanted to project: that of a correct and obedient schoolgirl. The navy outfit which Olivia wore at the pretrial hearing had been her own in-terpretation of it, and it wasn't quite right. The jacket hung awkwardly on her shoulders, and gave her a waiflike appearance. She needed to do better than that. She needed to look comfortable in these clothes she wasn't used to wearing.

Linda chose matching skirts and jackets in quiet colors, of a flattering cut and classical design: one each in navy, cream, and a light silvery gray, with flat-heeled pumps to match. "I spent eight hundred dollars on Laura's credit card buying those clothes for her," she said.

It was also an important part of defense strategy that Olivia should wear her hair long and loose, with bangs almost to her eyebrows. "That girl should have it cut, or wear it braided," a woman in the court's public section was heard to remark. Esthetically she was right, but miss-ing the point. So long as a jury could see all that hair surrounding Olivia's face, Laura Brevetti could minimize, even ridicule, Bruce John-son's testimony about her eyelashes. How could they have been singed, and not her hair? Even when a scientific explanation was offered to a jury, the presence of so much hair would strain their credulity. By leav-ing it long and loose, Olivia was offering constant visual testimony that she could not have been close to a flame without doing more harm to herself. Only on weekends, when the court was not sitting, did she braid her hair down her back, the way she had often worn it at the Fischers' home.

The jury and the court-watching public had no sense of this other Olivia. They saw only a virginal young woman dressed like a little girl, with her hair brushed until it shone, and shiny as her face. When pho-tographs of this new image of herself first appeared in the newspapers and on television, the Fischers barely recognized her. From the beginning of the pretrial hearing, only Linda, Maya, and the defense team glimpsed the young woman Bill and Denise had known, one who at the end of every court day could barely wait to get back to her lodgings and change into rumpled jeans and sweatshirt. As Linda phrased it, "She either looked slovenly and disheveled, or scrubbed and cutesy, the way I dressed her for court."

Sometimes in the evenings Linda took her out to eat. Always fashionably dressed herself, she felt uncomfortable—for Olivia's sake as much as her own—about her guest's reluctance to dress for dinner.

"I would say to her in advance: 'We are going to a nice restaurant; dress up.' But she would come in jeans and a baggy sweatshirt, with never a scrap of makeup."

Over one of these meals Linda asked Olivia if she had a boyfriend. The response was a firm no, emphasized by a shake of the head.

"I am a virgin," she insisted.

"You have never been with any man?"

"Absolutely not." Olivia seemed to be very proud of her chastity. It was Linda's more pragmatic view that she was "screwed up about sex." And yet this girl's naïveté about the ways of the world made the charges against her seem all the more preposterous.

Her entire demeanor was that of a trusting child who had no doubt that people would believe her innocent. At the end of the pretrial hearing, the third week in May, she wanted to know if she would be allowed to go home in time for summer. As she saw it, the prosecution had not proved its charges, and the judge would soon dismiss them. Coming from a country that had no jury system, but rather magistrates to weigh evidence and hand down verdicts, she assumed that the police testimony before Judge Silverman was all there would be to this case.

"Honey, don't count on there being no trial," Linda told her. She felt sad for this girl's vulnerability.

Olivia was not privy to the painstaking preparation for her defense, and had little sense of its complexity. Linda did. Her relationship with Laura Brevetti gave her a privileged insight into the way a skilled attorney plans for a major trial. She was included in conferences behind closed doors, the kind to which journalists are rarely privy; in turn, she brought in information, like the gossip she was picking up about John Gallagher, and about certain young men engaged in illegal activities who were said to be his friends, all of which might be used to deflect suspicion from Olivia Riner.

This was Linda's first experience of the private society of lawyers, and she entered it on the naive assumption that defense attorneys are wholly committed to their clients' innocence. She had yet to learn that it is not their job to make judgments about a client, only to ensure that he or she gets a fair trial. The crucial question "Did you do it?" is one which a defense attorney may choose not to ask. Culpability is for a jury to determine. And while the prosecution must prove its case beyond a reasonable doubt, the defense has in many ways the easier task of presenting alternative scenarios which will raise enough doubts among the jurors.

One day Linda was curious enough to inquire: "If you were prosecuting this case, could you win?"

She worried about the unhesitating response, "Yes, absolutely," unaware that Laura Brevetti was expressing confidence in her own courtroom skills, rather than commenting on the merits of this case.

Linda was again surprised, and again a little shaken, when she attended a mock trial, staged in the conference room of Laura Brevetti's law office, about a month before the pretrial hearing.

"Laura played the prosecutor, and her assistant, Elan Gerstmann, played the defense attorney," she recalled. "I was sitting there, knowing what I knew, and listening to her summation. She went into details of how small this house was, how difficult it would have been for someone to break in and set those fires without Olivia knowing, who but she could have committed the crime. I thought to myself, Holy cow, when you hear it in those terms, the girl has to be guilty. But none of us wanted to believe it.

"There were about thirty people in the room, and afterward we broke up into groups and discussed the case. I remember an older man in my group who said: 'I don't believe that this girl didn't hear or see or smell anything. Paint thinner stinks. Give me a break!' And yet, when we were asked to come up with a verdict, we all voted not guilty because there was no hard evidence. We wanted to believe that she did not do it, and I was the biggest believer."

Linda's allegiance did not fail even after her reading of pretrial depositions raised some troubling questions.

"One day I was lying on the floor in Laura's office, going through the evidence. It came out that there was a baby monitor in the nursery. I said, 'Laura, there was a monitor. Do you know what that means? There's no way Olivia couldn't have heard what was going on in that nursery.'

"She didn't answer me at first. Then she said maybe the transmitting end was switched off. I have done that myself, so I know how it works. When you turn off the transmitting end there is a loud static noise at the receiving end, and that was right in Olivia's room.''

Of all those who studied the pretrial evidence, Linda was probably the only one with the recent experience of a young mother. It led her to pick up another serious discrepancy which everyone else missed, including the police. During his interrogation of Olivia, Bruce Johnson had asked her about the clothes Kristie was wearing when she was set down to sleep in the nursery for the last time, about half an hour before the fire broke out. Olivia had described a light-green one-piece suit, worn over a diaper and a white undershirt. She was precise in her recollection, down to green-and-white-striped ruffles at the wrists, which was strange, given Denise's certainty that there was no such outfit in Kristie's wardrobe. What struck Linda was that not a shred of this or any other outer garment was found on the baby's burned body, although those pieces of clothing that had been pressed between Kristie and the infant seat—the back of her undershirt and the rear section of her diaper—remained intact. Hence the unburned section of diaper, soaked in paint thinner, which fell from the body when the medical examiner's assistant lifted it from the carrier. If Kristie had been wearing an outer garment, a portion of that would surely have been preserved too.

The absence of these fragments raised some disturbing questions. On a damp December afternoon, chill enough for Olivia to be wearing a long-sleeved sweatshirt around the house, did she really put a small baby down to sleep dressed only in her underclothes, with nothing covering her? Was the green ruffled outfit an invention to explain away her neglect? Or, worse, had she decided that this child was about to die, so what she wore didn't matter? The only other explanation for the missing outer garment was incredible beyond belief—that there was an intruder who, for some obtuse reason, took the time and the risk to pick up and partially undress Kristie, then put her back in her carrier before setting fire to the rug around her; and that during this entire operation neither the arsonist nor the baby made a sound which Olivia could hear from a few yards away, with or without the amplification of a monitor.

Linda did not want to think of Olivia inventing an elaborate lie. But her journalistic curiosity demanded an explanation.

"The jumper, Laura," she said, referring to the green-striped outfit. "What happened to the jumper?"

She understood the response to be that maybe the jumper just burned up.

"I wasn't satisfied with Laura's explanation about the monitor and the jumper," Linda related. "But I was so psychologically connected to Olivia that I let it go."

She would leave the law office with these doubts in her mind, and then go back to Westchester where one piece of gossip about various young people of John Gallagher's acquaintance would lead to another; where there would be dark hints about break-ins and undercover deals and motives for revenge, all seeming to point to the possibility of the arsonist being someone other than Olivia.

"They were pieces of a puzzle, but it was the wrong puzzle," Linda acknowledged, months later. At the time she felt the excitement of discovery, of being the researcher and the crusader who would ferret out the truth and set Olivia free.

"I was finding out more for Laura than the private investigators she was hiring," Linda claimed. "She was spending tens of thousands of dollars on them, but I was consistently bringing more stuff in for her." In return Linda understood that she was promised an exclusive television interview with Olivia, as soon as the trial ended. Given the publicity this case was generating, the prospect of that interview was a journalist's dream.

In the meantime she continued researching. "I would go to the town of Mount Pleasant and be there until all hours of the morning, in different bars, looking over my shoulder, afraid to turn on the ignition of my car when I left. I was hearing too much for my own safety about the corruption and the drug scene in this area. But I thought it was worth the risk if it would lead me to the killer of an innocent baby."

She had become even more dedicated to her work since her twins were born. As she expressed it: "I have more reason to do well in my professional life than ever before. Before, it was about personal satisfaction. Now it is about coming home at the end of the day and seeing four little eyeballs looking up to me, knowing that these children think I am great no matter what. Now, whatever story I get, I am out there doing it for them. And this one I was also doing for my nanny, and for all nannies. I kept thinking of that film, *The Hand That Rocks the Cradle,* and all the fear and paranoia it provoked, and I wanted to set the record straight."

Temperamentally as much as geographically, Linda Sawyer and Maya Hess came from different places, and were drawn to this case for very different reasons. Maya was less emotional about it, yet for a time her involvement was almost as deep. When she realized that their enforced stay in New York was causing the Riner family severe financial hardship, she enlisted the support of the Swiss Consulate in soliciting contributions from Swiss residents of the New York area. She even wrote some of the appeal literature. Over the next few months the Swiss Benevolent Society, in conjunction with the Swiss Consulate, collected more than $20,000.

"I felt badly for the Riners because they did not have a lot of money, and they were spending so much on living expenses," Maya explained.

She felt drawn to Olivia, detecting beneath her grave exterior a certain sweetness and a wry sense of humor which, with gentle encouragement, she was able to bring out. She also admired the way this girl held herself together under the enormous strain of a murder trial. Whether it was stoicism or dissociation seemed irrelevant; her composure was impressive. It would have seemed callous not to befriend her. With Laura Brevetti's approval, Maya began to invite the Riners to her home at weekends, and to plan little outings for them.

She and Linda were not alone in their empathy with Olivia. The trial attracted an unusual group of supporters who, for a variety of personal reasons, made her cause their own. Day after day they filled most of the seats in the public section of the courtroom, smiling approval at her. At least two of the women were Swiss, demonstrating their solidarity with a fellow citizen. Then there was a young man who had seriously dated a Swiss au pair, seeking reassurance that none of her kind was capable of such a horrible crime. There was a retired Irish-American couple who seemed to regard Olivia as a kind of surrogate granddaughter, and themselves as her committed champions. There was a woman who had been badly hurt by a couple of ugly divorces, determined to ensure that no other woman would be victimized by the judicial system. And there was an Englishwoman named Margaret Albore who had come to the United States as an au pair twenty-six years earlier, still carrying the painful memories of a lonely young girl in a strange land.

Her empathy with Olivia was strong, and very personal. "I became psychologically fixed on this case as soon as I started reading reports of it. It was not just a gut feeling. It was much more than that. It went deep into my soul. I knew that if this girl was found guilty she would lose about twenty years of her life, and I had no doubt of her innocence. No doubt at all. I had never taken a stand like this before, but I started going to the trial every day. I postponed medical appointments to be there. And I kept remembering how I felt when I was only eighteen, facing my first Christmas away from home, just as she was. I had never been out of my village before, never even been to London, and here I was in a strange environment caring for a two-year-old and a three-year-old whose parents were out a lot. It was such a responsibility. Although I was excited about being in a new country I was very homesick in those early weeks. I could fully relate to Olivia Riner, and I knew I had to be there for her.''

All of Olivia's supporters had a personal story of this kind; otherwise their unquestioning defense of her made no sense. On the face of it, she was an unlikely focus for sympathy: a foreigner and a stranger accused of the vilest kind of murder. Yet, influenced by pretrial television coverage and by their own emotions, many people perceived her as a victim even before her trial began. They came to court to see justice done, and genuinely believed that meant her acquittal.

In the meantime, the real victims, the baby's parents, were ignored. Following George Bolen's advice, they had declined to deal with the media; as a result, people had no sense of who they were or what Kristie's death had done to them. Several reporters had called at Fischer's Garage, asking for a photograph of Kristie, or a comment from Bill, and he had adamantly refused. He and Denise could not have borne to see their baby's living, smiling image sensationally reproduced in a mass-market publication. Nor did they want to talk about her death. Thus the Fischers never connected with the general public, never became real to them, never told their story, and all the sympathy which should have been theirs went to Olivia.

26

A few weeks before the trial, Bill and his immediate family had to move out of the Thornwood condominium and find another temporary home. They were offered the use of a large old house in the neighboring village of Valhalla; a gray and shadowy Colonial-style building which stood back from the road behind an overgrown garden. The owner, a colleague of Bill's, had bought it several years earlier but had never lived there, and in its desertion the house had grown colder and shabbier and spookier.

It was the antithesis of the house on West Lake Drive, still being rebuilt, which in happier times seemed to have been filled with sunshine and children's laughter. This place had a dark winding staircase, and peeling paint, and holes in the plaster. Eerier yet, Bill, Denise, Leah, and John came to believe that it had a ghost.

None of them saw her, but they were positive this was a female ghost because they could smell her perfume. There was a woman who had owned the house soon after it was built, more than fifty years earlier, and after she died there were reports of her footsteps being heard around the building. If this was her spirit, checking on the place, it meant no harm. It was simply there, uneasily hovering, adding another uncomfortable dimension to their lives.

The ghost never manifested herself when they were all in the house together. One day when John was home sick he was wakened by a feeling of someone poking him in the ribs, urging him to get out of bed. Then he heard the front door slam, as though his visitor was leaving. He assumed it was Bill and was later shocked to learn that Bill was at work at that time, as were Denise and Leah.

Bill had his own supernatural experience when, alone in the house, he heard the clinking sound of dishes being washed. He went into the kitchen but no one was there, and the last meal's dishes were still in the sink. Another time he and Denise were in their bedroom, certain that Leah and John were out, when they heard someone walking around. Bill checked every room, but they were all deserted.

Leah had a frightening experience when she was alone, using a vacuum cleaner. Over the noise of its motor she thought she heard a woman scream. Terrified, she fled the house for the sanctuary of her car. Then she realized she had left her car keys indoors, and ran back to get them, heart pounding. For the next half hour she sat in her driver's seat, quaking, until somebody came to rescue her. After she had calmed down she acknowledged that it might have been an oddity of the vacuum cleaner which sounded like a scream. But the experiences of the others were not so easily explained.

Grada, her mother, theorized that the ghost was a manifestation of the trauma they were all still suffering, intensified by the gloomy atmosphere of the house. That summer she had an insight into how severely John was affected when he and Leah came to visit her at a Long Island seaside cottage she had rented for the season. She could not be there for their arrival, and told them where to find the key. Afterward John admitted to her that he felt very uneasy as he opened that locked door, fearful of what he might find on the other side.

In Grada's opinion, anyone that traumatized might easily imagine a ghost. But Betsy, who believed in the existence of earthbound spirits, thought that this one could be real.

"Ghosts," she explained to Leah, "are usually there because there is something they need to come back and do. Or else they are people who don't know they're dead."

She shared an experience which she had not found frightening. Some years earlier she had been living with her parents in a house rented from a man who had retired to the Midwest. Having built the place, he still felt a deep attachment to it, and told them that he planned to come back and see it again before he died.

"Twice in one day I saw a man at the back window, looking in," Betsy related. "My mother saw him at the kitchen door, but when she opened it he was gone. That's how ghosts are. They are there but they are not there. You feel their presence but you can almost see through them. A day or two later we saw an announcement in a newspaper that this man had died. It must have happened just before we saw him. So he did come back, as he had promised."

Betsy took the thought a stage further, into her own faith. "I tried to explain to Leah that if there was a ghost in that house, there had to be life after death. And that if this soul still floating around was real enough for her to hear and smell, then surely she could accept that Kristie—whose presence we could no longer feel—had gone to heaven, and that now she is a child in heaven where no one can hurt her anymore."

Olivia's trial was scheduled to begin on June 2, 1992, exactly six months after Kristie's death. A customary waiting period in the Westchester County court system would have been closer to a year, but there was a good reason for minimizing that time—the hardship to Marlise Riner, an innocent victim in this case, who was being kept away from her husband, her home, and her job. The Swiss authorities had hoped that conditions might be set for Olivia to live in Switzerland under some kind of supervision while awaiting trial. Since this was out of the question, it was politic to dispose of her case as quickly as possible.

The Fischers approached the ordeal hopefully, expecting a resolution which would bring them healing. None of them had ever testified in court, but several of them were very eager to do so.

Jim Donnelly wanted to state on the record that it was he who made the joke about the barbecue, not John Gallagher. Jan Menting wanted to tell what he knew about the house on West Lake Drive from his unique experience of having put it together: how it was so much smaller than it looked from outside, how loudly footsteps sounded on those vinyl tiles which he had laid directly on the concrete foundation, how the very openness of the structure made it virtually impossible for an intruder to prowl around outside, as well as within, without being seen. Grada, who had lived there longer than anyone else, wanted to talk about the sliding windows on the main floor, how the noise of them grating on their tracks was impossible to disguise.

They were all so anxious to help, but almost nothing they could offer was of value to the prosecution. George Bolen did not even want to mention the Geraldo Rivera program, let alone identify the voices on that misinterpreted police video. Jan and his daughter had known the house too long ago for anything they remembered about it to be relevant. Bolen could imagine Laura Brevetti's knowing look as she posed the question: "And when did you last inspect the premises, Mr. Menting?"

It was hard to get the Fischer relatives to accept their limitations. From the beginning, Bolen had determined that Bill, Denise, Leah, and John would be his only family witnesses. Individually, he liked them all, but he worried about the impression they would make in court. He judged that Bill would be the most effective of the four. He was the only one who could testify about the quantities of paint thinner and other accelerants which were missing from his utility cupboard; also he was the last member of the family to see Kristie alive. He was strictly truthful, and it showed on his face.

Denise was more complex: intelligent, analytical, and utterly devastated by her baby's death. During the three months of Kristie's life she had surprised the Fischer relatives by showing a warm and gentle side of herself which her shyness had previously concealed. This tenderness touched by mourning would surely elicit the jurors' sympathy. Predictably, she would weep on the witness stand. Bolen could not bring himself to put her through a public exposure of her grief merely for the dramatic effect of it—which, given the tactics the defense was using, as well as Denise's eagerness to testify, may have been overly protective on his part. But he was also looking beyond the emotional impact. He knew that her value to his case, for better or worse, would depend upon what she said, rather than how she behaved. She could give no direct evidence about the events leading up to the fire. And when he considered the questions that Brevetti would put to her and the answers Denise would feel constrained to give, he was worried. He could predict those questions: "Before the fire, were you happy with Olivia? Was her work satisfactory? Her attitude? Was she loving and attentive with the baby? Did you feel confident about leaving her alone with Kristie?" And Denise, who until the night of the fire believed she had found the perfect baby-sitter, would have to answer yes to every one. Her testimony might help the defense more than the prosecution. Bolen decided to defer a decision about calling her as a witness until the trial was under way.

Leah, he judged, would be controlled and straightforward. But her staunch defense of John was a serious hazard. She was a warm and giving person, eager to mitigate the damage he had suffered on account of her family. But if Brevetti could persuade the jury to suspect him of murder, Leah's loyalty to her boyfriend could make her look like his co-conspirator, and that could be bad for both of them.

227

On Judge Silverman's orders the jury-selection process took place behind closed doors, producing a predominantly middle-aged team of seven men and five women. Most of them were professionals, some were grandparents, a few had retired. It was just the kind of jury that Laura Brevetti wanted, intelligent and aging. Younger jurors, she had been advised, would empathize more strongly with Bill and Denise in their infant-care problems, and be quicker to blame Olivia. Older jurors might have less sympathy for a mother who went back to work so soon after the birth of her child, and be more reluctant to send a young girl to jail. They might also be more critical of the Fischers' life-style.

That was another problem for the prosecution. While Bill had the outward appearance of a traditional, even conservative, parent, his was a very unorthodox household. It was hard to predict what a jury might make of a father who condoned his daughter having her boyfriend as a regular overnight guest, then invited a woman of his own choosing to move in, delayed marrying her until two months before their baby was born, and subsequently told the daughter's boyfriend to move out to make room for a nanny. A jury could fit a variety of plots into that situation. The most likely one would have the displaced boyfriend staging a house fire to eliminate both the baby and the need for a nanny, while presenting himself as a hero who would be welcomed back into the family.

From the prosecution's viewpoint, this was a real danger. Jurors cannot possibly remember all the testimony they hear, and what they hear is never the whole story, so they try to make sense of the material presented to them by forming their own narrative, weaving the disconnected facts into an intelligible tale. When the evidence is circumstantial and the motive unclear, attorneys in the case try to create a narrative for them. Laura Brevetti had already laid the foundations for her version by imputing guilt to John Gallagher, but George Bolen could not come up with anything as persuasive for the prosecution. If Kristie had been dead before the fire was set, there would have been motive for a panic-stricken baby-sitter to start the blaze to cover up. But the autopsy findings had ruled out that possibility. If only the medical examiner had gone to the scene that night. . . . He might have noticed something about the body and the way it was placed to provide a better insight into the cause of death.

The challenge for Bolen was that "Olivia Riner did not fit the profile of a typical criminal. She was a young female, and there was a ready male suspect. Somehow I had to get the jury beyond that to look at all the bits and pieces of evidence which pointed to her."

He acknowledged that while "the prosecution is not required to show motive, people still want to know why." And he could not find that answer for himself.

"Did she mean to kill this child?" he wondered. "Or did something else occur in that household which Olivia intentionally or accidentally caused to happen? Maybe the baby was overcome by smoke in another room. Maybe Olivia set a fire to cover. Maybe that is the scenario, certainly the one most acceptable to a jury."

It was a theory Bill Fischer had also developed. The house was heated by a hot-air system with vents in every room. Most of them were at floor level. Some time previously, when Bill was enlarging the closet in Leah's bedroom, he had moved one of that room's two exhaust vents close to the ceiling "because," he explained, "there was nowhere else to put it." If, as Bruce Johnson believed, the fire in Leah's room was set first, Bill theorized that rising smoke could have quickly entered that vent because of its height. The next opening in the system was at ground level in the nursery next door, close to the place where Kristie was lying. Thus she could have died from smoke inhalation almost immediately—a belief to which Bill clung because he did not want to think of her being burned to death. Whoever set that fire may not have wanted to kill her, may in fact have intended to rescue her, but finding her either comatose or dead, may have panicked, and in that crazed condition the rest was almost inevitable.

When Bill suggested this explanation, naming Olivia, neither he nor anyone in his family was familiar with "The Heroine." When they eventually read it, Leah remarked that "it seemed so close it blew our minds."

The heroine theory was persuasive to George Bolen, and he would like to have presented it in court. "But in order to get that book admitted into evidence I would have had to establish that Olivia bought a copy," he explained. "If I could have proved that the kiosk owner sold it to her, if I could have placed it in her hands, that would have been enough to argue circumstantially that she was influenced by it. Without that proof I couldn't mention the book."

At one point he mused: "They say a trial is a search for the truth.

But is it really? The jury has only limited information. Some evidence is suppressed because it is hearsay or might be prejudicial. A prosecutor can rarely tell the whole story."

He did not share his concerns with the Fischers. It was not his way of working. And he wanted them to maintain the confidence of believing that justice would prevail.

Before and during the trial Bill, Denise, Leah, and John had a compassionate mentor and counselor in Marianne Walsh, who ran the homicide crisis program for Victims Assistance Services in White Plains. A strikingly attractive blonde in early middle age, she was a former investment banker who had been drawn to this unusual and sensitive work after her father was robbed and fatally stabbed near his home, six years earlier. When she and her family felt that the police were not doing enough to track down his murderer, they became their own detectives—held a press conference, generated newspaper articles, and organized community meetings. Their persistence led to the identification and eventual imprisonment of the murderer (although for another crime), and to a dramatic change in Marianne's career. She took courses in criminal law, constitutional law, police procedure, and counseling, and designed the innovative program which she now headed, specifically for the families of homicide victims.

She formed an immediate and deep bond with the Fischers, guiding them through the police investigation and the trial preparation, listening to their pain and their fears. She told them they were fortunate to be represented by George Bolen ("an honorable man who plays by the rules"), but disagreed with his insistence that they should avoid talking to the press.

"Weeks before the trial I told them that the way the case was being portrayed, it was going to be tried in the media whether they talked or not," she related. "I said that they should look for one person in the media whom they could trust, and give them a story—let them see you, let them visit you, let them into your life a little bit.

"Instead, the only photographs taken of them showed people running away. After the Geraldo Rivera program a television reporter tried to talk to John and he was photographed running back into his garage. Bill was seen on TV running into his workshop. It looked terrible, and I told the Fischers that they ought to try and counteract this. I could see that Brevetti was using the press, and I knew that would escalate when the trial began.

"There was no focus on the baby. I asked Denise and Bill if they could possibly release a picture of her. I knew they were not going to give interviews. But they said no, and I understood why. After my dad died we were making up posters and we had to decide whether to use his picture on them. And I too said no because I thought some of those posters might get thrown around and trampled on. It would have seemed like desecration. But at some point Kristie should have been given some reality."

Afterward she agonized about whether she should have argued more forcefully. She had been around courthouses long enough to know that justice can be perverted. Sometimes it was necessary to anticipate and bypass that possibility. "But in the agency we walk a fine line because we cannot undermine the prosecution, which is supposed to be supporting our clients."

Lacking her sophisticated knowledge, the Fischers held on to their trust in the judicial system. "They thought that once they got to trial all the ugly rumors would be dispelled, and people would see the truth," Marianne commented.

In that expectation Bill Fischer left his temporary and haunted home on the morning of June 2, 1992, to be the prosecution's first witness.

27

This is the point at which most journalists came into the story. In the six months since the fire, very little had been added to their understanding of what happened on the afternoon of December 2. The police had said all they intended to say during the week of Olivia's arrest. George Bolen had refused to discuss the case. All attempts, even by Swiss reporters, to talk with Kurt and Marlise Riner had been repelled. No one had been able to discover where Olivia was living. The Fischers were consistently unavailable. Approached at his garage, Bill repeatedly turned his back on reporters. None of them knew where Denise worked or what she looked like. Laura Brevetti was the only principal in the case who was talking, and to only a few reporters. But the scant information filtering out of her office strongly suggested that the wrong person was being prosecuted, and that the media ought to be taking a hard look at John Gallagher. He, however, was being as elusive as Bill Fischer, which gave the impression that he had something to hide.

One journalist raised the question with Brevetti: "What was he doing at the Fischers' home at the time of the fire?"

"You may well ask," she replied tartly. And left it at that.

Reporters try to keep open minds, but they speculate on the facts available. On that limited basis, this seemed to be less of a story about a murderous baby-sitter than a Gothic tale of family jealousies which had ended in disaster, and of an inept rural police department which had been too quick to blame an innocent foreigner. Perhaps the police had not wanted to look further than Olivia Riner, fearful of involving someone they knew. Perhaps some carefully hidden truth would come out in testimony. If so, "the nanny trial" could be an unusually good story.

In that expectation, on the morning of Tuesday, June 2, 1992, the press seats in Judge Silverman's courtroom were filled with American and Swiss reporters, television commentators, and (cameras being banned) artists. It was a relatively small and simple room on the fourteenth floor of a vertical modern white building which was so utilitarian in design that if the windows had been smaller it could have passed for a prison. Its elevators were never adequate for the crowds making their way to various courtrooms, and at this time the congestion was compounded by the fact that several sensational cases were being heard on different floors. Trial-watching was a popular hobby in White Plains. The pretrial hearings in the Olivia Riner case had coincided with the last days of the sensational trial of Carolyn Warmus, an attractive Westchester schoolteacher convicted of fatally shooting her lover's wife. Now there was the choice of a case centered on a videotaped sex act (was it fun or was it rape, a jury was being asked to decide), or the opening of "the nanny trial." Some people drifted from one unlikely episode to another, like switching channels on TV. Outside, the busy modern city of White Plains went about its business. Inside the courthouse was this kaleidoscope of human drama.

In the Olivia Riner case Judge Silverman had given his customary advice to jurors during the previous week: "The defendant is presumed to be innocent. She need not prove anything. She need not testify. If she does not it will not be held against her. . . . The burden of proof is on the prosecution. The prosecution has to prove beyond a reasonable doubt that the defendant is guilty. If they do not do so the proper verdict is not guilty. If the evidence satisfies you beyond a reasonable doubt you must convict. If it does not, you must acquit."

The morning session on this first day of the trial was taken up with George Bolen's opening statement. He began by bluntly telling the jury that the prosecution was relying entirely on circumstantial evidence. "You will hear no confession. You will see no videotapes of the crime being committed. . . . No one witness will be able to tell you what occurred on a dreary, rainy, dismal day in December of 1991. But by the end of the case it will come together like pieces of a puzzle, and then you will know beyond a reasonable doubt that this defendant, Olivia Riner, murdered Kristie Fischer."

It was fine courtroom rhetoric. Bolen went on to describe in detail the layout of the Fischers' house, and of the surrounding neighborhood. After the fire, he said, "there was no sign of forced entry, no door locks picked, no broken windows, zilch. . . . This house had no basement or attic, but the grade of the house was such that the exterior windows of the downstairs bedrooms were below a person's waist. Here you have raccoons, all sorts of things, so the windows of those rooms were kept closed. The baby's room windows were kept closed and locked. . . . There was only one entrance to the house, and on either side of it was floor-to-ceiling glass.

"You walk through that front door to a combination playroom, family room, living room. To the right was a fireplace with a couch and reclining chair. To the left was tile, and a series of closets which were for storage. There Mr. Fischer kept his fishing tackle, tools, containers of turpentine, paint thinner, lighter fuel. Additionally on the wall—you could not miss it—was a fire extinguisher. . . . Bill Fischer was a very neat and organized man. Everything had its place, and that was particularly true of that closet. If the paint thinner was used it would be securely capped and put back."

Bolen described the inhabitants of the house: "Bill Fischer, quiet, organized, and handy . . . divorced with two adult children, he first met Denise at his repair business in North White Plains. . . . Denise was a college graduate. Bill was not. She was an accountant involved in tax matters. . . . Leah is twenty-two, and was a secretary at an automobile dealership in White Plains. For several years she had dated John Gallagher, and they spent time in one another's homes. Gallagher worked as an auto mechanic for a firm in Greenburgh. . . . Kristie, the baby, developed normally and was healthy."

He explained how the Fischers came to employ Olivia ("quiet, reasonably intelligent, with a reasonable understanding of English"), and how Bill showed her the workings of his house including the contents of his utility closet, and the shelf by the upstairs fireplace where he kept his household matches. She was also told of the precautions in place for an emergency: three fire extinguishers, three battery-operated smoke detectors, six telephones with a list of emergency numbers, a baby monitor in Kristie's room with one transmitter in the master bedroom and another in the au pair's room across the narrow hallway from the nursery. Bolen went on to describe the new hollow-core door to that nursery, which, inexplicably, became locked from the inside. "One punch would have put a hole in it. If you were to take a fire extinguisher and wham it, you could punch a hole in that door."

All this was new to the press and the public who were hearing for the first time about the half-spent box of matches found on the nursery floor, identical to a box missing from upstairs, along with the twisted remains of a soda bottle, identical to some of the empty soda bottles in the laundry room's recycling can, except that this one had contained an accelerant.

Bolen alleged that Olivia took flammable liquids from the utility closet, transferred some of them to a discarded soda bottle, and using matches taken from upstairs, set fires in three separate rooms on the main floor, locking the doors to the nursery and Leah's room behind her.

He stated: "Olivia had the presence of mind to get the fire extinguisher and put out the fire in her room; yes, she had the presence of mind to get emergency personnel to that scene. But what about Kristie? She says she tried the door and it was locked, and that she had left it open." Earlier, however, "in an unguarded moment," she told Bill Fischer that she had shut it herself.

What really happened, he insisted, was that "between four and five o'clock the defendant set about intentionally, knowingly, and willfully in various acts that ended in murder and arson. No one else was in that house. No one came into that house by breaking windows, picking locks, entering through skylights. No one threw what might be called a Molotov cocktail into that house. In short, the defendant was the only person with the infant Kristie . . . and she intentionally, though inexplicably, poured flammable liquid accelerants on her." Bolen contended that Olivia did not make her emergency telephone calls in the hope of saving the baby "but for other reasons, including her own consciousness of guilt for what she had done."

He glanced across the courtroom at Olivia, dressed in the most demure of her new outfits, the navy suit with the plain white blouse, and commented: "As you look at Olivia Riner, the way she is attired, her apparently angelic face, you will be asking yourselves why. You will be thinking it cannot be her. It must have been Bill. It must have been Denise—postpartum depression. It must have been Leah—she was jealous. Or else some unknown murderer, some unknown arsonist."

Before this day's session began, Bill Fischer, waiting in the corridor beyond the courtroom, had encountered Olivia for the first time since the night of the fire when, on the patio outside the burning house, she had tearfully told him that she had shut the nursery door. He had never wanted to see her again, and now, forced to sit so close to her he felt affronted, all his anger focusing on her strategically changed style of dress. Bolen picked up on this.

"The Germans have a phrase," he remarked to the jury. "*Kleider machen nicht Leute:* Clothes do not make the person. We have the same in English: Appearances are deceptive.''

Olivia looked puzzled. So did the Swiss reporters. Bolen had negated the quotation and fractured the grammar. The saying, the title of a popular nineteenth-century tale, should have been *Kleider machen Leute,* which had the reverse meaning: Clothes can make people. But his perversion of Olivia's language did him no harm. In the next day's newspapers his most widely quoted remark was memorable: ''Some offenses are so askew of humanity, so devoid of rationality, that it is difficult to imagine what could possibly have motivated them.''

He had made a forceful and convincing presentation. During the lunch recess an American reporter remarked to a colleague: ''Until this morning I was certain that Olivia Riner didn't do it. But if I had to vote on this case right now, I'd vote guilty on the basis of what George Bolen said.''

It was a hard act to follow. The previous week, at the completion of jury selection, Laura Brevetti had done her best to overcome one of the weakest points in her case—Olivia's failure to try to rescue Kristie.

At that time Brevetti had asked the jurors: ''How many people here understand that you can have delayed reactions? That you can look back and say that you should have done this, or you should have done that, but in the panic of the moment you didn't?''

She left the question hanging, and never raised it again. Now that the trial was beginning, all her efforts were concentrated on attacking the prosecution's presumption of Olivia's guilt. On this opening day Brevetti was dressed more conservatively than usual, in a tailored navy suit worn with a striking pearl brooch and earrings, which made her look like an haute couture version of her client. She must have given a lot of thought to the impression she would make. Her manner was always assertive, but today she seemed nervous, at times addressing the jurors so softly that they had to strain to hear her above the sound of the air-conditioning unit, directly behind their double row of chairs.

''You will come to learn,'' she told them, ''that from the first hour the police department set out not to solve the crime, but to build a case against Olivia Riner. . . . Mr. Bolen has told you of a matchbox and a soda bottle, that doors were locked, that windows were closed. Listen to the conclusion that is drawn from this: She did it. Without any doubt.

End of story. But there will be no expert, no witness, who will tell you beyond all doubt that these items came from the house. This girl was not the only one who had access."

She pointed to Olivia's cooperative behavior on the night of the fire—how she telephoned for help, turned on the upstairs lights to guide fire trucks to the building, and was respectful and compliant during seven hours of intensive interrogation. Were these the actions of a guilty person?

Brevetti suggested that the police themselves had doubts, citing Bruce Johnson's unfortunate questions: Was she covering up for someone? John Gallagher? "This," Brevetti said cynically, "to the person who they are sure did it! And yet two hours after the arrest they are grilling her about whether or not she had help, or whether someone else was responsible."

She was making some strong points, but her speech lacked impact. She kept it brief, and sat down abruptly, exhausted by the effort. Then the prosecution called its first witness, William Fischer, and the story so many people had been eager to hear began to unfold.

28

Those who were seeing him for the first time were surprised when Bill walked stiffly up to the witness stand, treading warily when he approached the defense attorney's table where Olivia was sitting. He was an unlikely type to be the third-generation owner of an auto-repair shop. Except for his obvious discomfort in a city suit, dated in style but barely worn, he looked like a conventional businessman. He had none of the burly bonhomie normally associated with his job. This was a very private person, stoic and withdrawn, yet unable to hide his pain. The expression in his unusually light blue eyes was of one so deeply wounded that there was no joy left in him. It was impossible to look at him without feeling compassion.

Over the next three days he told his story. In response to George Bolen's sympathetic questioning, he came across as a responsible, caring husband and father; a model homeowner who could give immediate answers to a barrage of questions about the mechanism of all his door and window latches, the position of all the vents in his hot-air heating system, and the contents of his utility cupboard, including the number of cans of paint thinner, charcoal lighter fluid, turpentine, and other flammable liquids, and their approximate levels. He stated that these cans were always put neatly back on the shelves, never left uncapped or on their side, as some of them were found by the police. Thus he was able to confirm, with believable certainty, which accelerants had been taken from the utility closet, and the approximate quantities. He was specific about the missing paint thinner because he had used it only ten days earlier when he was finishing the new door to the nursery. After so much precise description, it seemed uncharacteristic of Bill Fischer to have hung that door in such a way that the locking mechanism barely engaged and could easily be popped open. But from the prosecution's point of view, the ill-fitting lock was a fortuitous error because it emphasized how easily Olivia could have opened that door, had she tried.

Bill outlined his daily regimen of getting up at 5:30 A.M. and working out at a gym before arriving at his garage two hours later. He usually stayed there until 6:00 P.M., with a break at about 1:30 P.M. when he often drove home for lunch. On the day of the fire he remembered saying said "Hi" to Olivia when he walked into the house, and "See you later" when he left. He spent the intervening forty-five minutes alone in the kitchen upstairs while she remained on the ground floor, near the baby. His version of their brief encounter conveyed his awkwardness with her, and hers with him. It also gave a sense of her isolation, alone with the baby in a rural area where she had no friends, did not know the neighbors, and where the only family member who came home during the day was not very communicative.

"Denise mostly would have conversations with her," Bill explained, as though that covered the need for verbal contact. Olivia impressed him as "acceptable and obedient," and he "did not see any problem at all" in her relationship with anyone in his household. But he did not seem to really know her. It had been Denise's idea to get an au pair, he said, and she did all the research. E. F. Au Pair sent a written profile and references, but no one from the agency had visited their home.

During her first month with the Fischers, Olivia was given time off during the day when she sometimes walked to the shopping center. But when Denise went back to work, the week before the fire, Olivia was required to stay at home with the baby. She had no household duties other than caring for Kristie and feeding the cats, and it was Bill's observation that she loved all animals.

He was asked whether he used his front-door key when he arrived home for lunch on December 2. No, he said, he just walked in. That door was never locked in the daytime. He assumed that Olivia heard him opening it, or perhaps the sound of his truck pulling onto the driveway; in any event, she did not seem surprised when he entered the nursery where she was sitting on the floor, folding baby clothes. At the end of the day's testimony Laura Brevetti made sure that the implications of that unsecured front door were fully understood.

"This house is not the fortress that is being portrayed," she remarked to a group of journalists in the hallway outside the courtroom. "Not just

Bill Fischer but anyone could have walked in without her knowing."

Brevetti latched on to her own phrase, and used it repeatedly through the rest of the trial. "That house was not a fortress." No one had directly claimed that it was, but her denial created the unspoken assertion, at the same time making it seem too extravagant to be true. It was a clever strategy which led the jury so far away from one of the prosecution's best arguments that as the trial proceeded it was virtually forgotten: the contention that although it was possible for an intruder to enter the house, no one could move around it without being seen or heard. Brevetti repeated her assertion so often that it began to sound like a mantra: "That house was not a fortress. Anyone could have walked in and lit those fires. . . ." And as the complexity of Bill's family relationships began to emerge, it was tempting to invent possibilities.

In his testimony Bill stated that Grada moved out of the house in the fall of 1987, and that he bought her half share of the property when they divorced in 1989. Leah had continued to live there with him, but Troy had moved to Manhattan. Denise moved in during the summer of 1990; they married in July of 1991, and Kristie was born that September. Bill said that Leah was happy about the new baby. But he conceded that she and Denise "did not always see eye to eye," and that when Olivia joined the household and John was told to discontinue his practice of sleeping over, Leah began to spend more nights in Mahopac with the Gallagher family. Although they had been dating seriously for some time, the relationship between these two young people had its stormy passages. Bill recalled an occasion the previous November, the month before the fire, when Leah came home angry and upset after an argument involving John. He added that the disagreement was soon settled.

He was questioned about another cause of friction in his family.

"Did you smoke?" Bolen asked him.

"I have never smoked," he replied.

"Did your wife smoke?"

"No, sir, she did not."

"Prior to December the second did you know if Leah smoked cigarettes?"

After an uncomfortable pause Bill muttered: "She didn't admit to it but she did smoke."

"Did you see her smoke?"

"No."

Outside the courtroom Laura Brevetti's private detective and chief investigator, Christopher Rush, hinted to journalists that there were other, more serious tensions in the Fischer family. None of us had heard the half of it, he said. Rush, a burly Irish-American who was formerly a New York City policeman, also proffered his theories about why Olivia was not aware of the alleged intruder: "This was a kid who could be so thoroughly wrapped up in what she was doing that you could set a bomb off behind her and she would not hear."

Toward the end of Bill's second day on the witness stand, George Bolen asked him to identify a photograph.

"Do you recognize what this is?" he asked.

His voice breaking, Bill replied: "Yes, my daughter Kristie's car seat." He was referring to the infant carrier in which she died.

There was a smiling Kristie cradled in the carrier, reminding him of the last time he saw her, but he couldn't bring himself even to mention that she was in the picture. Bolen wanted to get the photograph entered into evidence, knowing it would have an emotional impact upon the jury. Laura Brevetti objected for the same reason, and the judge upheld her objection. He asked what purpose the photograph would serve, and Bolen gave the convoluted answer: "To show what portions of the baby would be affected by whatever it was that burned her."

"There is no real controversy as to how this baby died," Judge Silverman observed. And so the jury had no sense of how Kristie looked, and was left to think of her only in the abstract, as a child unknown to them who died in a fire. With that, the emphasis of this trial shifted, and it became more a case about arson than one about murder. It was more comfortable to think and talk about in those terms, as Bill himself knew. It would be many months yet before he could bring himself to say: "Kristie didn't die in a fire. Kristie was set on fire!" And when he was finally able to accept and state that reality, he was shocked by the sound of his own words.

Bill's appearance in court was the beginning of daily television coverage of "the nanny trial." It brought out a new breed of journalists, slender young women of flawless appearance who seemed to spend as much time preparing themselves for the cameras as they did listening to testimony. Some of them had assistants to do the listening, and would appear only toward the end of the afternoons, in time to position them-

selves with their camera crews in the large open area on the ground
floor of the courthouse, waiting for Laura Brevetti. Sometimes they were
observed reapplying their lipstick and curling their eyelashes while they
waited. There would be a scuffle of activity as Brevetti came importantly
down the escalator with a retinue of aides and supporters at her heels;
microphones would be held up to her face, cameras trained on her.
Soon she too learned the value of replenishing her makeup first, of
appearing as fresh and groomed as her questioners. The ladies' room
on the fourteenth floor, next to Judge Silverman's courtroom, became
a regular hive of activity at the end of each day's proceedings.

This daily television exposure gave Brevetti a superb opportunity to
present her case to a large viewing public hungry for details of a story
almost too bizarre to be true. Her version was virtually the only one to
be aired on the nightly news programs since George Bolen, observing
protocol, was consistently unavailable to the media.

At the end of Bill's second day on the witness stand, one television
news program reported that Leah was jealous of the new baby—which
was exactly the opposite of what Bill had just said in court. But no one
on the prosecution side spoke up to correct the impression.

Laura Brevetti and her staff worked late into the night, analyzing Bill's
testimony, comparing what he stated at the trial with what he had said
before a grand jury almost six months earlier. It is an odd aspect of the
American criminal justice system that while the proceedings of a grand
jury (the panel of citizens which determines whether or not the prosecution has a valid case) are kept secret, certain relevant statements made
at that closed hearing may be quoted at a subsequent trial. When Brevetti's turn came to cross-examine Bill, she revealed several minor discrepancies, sufficient to cast doubt on Bolen's carefully presented image
of a homeowner who knew every screw in the place.

She reminded him that at the grand jury hearing he had not been
certain about how many boxes of matches there were by the upstairs
fireplace. Now he was positive there were four. He had told the grand
jury that there were three bottles of paint thinner in the utility closet.
Now it was "two, three, or four."

Bill tried to explain: "I don't believe they were all paint thinners.
There were different chemicals in the house."

Judge Silverman intervened: "Do you consider turpentine a paint
thinner?"

"Yes," Bill replied. "I included that the first time." Then he remembered: "There's a large bottle of paint thinner, a small bottle of turpentine, and a small bottle—I don't know what it was."

By now most of the jurors were looking confused. But even Bill's uncertainties left little doubt that someone had tampered with his utility closet, removing significant quantities of flammable liquids.

There was one question George Bolen would like to have asked but deliberately avoided because Bill had misunderstood it at the grand jury hearing. Now he would be answering correctly, and what he would have to say was important to the prosecution's case, but Laura Brevetti would inevitably point out that it didn't match up with his earlier response, and the truth could now be made to look like a lie. Initially there had been an innocent human error on Bill's part, like his early recollections about the quantities of matches and paint thinner, made when he was in a state of shock. But a jury would be unlikely to see it that way.

Bill recounted the incident, ruefully, months later.

"The wooden matches which I used for lighting the barbecue grill were kept in the bookcase cabinet by the upstairs fireplace. In the grand jury hearing I was asked, 'Subsequent to the fire were all the boxes of matches still there?' and I said yes. I got stuck on the word 'subsequent.' It's not a word I would use. Afterward Denise asked me, 'What does subsequent mean?' I said, 'It means prior to.' She said, 'No, it means the opposite.' Later in the hearing I made the mistake again. So Bolen couldn't ask me about the missing matches at the trial because Brevetti would have pointed out the discrepancy, and that would have made me look uncertain about everything else. But when I looked in the cabinet on the day after the fire, I knew that one of those boxes of Diamond matches had gone."

Through several hours on the witness stand, almost directly facing Olivia, Bill avoided any eye contact with her. But from time to time she looked across at him with a kind of detached curiosity. His pain was palpable, yet it did not seem to touch her. It was as if she had never known him or his baby; as if the tragedy he was describing was so far outside her experience that she could not begin to empathize with his loss. She was seated only a few yards away, slightly below and to the right of him. Maya Hess was next to her, whispering a translation into her ear. Laura Brevetti and her legal assistant, Elan Gerstmann, occupied the other two seats at the defense attorney's table. While the three of them frequently shifted in their chairs, easing their backs away from the places where the wood prodded, Olivia sat upright, hour after hour, feet side by side on the floor, hands in her lap, like an obedient child waiting for the next instruction. There was only one outward sign of her nervousness, and no one in the press and public section was close enough to see it. The hands which from a distance seemed to be quietly folded were in fact never still, the fingers constantly twining around one another, as pliable as if they were made of rubber. They were small for the rest of her, and her entire body language was concentrated in the continuous movement of those childlike hands. Otherwise she was a statuesque little figure who looked almost too good to be true.

This aspect of her public image was an ongoing concern of her supporters. Her hairstyle, her clothes, and her demeanor made her look young and innocent, but her lack of emotional response was troubling. Linda Sawyer urged her to act as though she was grief-stricken by Kristie's death, and she worried that Olivia did not seem to appreciate that she was likely to be judged by the way she behaved. In one television shot taken as she left court after listening to Bill's evidence, she had looked almost happy.

That evening Linda took her aside. "I sat down and looked into Olivia's eyes and I implored her to show emotion in court. I told her that she must no longer act like a Swiss because she was facing an American jury who would not understand. I was crying as I said this. I said, 'If you feel you can cry, you should.' I told her that her freedom was at stake. She listened to me as though she was a student listening to an authority figure. There was no emotional reaction. But her mother was there, and she knew what I was talking about. She told her, 'One tear, and you can go home.' "

The following afternoon, the tape recordings of Olivia's two frantic telephone conversations with the desk sergeant at the Mount Pleasant police station were entered into evidence as People's Exhibits 79 and 80, and played to the jurors. This was the first time they had heard her speak, and it was an odd experience to watch her quietly sitting there while her disembodied voice became more urgent and hysterical, trying to convince the desk sergeant that 5 West Lake Drive did indeed exist, and was on fire. Suddenly the Olivia at the defense table seemed overcome by this replay of her own anguished cry for help. She became tearful, and was ushered out of the room by her attorney. There was a sympathetic silence when she returned a few minutes later.

This incident made the next day's headlines, NANNY SOBS HEARING TAPED CALL, taking precedence over a brief report of Bill's testimony. "It was just too much," Laura Brevetti explained to reporters. "It was very, very emotional evidence for her to hear."

The next People's Exhibit was even more theatrical: a twenty-minute film of the fire itself. It was an amateur film whose sequences were only jerkily connected because the photographer, Henry Flavin, had switched his video equipment on and off as he moved around the burning house. If he had known that the film might be used as court evidence, he might have made a smoother job of it. But Flavin, an instructor of volunteer firefighters for Westchester County Fire Services, made the film solely for his own records, with the idea of replaying it during one of his training sessions.

He had been at the county's Fire Control Center when the alarm sounded on the afternoon of December 2. Picking up a video camera from his office, he hurried to the scene and took some dramatic shots while the fire was at its height. Then his videotape ran out and the film ended abruptly.

A large television set was wheeled into court, and the room darkened, so that the judge and jurors could watch it. What they saw did nothing to help them determine the cause of arson, or even the extent of the damage, but it did convey the drama of men bravely fighting to staunch a blaze which was surging out of control. The expressions on some jurors' faces mirrored their own fearful reactions: This could be my home burning. Olivia's mother, who had moved from her seat in the public section to a better viewing position by the far wall of the court-room, instinctively put a hand up to her face, and then over her mouth, as if to silence the shock she dared not express.

The film itself was a confusion of flame, noise, heavy smoke, search-lights stabbing the darkness, firemen dragging their equipment around the outside of the house, firemen hacking at the building with axes, firemen shouting instructions to one another, "You guys, take a hose and spray in there. . . ." At a point when the blaze seemed to be under control, a huge spurt of orange flame poured out of the side of the house—the previously unknown fire in Leah's bedroom bursting out of the window. Otherwise nothing seemed to differentiate this from any other house fire. There were no indoor shots. Viewers were spared the sight of Kristie's body, or the interior of the nursery. All told, there seemed little to be learned from this videotape. So it was assumed as the television set was switched off, and the next witness sworn in.

Later, Henry Flavin's film would become the most crucial piece of evidence at this trial.

29

Before John Gallagher was called upon to testify, his alibi was clumsily established. The Fischers were shocked that he needed one. They were in full support of him, and embarrassed that his heroic attempt to save Kristie had come to this. Nevertheless, it was important to satisfy the jury that John could not have reached the Fischer house in time to light three fires (or to stand on guard while someone else lit them) before Olivia telephoned for help at 5:10 P.M. He had told the police that he drove there directly from work, arriving at 5:15 P.M. Since it was a fifteen-minute drive from the White Plains Jaguar service department to West Lake Drive, the prosecution needed to demonstrate that he did not leave work before five.

Here the trial took a turn for the bizarre, with testimony from the White Plains Jaguar service manager, James Westbrook, about the quirky nature of his company's time clock. When Detective Bruce Johnson called on him a few days after the fire to pick up John's December 2 time card, Johnson noted that it showed the wrong time and date. Now Jim Westbrook was in court to explain that it wasn't wrong at all, it simply needed to be understood.

He stated that at the beginning of every year a new die with the date stamp had to be entered into the clock's mechanism. The die cost about $200, and installing it was a complicated procedure. Hence the company had not ordered one for the past two years, and all the 1991 time cards were stamped 1989. The clock was programmed for thirty-one-day months, and had to be manually moved forward at the end of every month in which there were fewer than thirty-one days. This should have been done on November 30, but that was a Saturday when the workshop was closed. After recording a nonexistent November 31, the clock switched itself back to November 1. It was not corrected when work resumed on Monday, December 2, 1991, which caused that fateful date to be registered on John Gallagher's time card as November 1, 1989.

There was yet another complication. For the purposes of calculating hourly pay, the hours on the clock were divided into one hundred segments rather than sixty. So it read differently from clocks designed to tell the time: What appeared to be fifty minutes on a stamped card was thirty in reality. After all this had been explained to the confusion of everyone in court, it was established that on December 2 John Gallagher arrived at work at 8:04 A.M., was out for lunch between 12:18 P.M. and 1:27 P.M., and punched out for the day at 4:42 P.M. That was the best that Westbrook could contribute to his alibi. The eighteen minutes between 4:42 and 5:00 were still unaccounted for.

Enter John Sunseri, a fellow mechanic at White Plains Jaguar, to confirm the story John had told the police—that he stood around chatting with three of his colleagues after clocking out from his job. One of them had spent the day at the company's training school "out in Jersey," returning to the service station at about 4:45 P.M., when he drove his car into the shop, opened the hood, and checked the engine. John Gallagher and another mechanic talked with him while he did the checking. Then, said Sunseri, "I turned my head, they were both gone. I assumed they left together." The time "give or take a minute" was about five o'clock.

None of John's other colleagues was called to back up this story. The man who presumably left when he did was not on the list of witnesses. Confirmation of John's time of departure rested entirely on Sunseri's memory. And Sunseri, who said he had known John for several years, was not a convincing witness. A slender young man with smooth, dark hair, he had the confident air of one who would tell a good story for a friend. Perhaps too good a story, a tale on the edge of the absurd. He plunged into it when he was asked about John Gallagher's driving style. Sunseri grinned, relishing the question.

"We had fun with him at times because he drives like grandpa," he volunteered.

He was asked what that meant. "Slow," he said.

Minutes later he acknowledged that John sometimes went race-car driving. Like grandpa? Not at all fazed by the question, Sunseri responded: "I think he just doesn't beat on the truck, that's all. If we're talking track, that would be different."

248

There was a stir in court when the next name was called: John Philip Gallagher III, the witness everyone in the public and press benches had been eager to hear. Almost no one had any idea what to expect. The few news photographs taken of him in his work clothes, dodging photographers, had been barely recognizable. Now he looked groomed and correct, dressed in a style which was rare for him, a silvery-gray suit, white shirt, and conservative tie, bought specially for the occasion. He wanted to make a good impression, and all his dress clothes had been burned with Leah's in her closet. Everyone in court stared at him as he took his place at the witness stand. They saw a tall, lean young man with a pale complexion and thick red-gold hair, slightly receding at the forehead and worn low on the nape of his neck.

Bolen's questioning began gently, then led into some of the controversial areas of his life. Brevetti was certain to probe them in her cross-examination, so it was politic for the prosecution to put them out in the open. There was the fact that twelve years earlier, when he was fourteen, John's swimming coach had been Lieutenant Louis Alagno of the Mount Pleasant police. It was an irrelevant detail, but the defense could make it seem significant.

Bolen moved to his witness's failure to graduate from Westlake High School. At first John told the court that he did graduate, then, shifting uncomfortably, amended his response. He was asked why he did not complete his senior year.

"I was asked to leave," he replied.

"You were asked to leave?" Bolen was giving him a chance to rephrase his answer. John had not been expelled. He was an indifferent student who dropped out of school at the age of seventeen because he found the life of an automobile mechanic more appealing. It was a natural choice, the work that his father did, learned in his own backyard. None of the Gallagher men equated scholarship with earning a living. They all worked with their hands. Brevetti had subpoenaed John's high school records, which showed a history of chronic absenteeism, but not the kind of behavior that leads to expulsion.

John did not explain this, but simply said yes, he was asked to leave.

Bolen tried again. "You were expelled? What did you do?"

"Cutting classes."

It did not seem reason enough for expulsion. The impression was left that there was something reprehensible in this witness's past which the

249

prosecution was covering up. Bolen moved on to broader biographical detail.

He had John tell how two years before the fire his family moved from Mount Pleasant, where the Gallaghers had lived for several generations, to Mahopac in Putnam County, immediately north of Westchester. By then he had been dating Leah Fischer for two years. They met in 1987, broke up for seven months in 1988, and had dated steadily ever since. John admitted that over four and a half years it had been "an up and down relationship" with "lots of squabbles," including the argument during the month before the fire to which Bill had alluded.

"How serious is the relationship?" Bolen inquired.

"Serious relationship," John replied.

Bolen stumbled over his own embarrassment with the next question. "Would you say that you and Miss Gallagher have been intimate? Understand what I mean by intimate?"

John looked surprised. "Miss Gallagher?" he inquired.

Bolen corrected himself. "Miss Fischer. Have you been intimate?"

"Yes."

Seated in the back of the courtroom, Carol Gallagher looked flustered. She was very fond of Leah. But the Gallaghers, who were Catholics, had stricter views than the Fischers about premarital sex. Certainly about the public acknowledgment of it. "You can always come home," Carol had told John, knowing that he wouldn't, when he moved in with the Fischers after the fire. Nevertheless, she was proud of him, and of his brave attempt to save Kristie. She had taken time off from work to be in court, supportive as ever, through his testimony. Her husband did not accompany her. He said he was fearful of losing his Irish temper and saying something regrettable. He had the same reddish hair as his son, with a heavier, muscular body. Carol seemed to be the linchpin of this family.

"I'm here for you, hon, no matter what it takes," she had said to John before he began to testify.

Bolen went on to ask him about the vehicles he owned, the Ford pickup truck which he always drove to work, and a 1989 Ford Mustang which he shared with one of his two brothers. The brother sometimes went racing in it, but John said he had given up the hobby. He also owned a Dodge Dart which had not been used for four years. "It just sits. It's off the road. It's kind of like a project."

He stated that he smoked cigarettes, and sometimes lit them with matches. When he was in the truck, where he usually kept a pack above the driver's seat, he used the cigarette lighter. He was allowed to smoke in his parents' home, but not at Leah's. That seemed to diminish the possibility of his walking into the Fischers' house with a box of matches in his hand. He was asked if Leah smoked. No, he said. Had she ever smoked? Yes.

He had been employed by White Plains Jaguar since it came into business in June 1991. Before that he had worked at two other Jaguar service stations. His hours were from 8:00 A.M. to 5:00 P.M., Mondays through Fridays. When he slept at the Fischers' house he always parked his truck on their driveway. And he left it there when he and Leah made overnight visits to the Gallagher home, driving to Mahopac in her Toyota Corolla because it was easier on gasoline. It was a 1989 model with a stick shift.

"What kind of driver is Leah?" Bolen asked.

"Decent driver," he conceded. But he always took the wheel when they traveled together.

On Sunday, December 1, he and Leah spent the night at Mahopac. He drove her home the following morning, arriving there between 6:45 and 7:00 A.M. He testified that he did not accompany her into the house but picked up his truck and went directly to work.

This left a gap in his account of the day which Brevetti would be sure to seize upon when she cross-examined him. Given the facts that John Gallagher clocked in for work at 8:04 A.M., and that it took fifteen minutes to drive from the Fischer house, there remained about an hour of unexplained time.

Ignoring it, Bolen quickly moved the narrative to 5:00 P.M. when John left work and drove back to West Lake Drive. He had him tell about pulling into the driveway, seeing a burst of fire from the hole in the nursery window, running up to the house, taking the fire extinguisher from Olivia, yelling a question at her about the locked nursery door, but being unable to make out her response before he kicked it open.

"The baby was on the floor in front of me," he recounted. "On fire."

There was a long pause before he was able to continue. Yet his emotions were so tautly controlled that his telling of the tale seemed almost dispassionate. The more gruesome the narrative, the harder it was to read his facial expression. Finally he described kneeling down beside the remains of Kristie, and spraying foam from the extinguisher around her, in the path of the circle of fire. "But I knew it was too late. I then backed out."

"What motivated you to leave the room?" Bolen asked.

"The smoke," John replied. "And the smell of the burned baby."

Bolen had no more questions. This was a propitious moment to let his witness go, allowing the horror of that scene to sink in. It was a few minutes after noon on a Friday, and if Judge Silverman followed his usual procedure he would call a lunch break and have Brevetti's cross-examination occupy the afternoon. John Gallagher's ordeal should be over before the weekend. Instead the judge made the unexpected announcement that he was adjourning court for the day.

"Some things have arisen that are beyond our control, and we do not know yet if we shall be able to proceed on Tuesday," he said. (The court did not sit on Mondays.) No explanation was offered, but later some of Laura Brevetti's aides let it be known that she had requested the break because she felt ill. She was reported to be feverish and in severe pain from a viral infection.

It was Wednesday before the court resumed.

That Tuesday evening the Fischers and the Gallaghers were shocked and appalled when, on Geraldo Rivera's *Now It Can Be Told,* there was a replay of Linda Sawyer's program suggesting that John should be a suspect in the murder of Kristie.

"Are you going to tell me that they can allow *this* ???" Jim Donnelly asked his brother-in-law, outraged. They had no idea that the show would ever be aired again. At their home in Mahopac the Gallagher family switched it on by chance.

"What the hell are they trying to do?" John senior demanded. He was so angry that he had to be dissuaded from calling the TV station in the middle of the program and demanding that it be immediately taken off the air.

"We can't do that, hon," Carol told him. "We have to play it cool." But she was just as furious.

So, on the evening before he went back on the witness stand, John Gallagher was again identified on a popular television program as the man who joked about barbecues while sifting through the ashes of the fire that killed Kristie. The nervous laughter in the background was again described as Leah Fischer's. Yet again, viewers were treated to Rivera's innuendos about "this guy Gallagher," and to his suggestion that the police and the press should take a harder look at him, instead of at Olivia Riner.

(Later Linda Sawyer explained: "After my program was aired the first time, in February, the show *Now It Can Be Told* was canceled in mid-season. That was April, and the contracts with the stations ran until September. So they had to do reruns to fill in airtime. On June 9 the Geraldo people, thinking this was a topical subject because the trial was on, decided to do a wraparound about the nanny case, and dump in my twelve-minute package. It was entirely their decision. I was no longer working for them.")

That was not the end of it. As if by collusion, the following morning's *Newsday*, a New York daily newspaper widely circulated in White Plains, carried a prominent article by one of its columnists, Carole Agus. Headed A NANNY VS. A LIAR: WHO TO BELIEVE?, it named John as the liar, and the misinformation he had initially given about his high school record as evidence of his mendacity. The article opened with the challenging question: "The man on the stand today as the Nanny Trial resumes is John Philip Gallagher III, an auto mechanic. Should he also be a murder suspect?" Copies of this newspaper were on sale in the streets of White Plains, and at the newsstand in the courthouse building before "the nanny trial" resumed that day.

Against this background of renewed suspicion, John returned to the witness stand—agitated, angry, and exerting all his energy to keep his negative feelings in check.

Apparently restored to health, Laura Brevetti began her cross-examination with an acerbity which jurors had not previously seen in her. She had been relatively gentle with Bill Fischer. But John Gallagher was a witness she wanted to discredit, and she knew exactly how to do it.

If he was expelled from school, why did he at first say he graduated? she wanted to know.

"It was a mistake on my part," John replied. He was wearing his only suit again, with a different tie. Olivia was in her cream-colored outfit, the one she wore least often. It was an impractical color, but the pallor of it, enhancing the gold in her hair and her wan complexion (white would have been too harsh for her), made her look almost untouchably pure. Was it happenstance, or did she save this suit for the days when she most needed to impress the jury that she was innocent?

Brevetti wrung an admission from John that he was expelled from school after cutting classes "four or five times." He was underestimating by far.

"Nothing else?" she asked. After a pause to allow jurors to share her incredulity, she went on to probe another dubious area of his life.

There was the matter of the insurance on his pickup truck, with Leah named as the primary driver, although it was registered as a commercial vehicle. Under relentless questioning John admitted that he had used Leah's name for insurance purposes because of his own poor driving record. He "didn't recall" signing his own application for insurance and being refused until Brevetti produced papers showing that he had amassed five traffic violations in as many years, for speeding, for driving through stop signs, and for driving while his license was suspended. He told her he "didn't remember" to include these violations on his insurance application, as required by law.

"Sir, are you aware of friends saying you drive like grandpa?

He smiled. "Yes."

"Are they aware of your speeding and going through stop signs?"

"Yes, they are." So much for John Sunseri's assistance with his alibi.

Under Bolen's interrogation, John had been clear and prompt with his answers. Now, with no prior warning of what he would be asked, he was flustered and confused.

At the opposite end of the courtroom, Carol Gallagher looked anxious. Today two of her other three children, Shawn and Renee, were with her, along with her sister-in-law, all of them agonizing as John flubbed Brevetti's searching questions. "Johnny was nervous before he went on the stand," Carol explained. "He was pacing the room, and I had never seen him do that before."

She knew, perhaps better than he did, what was now happening to him. "This is just a normal kid who got out of high school and went straight to work as a mechanic, and who doesn't know the ramifications of the big long words, the hundred-dollar words, that he does not hear every day. And to have those hundred-dollar words thrown at him by an attorney who is doing a damn good job of trying to convict him instead of Olivia . . . how do you expect him to react?''

Across the aisle from John's relatives were Olivia's self-appointed supporters, several rows of them, mostly women, exchanging knowing looks as he sank deeper into his own confusion. His most frequent responses were, "I don't know," "I can't recall," "I don't remember." He didn't even recall Denise objecting to his overnight visits until he was reminded that this was the cause of the big argument in which he and Leah were involved in November. As to his own feelings about Denise: "It was not a great relationship, but I got along with her." He would have done better to have omitted the first half of that sentence.

Brevetti picked up on it instantly. "You did not have much in common?'' she pursued.

"No, we did not." Outwardly impassive, George Bolen must have been wincing.

John was asked about his activities on the day before the fire, Sunday, December 1. He said he arrived at the Fischer house in the early afternoon. The front door was unlocked, as usual; he walked in and found Leah alone. He had planned to take her out to brunch but they sat around talking until it became too late for a restaurant meal. Instead, they drove to his home where they stayed overnight.

Brevetti led him into the events of the following morning, where he had already laid a trap for himself. She asked him to account for that unaccounted hour between dropping off Leah and checking into work at 8:04 A.M. Although he had testified on the previous Friday that he did not enter the Fischer house at that time, she prodded him into remembering that "it was possible" he did go in and have a cup of coffee while Leah showered and dressed. He had sometimes done so in the past. He also admitted to being in the habit of going into Leah's room. This time he "believed" he didn't, and that he left the house before she finished showering.

Again Brevetti was several steps ahead of him. She was laying the foundation for a theory that, alone in Leah's bedroom on the morning of December 2, he could have slipped the catch on her window so that later in the day he or someone else could have entered the house undetected. He had an excellent opportunity. Leah was taking a shower. Bill had gone to work. Denise would have been preparing to leave for her office. Olivia was not yet up.

"Is it not a fact that on Friday you said that you arrived at the Fischer household, exchanged cars, and went directly to work?" Brevetti demanded.

John was turning red, and shifting in his seat. "I don't recall," he said.

After the trial, he explained: "When I said I didn't remember it was because I didn't remember. After the fire, I couldn't place when things happened. At times when Brevetti was talking to me, everything that went on in Kristie's room that night would be going through my head, and there was this murderer sitting five feet away from me, and I was wanting to say to her, 'What the hell did you do that night?' But I couldn't. I didn't want to screw up. I wanted to hold back my temper."

The effort of masking his emotions translated into a facial expression which at times resembled arrogance. Brevetti was baiting him, and he didn't appreciate this smart lady attorney trying to trip him up. Sensing his antagonism, she pressed on relentlessly. "Did you make any plans with Miss Fischer that morning?"

"No, I don't recall making any plans with her." He seemed to have forgotten their arrangement to have dinner with his mother before she went into the hospital.

"Did you call her at lunchtime?"

"It's possible that I did, and possible that I didn't."

Now he was really doing badly. And so it went on until Brevetti led him into the episode of the fire, which again he was able to recount with considerable clarity. He knew every detail at the heart of the trauma. The rest eluded him. And it was the rest she was grilling him about, in such a way as to avoid any suggestion of his own heroics that night. She insisted on his telling her the exact wording of the question he had yelled at her client. Was it "Why is the baby's door locked?" Or was it "Why did you lock the door?" She made the distinction seem of crucial importance, as though, in a moment of panic, he should have paused to consider the implications of his own phraseology.

"I don't remember," he said.

"No recollection of which of those two statements you made?" She looked at him, coolly appraising.

"That's correct."

She wanted to know whether he grabbed the fire extinguisher from Olivia, or whether Olivia offered it to him. He said he took it from her, whereupon Brevetti reminded him that he had told the police he grabbed it. He conceded that maybe the word grab "was a bit much."

Finally she apprised the court of how many Mount Pleasant police officers he knew. Scott Carpenter and his brother Jeff. Louis Alagno, who taught him to swim. ("He didn't ask you much, did he?" Brevetti prodded, referring to the night of the fire.) She mentioned the recently retired police chief, Paul Oliva, who knew his grandfather. (Of course he did, since the elder John Gallagher was custodian of the only high school in town.) And—her moment of triumph—the new acting chief, Anthony Provenzano. "You call him Uncle Tony?" she asked, with a meaningful look.

He conceded that he did. All these relationships were small-town stuff. Provenzano had known John's parents since the three of them were in Westlake High School together, almost thirty years ago. John had called him Uncle Tony since he was knee-high to the man, but the friendship between the two families drifted after the Gallaghers moved to Mahopac. Now it was being made to appear too close for justice to be done, although Provenzano did not inherit the Olivia Riner case until after it was scheduled for trial. But the impression of a police cover-up had been registered, ready for Brevetti to exploit when the police witnesses were called.

On this second day of John's testimony every seat in the courtroom's public section was filled. Two rows were always set aside for people attached to the defense team, which meant there was always a place for Marlise Riner, and for friends and colleagues of Laura Brevetti, including Linda Sawyer. But the Fischers and the Gallaghers were often obliged to stand in line with the general public. At times even Bill had to argue his way into court—although, having testified, he was free to attend the rest of the trial and did not want to miss a moment of it. Today he was in his usual seat in the back row. But after the lunch break, Carol Gallagher, who had been in the courtroom all morning, was refused readmission by the uniformed court officer guarding the heavy swing door.

"You'll have to wait your turn," he told her. Most of the public seats had been taken, and there was still a line of people in the hallway. Some of them recognized her.

"I hope you're not going to let *her* back in," one woman said to the court officer, loudly enough for Carol to hear.

"Excuse me, I happen to be the mother of the young man who is testifying," Carol insisted, standing her ground.

"I don't care who you are," the woman said. "You have to stand on line like the rest of us."

Through the glass panel in the door, Carol could see that the afternoon session was about to begin. The court officer was not budging. She started to cry. Shawn and Renee led her to a side bench. Finally the three of them were let into the courtroom, just in time to hear Bolen's redirect examination. He kept it brief, and ended it dramatically.

"You were asked about your relationship with Leah Fischer. At some point after Olivia entered the household it was made clear to you by Bill and Denise that it would be better if you did not sleep over?"

"Correct," John replied.

"Did you dwell on that for a long time—?"

"No."

"—to such a point that you came into the home, set three separate fires, doused an infant in some flammable liquid, and set fire to her. Did you do that, sir?" He was shouting now.

"No," John replied, almost shouting back.

It was a staged effect, designed out of desperation. Bolen was trying to redeem all that had gone before, but some of it was beyond redemption. One of the few family members to recognize this, so early on, was Barbara Donnelly, seated near her brother, attending her first trial, increasingly disenchanted by the discrepancy between what she was hearing in court, how the media was presenting it, and what she believed to be the truth.

"I think we lost the case when John was on the stand," she observed later. "He got flustered and couldn't remember a lot of stuff. And I think George Bolen gave up after that."

She was wrong about Bolen. He was too stubborn a prosecutor to give up. But he did appear to change direction. From now on he seemed to be defending John Gallagher, rather than prosecuting Olivia Riner.

30

The next three witnesses were volunteer firemen, describing the scene before the police investigation began. Thornwood's second assistant fire chief, Joseph Rod, confirmed that the window in Olivia's room was closed when he arrived there, which contradicted her statement to the police that she had found it open by several inches when she put out the fire on her bed. She had said nothing about shutting it, and according to the firemen, all the windows in the house were fully closed before they began to vent the place. The laundry room and bathroom windows were not merely shut but stuck, and it took an effort to open them. Axes were used to bash at doors and windows as the men fought to get the blaze under control.

Rod told of kicking Leah's door open and causing the flash fire which sent both him and James Lawrence running back down the hallway. Lawrence was asked by George Bolen: "What does it mean when a fire flashes?"

"It means," he replied, "that there was not sufficient oxygen in the room for the fire to continue burning. It reignites when you let oxygen in by opening the door, and that would blow the windows out." It was an important point, in light of later developments at the trial.

The firemen's evidence left no doubt about the extent to which the crime scene became contaminated as they fought to save the building from total destruction.

"How much water was poured into that house?" Judge Silverman asked Joe Rod, who had fifteen years' experience as a volunteer fireman.

"A lot," he replied.

"How much is that?"

259

"There were three hoses operating for about three hours, pouring in twenty-five gallons a minute."

Police Officer Robert Miliambro recounted his part in the story—of finding the nursery door locked from the inside in such a way that when he shut it on leaving the room it became locked again, of smelling paint thinner on the only fragment of Kristie's diaper which had not been touched by fire, and of noticing that several containers of accelerants had been almost emptied and then put back carelessly in Bill's neatly maintained closet—including a two-liter plastic flask of paint thinner left lying on its side. Again Laura Brevetti led the witness away from the focus of his testimony, into peripheral details.

After Miliambro described the evidence he collected on the night of the fire—the partially melted soda bottle, the charred box of wooden matches, and the diaper fragment from the nursery, plus the residues of paint thinner, Coleman appliance fluid, and charcoal lighter fuel from Bill's utility closet—Brevetti asked what else he had looked for. Hair samples? Bloodstains? Did he remove the knob from the nursery door? No, he said to all three.

"Did you secure the crime scene before you left?"

"No, it was not my responsibility." He was a good witness, but she was making him look inept.

He had been told to answer the questions, and only the questions. After five years as a police officer, this was his first experience of testifying in court, and he was following the rules. If he didn't, she would undoubtedly object. What he wanted to say was that the reason he didn't secure the crime scene was because other police officers had been delegated to the task, that a guard would remain there all night, and that it was no use looking for hair samples or bloodstains in a waterlogged house in the dark. That search would be made after daylight when the door locks and other items would be removed. In the meantime, nobody could disturb them. He had been assigned to help Sergeant Brian Dwyer in the collection of evidence and had done the job to the best of his ability. He had only one regret, the same as Detective Bruce Johnson's, that of leaving Kristie's infant carrier in the ruins of the nursery. Even though Joe Butler didn't need it as proof of arson, he or some other officer should have taken it as evidence of murder.

After Miliambro's testimony, the carrier was brought into court and placed in front of Judge Silverman's bench. At the judge's request the jurors got up and walked around it, silently, in single file. What they saw, in the poignant moment before they all felt impelled to avert their gaze, was a twisted mess of metal and plastic, still attached to the portion of burned carpet into which it had melted. The handle of the carrier, badly bent, was just about discernible. Otherwise the object had been incinerated beyond any recognizable color or shape. Nothing—except the police photograph of how Kristie looked in death, which the judge had banned as a court exhibit—gave a more graphic sense of what happened to this baby. When the exhibit was removed, it left a trail of ashes on the beige carpeted floor of the courtroom. Olivia turned her head from the sight.

The next police witness was Brian Dwyer, the sergeant whom Miliambro had assisted in collecting evidence. Tall and slim, with graying hair, clean-cut features, and a military bearing, he gave an immediate impression of competence. He was forty-seven years old and had spent virtually all of his adult life in the Mount Pleasant police department, while also serving as a volunteer fireman. Consequently, the expertise which he brought to an arson case was much broader than that of most police officers. He was one of the first firemen to arrive at the scene on December 2, reverting to his police role during the evening. He confirmed Miliambro's testimony and described his first glimpse of the dead baby through the nursery window. He saw no signs of an attempted entry, but noticed that the glass had fractured, creating the hole through which Bruce Johnson stuck his head to peer inside. Later, Dwyer said, he used a folding ladder to break out the rest of that window in order to vent the room.

Bolen asked him about the hole in the window. When he first saw it, were the fragments of glass inside the nursery, or outside on the ground? It was a crucial question. If the window had been ruptured by the heat of the fire, shards of glass would have been blown outdoors. If the break was caused by an intruder, they would be inside the room.

Dwyer said they were inside. Baffled, Bolen repeated the question, and got the same reply. As he left court at the end of the afternoon Dwyer realized that he had momentarily lost his concentration and was thinking of the glass fragments he saw later, after he smashed the remains of the window from the outside. He had the images confused. It was a mortifying mistake for a veteran police officer to make. He went straight to Bolen's office, on the third floor of the courthouse building.

"George, I messed up," he said. He was due to go back on the witness stand the following morning and had to decide how to deal with his mistake. There was a temptation to let it go, rather than risk further damage to the prosecution's case by drawing attention to it. But, honorably, he didn't have a choice.

"It was tough on me," he said later. "I was about to change my testimony, and I knew what the media would make of this, and that my kids would watch it on TV. I have two in high school and one in college, and their friends would see it too. My wife is a teacher, and the people in her school would all ask questions. But I would never tell a lie to get a conviction."

He could predict that Laura Brevetti would capitalize on his mistake. In fact, she was doing so already. While he was talking to George Bolen she was giving her usual informal press briefing downstairs, pointing out that Dwyer's testimony about the window was significant to the defense case.

"The prosecution stated the broken window occurred other than someone breaking in. But this evidence, elicited by the prosecution itself, is contrary to their position. The defense theory is that this was not a thermal break but a mechanical break." Now, she added triumphantly, Brian Dwyer had confirmed this.

In court the following morning, Dwyer did his best to backtrack. He stated that he had made an error about the nursery window. The broken glass was on the ground outside the house.

"Who or what refreshed your memory?" Brevetti asked.

He replied: "When I walked out at recess it dawned on me what I had said, and I knew I was wrong."

She stared at him, incredulous. "Did it dawn on you because you realized the significance of what you said, that it was not a heat break because the glass was on the inside? Is that what dawned on you?"

"It dawned on me that I made a mistake."

He had done his best to correct his error, but the damage was done. The media took up the story, and presented it as he had feared. A four-column headline in *Newsday* read, NANNY COP RECANTS. Laura Brevetti was quoted as saying that Dwyer's amended testimony was "too convenient." And that was what was widely believed—that his first statement about the window was correct, that there had indeed been evidence of an intruder, but now the police wanted to cover it up.

Very little else was reported about Brian Dwyer's evidence. Looking back on the trial, months later, he remarked: "I was on the stand about four hours one day, and eight hours the next, and the only thing the newspapers brought up was my change in testimony. But what was important was my evidence about the way those containers in the closet had been disturbed, and the paint thinner on the baby's diaper, and the fact that the accelerant was poured around her in such a way that it must have been done from inside the house, and not through the window.

"Brevetti criticized the police for not collecting more evidence. But you can't collect evidence while you're fighting a fire. It's organized chaos. Basically everyone knows what they are doing, but the guys are going off in all directions. That night they did a good job. That house could have been lost. Windows were torn out, and that's normal. Furniture was ruined. And there was intense smoke damage. But within an hour the fire was completely out; then there was a lot of cleaning up to be done. In all that mess we're supposed to dust for fingerprints? Even if we had, what would it have proved—that Olivia Riner and John Gallagher were in the house? We knew that already."

His point about the inevitable loss of evidence in an arson case was never made clear during the trial. Through several more witnesses Laura Brevetti was able to strengthen her argument that the police had done a sloppy job. She capitalized on their mistakes—the failure to remove the infant carrier, the lapse of time before materials were sent to the laboratory for testing, the desk sergeant's delay in calling the Thornwood fire department because he doubted the address which Olivia gave him, leaving the record of a taped conversation in which she sounded frantic, and he inept. These became Brevetti's themes for the trial: her allegations of police incompetence, and her contention that the house was not a fortress. It was just what the media needed to give new interest to a tale which seemed made for the movies. She couldn't lose.

Fate also played into her hands in a way she could not have predicted. The morale of officers involved in the case was at a low ebb. They believed they had done a good job and had the support of the man who had been their chief throughout the investigation, Paul Oliva. He had retired at the end of March, a little more than two months before the trial began, expecting to be succeeded by one of his two lieutenants, Louis Alagno or Michael Mahoney. The results of last year's state civil service examination which qualified them for the job of police chief would cease to be valid after July. By retiring well ahead of that date, Oliva was taking the long view, planning for a smooth transition; otherwise he would have stayed on until the Riner trial was over.

What he didn't envisage was that his old adversary Robert Meehan, the town supervisor, would override his recommendation by appointing an acting police chief and maintaining that man in the job until he could qualify for the permanent appointment by taking the state test. By that time the lieutenants' test results would no longer be effective. Meehan picked his own candidate, rather than following the traditions of Paul Oliva, promoting Anthony Provenzano, a sergeant, over the two lieutenants. It was a total break with the Oliva tradition of promotion through the ranks, demoralizing to senior members of the force.

Provenzano's appointment was announced at a town board meeting at the beginning of April. The reaction of Oliva and his supporters was bitter and vociferous. Several ensuing meetings in this contentiously governed township were memorable for their noisy dissension and naked spite. At one session Paul Oliva, now a private citizen, told Robert Meehan precisely what he thought of him, and Meehan reciprocated in kind. These were no mere party political arguments. Effectively, there was only one party in Mount Pleasant, and that was Republican, but the factions which divided it were so deeply rooted in old animosities that the combat had become as vengeful as an ancient blood feud.

This was the state of the Mount Pleasant police department when the trial of Olivia Riner began. The department's witnesses for the prosecution felt deprived of the advice and encouragement of their old chief, or of a successor familiar with the case, and were angrily aware that some of Robert Meehan's supporters were saying in private what Meehan himself would soon be alleging in public—that Paul Oliva retired before the trial because his department's investigation of the case was an embarrassment to him. This looked like strong confirmation of Laura Brevetti's charges about police ineptitude. She also capitalized on the uneasy situation at police headquarters. At one of her informal daily press briefings, a question was asked about the police video which had ended up in the Geraldo Rivera program. Since Bolen had denied that his office was the source, Brevetti was asked about hers.

"Mr. Bolen should check his own people," she asserted, "those in the police department and elsewhere who are dissatisfied with this prosecution as to where that tape came from.'' What was remembered about this comment was her suggestion of mutiny in the ranks of the police. It passed almost unnoticed that she had not directly answered the question.

31

"The prosecution didn't get a break," George Bolen complained after the trial was over. "Not one."

The defense had lost all its pretrial motions, but this early advantage soon slipped away from Bolen. Laura Brevetti had the superior resources, both in finances and organization. Hundreds of thousands of dollars were spent on the preparation of her case. Consultants were hired, and quantities of sophisticated tests ordered. Nothing was left to chance. Upstate, in a building due for demolition, arson experts reproduced and filmed the fatal fire with such attention to detail that furnishings and carpeting similar to those in the Fischer house were brought in for destruction, the same kind of accelerants were used, and an actress of Olivia's approximate height and weight was hired to recreate her role. This reenactment was carefully timed to check whether the fire could have burned and spread in the way Olivia described.

Henry Flavin's amateur film was taken to a studio and run in slow motion on a large screen, so that it could be studied frame by frame, many times over, in the hope of picking up some clue which the prosecution had missed.

At the beginning of the trial the entire defense team moved into a White Plains hotel, not merely to save commuting time, but to enable them to confer together several times a day, shaping and reshaping strategy on the basis of the latest developments in court. Despite the reports of her health problems, Laura Brevetti had the tireless ability to continue working far into the night, and to return to court next morning looking fresh and groomed and rested.

"It was like Gethsemane," Chris Rush related. "She could keep going

266

after we had all fallen asleep around her. She did the work of five at-torneys. I have never worked for anyone like her."

His own days began at 6:00 A.M., checking security around the hotel before Brevetti and her aides left the building. There were two body-guards to assist him, one an ex-wrestler of formidable stature. "You wouldn't want to mess with Carmine," Rush remarked. One of the body-guards always drove with Brevetti to the courthouse. Rush waited there for the limousine that brought Olivia from Manhattan, and stayed near her all day. Most news photographs taken of her during the trial picture him at her side: a burly man in dark glasses, stolidly planting himself between her and whoever might be trying to get close. He developed a protectively avuncular attitude toward her, affectionately referring to her as "the kid." You wouldn't want to mess with him either.

Olivia was never part of the strategy meetings. She wasn't needed, and it was politic to get her back to the city as soon as court was recessed for the day. A limousine was always waiting, with Chris Rush on hand to shepherd her and Marlise into it. Sometimes reporters tried to follow, hoping to discover where the Riners were living, but the drivers hired by Brevetti's law firm were skilled at avoiding pursuit. Olivia was always eager to get back to her Manhattan lodgings because every evening at six o'clock (midnight in Wettingen) there would be a telephone call from her father. She seemed closer to him than to her mother. Twice during the trial he flew to New York for a few days, and her face lit up when she saw him: daddy's little girl.

Olivia's only part in the presentation of her case was to project an image of innocence. Brevetti had no intention of having her testify. Chris Rush instructed her about her behavior in court: "Do not show your feelings either way when the topic is being discussed, whether it is going for or against you, because people are watching you. This is such a hideous case that a smile on your face at the wrong time can be misinterpreted. Just sit there like a lady and listen."

It was part of defense strategy that her understanding of English should appear to be minimal, it having been argued in the pretrial hearing that she did not understand the Miranda warning. So there was some consternation when one day, in the hallway outside the court-room, she picked up a copy of *The New York Times* and began to read the latest report of her trial. Immediately one of Brevetti's aides told her to put it down.

As to her general demeanor, Rush admitted: "At times we were bothered by her lack of emotion, but we couldn't have it both ways.''

Linda Sawyer, still working with the defense team, did not give up trying. During the trial Maya Hess asked Laura Brevetti's permission to invite Olivia to her home for a weekend meal, as relief from the stress of being in court, and Linda followed up with a proposal of her own. She asked Maya to rent a home movie for Olivia to watch: specifically, *A Cry in the Dark*, the true story of an Australian couple whose baby mysteriously disappeared during a family camping trip. The mother, played by Meryl Streep, insisted that the infant had been carried off by a wild dog. She was not believed and, despite her protests of innocence, was convicted of murdering her own baby, largely because her public demeanor was so emotionless that she was assumed to be guilty. After she had spent some time in prison, evidence emerged which proved her right. Linda saw a lesson in this for Olivia.

Maya rented the film. She also took Olivia to Washington Square Park, near her home, and they sat there one fine summer day reminiscing about their Swiss childhoods. Comfortable in Maya's company and freed from the stresses of court, Olivia spoke freely and naturally, giving the impression of an introspective young woman who could set unattainable goals for herself and feel inadequate when she failed to reach them, and who had not yet resolved her adolescent uncertainty about what to do with her life. She seemed to be searching for something without knowing what. Maya was poignantly reminded of her own teen years.

"Getting to know her triggered for me things about my personal history; about my own growing up, about being Swiss. I could understand why she would come to America, perhaps running away, and I felt an empathy for her.''

She continued to believe in Olivia's innocence, although not with the unquestioning passion of a Linda Sawyer who had her own emotional reasons for wanting an acquittal. For Maya, it was more like a quiet and deep sense of knowing. Or rather, thinking she did.

Brevetti did not take weekends off. Rather than go home to her Manhattan apartment, she remained in her hotel suite, working with a driven dedication. This case had fallen into her lap through her personal contacts with the attorney for E. F. Au Pair, and it was obvious from the beginning that it would attract national publicity. Trial lawyers dream of being handed opportunities like this which, overnight, can turn them into public figures. Stimulated by the challenge, Brevetti made sure that she was superbly prepared for every day's interrogation in court and worked with a driven desire to succeed.

As adversaries, she and Bolen could not have been further apart. She was aggressive, and he withdrawn. She used the media constantly, judiciously, and boldly, feeding information to the journalists likely to do her most good. He kept his own counsel, ignoring, even alienating, the media. Her method of interrogation was dogged and incisive, pursuing a line of questioning until even the most stubborn witnesses had told her more than they intended. His could be so convoluted that it was easy for his listeners to get lost. Bolen had a unique reputation around the Westchester County Courthouse, that of a skilled prosecutor, one of the best, who could nevertheless confuse witnesses by his random method of interrogation, jumping from one topic to another for no clear reason. He was like a conjuror plucking tricks from down his sleeve and out of someone else's pocket, bringing out stray pieces of information which didn't appear to relate until he had patiently accumulated enough of them. Then, seen together, they usually made astonishing sense.

He appeared to be making that kind of labyrinthine journey through this trial, his direct examinations dodging around in time and place, sometimes complicated by a tortuous phraseology which the trial reporters dubbed Bolenspeak. Occasionally the judge stopped him to act as interpreter, as he did after Bolen's question to Bill Fischer about the nursery door: "During the time when you purchased it, and while you were working on it, and during the process of your hanging it, were you able to determine the depth of the inside and the outside of the door that was hollow between the two?"

"How thick was the door?" Judge Silverman translated.

In contrast with the considerable resources of the defense, Bolen was relying upon a police department and a district attorney's office with such limited budgets and vision that both of them had decided against the expense of sending an investigator to Switzerland. While Brevetti's team had researched the backgrounds of all the witnesses, particularly John Gallagher, Bolen was prosecuting a total stranger. He went to trial knowing nothing about Olivia Riner. Publicly, District Attorney Carl Vergari blamed the Swiss for a lack of cooperation, but his own office already had the material at hand for its prosecutor to be better informed than he was about the young woman on trial.

Olivia's diary, which the police passed on to Bolen, covered the entire year. But, like the police, the D.A.'s office translated only her entries for the last month, starting with her arrival in the United States—a period that reflected her eagerness to learn more about the country, her homesickness, her impatience with the Fischers' indulgence of Kristie, and her own growing affection for the baby. On the basis of these entries, the prosecution decided not to introduce the diary as evidence. But there was earlier material in that diary which might have helped Bolen's case but which remained untranslated. Like this comment about a doctor for whom Olivia worked in Switzerland:

"He is sometimes unbearable, and every day I hope that he will have a fatal accident and we will get time off. This is not nice, but anyway. If I believed in God I would even pray for that! But nothing has happened so far. Unfortunately."

Bolen also seemed unaware of the contents of the brief telephone conversation between Olivia and her father on the morning after her arrest. Kurt Riner's call to the Mount Pleasant police station was routinely taped. But no written translation appears to have been made of it. Months after the trial it was revealed that Riner asked his daughter: "How did you see the fire?"

Sobbing, she replied: "I don't know how the fire traveled, but somehow there was a liquid there."

"Somebody threw a liquid there?"

"Yes," she told him.

It is possible, but unlikely, that she had heard about the use of a liquid accelerant during the few hours since her arrest. Bruce Johnson was positive that he did not tell her during the long interrogation which led up to her being charged. Nevertheless, no attempt was made to enter that tape as evidence, or to raise the question about Olivia's knowledge of the arsonist's methods.

The prosecution also lost the opportunity to show the jury the largest and most telling piece of evidence. Bolen tried hard to get Judge Silverman's approval for jurors to visit the Fischer house, believing that they could not fully comprehend the dimensions of that ground floor, and the proximity of the rooms, without walking around it. A floor plan had been hung up in the courtroom, but it gave no sense of the house's acoustical qualities, and the flow of its rooms. Its builder and architect, Jan Menting, sat through the trial, frustrated that he could not take the jury there himself.

"Seeing that plan was not enough," he said. "Very few people can look at a plan and get a three-dimensional view. I have that problem with my clients. I show them sketches, but they cannot visualize."

Bolen knew that, too. One morning after the jurors had been excused, he told the judge that it was crucial to the prosecution's case for them "to get a true, overall picture of what the People consider to be a very unique house with a very unique layout. . . . Without seeing it, it is hard for the jury to grasp how open this house is. . . . It is important for them to have the benefit of seeing the close relationship and juxtaposition of the rooms."

He did not seem to have anticipated Brevetti's argument that the recently rebuilt house was no longer the crime scene. Things had been altered. Different construction materials had been used. Bill had decided to enlarge Leah's bedroom by reducing the length of the hallway. The shape of her closet had been changed. The new window frames were not quite the same size as the old ones. The new floor covering gave footsteps a different sound. While the house was visually unchanged on the outside, the interior renovations had made enough of a difference for Judge Silverman to rule in Brevetti's favor.

"We run a danger in taking the jury to that scene," he conceded. "Rather than having the benefit of seeing what could have been seen on that day, we would be giving them the opportunity to speculate on how it might have been. I wish that were not so. I think there would have been some benefit if the scene had been preserved as it was, but that benefit has now gone."

Seated in his accustomed place in the back row of the courtroom, Bill Fischer was utterly dismayed. Why hadn't anyone warned him of this? If he had had any idea that he could hamper the prosecution's case by making those small structural changes, he would never have suggested them. He would have gone to endless trouble to restore that house to the way it was, down to the final screw on the last window latch. He doubted if he and Denise would ever want to live there again. His intention had been to make the house as attractive as possible, in the hope of finding a buyer. Now he felt angry with himself for what he had done, and with George Bolen for letting him do it.

This was yet another defeat for Bolen, perhaps the most decisive. As if that weren't enough, there was an important piece of evidence which he did not learn about until shortly before the trial: an accelerant-soaked diaper found under Olivia's bed. Unfortunately for him, it was not the police who found it.

On the night of December 2, after they had extinguished all the flames, firemen had gone through the Fischers' house tipping up pieces of furniture to make sure that nothing was still smoldering beneath them. This is normal firefighting procedure. There was a partially burned cloth diaper on Olivia's bed which fell to the floor when the bed was tipped on its side, and became hidden beneath the upturned mattress. The police failed to notice it, and it remained there until the defense team's investigators were given access to the house several days later. Discovering the diaper, they had it analyzed and learned that it had been soaked in paint thinner. Subsequently, as part of the process of legal discovery, Laura Brevetti had the diaper delivered to the District Attorney's office which ordered its own laboratory tests. These revealed not only paint thinner, but the same kind of charcoal lighter fluid which was kept in Bill's closet.

It was further evidence of an inside job. So far the police had found only paint thinner in the materials taken from the nursery. They had not thought to remove bedding and carpet samples from Leah's room where the fire damage was heaviest, where other accelerants may have been used. At the time it seemed sufficient to have evidence of arson. Only later, too late, did they realize the importance of proving that the same accelerants were used to set the fires as were missing from Bill's closet. Paint thinner alone could have been brought in by an intruder. The discovery of charcoal lighter fluid in the diaper under Olivia's bed could have been a gift to the prosecution, except that Bolen would have to call the defense's witnesses to testify how and where that diaper was found. This would be embarrassing and not very productive since they would argue against the presence of the charcoal lighter fluid. And who knew what else they might say? They could be counted on to use the opportunity to make the police and prosecution look inept, reiterating Laura Brevetti's theme.

"Her defense was right out of the manual—criticize the police," Paul Oliva observed. "What else did she have to criticize?" Oliva had continued to live in the neighborhood after his retirement, and was closely following the case. He was as defensive as ever about the department which he had run his way for so long. Even now, an attack upon the Mount Pleasant police felt like a personal blow to his gut.

He and Bruce Johnson and George Bolen were all convinced that the accelerant-soaked diaper was the object which had been in the middle of the burned patch on Olivia's bed, protecting it from the deeper burn around it. Olivia had told Johnson that when she put Kristie down to sleep for the last time she rolled up a clean gauze diaper and used it to prop the side of the baby's head. This could have been that same diaper, removed from the infant carrier when the circle of fire was set. Perhaps it was used to hold the cans of accelerants, to avoid leaving fingerprints. Or else as a wick, then flung in panic on Olivia's bed while it was still smoldering. If she was the arsonist, that would account for the least explicable fire of the three, the one in her room, which did the least damage, the only fire she attempted to put out.

Joe Butler would not be shaken from his theory that it was the infant carrier that had caused the protected patch on top of Olivia's bed, and that the baby was fatally burned there. This belief did not fit any scenario that made sense to the police or the prosecution. Butler could offer no explanation for how the baby carrier might have been taken to the nursery while it was burning. Creating a script for this drama was not his job. His responsibility was to describe what he saw, and how he thought it happened. Bolen worried that Butler's theory might raise more questions than it would resolve. He also wished he could apprise the jury of the charcoal lighter fluid his experts had discovered on the diaper, and speculate on the purpose that piece of cloth might have served.

All he felt able to do, in his direct examination of Butler, was to ask whether the article on top of Olivia's bed could have been a folded diaper.

"It could have been, yes."

Would it fit the protected area on the coverlet?

"It might fit," Butler conceded.

That was as far as Bolen felt he could go, which was a long way from making his point.

32

Joseph A. Butler, Jr., was one of the memorable witnesses of the trial. His experience as an arson expert went back more than half a century and had been so fully documented that it took George Bolen about twenty minutes to lead him through his list of personal credentials and public appointments—the most recent as criminal-arson investigator for the district attorney of Westchester County. Another witness might have covered the ground in half the time, but long ago somebody must have instructed Joe Butler in the art of giving evidence: Don't simply say yes or no, but spell out your answer. Don't enlarge upon it, but wait for the next question. Don't say any more or less than you are asked. Speak loudly and clearly. Don't mumble, and above all, don't rush.

It made for tedious listening, but there was no misunderstanding him. His style came out of another era, before microphones and stenography were invented, his voice raised to overcome the quirky acoustics of this courtroom, his speech clearly enunciated and ponderously slow. The effect was like that of a deaf man dictating to a secretary who was writing it down in longhand. This was a gift to reporters, and to Maya Hess, who needed a break from translating Bolenspeak.

Butler's knowledge of fire was encyclopedic. He spent his first few hours on the witness stand treating the court to a primer on the dynamics of combustion, the ignition of gases, and the patterns of smoke. He described the scene at the Fischer house room by room, and confirmed that there were three, possibly four, fires set from within the building in the three downstairs bedrooms, but no fire in the connecting hallway. He could not determine the order in which they were lit. He described "a very pungent odor" of some flammable fluid on the baby's carrier,

274

the nursery rug, her clothing, and on the infant herself.

His mention of this infant seat touched on another weakness of the prosecution's case. During the trial it emerged that when the carrier was eventually removed from the fire scene, it was dumped in a corridor of the police station where it lay unprotected for more than a month before being sent to the county laboratory. The casual treatment of this dramatic piece of evidence was a tactical error, even though there was little point in testing it. Traces of volatile fluid do not remain on plastic, only on porous material like the fragments of diaper, carpet, and bedspread which the police had taken. But a jury could not be expected to know that.

Butler asserted that flammable liquid had been poured on the carpet around the carrier by someone standing close to the baby, out of a container like the soda bottle which was left on the nursery floor. If the liquid had been thrown from across the room or through the window, the burn on the carpet would have been fan shaped. "But if you pour it you will get a more or less perfect circle." Which is what he saw.

He confirmed the amended testimony of Brian Dwyer, that the nursery window was initially blown out, not broken in. And he said that he had not suggested taking samples from Leah's room for analysis "because of the volume of debris" and because he judged her fire to be the same kind of arson as the other two. Viewing the scene as an arson (but not a homicide) expert, "We already had unusually good evidence from outside Leah's room, much more positive than the materials in there."

In cross-examination Brevetti brought out the fact that Butler took no notes at the fire scene. He left Thornwood at midnight and wrote his report the following morning. Later he explained: "From years of experience I can easily do it from memory, and I have an excellent memory. That night there was a poor light, it was raining cats and dogs, there was water coming down inside the building, and if I had tried to take notes they would probably have been illegible." Outside the courtroom Brevetti hinted that a man of his age should not be trusting his memory. She commented to reporters: "It's very significant that a total investigation was made by this individual with nothing to refresh his recollection—no notes, no photographs. If that evidence had been carefully documented it would have led away from my client to another individual instead. . . ."

With television cameras focused on her, she was back to the attack on

John Gallagher. It made good copy for the evening news. The TV reporters had turned out in force for Butler's testimony, but seemed less interested in his findings than in what Laura Brevetti thought of them, adding a little color of their own. "How are you holding up, Olivia?" Channel 4 asked, aiming a microphone toward the accused young woman as Chris Rush ushered her out of court at the end of the day. No luck there, so back to Brevetti. She had got the hang of this media business by now, and seemed to be enjoying the exposure.

During his second day of testimony Butler stated that although he saw fire-extinguisher residue in Olivia's room, he found none in the nursery. He explained that this was not necessarily significant. "It leaves a dry powder, and air and water could blow it away."

This became the subject of Brevetti's next impromptu press conference.

"The truth will come out," she told the reporters who had gathered around her in the courthouse lobby for a second session on Joe Butler. "We heard that John Gallagher sprayed residue all over the nursery, but now we hear there was no fire-extinguisher residue in that room. It may be that the fire was self-extinguished. There was hysteria that night, and fingers were pointed incorrectly at my client where no evidence exists. Mr. Butler was the authority on the scene, and the prosecution has no choice but to take his word. But we found out today that his opinions have no forensic basis, and are nothing but his opinions, and as the result of those opinions my client is sitting there today in that courtroom. And that is why I am upset."

It was another performance for the cameras. Privately she felt kindly toward Joe Butler. "He's a nice man. A loyal public servant," she remarked in conversation earlier that afternoon. At a human level she respected him. In public, he was the logical target for her latest attack.

Meantime, from the high vantage of the witness stand, Butler had been making his own assessments. Looking down and slightly across at Olivia, there was a moment when he caught her eye. "She gave me an aberrant look," he said. "It was only a quick observation, but I felt she was not normal. She had a deadpan, expressionless face, a face with no feeling and no emotion. It was more like something molded in plaster than a living skin. She fit the crime. Absolutely."

Butler had testified in more courts than any of the other witnesses, but this trial was unique in his experience.

"It appeared to be the easiest case I had ever had," he reminisced.

"There was absolutely no doubt that it was arson. There were three separate fires, obviously set by an amateur. There was a suspect, and the evidence of her guilt seemed incontrovertible. Yet in court we were losing ground every day. The media was against us, and it floored me that Brevetti could introduce another suspect who had never been charged. But this case went wrong from the beginning, from the delay after the au pair's telephone call to the police, to my delay in getting to the scene because I was trying to reach my boss, and so it continued through this trial. It was a foolproof case which exploded."

If there was a moment when George Bolen began to feel despair, it must have been in the middle of Joe Butler's testimony when, with his back to the witness, Bolen turned and faced the press and public benches, raised his eyes and spread his hands in a hopeless gesture. Neither the judge nor Butler saw it. Those who did had a growing sense of what it was about. The way it was coming out, some of the testimony of Bolen's witnesses was more helpful to the defense, and he had to keep digressing from the prosecution of Olivia Riner to paste over the cracks in his own case.

His next witness was a twenty-six-year-old volunteer fireman, Thomas Kelsey, who had cut his finger on the shattered nursery window. It was a minor injury which bled a lot, soaking through the gauze which a paramedic applied. Two weeks after the fire the defense's investigators found a smear of blood on the nursery doorpost—another possible clue which the police missed—and were suggesting that this might be the blood of an intruder. They knew it wasn't Olivia's because she was checked by paramedics at the fire scene. Again the prosecution had to digress by having Tom Kelsey tell about his lacerated finger, and how he went back to firefighting after it was treated.

Next Bolen questioned Mary Eustace, the forensic chemist who was asked to analyze a blood sample taken from the doorpost. The District Attorney's office had presented it to her on the end of a small wooden stick with a white cotton tip, sealed in a manila envelope. Adding to the prosecution's embarrassment, she told the court that this was too small a sample for her to determine anything about it, except that it was blood. She was not even sure it was human.

Still prodding, Laura Brevetti wanted to know what happened to the swab. The witness replied that she threw it away. That was standard procedure. Brevetti asked, with an edge to her voice: "Did you ever consider, Miss Eustace, that other people might want to test that swab?"

Quietly defensive, Mary Eustace replied: "There was no way anyone else could have tested it."

Another gap in the investigation was revealed by Christopher Chany, the arson specialist at the Westchester County Forensic Science Laboratory, who stated that when the charred infant seat was delivered to his office in a brown plastic garbage bag, more than a month after the fire, "there was no examination other than a visual look-see." He judged it pointless to do more. The rationale for this decision was not explained to the jury.

Chany confirmed that Brian Dwyer's nose had informed him correctly: The fragments of Kristie's diaper and undershirt were indeed soaked in paint thinner. He also found traces of paint thinner inside the partially melted plastic soda bottle, "basically the same" as the paint thinner in the tampered-with flask from Bill Fischer's closet. A positive identification was not possible. Once again the prosecution had come close to proving that this crime was an inside job. But once again it was the gaps in the investigation which made the popular newspapers—the police's disregard of the charred infant carrier, and the fact that Mary Eustace was unable to find evidence of accelerants in clothing taken from Olivia seven hours after the fire and not submitted for laboratory testing until several days later.

A typical (*Newsday*) report of the day's testimony was headlined WITNESSES SUGGEST COPS BOTCHED CLUES.

That same evening another national television program, *Hard Copy*, replayed the videotape of the fire scene with the same interpretation as Geraldo Rivera's: that John and Leah had been laughing about making a barbecue as they sorted through the ruins of her home. It was the third time this damaging film had been shown, the second since the trial began. Its clear intention was to persuade viewers that Olivia was innocent.

"It's much too early to know what the jury will do in this case," commented Doug Ruttner, the show's reporter. "But those who have followed the trial seem to be convinced that the wrong person has been charged with murder."

Yet again John Gallagher was named as a likely suspect. As to why he was not arrested, Ruttner remarked that John had "close ties to the police department involved in the arson death of baby Kristie."

Astonishingly, Laura Brevetti was a participant on the show, claiming that Olivia was not fairly investigated and contributing her own dark hints about John.

"There were fights in that house over his being there," she said. "They were changing rules abruptly at the time of my client arriving there. . . . Routines had to be changed, habits had to be changed, so . . . that house was not a fortress, and that house was not without arguments."

The program ended with three unidentified women, apparently chosen at random, being asked how they thought the trial would end. Their views reflected what had become widespread public opinion:

"I think they're going to find her innocent, no doubt."

"I really think that she was framed. Somebody set her up."

"I don't know how it could get this far. They've got the wrong person."

The trial was nearing the end of its third week. Arriving in court the following morning, George Bolen looked preoccupied and angry. At that hour, around 9:00 A.M., the courthouse elevators were always overcrowded; the tedium of waiting one's turn in the lobby was usually the occasion for a friendly comment or a tired joke. Even Bolen, never very communicative, would usually acknowledge journalists covering his case with a curt nod or a thin smile. Today he ignored them.

"What's that about?" one of them asked on the ride to the fourteenth floor. In the courtroom a few minutes later, before the jury was called in, Bolen answered the question with a tirade against the media. Focusing on Geraldo Rivera's interpretation of the police videotape, he charged that it was full of "outright lies and distortions." His voice rose to a shout as he described the repetition of part of this program during the trial as "an incredible act on the part of a section of the media, without any attempt to verify the accuracy."

He added: "I would like to state that the voices and the laughter in question are not those of John Gallagher and Leah Fischer."

In four months since the Geraldo Rivera show was first aired, this was his first public denial. His initial reaction, to let it pass, had been a misjudgment. Now he was furious. At one point he turned his back on the judge and addressed the reporters directly, accusing them of "misrepresentations, distortions and falsehoods." Glaring at Laura Brevetti, he added, "I'm biting my tongue and not stating what I surmise."

Judge Silverman agreed to ask the jurors, one by one, whether they had seen the previous night's TV program. Assured that none of them had, he repeated his warning to them not to read, watch, or discuss anything about the trial: "The best information about this case comes right here in this courtroom. Nothing has been withheld. Nothing has been suppressed." He had some harsh words for George Bolen: "I do not think that most members of the press are interested in reporting what is not true." Perhaps, he suggested, they were unable to verify the accuracy of the videotape "because of the policy you have adopted" in refusing interviews. He challenged Bolen to identify the couple who seemed to be joking in the ruins of the house. "It is entirely up to you."

It had become a game of legal strategy, in which reputations of people unsuspected by the police and the prosecution were being attacked, dragged down, virtually destroyed in the cause of disproving the charges against Olivia Riner. The next victim was Eric Trimpe, an easier target than John Gallagher because of his history of arrests for petty crimes, mostly burglary. But despite the police's suspicions about his connection with fires in old barns and trash cans around Thornwood, Trimpe had never been charged with arson.

With the jury again absent, Brevetti argued before Judge Silverman that testimony about these other local fires should be brought into the trial. Like the Fischers' fire, most of them were started after dark by the ignition of a flammable fluid. However, most of them caused only minor damage, and none was a threat to human life. Although she had no evidence that Trimpe was directly responsible, Brevetti described him as "a pathological fire setter" whose modus operandi was to involve at least one other person as a lookout. She suggested a close association between Trimpe and Gallagher, based on the facts that they attended the same high school and shared an interest in car racing. She theorized that Gallagher could have "used" Trimpe, three years his senior, to set fire to the Fischers' house. Citing several other troubled young men from the neighborhood, those whose names Linda Sawyer had picked up in her late-night barroom conversations, she implied that they too might have had a hand in the Fischers' fire.

Then she made the direct accusation: "It is our submission and analysis that Eric Trimpe was involved in the fire at Five West Lake Drive, and that there is a connection between Trimpe and Gallagher.''

It was a bold claim which sent the district attorney's staff chasing down another tangent, researching the background of Eric Trimpe and other petty criminals who from time to time had disturbed the peace of Mount Pleasant, but who seemed unlikely to have any connection with this case. It was a tiresome task, but Brevetti's allegations had to be answered, creating another unwanted diversion for George Bolen. It was becoming harder and harder for him to follow his own agenda.

One man in the public section of the courtroom took this procedural debate very seriously. Eric Dardenne, the Swiss vice consul in New York, was there most days, a silent, hovering presence, keeping a watching brief on the trial. When he could not attend, a colleague took his place. This intense, ongoing interest from a consulate was highly unusual. But in Dardenne's view, so was this case. He was concerned about the extreme youth of the defendant, and the certitude of those who knew her in Switzerland that she was incapable of violent crime. From the beginning of his involvement, the day of Kurt Riner's first telephone call to the consulate, he had a sense of justice being subverted. Inevitably, he compared the American judicial system with his own, and found it wanting.

Like many other European countries, Switzerland does not have a jury system. A judge alone would determine the outcome of a trial such as this, after examining all available evidence. In Dardenne's opinion, the increase in mischievous arson incidents around Thornwood, beginning several months before Olivia arrived in the United States, should have been included in that evidence. He also thought Eric Trimpe and John Gallagher should have been investigated as possible suspects. Under such scrutiny, Dardenne suspected that a link between the Fischers' fire and others in the neighborhood might have been established, exonerating Olivia. Filtering what he heard in court through his Swiss legal experience, he felt impatience with a system in which the person indicted by a grand jury was tried as the only likely perpetrator.

Operating under a very different set of precepts, Judge Silverman ruled against Laura Brevetti's request for the admission of evidence about the other fires. His explanation, that ''under our system of law there must be more than mere suspicion that there is evidence which links a third party to the crime,'' could have been composed with Eric Dardenne's doubts in mind. But it did not ease them. Silverman pointed out that one of the worst fires cited by Brevetti, at the local volunteer ambulance headquarters, was thought to be an inside job, which surely ruled out Trimpe as a suspect. He saw no pattern of arson which might link the Fischers' fire to him, or to the other fires. If the defense could establish a connection, Silverman said, he would admit the evidence. In his judgment it had not, so he was proceeding with the trial.

All this was no doubt reported, and the import of it interpreted, to the Swiss government. At the same time, the Swiss people were being fed a popular version of Olivia's trial by their own newspapers which, for the most part, are less investigative and less intrusive than the American. Governed by stricter libel laws and motivated by national pride, they did not make a serious effort to research the background of Olivia and her family. They assumed her to be innocent, and her parents to be law-abiding people whose rights of privacy should be respected.

Swiss journalists must have been aware of a fact that the American reporters did not learn until after the trial—that, as a civil defense official for his town, Kurt Riner would have been experienced in firefighting and fire prevention. He was one of the senior firemen in his canton, a man fascinated by the art and science of his profession. Like many such enthusiasts, he had firefighting equipment on display in his home, hung around the walls of a spare bedroom. Growing up in that household, an only child close to her father, Olivia would surely have acquired more knowledge of arson methods and fire prevention than most. Perhaps it was for him that she took the snapshot which puzzled Bruce Johnson, of the stubby fire hydrant protruding through a drift of fallen leaves outside the Fischers' house. It would have intrigued him, as a professional curiosity. Perhaps it was because of what she had learned from him that Olivia switched on upstairs lights to guide the fire trucks to the Fischers' house. Most people would not think of that. A fireman's daughter might know.

All this should have raised questions that Swiss journalists did not ask. Instead, their focus was on Olivia's indictment as an affront to their national image. Taking their cue from the American media, they concentrated on the gaps in the police investigation, and on the speculations of guilty involvement by John Gallagher and Leah Fischer. Typical headlines in Swiss-German newspapers read: RINER ATTORNEY CRITICIZES POLICE. RINER TRIAL—NEW CONTRADICTIONS. AU PAIR TRIAL UNCOVERS POLICE SLOPPINESS. EVERYTHING IS GOING WELL FOR OLIVIA.

Laura Brevetti saw to it that no reporters, not even Swiss, were given an opportunity to question the Riners. But Swiss journalists in their own country had the resources to learn more about Olivia than the fact that friends and neighbors had a good impression of her. The possibility of her guilt was never seriously considered. "Swiss girls wouldn't do such a thing," one of their journalists remarked during the trial. "They come from a more carefully sheltered environment than Americans."

Using some of his vacation time, Kurt Riner was on a flying visit to White Plains through the testimony of Joe Butler. Laura Brevetti had arranged for an additional interpreter to sit with him and Marlise in court, and their heads were bent toward hers, concentrating on every word.

Riner's inner tension showed only in the rhythmic flexing of his jaw muscles. He was wearing sports clothes, the jacket short by American standards, like a fast-growing schoolboy's, and rumpled across the shoulders as though it had been packed in a hurry. The bleak expression on his face reflected Bill Fischer's, seated a few rows farther back and across the aisle. They did not acknowledge one another. Seen in such proximity, their likeness was striking—not that of a mirror image, or even of a relative, but of a physical type—blond, muscular, Germanic, withdrawn, controlled, loyal, and stubborn.

The thought nagged: When Bill came in for lunch, did Olivia expect him to behave like her father, brightening her day with familiar conversation? And did her loneliness and her longing for home become less tolerable when he didn't?

33

Denise Fischer drove to the courthouse with her husband every day of the trial. Arriving there at 8:30 A.M. they parked their car in the building's underground garage, took an elevator to the district attorney's suite on the third floor, sat there together for a while, then parted. Bill went to Judge Silverman's courtroom, eleven stories up, to hear the day's evidence; Denise remained in the room reserved for prosecution witnesses, and waited. Prospective witnesses are not allowed in court until they have testified, and George Bolen indicated that he was saving Denise's testimony until last. She assumed he was thinking in terms of dramatic impact. The jurors would retire to consider their verdict, wrenched by a mother's tears. In the meantime, Denise wanted to be close to the action.

There was little for her to do all day except browse through law books in the district attorney's library, pace around, and drink coffee. Even with her friends dropping by to chat, time hung heavily. She badly wanted to take part in this trial, and felt unjustly excluded. Marianne Walsh of Westchester's Victims Assistance Services tried to ease Denise's anxiety by going back and forth between the court and the waiting room, reporting on the latest testimony, but that meant missing much of it herself, and lining up to get back in.

"My heart went out to her," Marianne said. "She had this constant feeling, 'I have to fight for Kristie,' but she wasn't even allowed to hear what the witnesses were saying."

As a mother, and as the daughter of a homicide victim, Marianne understood Denise's pain. At times she wondered how this woman and her husband could get up in the mornings and force themselves through another day, grieving, and not knowing how this case would end, and being surrounded by people who thought that John Gallagher and Leah Fischer had conspired to cause their baby's death, and having no home but that moldering house which seemed to be possessed by someone else's spirit. It was so unjust; Bill and Denise struck her as "such a lovely couple, a truly caring couple." Once when they were visiting in her office, Denise briefly removed the aviator-style glasses which dominated her face, and for the first time Marianne noticed the vibrant blueness of her eyes. It was different from Fischer blue, and just as startling, in contrast with the rich chestnut of her hair. The thought flashed through Marianne's mind: "Kristie must have been a beautiful baby." It pained her that the image of this lovely lost child, which should have been central to the trial, had been replaced by the image of Olivia Riner.

Her sadness was turned to anger by the court officers' treatment of the Fischer family. Every day some of Bill's relatives came to court and, like Carol Gallagher, were ordered to stand in line with people who had no reason to be there, other than curiosity. Waiting, unrecognized, in that crowded fourteenth-floor lobby, sometimes for an hour or two, they could not avoid hearing what some of the spectators thought about people they knew very differently.

"It was horrendous," Jim Donnelly remembered. "We had to stand there and listen to the general public saying that John Gallagher committed this crime because he was not allowed to have sex anymore with Leah, which was absolutely ludicrous."

Marianne Walsh concurred: "People were saying horrible things. I have never seen victims' families treated so badly. Generally seats are reserved for them behind the prosecutor, and they can go straight into court. It is highly unusual for court officers to make them wait, or to turn them away. I think the judge was unaware that this was happening, but when I tried to get a message to him, none of the officers would take it."

Nevertheless, Fischer relatives continued to show up. Some were so distantly related that they had not been seen in a very long time. One day Bill's ex-father-in-law, Jan Menting, was surprised when a younger woman in the waiting line said hello to him. Her face was familiar, but he could not immediately place it.

"Have I met you before?" he asked.

She smiled. "I was your daughter-in-law for two years."

Her presence was further proof of how the emotional ties of this uncommunicative family survived its complex web of divorces. This woman, the ex-wife of Bill's ex-brother-in-law, had not been heard from in about twenty years, yet she was there to show support. The only close relatives who were not at the trial were Troy, who couldn't get time off from work, and Willie, who felt the same way about courts as he did about hospitals. He continued to deal with the pain of losing a second grandchild by keeping busy around his workshop, and going fishing.

The family turned out in force when it was Leah's turn to testify. For several days she had been waiting with Denise for the ominous telephone message from the fourteenth floor, "You're on in a few minutes." It came at the end of the trial's third week, later than she had anticipated, and her apprehension had grown with the wait. By now she was so pale and tense that Marianne advised her, "Put on a bit of blush before you go up to court." They took the elevator together and were told to sit on a bench in the hallway until Leah's name was called. Scanning the line of spectators, Leah was shocked to see two young women she had known in high school. They were not her friends. Panicking, she grabbed Marianne's arm.

"My God, they're just here to look at me," she said.

She had dressed carefully for her day in court. With a navy blue suit she wore a white V-necked blouse, framed by the lines of her jacket, some discreet jewelry, and high-heeled navy leather pumps. Her lightly waved brown hair, a little below shoulder length, was drawn back and tied with a white bow high on the back of her head. The effect was ladylike and conservative, as she might dress for a job interview. She looked older than twenty-two, and of a different generation from Olivia who, only two years younger, was more child than woman. At a future date Laura Brevetti would boast that she had changed her client's public image "from a murderess in December to Heidi in July." Leah Fischer could never have metamorphosed like that. She looked the person she had always been, an attractive middle-class girl from a small American town.

She was nervously conscious of her appearance, and its impression on others, as she went into court a few minutes before 11:00 A.M. At one point during the trial she was in the same packed elevator as George Bolen, stopping at every floor for people to get out and in. The long journey up seemed to be taking forever, and she smiled at him to ease the tension. He made a gesture with his hand for her to stop, and afterward told her, "Don't ever smile like that in public. One of the jury might see." She understood, but felt very inhibited. "We were all afraid to say anything, or to show any emotion."

Bolen had also advised John Gallagher to stay away from court after he finished giving evidence. "He wanted the jury to get him out of their minds," Leah said. "But John wanted to be there for me and for all of us, so he came anyway."

He sat at the back of the courtroom throughout her testimony, along with Bill, and Leah's mother, Grada, and Grada's parents, Jan Menting and Ann Scheller: two divorced couples with a united concern for this young woman on the witness stand.

Bolen began his interrogation by dealing with the unfortunate matter of the insurance on John's pickup truck. He wanted to get that, too, out of the way.

"Miss Fischer, your boyfriend John Gallagher drives a truck, right?"

"Yes."

"In whose name is it registered?"

"It is registered in my name."

"Nevertheless he is the principal operator of that truck?"

"Yes."

"Yet in connection with the insurance, you have been named as the operator of that truck?"

"Yes."

"When you failed for whatever reason to list him as an operator, you knew that he would be?"

"Yes."

"And you have since corrected that?"

"Yes, I have."

That, Bolen hoped, disposed of John and Leah's subterfuge to "get a break on the insurance," as it was described in the Gallagher household. But not quite. Jurors were left with the impression of a couple who didn't mind bending the law a bit, and of a young man who might be under a heavy obligation to his girlfriend. Bolen moved on to the safe territory of Leah's biography.

He elicited that she had grown up in the house at 5 West Lake Drive, and that after her mother moved out in 1987 it was her decision to continue living there with her father. "I did not want to change," she explained. She seemed accepting about Denise's entry into the household three years later, and mentioned the baby shower which she gave for her new stepmother before Kristie was born. It had been her own idea, she said.

She had attended the same high school as John, graduated on schedule, and in addition to a full-time secretarial job, she was currently taking college courses, three nights a week, at Pace University in White Plains. The discrepancy between her education and John's was noted and wondered about by many people in court, yet understood and accepted by those who knew them. This was a relationship which flourished on other levels. Bruce Johnson had remarked, quite fondly, about seeing Leah and John together "stupid in love," and Marianne Walsh was touched by John's expressions of tenderness toward Leah, following her around like an affectionate puppy and rubbing the back of her neck when she was stressed. Knowing none of this, the jurors were left to wonder what these two really meant to one another.

Questioning Leah about her daily routine, Bolen asked whether she usually closed her bedroom door before leaving the house. No, she said, she always left it slightly open in case one of the cats was trapped inside. This was contrary to Olivia's assertion that Leah's door was kept shut. Early on the morning of December 2, Leah related, she came home from her overnight visit with John's family to have a shower and change her clothes. She reached her office at about 8:30 A.M. and left at 5:10 P.M. On her return at 5:25 or 5:30 P.M. she saw fire trucks in the front yard. John was standing in the driveway, waiting for her. Her father and Olivia were in the patio area.

Bolen asked whether she heard her father say anything to Olivia. Brevetti objected to the question, but the judge allowed it.

"My father asked her what happened," Leah related. "She said she fed the cats, and she closed the door to the baby's room so the cats would not go into the room because the baby was on the floor. She sounded hysterical. . . ."

Leah's memory of this incident was better than her father's. She recalled not only hearing Olivia say that she closed the nursery door but explain why she did so. It was an important piece of testimony which passed almost unnoticed.

Leah became even more apprehensive during the lunch break. Laura Brevetti had barely begun cross-examining her when the judge called the midday recess; the testing time would come in the afternoon. Bill and Grada tried to reassure her. Marianne offered comfort: "Brevetti can't be too harsh on you." Her experience of shepherding victims through trials had taught her that the defense attorney would not risk alienating the jury by provoking Leah as she had provoked John Gallagher. John was fair game; members of the Fischer family were probably not.

But Leah felt victimized already. Ever since the first Geraldo Rivera program, four months ago, people had been making her aware, overtly or by innuendo, of their suspicions about her and John. In the small community where she had lived all her life she was stared at and talked about. Whenever she appeared in public with John she could feel the conversation stop. Yet she felt safest with him because they had shared an experience which no one else could understand.

Leah was angry with Laura Brevetti on account of her treatment of John, and afraid that she might endanger the prosecution's case by showing her anger at the trial. Or, the worst humiliation, that Brevetti's needling questions might make her cry. She had cried a lot since Kristie died. She had to hold herself together this afternoon.

Bill, rarely demonstrative, patted her hand before he left the waiting room to go up to the fourteenth floor for the afternoon session. Marianne went up ahead to reserve his usual seat in the back row. She saw it as part of her job to ensure that victims' families were as comfortable as possible.

The afternoon crowd was larger than usual. Word had gone around that Leah was on the witness stand, and the courtroom had filled early. At the double swing doors a court officer blocked Marianne and refused to move. She explained who she was, and why she was here, but he would not admit her.

"There's no room," he insisted.

"Just a minute," she said firmly. "Are you telling me that this dead baby's father cannot be in the court when his daughter is testifying? Are you telling me there is no room for Mr. Fischer?"

"That's it," the court officer replied.

It was too much. She lost her temper. "I am going back down to get Mr. Fischer," she announced, "and let me tell you this. If you don't let him in, I am going to bang on these doors and make so much commotion that either the judge lets him in, or I get arrested."

Grudgingly, Bill was admitted. Grada and her parents had been let in after waiting in line through the lunch break. Leah, back on the witness stand, sat tensely upright, prepared for the onslaught.

It started almost gently, like a woman-to-woman conversation, except that Laura Brevetti was in charge. She led Leah through the circumstances of her life since her parents separated. Much of it had been said before, but Brevetti wanted to be certain that the jury understood how the life-style of this family had changed since Denise moved in, and how there might be grounds for a daughter's jealousy, and a boyfriend's desire for revenge.

In response to Brevetti's unabashed questions, Leah stated that her father had given her a full-sized bed (his own?—it was not made clear) when Denise joined the household; later she was allowed to move it into the existing master bedroom and make that hers, after her father had created a new bedroom upstairs for himself and Denise. Brevetti dwelt on the details of Leah's platform-style bed with its foam-rubber mattress, making sure that the jury had a mental picture of it; then, with no pretense of subtlety, shifted directly to John's overnight stays at the Fischer house, four or five nights a week, and how her father and Denise determined that these must end with Olivia's arrival.

Brevetti asked where John used to sleep.

"He slept on the couch," Leah replied.

"Never anywhere else?"

"No."

"Are you engaged?"

"No."

"Are you going to marry him?"

Leah was offended by the question. "Maybe," she snapped.

Her antagonism was beginning to show. Brevetti was doing the same thing to her that the gossips had done in Mount Pleasant, only out in public, with reporters taking it all down. Defensively, Leah was beginning to sound tart and snippy. From their places at the back of the courtroom her parents and grandparents agonized for her.

"What I saw in Leah, up there on the witness stand, was a young girl in a lot of pain," Grada said afterward. "She had lost her sister. Her boyfriend had been accused, and now she was being accused too. She had been harassed by the press. Brevetti was badgering her. She was hurt and angry, and trying to control herself. With all that going on, how do you expect a young girl to react?"

Grada felt as frustrated as her daughter. "Everything that you teach your children about morals and truth and being good to one another goes to the winds in a situation like this. . . ." There was a strong resemblance between them: the same soft brown hair, clear skin, oval face, a look which was indefinably Dutch. Usually both of them projected warmth and openness. But the more Brevetti prodded, the more Leah became closed off.

Referring to the cancellation of John's overnight sleeping arrangement after Kristie was born, Brevetti asked her whether she recalled having an argument about that time.

"It's possible," Leah replied.

"Do you recall coming home one night before Thanksgiving and being very angry?"

"It's possible. I don't recall." Her answers were beginning to sound like her boyfriend's.

"Both you and John Gallagher smoked?" Brevetti inquired.

"At one time, yes."

"John used matches and a lighter?"

"Yes, he did."

"Your father did not permit smoking in the house?"

"Correct."

"But you smoked in the bedroom, didn't you?"

"No."

"You left the window open to smoke, didn't you?"

"No."

This could have been a dialogue between a frustrated parent and a wayward teenager. In response to Brevetti's questions, Leah stated that she kept her bedroom window locked and the blinds closed. She wasn't sure whether John came into the house on the morning of December 2 while she took a shower. "He must not have been there," she finally decided.

"Before you left that morning, did you check the lock on the window?" Brevetti asked.

"No."

What about her bedroom door? Did Leah really leave it open for the cats, or did she close it to avoid Denise's criticism about her untidiness. "You kept it closed to hide the mess," Brevetti accused.

She questioned Leah about the day before the fire, when John had testified about a brunch plan which did not materialize because the two of them sat around until it was too late to eat out.

"On Sunday, December first, John came over to your house to take you to brunch, right?"

"Yes."

"Isn't it a fact that you did not go out that day?"

"Yes, we did."

Where? Without hesitation, Leah replied that they ate at the Travelers Rest in Millwood, an elegant restaurant in the Westchester countryside, not the kind of place where a young couple on a budget would eat regularly. How could John have forgotten that meal? Now a spectator in the courtroom, he felt mortified. "When Brevetti asked me about it I couldn't remember for the life of me. After the fire, stuff like that didn't seem very important."

The questions probed relentlessly on, then back to the insurance on John's truck. Leah acknowledged that it was put in her name "to save money." She "didn't remember" attesting that the operator of the vehicle had no traffic violations in the past five years until Laura Brevetti brought out a copy of Leah's signed statement. Faced with it, she admitted, "Okay, I did."

Using the same tactics that he had adopted for his redirect examination of John Gallagher, George Bolen hurled two final dramatic questions at her. He had not warned her, and the shock registered on her face.

"Did you murder your half sister?"

"No, I did not."

"Did you set fire to your own house?"

"No!"

It had been a worse ordeal than she had feared. Leaving the witness stand, she walked down the center aisle of the courtroom, past the rows of jurors, reporters, and spectators to the swing doors. All of them were watching her. She held her head high, and her facial expression was frozen. It felt like the longest walk in the world.

Outside the courthouse at the end of the day, Laura Brevetti shared her impressions with a small group of reporters. Without the television cameras focused on her, forcing her to be conscious of her image, she was more forthright than usual.

"You have to feel sorry for this girl. She's stuck with this bum. Some of the discrepancies in their stories are so glaring. None of them is much in itself, but it all adds up to a couple who have tried to agree on a story, and haven't got it right. She even gave me the same kind of answer as he did, 'I don't remember,' over and over. How can neither of them remember, on the day this thing happens, whether or not John came into the house that morning when it could be vital evidence?

"Why is he keeping clothes in her closet if he doesn't sleep there anymore? Then about lunch that Sunday. Gallagher was not sure whether it was lunch or brunch, and said they left it too late to have any. Then she comes along and not only says they went out together but she gives me Travelers Rest. *She gives me Travelers Rest!* I could have kissed the girl."

34

Leah and John left the building hand in hand, with everyone staring at them. Jan Menting hurried to the public telephones outside the courtroom to call his wife, Mary, found several reporters ahead of him, and, waiting his turn, was pained to hear their versions of his granddaughter's testimony. He caught their mood more than their words, their badinage with colleagues on city desks about how it was looking more and more as if this young couple could have committed the crime. When Leah walked down that aisle he had felt a strong urge to jump to his feet and put a protective arm around her, but the watchful presence of the court officers was intimidating—he feared they might lay hands on him—not that he minded for himself but he didn't want to risk a scene that would add to her embarrassment. Now he was wishing he had followed his instincts.

For months to come he and his relatives would be haunted by their memories of Leah's ordeal. "That was a terrible day when George Bolen asked her, 'Did you murder your sister?,'" her grandmother, Ann Scheller, recalled. "It was shocking. Grada almost broke down. John's mother tried to comfort her. And yet I was sure the truth would come out, that Olivia was guilty."

All of them held on to this belief. It was the only logical conclusion to the story as they knew it. Their inside view of this case was an inversion of the way it appeared to the outside world; they also had George Bolen reassuring them, keeping their spirits up.

Troy related: "I would call my father and he would say that the trial was going well, that Brevetti was asking ludicrous questions, that she was being unethical, and that the D.A.'s office had everything under control.

He thought it would be a tough struggle but that Bolen would prevail. But from what I was getting from the media, it didn't seem that way at all.''

Barbara was in court almost every day, still reliving her own bereavement, frustrated because so much evidence related to the mechanics of the fire, and so little to the murder of Kristie. The essential truth of this case had been softened, even circumvented, to avoid the cruel reality that a baby was deliberately torched. Nobody wanted to talk about that, much less deal with it. Even the police photograph of the burned-out nursery was not shown to the jury until a strip of manila-colored tape had been pasted diagonally across, obscuring the image of a dead Kristie.

"Put Denise on the stand," Barbara kept urging Bolen, clinging to the hope that a mother's testimony could break through all this denial.

Instead, the prosecution's next witness was an officer of the Concord Beverage Company, John Marble, summoned from Philadelphia to identify the partially melted soda bottle found in the nursery as one of his company's Vantage brand. The transparent plastic had turned a milky white in the heat, but its code mark, still legible, indicated that it was one of hundreds of thousands of identical bottles marketed in the greater New York area during the few weeks before the fire. The only apparent purpose of Marble's testimony was to show that this bottle could have been taken from the recycling bin in the Fischers' laundry room. But it was just as likely to have come from many other places for miles around. Rather than pulling the threads of this case together, George Bolen seemed to be clutching at straws.

Next came Marie Solimando, the civilian dispatcher for the Mount Pleasant police who kept watch over Olivia on the night of her arrest. She had been summoned to confirm Bruce Johnson's observation about her prisoner's singed eyelashes; everything else she said was more helpful to the defense.

She was a pleasant, middle-aged woman who looked motherly and flustered. She had been apprehensive about this, her first court appearance, and it showed. She stated she had watched Olivia undress, but saw no injuries to her body, and no stains on her clothes. Her eyelashes were the only sign of her contact with fire. In a few minutes of incisive cross-examination, Laura Brevetti made those eyelashes seem insignificant compared with the police's treatment of her client. Conditions in a police station's overnight holding cells are always spartan; drawn by

Brevetti's questions, Marie Solimando made Mount Pleasant's seem brutally archaic.

She stated that after Olivia was locked up at about 3:00 A.M. she lay on her stomach, her face hidden from view.

"She had her face in the pillow?" Brevetti asked.

"There is no pillow."

"Just a mattress?"

"A bench."

"She was sobbing?"

"No, she was quiet."

As to the following morning, "Was my client allowed to take a shower?"

"We do not have a shower."

"Was she allowed to go to the bathroom?"

"In the female cell there is a bathroom with a screen for privacy."

Guilty or not, it was hard not to feel compassion for the grown child at the defense table, today wearing her navy blue suit, the one in which she looked most like a schoolgirl.

Kristie's autopsy report was presented by Dr. Kunjlata Ashar, as assistant medical examiner for Westchester County. She was an unlikely-looking pathologist, with thick dark hair braided down her back, Indian style, in odd contrast to her sporty glen-plaid suit. Her gentle manner softened the grisly details of her examination, revealing that between 80 and 85 percent of Kristie's body was severely burned. The only uncharred portion of her skin was on her neck and back, protected by the infant carrier, where a portion of her undershirt remained. She had been a healthy, well-nourished baby, weighing thirty pounds five ounces and twenty-four inches long.

Bolen asked whether Kristie had been injured before the fire. Dr. Ashar said she could not tell about bruises or abrasions because so much of the skin was destroyed, but there were no fractures. The infant died from burns, and from asphyxia due to the inhalation of smoke containing carbon monoxide. She had ingested a lethal amount of the gas, which meant she was still breathing when the fire started.

Some jurors were looking pained at this prosaic description of an agonizing death. Judge Silverman asked: "If the baby was alive at the time, she did not have to be conscious?" He sounded like a concerned father seeking reassurance, but he really wanted to know whether Kristie would have screamed. The doctor's answer left that question in doubt.

"That is correct," she replied.

Bolen followed up: "And carbon monoxide can produce unconsciousness, but not necessarily right away?"

"That is true." So whether the baby died from burns or from asphyxia remained indeterminate. "Either one could cause death, or both of them together," Dr. Ashar stated.

"Is it possible for a baby that size to lose consciousness in two or three breaths?" Judge Silverman asked.

"Yes."

Her response strengthened Bill's hope that this was how Kristie died. A few quick breaths, then oblivion. He tried to put the rest of that autopsy report out of his mind, thankful that Denise was not in court to hear it.

Although neither of them yet knew it, George Bolen was close to a decision not to call her. His last witness, and in evidential terms his most important, would be Bruce Johnson.

Johnson's testimony was spread over four days, longer than anyone else's. As at the pretrial hearing, he was calm, cooperative, and unemotional. He wore a civilian suit, the status symbol of a police detective, and his usual impassive expression. His largeness seemed to fill the witness box, but not aggressively. He left a memory of a moon-shaped face, impossible to read, with mild blue eyes focused straight ahead, avoiding Olivia's interested gaze.

He was remembering his former chief's injunction, to make sure that his evidence about her singed eyelashes came out right: "This whole case hangs on those eyelashes." Johnson was unhappy with the photographs he took when he arrested Olivia; the black-and-white film had not shown her damaged eyelashes any better than the Polaroid. But there was his evidence and Marie's, and he had urged George Bolen to subpoena an ophthalmologist to explain how combustible vapors will pool in the eye sockets before they affect eyebrows or hair. Calling that kind of expert witness made more sense to Johnson than bringing in a man from a bottle factory. Otherwise, he was prepared to do the explaining, provided he was asked the right leading questions. Trial witnesses may not volunteer information of their own.

The direct examination began, as he had anticipated, with a detailed description of the Thornwood area, the layout of the Fischer house, and what he saw when he was summoned there in the late afternoon of December 2. Asked about the windows, Johnson stated that when he went back to the house a second time, between 7:00 and 7:30 P.M., the center catches of the broken nursery window and Leah's window were in the locked position. The window of Olivia's room had been opened to its full extent (apparently by the firefighters), and all upstairs windows were closed.

From here on Bolen's questions moved from one unrelated topic to another, defying chronology. It was hard to tell whether he was developing a line of thought, or searching for one. Did Johnson know Thomas Kelsey as a volunteer fireman? Were there tree houses in the immediate vicinity of the Fischer house? What were the responsibilities of the desk sergeant at the Mount Pleasant police station? On the day of the fire, were any suspicious cars seen in the neighborhood? When did Johnson take his three separate videotapes of the fire scene? Followed by "How is your hearing?"

"Good," said Johnson, surprised.

Then on to the crucial question, phrased in Bolenspeak: "I want to take you back to a point in time between eleven-thirty and twelve midnight, a point in time when you were in the detective division with Marie Solimando—around that time did you have occasion to utilize a certain type of camera?"

Johnson replied that he took one or two Polaroid pictures of the prisoner's eyelashes, which were singed.

"Did that picture represent fairly accurately what you saw that evening?"

"No," Johnson admitted. "The picture came out dark, and the eyelashes did not show."

He wanted to say more about those eyelashes; instead, Bolen was asking who else was in the detectives' office when the photograph was taken. Was Betsy Hoagland, the civilian dispatcher? No, Johnson replied, wondering why the subject had been changed, and whether the prosecutor had forgotten that by this time Marie had taken Betsy's place. The next question was about the Miranda warning, followed by: "Now I want to go back to the scene of the fire . . ."

Olivia's eyelashes were not mentioned again until toward the end of the following day, after Johnson had recounted her story in all its variations, from her being in the living room, or maybe the laundry room, when a frightened cat warned her of the blaze on her bed. Finally he had the opportunity to say: "I asked her if she knew how she singed her eyelashes. She said she did not know. Then she thought for a minute and said she probably did it when she put out the fire on her bed. I asked her if she put the fire out from the foot end or the side. She said the foot end . . ."

He had given the lead to Bolen, and was expecting some follow-up questions which would bring out the significance of where Olivia was standing, how she could not have leaned over that small blaze far enough to get her eyelashes singed with the footboard in the way. But Bolen moved on to another topic, and the police's one piece of direct evidence linking Olivia to the crime, the clue that had determined her arrest, fell between the cracks in the prosecution's case. Paul Oliva would be mortified.

While Bruce Johnson was on the witness stand, his tape-recorded interview with Olivia was replayed, and again a courtroom was hushed by the sound of her high, small voice relating how she cared for Kristie on the last afternoon of this baby's life: "And then she a little bit hungry and I give her a bottle . . . and then I make the light on. Comes a little bit dark and she likes the light . . . and then I play with her, talk with her, change the diaper. . . ." And on through a mass of finely remembered trivia to the mysterious fire on her own bed and the locked nursery door, her voice rising with every repetition of the words: "And I try. It's locked. I try. It's locked. . . ." Then, later, "And I never closed the door. . . . I don't know how the fire start."

As at the pretrial hearing, Johnson was hearing the replay from his seat in the witness box, and Olivia from her place at the defense table. Finally he glanced across at her. She was still sitting upright, both feet on the floor, elbows lightly resting on the arms of her metal-framed chair, hands in her lap, in the same position she had held from the beginning of the trial.

After the recording was finished, Laura Brevetti, beginning her cross-examination, asked Olivia to stand up. "Would you say that she looks the same as on December the second?"

"Essentially the same," Johnson replied. Except, he recalled, that then her hair was pushed back behind her ears. "It is longer now. An inch, maybe."

Olivia was looking at him gravely, as if expecting his approbation.

"Eyebrows essentially the same?" Brevetti inquired.

"Yes."

"When you saw her, she had on slacks?"

"Yes, black pants, a purple top, and cloth sneakers."

"Did you notice anything unusual about her clothing?"

"No."

"Did you smell any flammable liquid on her?"

"No."

After the jury had had a good look at Olivia, surely the purpose of this exercise, Brevetti motioned to her to sit down, and began to pick away at Johnson's recollection of his interview with her. He had already said she told him, "If anyone else was in the house I would either hear or see them from anyplace I would be downstairs," contrary to the defense's contention that there had been an intruder. Now Brevetti tried to discredit his memory of that statement. She asked if it was an exact quotation.

Johnson replied that it was. Was he sure that such a grammatical sentence was spoken by the same young woman who insisted: "I don't light no fires"? Yes, he was sure.

She looked at him dubiously. "Inspector Johnson, did you write that quote down?"

"No."

"So you are relying on your memory?"

"Yes." But he was not to be budged.

Laura Brevetti had a way of smiling to herself, with her lips pressed together, slightly upturned at the corners. It seemed to express an inner satisfaction, as of one who had access to important information, denied to everyone else.

A few minutes later, during the midafternoon recess, five television sets were rolled into the courtroom. Members of the Brevetti team had been out hiring bigger and newer models than the single set George Bolen had used to show Henry Flavin's videotape of the fire scene. Now four twenty-seven-inch TVs were strategically placed by Chris Rush so that the judge, jurors, reporters, and spectators all had excellent views. A fifth, smaller set was put directly in front of the witness stand for the benefit of Bruce Johnson.

After Rush had put all the cables in place and the courtroom blinds had been closed, Laura Brevetti announced that she was going to replay Flavin's eleven-minute film. She reminded the court that it was shot before Bruce Johnson returned to the fire scene between 7:00 and

7:30 P.M. to take a second look at the damage, leaving Olivia in the Fries house. Enhanced by the superior equipment, this film showed a fire that looked more fearsome and overwhelming than it had when Bolen showed it, with an orange inferno spilling out of a huge hole in the fabric of Leah's bedroom. In the background, searchlights picked out the sharp lines of bare trees against the night sky. Standing in the middle of the courtroom with a remote-control switch in her hand, Brevetti stopped the film abruptly, freezing the scene with a shot of Leah's window lit by raging flames from within. She had rehearsed for this moment, and her timing was perfect.

Addressing Bruce Johnson, she said: "Now concentrate on the frame of the window in Miss Fischer's room with particular regard to the middle bars. Looking at the center bars of that window, would you tell me what position they are in relation to each other?"

He gulped. What he was seeing on the screen was not what he remembered seeing that night, after this video was filmed. At that time he was certain that this pair of sliding windows was so firmly shut that the center catch was in the locked position, and the inside frames of both windows were flush. Now he was looking at a picture of a gap between the two glass panels, as though one of them had been slid across by three or four inches.

"I don't know," he said, hesitantly. "They look like they are back to back, but separated."

It was an illusive image. At first glance the windows looked closed. Then they were slightly open. He had to stare hard at the film because the smoke and the fire and the movements of Flavin's hand-held camera prevented the window frames from being sharply delineated. They had looked shut when the videotape was run straight through, earlier in the trial. But the longer one stared at this frozen shot of them, the more obvious was the center gap between the two panes.

"As you look at them now, Inspector Johnson, do those windows appear to be separated?" Brevetti persisted.

"Yes," he agreed.

Addressing the court stenographer, Judge Silverman remarked: "For the record, there is a space between the two bars, but you do not know if they are lined up back to back or if they are open."

Flicking the control monitor, Brevetti ran the film back and forth, repeating the view of Leah's slightly open window silhouetted against the flames. She was relishing the witness's discomfort.

"Who closed the window, Inspector Johnson?"

"I don't know."

"It was open before you saw it?" She framed this as a question, but she was making a statement.

"I can only tell you what I saw," he replied. He looked very uncomfortable.

She let the film run to its conclusion. But she had not finished with Bruce Johnson.

"Who was opening and closing the windows that night?" she demanded.

Given time to think, it occurred to him that the two wooden frames may have been burned or warped apart as the heat intensified.

"The fire," he said.

She looked incredulous. "The fire was opening and closing windows? . . . When you saw that window the center bar was closed?"

"Yes."

"So if you made that observation at seven o'clock, you had no idea what the status of the window was at the time of the fire . . . and when you testified that the window was closed and locked, you had no way of knowing if it was closed and locked before the fire—is that correct?"

Her voice had risen to a triumphant shout. It was the only sound in the courtroom. She had everyone's rapt attention. All those hours when Chris Rush had scrutinized this film, larger than life and frame by frame, had paid off. Rush had noticed this one quick shot of the gap down the center of Leah's window where the two panes normally met, and everyone on the defense team had kept quiet about it, hoping that none of the district attorney's staff would make the same observation. It was not discernible on a normal run-through of the videotape, which left an impression of fast movement and blurred images. Cleverly, Brevetti delayed bringing it to the jury's attention until her cross-examinations had revealed that Leah did not check her window latch that morning, and that John may have gone into her room while she was taking her shower. It did not take much imagination for jurors and reporters to fill in the gaps.

Johnson was abashed. "When I saw Leah's open window on that video I felt like someone had punched me in the stomach," he admitted later. "I am one hundred percent sure that the latch was in the locked position between seven and seven-thirty. The only way I can explain it is that the hasp became burned, and melted down to make the windows spread apart when the fire was raging. But after Leah's fire was put out, before I got there the second time, the window frames must have gone back into place. What I saw on that video was like an optical illusion. At first the window looked closed, then halfway through the film it was slightly open, and at the end it looked closed again. Leah's room was such an inferno that the heat could have made it happen."

This was not an explanation that jurors and reporters were likely to accept. Weighing the memory of a detective against the evidence of a photograph, they would conclude that the window was open all along. It was the window that an intruder with knowledge of the house would choose—low to the ground, at the back of the building, opening into the one room where Olivia was not likely to be. Leah's room would make an ideal hiding place until it was possible to slip into the nursery next door, unobserved. All that was needed was the inside assistance of someone who would leave the window latch undone. Henry Flavin's film seemed to confirm that this could have happened.

The television sets were rolled away, and Brevetti continued her questioning. The script she had written for herself was impeccably timed. She led Johnson directly back to the subject of John Gallagher.

"After my client was placed under arrest, did you ask her if she was covering up for someone else who had committed the murder? Did you mention the name of John Gallagher?"

"I believe I did, yes," Johnson muttered. He was heartily wishing he hadn't.

"Did you ask her if she helped someone else, and if that someone else was John Gallagher?"

"Yes."

"And the answer was no, right?"

"Yes."

"Was anybody else, that evening, taken to police headquarters for questioning?"

"Not to my knowledge." She had amply made her point.

From the beginning of Johnson's testimony it had become his habit, every time the judge announced a recess, to nod in the direction of Bill Fischer as he walked down the center aisle and out of the courtroom. More than a friendly greeting, it was his indication that the case for the prosecution was going well. At the end of this afternoon, for the first time, he avoided Bill's questioning gaze and strode straight to the swing doors, and into the lobby.

The following morning, George Bolen tried to demonstrate Bruce Johnson's interpretation of the Flavin film. But instead of the defense's five state-of-the-art televisions, he had only the single set provided by the court. On its smaller screen the shot of Leah's bedroom window was again blurred and indistinct.

"Can you go back a frame or two?" Judge Silverman inquired. Bolen fiddled impatiently with the knobs. Brevetti had known exactly where to stop the film with a flick of her hand-held switch, controlling all five televisions at once, and she did it with a flourish, standing in the center of the courtroom like a leading actress on stage. Bolen was down on one knee, trying to coax this single piece of elderly equipment into stopping at the right place, visibly annoyed about the indignity of his situation, with everyone in court staring at him.

"In the middle of the window you see two bars coming down. They are separate?" the judge asked.

"No," Bruce Johnson replied, peering at the screen. "That is the reflection, your honor."

It was almost anybody's guess. Jan Menting was convinced that the small overlap of the window's sliding panels, and the angle of the photograph, gave the appearance of a center gap where none existed; that this was an instance where the camera lied. He had fitted those windows himself and could understand how it might happen.

It could be argued that the fire in Leah's room would not have subsided to a smolder, and flared back into an inferno when the door was kicked open, if there had been a continuing supply of oxygen from an open window. In rebuttal, it could be argued that the window was not open wide enough to make a difference. The debate could go on indefinitely, with no way of ending this ongoing trail of doubt spread by a cleverly organized defense. Afterward it was said of George Bolen that he had always played by the rules, and that when the rules were suddenly changed he was lost. At the end of Bruce Johnson's evidence he rested his case.

The court was unprepared for Laura Brevetti's announcement that there would be no defense witnesses. "The defense rests," she said, almost echoing her opponent's words. She submitted only one piece of evidence, the single-page report of the ambulance worker who briefly examined Olivia at the fire scene. It stated that she had a pulse of 120, was hysterical and hyperventilating.

Brevetti's bold decision was made, she told reporters, "as soon as I heard Detective Johnson. He was Bolen's strongest witness, but on cross-examination he became a witness for the defense."

She added: "I have saved a lot of subpoena bills because most of the witnesses I would have called have been called by the prosecution. What they had to say is extremely favorable to my client, and they cannot say otherwise because there is not a shred of evidence that she committed this crime."

35

There is a perceptible shift of gears at this point in a major trial. The witnesses relax, their duties done, and all their discarded tension is taken on by the attorneys as they prepare for the last stage of this marathon. Their summations must somehow catch and distill the essence of their cases, in speeches powerful and succinct enough to leave an impression. No juror can recall everything that is said over several weeks; it is the statements most recently heard, including the summaries of the attorneys, which are most discussed in a jury room. As the time draws near for them to deliberate, the jurors themselves regroup, emerging as twelve individuals with positive and divergent opinions, rather than the collective mass which has sat, fidgeted, and occasionally nodded off through all those unrelieved days in court.

That, and much more, happened as the trial of Olivia Riner drew toward its close. In the public section there was a spontaneous convergence of her supporters, strangers with a common faith in her innocence and a desperate desire to see it proved. They began to introduce themselves to one another, and to lunch together in The Galleria, the large shopping mall one block down Grove Street from the courthouse. They exchanged stories, and as the tension of an approaching verdict mounted, talked about staying in touch, and did. They even invented a name for themselves, The Fifth Estate, and for weeks after the trial continued to meet in the same restaurant, sharing their private writings about this case, writings that spoke of their individual needs to believe in Olivia. In these last days of the trial some of them brought flowers and tried to present them to her outside the courthouse. Two handsome bouquets were intercepted by Chris Rush before she could grasp them.

He handled them gingerly, as if they might blow up. He need not have been concerned. The donors of a large bunch of peach carnations had attached an unsigned note, "We are with you all the way," and truly meant it.

On the other side of the courtroom the Fischer relatives rearranged themselves as Denise was finally permitted to join them. She had been excluded from most of the trial in vain, and neither she nor her in-laws could understand George Bolen's decision not to call her. They vehemently disagreed with him, but continued to trust that he would pull all the loose ends of evidence together, Bolen style, and bring his case to a successful close.

In a move both actual and symbolic, Linda Sawyer shifted sides. Detaching herself from the defense team, she began to sit across the aisle with the journalists and the Fischer relatives. She had little to say to them, or they to her. There had been a falling-out with Laura Brevetti, and the exclusive television interview which Linda believed she was promised was no longer likely to materialize. She felt hurt and angry and betrayed. Six months of her life had gone into this story, and she was losing her edge on it. But she was determined not to let go.

Seated with members of Laura Brevetti's team, Kurt Riner was again in court, on his third visit from Switzerland. He and Marlise had logged up a considerable sum in transatlantic airfares, which would be covered out of the money raised by Swiss citizens in the New York area. This had been a strange time for Marlise, living in a place where she was at a loss with the language, with little to do but think and fret. During these waiting months she had found her emotional outlet in compulsive shopping at New York's discount dress stores, acquiring enough clothes to fill the hanging space in the room she shared with her daughter, and overflow into the next. She also bought an unusual amount of makeup, perfume, and inexpensive wristwatches, which she hung from a pegboard on the bedroom wall, like trophies. Inwardly she worried about her daughter, and sometimes in court the strain made her feel faint and ill. Yet even now, with Olivia's future perilously in the balance, she seemed unable to get close to her. During breaks in the trial there were no reassuring hugs, and only an occasional exchange of glances. Marlise often spent those times on the back stairs with the other cigarette smokers, seeking her own kind of solace. When Kurt was in town, her daughter seemed to have even less need of her.

Olivia herself had changed since her arrest. She had lost her pudginess and was very conscious of her slim new figure. This young woman who had tried to assuage her loneliness with marshmallows and chocolate bars was now restricting herself to half a small sandwich at lunchtime, worrying about her weight. But she always carried a supply of Swiss candy to pass around among members of the defense team.

There had been a change, also, in the life of Judge Silverman. On a day when Bruce Johnson was on the witness stand, it was announced that Silverman would soon be campaigning for a place on the state supreme court. He had done well to be a county court judge in his early forties, and could have settled into that position for some time to come, but ambition drove him on. As a Democrat in a heavily Republican district he had a hard campaign ahead, but he had prevailed in those circumstances before. The possibility of advancement seemed to energize him; perhaps he was already realizing how much his visibility as "the nanny trial judge" might help his career. For him, the media's attention was positive and to be encouraged. Bruce Johnson, finishing his testimony, had a very different viewpoint: "We were all dead in the water with the media. Myself looking at the jurors, I could tell they were reading the newspapers."

By the afternoon of Thursday, July 2, one month after the trial began, all evidence had been heard and all the attorneys' motions had been dealt with. The charges were reduced to three counts of murder and one of arson, and the trial was adjourned for the Independence Day holiday, to resume the following Monday. Jurors were again told not to read or discuss anything about the case.

Over the long weekend, however, the pro-Olivia journalists continued to keep "the nanny story" in the news. Mike Taibbi and Carole Agus, who had been close to the Brevetti team throughout the trial, came out with exclusive reports, strongly favoring Olivia. Taibbi, a senior reporter for the CBS Television Network, had obtained some favorable excerpts from Olivia's diary which he quoted on Thursday's 11:00 P.M. national news. The diary had been kept secret up to this point; it was not entered as evidence at the trial, and the only known copies were with the two attorneys. Taibbi surprised his viewers by quoting three recent passages, one expressing Olivia's growing affection for Kristie, one telling of her homesickness, and a later, conflicting comment that "I do not regret for one second that I am here."

His newscast included a brief conversation with Olivia as she left court that afternoon. It was the first interview that Laura Brevetti had permitted since this case began. Taibbi, who had hounded Bill Fischer and John Gallagher for months, was excessively gentle with Olivia. His only question assumed her innocence. "Are you angry, Miss Riner, at what has happened to you?"

After a moment's hesitation she replied: *"Nein."*

The following Monday, the entire front page of *Newsday* was filled with a close-up photograph of Olivia looking fresh and pretty and thoughtful, alongside a headline-sized quote from her diary: I FEEL CLOSER AND CLOSER TO HER . . . I REALLY DO LOVE HER. An inside page was filled with more diary excerpts about her tender feelings for Kristie, introduced by Carole Agus. This section was headed: ACCUSED NANNY'S DIARY UNLOCKED—BUT NOT FOR JURY. Theoretically, that was true. But any juror who passed a newsstand on the way to court that morning could not have failed to see Olivia's photograph and her quote about how much she loved the baby.

The attorneys' summations took most of that day. The leading participants in this drama had dressed for the occasion, except for Olivia who was back to wearing the dreariest of her two navy suits. Laura Brevetti was as elegantly tailored as ever, in a double-breasted navy blazer with gold buttons, brightened by navy culottes with white polka dots, and a large but discreet pearl brooch at her throat. George Bolen had a lawyer's unvarying wardrobe of white shirts and distinctive gray suits, which he wore well, being tall and slim and erect. His personality was expressed only in his choice of tie. Today's was red silk paisley, one of his brightest.

Brevetti spent the entire morning arguing the case for Olivia's innocence, and for the probable guilt of John Gallagher. It was transparent but effective strategy. She claimed that she had known "from the beginning" that the prosecution's evidence would exonerate her client and "point the finger at others, known and unknown."

Much of this evidence, she insisted, lacked substance. "You are being told that a window is closed when it is open, that something is up when it is down . . . and you are led to believe that mere accusation is guilt. . . . The police never set out to solve a crime. They set out to build a case against Olivia Riner."

Brevetti pointed out that Bill Fischer saw no problem with Olivia.

Would he have left his baby with her if he had? "Of course not. Olivia was a good kid, an unlikely killer." Moreover, she had no motive. Bruce Johnson must have been searching for a motive when he asked if she had had sexual relations with anyone, and if she was covering up for John Gallagher. "Two hours after arresting this girl—thinking that someone else who was the logical suspect had done it, and that she was covering up!"

This led into an attack on John. "This is a man who, when he cannot get insurance, he lies on his application. But no problem. He has Miss Fischer to cover up so he can drive a truck with commercial plates. Why does he drive without a license? Because he knows all the cops. Carpenter questions him in the comfort of his patrol car, smoking a cigarette. He knows Carpenter. He knows Alagno, his old swimming coach. And he knows the new police chief, Uncle Tony. . . .

"This is a man who forgets being expelled from high school, who then remembers he cut classes. Who in the world is expelled from high school in this day and age for cutting classes four or five times? What is being covered up? Why is an alibi needed for Mr. Gallagher?"

In response to her own rhetorical question, Brevetti invented a new scenario. She stated, as if it were fact, that on the morning of the crime John "admitted he was in Leah's bedroom, that he waited there while she was in the shower." (In fact, he had testified that he doubted if he went into her room that morning.) "Well, what was he doing while she was in the shower?" Brevetti implied that he was opening the window.

She took her tale a stage further, imagining an episode to explain the melted soda bottle on the nursery floor. The prosecution had been unable to suggest why, if Olivia was the arsonist, she would have transferred paint thinner from the can in Bill's closet to a soda bottle. Why not pour it straight from the can? Brevetti had an artful explanation, implicating John Gallagher, whom she described as "a walking reasonable doubt." Paint thinner, she stated, was a clear liquid. The soda bottle, taken from the laundry-room recycling bin, was "used to transfer it out of the house, and then to transfer it back in without anyone knowing it was paint thinner rather than seltzer." Thus, she theorized, John could have come in unsuspected, openly carrying his stolen arson equipment.

She reiterated that 5 West Lake Drive was not "an impregnable fortress," and claimed that the prosecution had set out to prove "that no other human being could possibly have entered that house." Again, she was bending the truth. But she concluded by frankly facing Olivia's failure to try to save the baby.

"Ladies and gentlemen, she is not a heroine. She is just innocent of murder, that's all. She is not Superwoman who busted through walls and doors. She did what she could in those circumstances. . . . There is abundant evidence that Olivia Riner loved the child, treated the child well, and was cooperative. And there is something rotten when the police do not look far, and base their initial actions on what seems to be wild speculation."

George Bolen had a neat introduction to his closing speech, a quotation from one of Sir Arthur Conan Doyle's classic detective stories, *The Sign of Four.* Sherlock Holmes, lecturing his devoted disciple, Dr. John Watson, remarks: "How often have I said to you that when you have eliminated the impossible, whatever remains, *however improbable,* must be the truth?"

This had been Bolen's strategy throughout the trial, to eliminate the impossible, and the enormity of the task was overwhelming him. It was also unnecessary. Whether or not the Fischers' house was a fortress, or Leah's window was open, or the police had examined John Gallagher's clothes—none of those things was as significant to his case as the improbability of the tale that Olivia told. If her story was to be believed, a stranger entered this small house unheard and unseen, picked up matches from a cupboard on one floor and paint thinner from the closet in another, opened and closed doors and windows, went up and down the stairs and hallway, set three separate fires with accelerants whose odor must have penetrated the building, and finally lit a blaze around an active, healthy baby within earshot of a monitor which amplified every sound—all this while Olivia was no more than sixteen feet away, either in the living room or the laundry room, oblivious. In addition there were her own conflicting statements that she had no idea how the fires started, that she was alone with the baby and would have known if anyone else was in the house.

Instead of stressing the incredibility of this story, Bolen argued defensively. He even came close to apologizing for some of his witnesses. Of the firemen, he said: "No matter what you say about this case, about what they did or did not do, all of them did the best they could."

Of his arson expert: "I will acknowledge that Joe Butler made no notes. I don't know how old he is, been around a while, but he has a damn good memory."

Of Sergeant Dwyer's changed testimony: "We all make mistakes."

Brevetti's theory about the soda bottle was material for ridicule, but Bolen addressed it seriously, thereby conceding that it was plausible. "Is Brevetti suggesting that Gallagher would get a jug of paint thinner, pour it into a clear plastic bottle, get into the house after work, set a fire, exit by Olivia Riner's window, get back in the truck, and then get out and go to the front door? This is what she surmised. But if you look at the remaining liquid in the paint thinner container, it is not clear, it is yellow. Take it into the jury room. . . ."

Reflectively, as if still pondering the question himself, he asked: "If you wanted to do a really good torch job, wouldn't you use gasoline? Paint thinner is a kind of strange thing to use. Gallagher works with cars. If Gallagher really wanted to do this, wouldn't he use gasoline?

"Oh, yes, you say, but he wanted to set up Miss Riner. Well, if he wanted to set up Miss Riner, wouldn't he have said that he saw her pour paint thinner on the baby's diaper?"

Again he had fallen into the trap that Brevetti cunningly set for him; he was so involved in explaining why John was not a walking reasonable doubt that he was forgetting to prosecute Olivia. He could not even suggest a motive for her.

"No one," he acknowledged, "could possibly have a logical reason to do what was done in this case. . . . But I submit to you, ladies and gentlemen, that the police did not overlook any other suspect. It had to be Miss Riner."

Most members of the Fischer family were satisfied with George Bolen's speech. They had come to this trial with their own kind of innocence. They believed that Bolen stood for truth and justice, that Brevetti was the enemy, that Olivia murdered Kristie, that the American judicial system was evenhanded, and that right would prevail. A terrible wrong had been done to them, and they looked to George Bolen, and to this court, to give them satisfaction and peace. They appreciated his efforts to clear John's name. They felt it was John's due, and that once the jurors were convinced of his innocence they would automatically convict Olivia.

"We all thought we had a very good case," Leah said. "What we had was the missing matches, the missing paint thinner, her eyelashes, the layout of the house, and the fact that she was alone there. Who else could have set those fires?"

36

On the morning of Tuesday, July 7, the jurors began their deliberations. Warned that they would be sequestered until they reached a verdict, they brought overnight bags to court. It was a hot day, and like most spectators at the trial they came casually dressed, prepared for a long session. In contrast, Olivia was wearing her most formal outfit, the cream-colored suit, with matching shoes and stockings. There was a touch of pink at the neckline of her blouse; otherwise she was a study in unadorned off-white. A jury might have a hard time convicting a girl who looked so startlingly pure. Her supporters were out in force, filling the public section. Bill, Denise, Leah, and John were again in the back row, accompanied by Marianne Walsh, and the Reverend Steven Yagerman, the Episcopal priest who conducted Kristie's funeral and who was again there to support the family.

Judge Silverman explained the charges in detail: three second-degree murder charges, and one first-degree arson. The first two counts were alternatives, describing either reckless or intentional conduct resulting in loss of life. The third was a felony murder count, based on the assumption that in the course of a deliberate act of arson a person was killed. The fourth, the most serious of all arson charges and the one on which Bolen was pinning his hopes, presumed that the defendant set a fire knowing that it posed a serious threat to the life of another person.

"This will be one of the most important decisions you may have to make in your entire lives," Judge Silverman told the jurors. "I would urge you to take your time. Be patient with one another. . . . Take a few minutes or a few hours. It makes no difference at this point." At 10:47 A.M. they withdrew to the jury room.

At 11:50 A.M. they sent a note to the judge, requesting several exhibits from the fire scene, Bruce Johnson's taped interview with Olivia, a replay of Henry Flavin's video of the fire, and a read-back of large portions of testimony. Obviously they would not reach a verdict for hours.

At the beginning of the lunch recess, Denise decided to break her silence. She had picked her time carefully, too late for her to be accused of trying to influence the jury, and while reporters were hanging around with not much else to do. She chose a few whom she trusted and, accompanied by Bill, Leah, and John, took them to the third-floor waiting room. There she told them what she knew about the other side of Olivia; about the missing baby clothes, and the lie she told about whom she saw and what she did on the day after Thanksgiving.

"She is not as unimpeachable as she looks. Not as sweet as you might think. . . . She stole baby clothes, a whole shopping bag full. They were found in her closet after the fire," Denise expostulated, on the edge of tears. It was still too hard for her to talk about the crime itself. For seven months she had respected George Bolen's advice, and kept quiet. Now that she could contain herself no longer, what was coming out of her was the verbal equivalent of a puff of hot air when what was going on inside her was a festering volcano. The murder of her baby, and her own anguish about trusting the person she believed responsible—all that was too painful to put into words.

A reporter asked whether she thought Olivia was guilty.

Bill responded for the two of them: "Absolutely. No one else could have gotten into the house without her knowing it. And she never tried to get the baby out."

"She ran out from the fire," Denise added. "The baby was twelve feet away from her, and she did not get the baby. . . . Nobody can understand how we feel about losing Kristie. People can sympathize but not empathize. . . . I would like to talk to the jurors. I would like to play on their sympathies, but it wouldn't be fair."

"The media is trying this case," Bill complained, "and the reason we did not want to talk to the media was because we wanted this trial in the courtroom."

All of them insisted that there was no discord in this household. "We are a happy family," Leah said. "We have normal disagreements but no major problems," Denise added, making clear that her statement included John.

Close to tears, Leah spoke up for him. "You sit and watch a man dragged through the mud. . . . Brevetti made him look like an idiot for nothing."

314

John had been standing there, looking distressed. "She made up a very big fictitious story about me," he said.

"What would you like to say to her?" a reporter asked him.

"I would like to get up and punch her in the mouth," he replied.

Ignoring Bolen's advice, John went back into the courtroom with Leah after the lunch break. It took courage; yesterday he was booed out of the building, with Olivia's supporters yelling after him.

"How can you sleep at night? We all know you did this!" one woman had shouted.

The long wait for a verdict was punctuated by the jurors filing back to their places to rehear passages of testimony read to them in a fast monotone by Steven Sacripanti, the court reporter, then filing back to the jury room for more discussion. During the waiting hours it became a pastime among the spectators to guess their line of reasoning from the testimony they requested. First it was that of Joseph Rod, volunteer fireman. Then Police Officer Robert Miliambro, followed by Sergeant Brian Dwyer. Then the audiotape of Olivia's telephone call to the police station, with her frightened cry of "Fire!" and the aggravating response from the desk sergeant: "There is no Five West Lake Drive."

Kurt and Marlise Riner sat in the front of the public section, craning forward, trying to comprehend the language and the legal system and what was happening to their daughter. Olivia was seated with her back to them, rigidly upright in her chair, immobile and expressionless except for her twisting fingers. Laura Brevetti's tension was coming out of her feet. She began by tapping her toes on the floor, fast and rhythmically; then she crossed her knees and drew rapid little circles with the foot left dangling. She kept alternating the positions, up and down, round and round, as if a mechanical force was driving her from the ankles down, and the rest of her was unaware of it.

Shortly before 7:00 P.M. the courtroom was prepared for a replay of the Flavin videotape. The jurors had indicated that they wanted it stopped at the segment showing the separation of Leah's windows. Brevetti's feet, now moving up and down, slowed to a smoother tempo. This was looking good for the defense.

As if at a prearranged signal, the five handsome new rental TVs reappeared, courtesy of Laura Brevetti. She was taking no chances with the court's makeshift equipment. Again she stood up with the remote-control switch in her hand, in command: an imposing figure in a creamy-beige silk suit, with a softly pleated skirt that swished around her legs as she moved across the courtroom. Again she had that smug, compressed smile as she stopped the film at the shot of Leah's bedroom window. She was prepared to hold it there for as long as anyone wanted to look. People were craning forward, peering at the image of two sliding window panes which appeared to be spread some three inches apart. The judge got up and stood in front of one of the large screens for a better view. "Looks open to me," he observed. Brevetti went on smiling.

Shannett Yancy, the jury's forewoman, said afterward: "I felt from the beginning that she was not guilty, and after that film of the fire was shown, my mind was kind of made up." Just as Paul Oliva had determined that Olivia's eyelashes were "the clincher" in the police's decision to arrest her, so the gap in Leah's window was the clincher with the jury. At 7:40 P.M. they sent a note to the judge: "We are near a decision and think we can conclude deliberations tonight."

Again Silverman urged them to take their time. "If you feel the need to go overnight, we shall go overnight. This is too important a matter to rush a decision. No one—no one—should feel pressured." He emphasized his point by calling a dinner break until 9:30 P.M.

Several reporters left, realizing that Olivia's fate would not be settled in time for tomorrow morning's newspapers. Out in the hallway the judge made a surprising informal comment to some of the remaining journalists. He said that if the jury came back with a guilty verdict, he would probably set the conviction aside on grounds of insufficient evidence.

Spared from hearing this, the Fischers left the building and began to walk aimlessly along Grove Street. Stressed and drained, they all needed a change of scene and some fresh air. By now they had been joined by Barbara and Jim. Even though none of them felt like eating, they would like to have gone to a restaurant, as a convivial place to be together, but were afraid of being cornered by photographers. It had happened before. Instead, they strolled into the shopping mall, which was a quiet and anonymous place at this time of the evening, and sat in one of the big, open fast-food cafés. Urged by Marianne, they ordered coffee and cinnamon buns.

"I had been through this before," she recalled, "and I knew they should have something sugary, or there was a strong possibility of someone passing out."

With time still to kill and nowhere else to go, they went back to the district attorney's suite, now almost deserted except for the cleaning staff. George Bolen was hurrying down the hallway, looking preoccupied.

He nodded a greeting to Jim Donnelly, who had become separated from the others. Neither of them would ever mention it, but at the 8:00 A.M. mass on the previous Sunday, Jim had been surprised to notice George Bolen, alone, on his knees beside him. He had never seen him at Holy Name before; the church was some distance from Bolen's home, but a small detour on his drive to the district attorney's office, and Bolen had worked through the Independence Day weekend. That Sunday morning Jim glimpsed another dimension of this man who rarely let his defenses down—seeking the strength and guidance of his faith in the awesome responsibility of prosecuting a young woman for murder.

"Jim, I'm glad you're here," Bolen said, as they came face-to-face in his office hallway. "In case I don't get a chance to tell the others myself, the judge has asked them to remain seated after the verdict, no matter what it is. He wants to speak to the family."

Jim guessed what this was about, and so did Marianne when he told her: that if the verdict was guilty the judge was likely to overturn it, and would want to explain his reasons.

"Right up to this point we had all been hopeful, but now I began to prepare Bill and Denise for the worst," Marianne recalled. "I told them it did not look good, and that got them very nervous. We were all pacing around the third floor, not hearing any news, so after a while I said, 'Let's go up to the fourteenth floor and see what's going on.' "

There was still some time to go before 9:30, and they did not expect to find many people around. But as they got out of the elevator they walked in on a scene that surprised and shocked them.

Marianne related: "There was a table set by the courtroom, right near the sign which says No Food or Drink Allowed, and I had an impression of twelve to fifteen people, gathered around, drinking and eating. It looked like a party for the defense team."

She was wrong. This was not a celebration. Brevetti's group had sent out for pizza and soda because they, too, felt uncomfortable about being seen in a restaurant. They were every bit as tense and stressed as the Fischers, but the sight of them pretending normalcy caused all the welling fears of Marianne and her companions to spill over into anger.

"We were all outraged," she said. "We had barely been able to eat, and they were having a party. We had to go out for our food, dodging the media, and theirs was brought in for them. Somebody authorized

317

it. Somebody gave them permission to use that courtroom when it was closed to everyone else. I was livid, absolutely livid. We went back to the third floor and waited.''

By 9:30 P.M. all signs of the defense team's supper had been cleared away. The public section was again filled. The Fifth Estate was determined to stay until this was over, either to see Olivia freed, or to protest if she wasn't.

At 10:10 P.M. the jury filed back into the courtroom for a read-back of part of John Gallagher's testimony. In all these months John had spared Denise and Leah the details of what he saw when he kicked open the nursery door; now they were hearing it for the first time, read in the hurried and expressionless tones of the court reporter. John himself had left the building.

"I told him not to be there," Marianne said. "I was afraid that the crowd might turn on him after the verdict, and there would be no more reason for him to hold his temper.''

She went out on to the back stairs for a cigarette, and found smokers from both sides of the courtroom, tensely puffing and barely speaking: among them, Marlise Riner, Linda Sawyer, and Barbara Donnelly. While they were standing around, a television reporter approached them, wanting their opinions.

"Oh, please," Marianne said, and left to join the family.

At 11:00 P.M. the jurors withdrew for a final conference. Theirs was a thoughtful, well-educated group, mostly of an age to regard Olivia as their child, in some cases their granddaughter. The forewoman, Shannett Yancy, the only black juror, was a grandmother and a secretary, and through most of the discussion she defended Olivia strenuously.

"Two of the men brought up the point that she should have tried to break into the nursery somehow. I said that she was only a small girl, frightened, and that she did go for help, the best help she could think of. One man was upset because she didn't tell the fire department that there was a baby in the house, and I told him, 'That wouldn't get them there any faster.' ''

Along with several other jurors, Ms. Yancy discounted all of John and Leah's evidence. "Nobody said 'I don't remember' so many times as they did, and that disqualified their testimony so far as I was concerned. I couldn't believe anything else they said.''

Early in their discussions, ten jurors voted for acquittal. The two favoring conviction were men. "They voted guilty because she was the only one in the house and they thought no one else could have gotten in," said Alfred Carapella, a juror who had recently retired from being dean of students at a large public high school. "The rest of us said yes, that was probably true, but you have to go beyond a reasonable doubt. We were impressed by the audiotape of her call to the police dispatcher, that her tone was one of deep concern, and then we looked at the film again showing Leah's open window. The only evidence that Olivia's window was not open too was that the police said it wasn't.

"There were so many gaps in the story. We wanted to know: If her eyelashes were singed, why wasn't her hair also? Could Gallagher really see flames from the nursery if he was bending down and there were trees in the way? I tried it in my own driveway. When I bent down I could see nothing but the tops of buildings. Was that a minor discrepancy, or was it really important? Why didn't the police inspect Gallagher's truck? Why did the firemen take so long to discover the fire in Leah's room? Why didn't we have testimony from Lieutenant Alagno, who was in charge of the crime scene, or from Scott Carpenter, who was the first policeman to arrive, or from George Fries, who went in right after John Gallagher? Why was the bottle expert called at the trial? Why were the police in such a hurry to arrest Olivia? If she had used paint thinner from the house, wouldn't there have been some residue on her? When the fire broke out, why didn't she go to the neighbors for help? Why didn't the prosecution send someone to Switzerland so that we could have known more about her mental state?

"What disturbed everyone on the jury was that every question we raised came to a dead end. After listening to the evidence, most of us could come up with several scenarios, all of which may have been wrong. I don't know how anyone will ever get to the bottom of this case, I really don't, not unless at some future date Olivia decides to come out with a statement."

Their questions ranged all the way down to domestic details of the Fischer home. From a woman juror: "Why put a baby on the floor? With cats there?" It really troubled her.

Inventing their own narratives, several jurors had an intruder entering through Leah's window while Olivia was distracted by some other sound, the television or the washing machine, although no such distraction had been suggested in evidence. Ms. Yancy's scenario went like this: "Whoever got into the house got in through Leah's window after Olivia went into the laundry. They would have waited until she started the machine, then they went into the baby's room, fixed the lock so it would close, and started the fire there. The diaper that had been by the baby's head was put on Olivia's bed, still burning. They opened her window, went back into Leah's room, started that fire, and left the way they came in." She could not imagine a motive, and saw this as an unsolved crime, with the murderer still at large.

The jury's discussions focused on the arson charge, on the theory that if Olivia was not guilty of arson, the three murder charges were irrelevant.

"The baby never became part of the issue," one juror admitted. "This baby was dead, and we were not talking about it. We concentrated on whether or not Olivia set the fires."

At 11:10 P.M. a note was sent to the judge stating that the jury had reached a verdict.

When they filed back into the courtroom at 11:25 P.M. Laura Brevetti was so tense that she was hyperventilating. From his seat almost directly above hers, Judge Silverman glanced down in concern. At the back, Bill and Denise held hands, and in a chain reaction other hands were grasped all the way down the row, as the Fischer family and their few supporters braced themselves for whatever they would have to hear.

Slowly the three murder charges were read.

"Not guilty . . . not guilty . . . not guilty," Shannett Yancy replied.

Then the arson charge, the most likely one, the charge that hung in the balance.

"Not guilty."

In the public section a gray-haired woman in an orange dress stood up, let out a jubilant cry, and clapped her hands. Everyone around her joined the cheering. Judge Silverman called for silence but the applause was deafening, so he smiled and let it happen. Laura Brevetti hugged Olivia, and Olivia was suddenly transformed into a radiant young woman with sparkling eyes and a joyous smile. Judge Silverman stepped down to congratulate them both.

The group in the back row continued to hold hands, not looking at one another. Denise's body sagged visibly, all energy drained from it. Bill stared straight ahead, expressionless, in shock. All this had triggered the memory of another trauma, several years earlier, when on a visit to New York City he was overpowered by three men and forced at gunpoint to hand over his wallet. "What made me maddest of all was that people were passing by, pointing at me, saying that this man was being mugged, but not doing anything to help me." The rejoicing of Olivia's supporters was like the callous indifference of those passersby, and he felt as helpless and overwhelmed as he did then. It was torture to sit there and listen to their cheering while trying to comprehend that the murder of his child might never be resolved.

Judge Silverman dismissed the jury, and gave Olivia permission to remove the electronic monitor from her ankle. She bent down to unstrap it, smiling again at the relief of being freed. As the spectators began to leave, Denise wondered whether Laura Brevetti would come across and express sympathy over Kristie's death. Although it would not have been an easy encounter, she would have appreciated the gesture. But neither Brevetti nor anyone else on the other side of the courtroom had anything to say to her. The atmosphere was entirely one of celebration. Bitterly Denise remarked: "People seem to have forgotten that a baby was murdered."

She would have walked out, but for the judge's request for the family to wait. He had gone into his chambers to disrobe, and they assumed he would be back. Marianne Walsh and Steven Yagerman waited with them. As Olivia's supporters prepared to leave, Marianne was shocked to see a woman glaring directly at Leah, baring her teeth, and clenching her fists. She had never seen such hatred on anyone's face, and was glad that Leah was staring into her lap.

Eric Dardenne had dutifully stayed until the end. Even after a long, hot day in court he looked cool and immaculate in his pearl-gray summer suit, the epitome of the European diplomat. He picked up his briefcase, glanced at his watch, and remarked sadly: "Today is the birthday of my wife." He had planned a celebration for her, but the evening was gone, and he would not reach home before tomorrow.

The court emptied, and the Fischers stayed in their places, expecting the judge to return.

"You have to leave," a court officer told them.

They explained why they were waiting. "I'm sorry, I've had no instructions about that," the officer replied. "I've been told to escort you out."

Denise got up. "I've had enough," she said. "Let's get out of here."

Back in the district attorney's office, the Fischers encountered George Bolen. He looked exhausted and sad.

"I'm very sorry," he said. "If you're going to blame anybody, blame me."

Marianne felt for him. "This case wasn't tried in the court," she told him.

"I suppose that's true," he said. On his way out of the room he added: "Now I have to put on my smiling face for the reporters. . . ." And was gone.

Steven Yagerman tried to console the family. "You didn't lose this case," he told them. "The justice system failed you."

"Come on, Steve, don't pull that religious stuff on us," Denise responded. He didn't think he had, but he understood her anger. He had seen her like this before, seven months ago when they were planning Kristie's funeral.

Barbara was crying. "We should have worked through the media. Maybe then people would know what we have been through, what this girl did. It didn't come out in court. We should have talked to the reporters." Jim put his arm around her, consoling.

"The Fischers have no luck," she sobbed. "No luck at all." Once more she was back in her own tragedy.

Leah kept repeating: "It's not fair, just not fair. We do everything we are supposed to do, and look at what happens."

Marianne tried to comfort them. "I know this isn't going to make sense to you right now, but what goes around comes around. I really believe that."

Denise looked at here strangely. "What do you mean?"

"I'm not talking about the hereafter," Marianne replied. She was remembering the man who was never charged with her father's murder because of an inadequate investigation, but who later went to prison for armed robbery. "I am thinking that we have not heard the last of Olivia Riner."

"You mean she will do something to someone else?" Denise looked stricken.

"No, not that. I was thinking of something I have seen in other cases, including my own. I can't put a finger it, but in some way, shape, or form, there is a kind of justice. For you, it did not happen in this court, but in time it will.''

Ready to leave, they waited while Leah used one of the desk telephones to call John at the friend's auto shop where he was working late, trying to take his mind off the trial.

"They've come out with the verdict," Leah told him.

"Yeah?"

"They found her not guilty."

"What???"

"Not guilty." She waited for a response which didn't come. "I'm telling you not guilty."

"That figures," he said. He turned to his friend and mouthed the words "not guilty."

"After all you have gone through, they let her off!" the friend exclaimed.

Leah hung up, and the group in the district attorney's office prepared to leave. Their cars were in the basement garage, which necessitated changing from an elevator to an escalator on the main floor. In the large lobby they had to walk past a triumphant press conference being given by Laura Brevetti, seated at a table beneath a battery of television lights, with Olivia at her side.

Brevetti was having her last word about the Mount Pleasant police: "They should not close the book on this case. There is an arsonist running around in that community, and at nine A.M. tomorrow they should start pounding the pavements like good policemen to try and solve this crime."

Asked about her reaction to the verdict, Olivia replied through a woman friend of the Riner family, not an impartial translator such as Maya Hess had been but one who gave her own interpretation to Olivia's monosyllabic replies.

"She is happy. She is very relieved. . . . She says she had the best defense lawyer she could have had. . . . She learned a lot about the nice side of America. This has been a very positive experience. A lot of people wrote in support of her, and she met a lot of wonderful people."

How did she feel about the Fischers? "She has not seen them since it happened. She is very sad that they lost their daughter."

Of the crowd of reporters, only two saw the Fischers hurry by, and followed them down the escalator. Again the question: How did they feel about the verdict?

Bitterly Denise replied: "I felt as if they were all cheering at my baby's funeral."

It was past midnight when, in the shadows of the vast garage, the weary little group of relatives and friends parted, and walked to their separate cars. On most of the windshields there were parking tickets.

37

Olivia went home a heroine. Eight days after the verdict she was greeted at Zurich International Airport by relatives, friends, reporters, photographers, rounds of applause, and bouquets of flowers. In the space of a few weeks she had become the kind of celebrity who is recognized by her first name alone. OLIVIA FREI! the front page banner headline of one Zurich newspaper declared, alongside an account of her acquittal. All the Swiss-German newspapers saw the verdict as a vindication of her innocence, and rejoiced in it. Olivia herself had little to say, except that "being suspected of killing Kristie Fischer was totally unreal, like a bad dream," and that she wanted to put the ugly experience behind her.

In her hometown of Wettingen her father's colleagues drove her through the streets on a fire truck, like a carnival queen, with a striking absence of awareness as to how this might offend an American family whose baby had burned to death in her care. Relayed to the United States in a television newscast, this scene was the first intimation to the Fischers, the Mount Pleasant police, and the Westchester District Attorney's office that Olivia was a fireman's daughter, and they were shocked.

Laura Brevetti traveled to Zurich with the Riners, ensuring that her client said as little as possible to the press.

"My advice to her is not to speak to anyone," she said. "I am protecting her monetary interests." There was an American television-film contract pending, with the bulk of the money promised to Brevetti and a sizable sum for the Riners. That was not all. Three months later, Olivia, acting through Laura Brevetti, initiated a $20 million lawsuit against the town of Mount Pleasant for "unlawful and malicious" criminal prosecution.

Implicit in this action was an assumption of Olivia's innocence, although her acquittal left it in doubt. Judge Silverman explained that although he might have overturned a guilty verdict for legal reasons, he was still puzzled by the case.

"It is very rare for me to end a trial without having a strong feeling that the person is either guilty or not," he stated. "This time I don't know. I spent a lot of time looking at Olivia Riner, and did not observe much that I could draw upon. I was especially looking for her reaction to certain testimony—testimony about her, about the baby, and the condition of the baby—and she was expressionless. It would be weird with some people, but not with others. I would look at her for periods of time, and every so often she would catch me looking at her and put her eyes down. There was no smile. Nothing."

During the trial the press and the public saw only the back of Olivia's head, the jurors her profile. But one man was able to observe her, almost head-on, at close quarters for long periods: Steven Sacripanti, the senior court reporter who produced the official transcript. For more than twenty years Sacripanti had been sitting in courtrooms, at the heart of the action, only a few feet away from a variety of accused felons.

"I don't have to look at my hands, or at my notes, when I am writing," he explained. "I'm an observer. I sit and watch body language. I stared at Olivia Riner every day of this trial for more than a month, and I felt uneasy. It was a gut feeling, something I can't describe, but what I was looking at was not normal. I saw on her a look that I have never seen before, a look that was psychotic.

"In this case there were none of the usual motives for murder: love, hate, revenge, or money. It was not an act of vindictiveness, it was an act of madness. And that says to me that there doesn't have to be a motive. This girl comes from a small town; she could have deep psychological problems that were not recognized."

Sacripanti felt sympathy for George Bolen. "He was going upstream all the way, and he didn't have a day's break. This case was so difficult to prove, with such a lack of motive, and with public opinion insisting that she didn't do it. It was the most baffling that I have ever been on."

"Laura Brevetti manipulated the press skillfully," Judge Silverman commented. "She did a good job of steering public opinion toward her client. There was a spin put on this case, a distortion of there being great turmoil in the family, enough to make John Gallagher commit a horrendous murder in the household of people who had opened their home to him. But it was only a theory, and there was no evidence to support it. Brevetti subpoenaed a mountain of material, and I signed every subpoena she gave me—for Gallagher's school records, records of people not mentioned in court, which she thought might give a possible lead, police files of every arson in the area. She had investigators working around the clock, and the financial means to carry this out. Everything she wanted she got."

None of this material, the judge indicated, substantiated the theory of a plot to kill Kristie, or provided a link with other fires in the area. "There was an extraordinary number of them, but this fire was completely different. Here there was intent to kill a baby—not someone tossing something through a window, but a definite pour pattern around her, and no rational explanation for this act. No one benefits from it. No one could be seeking revenge against a baby. But if it was only the baby, why set other fires in that house? Why run the risk of being caught setting them?

"All these things point toward Olivia Riner having done this. . . . But Brevetti was able to play the case in such a way that if all the windows of that house were not locked someone else could have committed the crime. She did this so successfully that by the time the prosecution rested, the defense was won. There was nothing that Riner could have done by testifying, except lose the case."

The judge was severely critical of the media coverage. "*The New York Times* was very accurate, the Gannett newspapers were fairly okay, *Newsday* was emotionally driven. The TV people were off the wall. They made no effort to be accurate or objective, but saw the defense theory as a good story, and ran with it as though it were fact. They destroyed the character and reputation of John Gallagher, then moved out of the community without a care in the world."

Even after Olivia's acquittal the onslaught continued. *Newsday*'s columnist Carole Agus published an extraordinary allegation, one she asserted Brevetti refrained from making at the trial only "because good taste precluded her doing it." According to Agus, there was a shot in Henry Flavin's film which showed the body of Kristie Fischer, treated with such disrespect by the police and firemen that it was "thrown out on to the lawn like a discarded chair."

Brevetti repeated this charge in an interview with another writer.

"Every time I would see that scene on the video, I would cringe," she said. "Toward the end of the tape, in the middle of the lawn you see the body of a baby with its legs stuck out, and ten or so firemen gathered around, just gawking.''

What she actually saw in that dimly lit film, according to all the firemen who were there, was one of their oxygen packs, oblong in shape, and rounded at the ends with short attached straps protruding at odd angles. Some of the firemen were changing air packs, and this one had been discarded on the lawn. It was about the size of a baby. Everyone who was on duty in the room with Kristie's body verified that she remained untouched in her carrier until the man from the Medical Examiner's office arrived, after Flavin's film was completed. Brevetti's misinterpretation of the scene gave her another reason to castigate the police and fire departments. It also added to the agony of the victims.

"The Fischers *ought* to know about it," Brevetti insisted.

The family had been numb and unprotesting through most of the trial, but the verdict and these ugly events surrounding it released an outburst of uncharacteristic rage. Marianne Walsh, who was familiar with the helpless intensity of their kind of grief, had warned them that this was a stage to be worked through. But there was an added dimension to their pain. They had not only lost Kristie, they had lost faith.

"I don't trust the courts," Bill said. "I don't trust the media. I don't trust anyone. It was not Olivia who was on trial. It was us."

And from Denise: "You trust someone with your baby, and they betray you. You trust the media, and they betray you. The D.A., the whole justice system, they all betray you. It's as though the world isn't working anymore."

"This is how a rape victim must feel," Bill added. "You are not believed. You have been violated, and yet you are made to feel that you should have known better than to let it happen, that somehow it is all your fault."

Jim Donnelly empathized with them. "So many times at that trial I wanted to scream out, 'Forget Olivia. Think about my brother-in-law. You have no idea what he and his wife are going through. And you don't care.' If I were John I would have blown my brains out. I couldn't handle it. He was part of our family, and there's no way anyone can convince me that he set that fire. But that man was crucified. He was brutally taken apart."

"I expected a conviction in this trial, and I did not expect Laura

Brevetti to slam into Johnny the way she did," Carol Gallagher complained. "She opened up his whole life history, and threw quite a bit of mud at him. When he said he wanted to punch her in the mouth, I knew how he felt. What did he ever do wrong that she made him look such a horrible, monstrous person?"

She was reminded of something she had seen at the same courthouse, years earlier. "On the back of one of the benches someone had etched with a knife the words *Fuck Justice*. And I thought it is still true, because of what I saw at this trial, and what happened to Johnny."

During the succeeding weeks the Fischers and the Gallaghers heaped their frustrations on the person who had invited blame, George Bolen. They argued that if only he had done this, or said that, Olivia would have been convicted. Bolen, meanwhile, was undergoing his own agony of self-doubt.

"I have tried a lot of circumstantial cases," he recalled. "Usually it's possible to come up with a reasonable scenario of what you think occurred. This time I racked my brains, and couldn't. I was hoping the jury would find it incomprehensible that Olivia Riner never heard anyone come in the house and set those fires. I was hoping that once they evaluated Gallagher, whether or not they approved his life-style, they would see him as a decent man who did his best to save the baby. And that they would see that only she could have done it, despite the fact that they could not come up with a reason. I was really hoping for that."

Bruce Johnson was devastated by the verdict. As the lone detective on an investigation which, so his past and present police chiefs agreed, should have been shared with at least one other detective, he felt overly responsible for its outcome. It was the biggest case he had ever worked on, he had anticipated a conviction, and felt he had failed the Fischers. His emotional attachment to them added to his burden. "We had a lot of evidence, but so much of it didn't get presented. You don't know how disheartening it was to me not to take the jury to the house. I was throwing things around George Bolen's office. I was saying, 'Dammit, this is very important. . . .' The Fischers have been done a great injustice, and I wish I could make it right."

In the contentiously governed town of Mount Pleasant, it was predictable that someone would turn the trial result into political capital. Olivia's acquittal gave Robert Meehan the opportunity to justify his appointment of Anthony Provenzano as acting police chief. If the department, under Meehan's old adversary Paul Oliva, had been more efficient, this murder would have been solved—so Meehan's supporters argued. They predicted that if Oliva were succeeded by a man trained in his tradition, errors would be perpetuated. It was easy to pave the way for giving Provenzano the permanent appointment by playing upon the fears of a community which had been badly shaken by an outrageous crime. At one of several crowded town meetings which followed the trial, a heavy-set gray-haired man rose from the audience to declare: "If, God forbid, this girl was guilty, then she has been allowed to go overseas because of something that was not done correctly, whether it was by the D.A.'s office or the police. And if she is innocent, my grandchildren are at risk because there is a murderer still running round this town."

He was applauded vociferously.

Meehan won approval for the expenditure of up to $50,000 in public funds for an independent investigation of his own police department's conduct of the case, and over the ensuing months the already demoralized department was probed, prodded, split apart, and found wanting. Very little came out of this exercise other than some useful recommendations for strengthening police procedures (some of which Oliva had already put in place before he retired) and for drawing more extensively upon the county's technical services (which theoretically had much to offer, but whose budgetary restraints had already hampered the Riner investigation). In a supplementary report of his own, Acting Police Chief Provenzano concluded that one of the problems of his department at the time of Olivia Riner's arrest had been his predecessor's territorial attitude, which made him reluctant to call in outside help. Subsequently, and to nobody's surprise, the Meehan administration appointed Provenzano police chief.

There were other political consequences of the trial. Four months later, Donald Silverman was elected to the state supreme court. For the second time in his judicial career he won on a recount, in a very close election. What undoubtedly tipped the vote in his favor was his public exposure as the "nanny trial" judge, and the praise he was given in Westchester newspapers for his skillful handling of the case.

Laura Brevetti's career was given an enormous boost. She became a frequently quoted public figure in the legal profession, and resigned from her law firm to set up her own New York City practice.

None of the controversial posttrial inquests produced a single clue leading to any other possible arsonist, and as time passed, an increasing
number of Westchester residents came to believe that Olivia Riner may
have got away with murder. This view was strengthened by the withdrawal of her lawsuit against the town of Mount Pleasant, only two
months after it was filed. In an exclusive CBS Television Network interview with Mike Taibbi (courtesy of Laura Brevetti) Olivia gave her reasons: "I must [would have to] go back to New York. I must go to court.
It would take a long time and I do not want to do it." She was photographed in Switzerland, back at her old job as a physician's assistant.
Again Taibbi treated her as though she had been unjustly accused.

"I am not angry," she told him. "I am sad. They may have made a
mistake but I am not mad about it."

"What would you say to Bill and Denise Fischer?" Taibbi asked.

She hesitated for a moment. "I did not do it. I do not know how it
happened."

Not all the media remained sympathetic to Olivia. In the weeks after
her acquittal, journalists who had thought her innocent at the outset
began to question her story. During the trial they had concentrated on
the daily evidence. Analyzing it afterward, they saw troubling inconsistencies.

Linda Sawyer, now separated from the Brevetti team, began to dwell
on details which, earlier, she had pushed to the back of her mind. The
baby monitor which Olivia didn't hear. The green-and-white-striped outfit in which Kristie wasn't dressed, which Denise said she didn't own.
The excessive amount of formula which Olivia said she had fed her. As
she thought about these things, it was as easy for Linda to imagine that
Olivia was culpable as it had once been to think her innocent. And that
brought her to the distressing question: "Have I been defending a guilty
person for all these months?"

She had invested a lot of time, money, and emotional energy in helping to secure Olivia's acquittal. Now she wanted to be assured of the
truth, and to go on researching until she found it. "I cannot let go of
this story," she admitted. "It is almost an obsession." The Riners had
invited her to visit them anytime, so on impulse she flew to Switzerland
and showed up on their doorstep. They were surprised to see her, and
as hospitable as they had promised.

In their apartment she saw a great deal of Kurt's firefighting equipment on display, much of it hanging from the walls of the spare bedroom in which she slept. Its presence made her so uncomfortable, and she was so scared that the real purpose of her visit might be discovered, that she took a fireman's ax from the wall and slept with it under her pillow.

"Olivia was happy to see me," Linda recalled. "She had come to think of me as the sister she never had." Sitting around the kitchen table in the evenings, the two of them talked for hours. Afterward Linda related that, in response to her questions, Olivia revealed a sophisticated knowledge of fire and the use of accelerants.

While in Wettingen, Linda tried to check on the two Swiss references Olivia had supplied to E. F. Au Pair. At one address the name given in the reference was not known. The other address did not exist. She also visited the bookstall whose proprietor had talked on the telephone to Bruce Johnson, and learned that Olivia was a frequent customer. But she could not discover whether a book containing "The Heroine" was sold to her.

Back in the United States, she shared her information with Bill and Denise Fischer. By now she had come to believe Olivia guilty, and wanted to make amends. A few months earlier, listening to Laura Brevetti allege in court that John Gallagher was a walking reasonable doubt, she had told herself with some pride: "I did that for her." Now she was eager to undo it. She told the Fischers that she was in a unique position to help them get justice done "because if I hadn't believed in Olivia's innocence so desperately I wouldn't know what I know now." They were contemplating a lawsuit against E. F. Au Pair, and she could be very persuasive.

In an extraordinary reversal of allegiances, they appeared with her on two editions of a national television program—the same *Maury Povich Show* that they had turned down during the week after the fire. By now Bill and Denise were ready to publicize their side of the story, even though it was too late to change the outcome. In the first of these programs Linda made an abject public apology to John Gallagher.

For the second, she made a return visit to Switzerland and arranged to have herself videotaped as she waylaid Olivia outside her apartment house as she arrived home on her bicycle.

Linda approached her bluntly, becoming more and more emotional as she spoke. "I have questions to ask you, questions that are haunting me," she said. "Did you buy this book, Olivia?" She was holding a volume containing "The Heroine." "How did you know how the fire was started? How did you know a liquid was poured, Olivia? When you talked to your father on the phone, how did you know a liquid was poured? Were those your fingerprints on the accelerant bottles, Olivia? Were they? . . . Eight months of my life, I protected you. I investigated for you. I believed in you. Olivia, I deserve the truth. Olivia. Tell me the truth, Olivia. Tell me what happened, Olivia. What happened to Kristie? What happened, Olivia?"

She was trying her utmost to get the confession the police had failed to achieve. It would have been a tremendous coup, and on videotape, too. But this time Olivia had nothing to say to her. Throughout the tirade she had her head bent down, padlocking her bicycle, and when she was done, she walked indoors without a sign of recognition.

Following up on Linda's lead, Bill and Denise hired an investigator to research Olivia's references. His report stated that "even the most casual screening" should have revealed that they were fictitious. Both signatures appeared to have been written by the same person, in a hand-writing resembling Olivia's. One reference was signed with the surname Meier, the other Reinert. No first names were given. The address for Meier was that of a commercial building where no Meier was listed; however, the telephone number was that of the doctor (at a different address) who was Olivia's last employer. This doctor stated that she was very good with children but that she had not asked him for a reference.

Reinert's address did not exist. The investigator located a man with a similar name, Olivia's last teacher in high school, who stated that she had not asked him for a reference, but that he, too, would gladly have given her one. Her school work had been conscientious and satisfactory. It was inexplicable that she, or someone else, would have gone to the risk of producing transparent forgeries when genuine recommendations were available to her.

On the E. F. Au Pair application form, "Meier" and "Reinert" had even used the same level and style of English as Olivia herself:

In response to the question "Why should a family choose the applicant and trust her to take care of their children?" these answers were given:

"She love children and can learn many. . . . She is perfect an [sic] an au pair"—"Meier."

"Because she is a beautiful girl and the children can learn many things from her and she can learn many things from the family"— "Reinert."

Asked the same question, why a family should choose her, Olivia herself had replied: "I want learn so many things and I can do that only as an au pair in a family. Because I know many things at about children and I think the children can learn many things from me. I work for a medical for children and I want work with children then that is my 'Dream job.'"

On the second anniversary of Kristie's death, December 2, 1993, in a news conference arranged by Linda Sawyer, Bill and Denise Fischer announced that they had filed a $100 million lawsuit against E. F. Au Pair. The suit alleged that despite the agency's advertised claim of a rigorous screening process, it sent them an au pair who was unqualified and psychologically unstable, and who caused the death of their baby.

There was no expectation of a speedy settlement.

38

There were certain immutable occasions when members of the Fischer family got together. There was Willie's birthday on the Fourth of July, when Barbara always gave a big party for him at the family home. There were smaller parties on the children's birthdays, when aunts and uncles and cousins showed up. And there was the Christmas tradition of gathering at one home or another, with Jim Donnelly, jovial, portly, and exuding good cheer, playing Santa Claus.

Kristie's murder changed the shape and atmosphere of family reunions. Willie's seventy-ninth birthday fell on the weekend before the jury began its deliberations. Bill and Denise were too distressed to attend the party, and the others too tense to enjoy it. Two months later was the first anniversary of Kristie's birth, so painful to her parents that they took a trip to Maine to try to forget what might have been.

"We just about got through that first birthday," Denise said. "There is that numbness. I wonder if it will ever go away; what it will be like for the next birthday and the ones after that, if I will always go on thinking how old she would be, and what she would be doing."

It was understood that Denise would find it too difficult to celebrate E.J.'s second birthday and Christopher's third, later the same month. A year earlier, and only a week after Kristie's birth, she had gone to Christopher's last party, carrying her tiny daughter in the folds of a shawl, which was draped around her own slender shoulders. She had walked around the room, unselfconsciously chatting to the other adults while her baby nuzzled sleepily at her breast. This was a Denise none of them had seen before, transformed by motherhood into a tender and joyous woman who radiated happiness. Two and a half months later that part of her seemed to die, along with Kristie. She had barely smiled since, and often became tearful in the presence of other people's children.

The family moved cautiously around her pain, avoiding bringing their little ones to visit, and curtailing the visits when they did. It seemed insensitive to discuss their own parental hopes and concerns in her presence, safer to talk about more trivial things. Fischers had never been at ease with their own emotions. But throughout the family the sense of loss was enormous; the gap left by Kimmy's death had widened into an abyss. Of the American Fischers, Kimmy and Kristie had been the only children of the third generation's middle age, cherished offshoots of a family tree which seemed so sturdy and unshakable before all this happened. That sense of security and continuity might not be recovered in their lifetimes.

This is how Betsy remembered the Christmas following the trial: "Jim was dressed as Santa Claus for a Christmas Eve party at his home. Barbara had decorated the tree, again with those ornaments showing pictures of Kimmy, the kind you can have made from school photographs. Most of us were there—my mother and dad, Bob and I, Debby and her husband, Rick, Jim's sister and her daughter and husband. And the children, Christopher and E.J.

"At seven P.M. the front door opened and Santa came in doing his 'Ho! ho! ho!' routine. Then his voice cracked. Tears ran down his face. And Christopher asked, 'Why is Santa Claus crying?'

"I said quickly, 'Santa got soot in his eyes coming down all those chimneys.'

"Jim tried to change his voice, but it was cracking again, and he made a quick departure. He came back wearing his usual clothes and said, 'I'm sorry. I had a flashback of Kimmy.' He always used to play Santa for her.

"Then E.J. realized that this hadn't been Santa but Grandpa, and Barbara, who looked like crying too, got mad instead, blaming Jim because now E.J. won't believe in Santa anymore, and he's only two."

The next day, Christmas, the family gathered at Bill and Denise's new home. They had moved again, permanently this time, to a spacious condominium with an adjoining apartment for Leah and John. Obliged to buy a houseful of new furniture, they had started with the basics in a simple modern style. Although tasteful and attractive, it was a home from which the usual curios and keepsakes were noticeably missing. All those household treasures, accumulated over years, had perished with Kristie.

"Denise had done a beautiful job with the tree," Betsy recalled. "They lost all their ornaments in the fire, so she had decorated it with white lights and red ribbon bows.

"She did not shy away from the children. She was teary, but she made an effort. I don't know who gave them toy guns, but at one point E.J. was whining and Christopher was shooting him, and E.J. was saying, 'I don't want to die.' Then Bill started to cry, and so did Willie."

When Denise was in the kitchen, preparing the meal, Jim took the opportunity to speak to her privately. He had been trying to find the right occasion for months.

"There's something I have to tell you," he said. "I don't want you to think I was intruding into your life, but that time when Barbara and I visited you in the hospital I baptized Kristie. I don't know why I did it, but I had this sense of urgency."

She grasped his hand, and there were tears in her eyes. Nothing was said. Others came into the kitchen, and the moment passed. He felt a sense of relief. Afraid that he might have overstepped a boundary, he had worried about how she would react. But it was all right. She understood.

The house that Jan Menting built was restored, refurbished, and put up for sale. Bill might have been able to go back to it, and to find healing among the memories of the good years spent there; years in which he had made his own mark upon the place, taking over where Jan left off, adding subtle improvements which respected the simplicity and openness of the design. Even after thirty-eight years, it was a house ahead of the times, one carefully intended for a life of light and joy and peace. Influenced by the Dutch minimalist style of his youth, Jan had understood the uplifting effect upon the human spirit of letting the sunshine in. But now Denise could think of it only as a house of gloom and terror, where her baby burned to death, and she could never return.

There were no ready buyers, so Bill rented the property until it could be sold. He continued to mow the lawn and tend the shrubbery, wishing he didn't have to because it forced him back into the moment when, standing on that same lawn in the fading light of a winter afternoon, he was told by a fireman: "You don't want to go in there." Now he couldn't go in, not without the tenants' permission.

It had been Jan's hope that the house would eventually pass to his grandchildren; that it would continue to be a family haven and a gathering place, just as the house now referred to as "Barbara's home" had been for four generations. After the fire neither Troy nor Leah tried to influence their father's decision; nevertheless, the prospect of losing their childhood home left them feeling rootless.

"I never thought I would see the day when someone in the family would want to sell the house," Troy said.

Jan purported to mind the least—not that he had lost his feeling for the place but because stronger emotions took precedence. During the trial, and while the rest of the family still trusted in a conviction, he already sensed that the prosecution's case was lost, and was utterly dismayed.

There had been a lot of injustice in his lifetime which he had been powerless to prevent; now he was stubbornly determined to see that the truth of this case should be known. He was not seeking vengeance against Olivia, but he could not let pass the lies that were told about his granddaughter Leah, about John Gallagher, and about what might have happened in the house he knew so well.

The trial triggered the same memories that were awakened by a priest's mention of the Holocaust at Kristie's funeral: memories of the injustice to his father, Gradus, a mining engineer, trapped in Sumatra when it was overrun by the Japanese, whose health was broken in the inhuman conditions of a prison camp, and who died within a year of his release. Memories of his Jewish friends who were taken away in the night during the Nazi occupation, with no one to speak up for them. His outrage over those injustices had never left him, and his strong reaction to Olivia's trial came out of it.

"It's all lies," he said one day, addressing a group of her supporters outside the courthouse. They ignored him, and he walked away, frustrated. It was not his style to make a scene. Or yet to give up.

After the verdict he used every public opportunity to tell how he believed the trial had been manipulated. Olivia could never again be charged with Kristie's murder, but that was less important to him than a public admission of what he believed to be the truth. He spoke out about it, wrote letters to editors, and encouraged the Fischer relatives to describe their perception of events for this book. Better than they, he realized that only if the whole family story was told could the full impact of the injustice done to them be understood.

Grada, named after the grandfather she never knew, often described her father as a humanist. Given his values, and his life experience, it was inevitable that he—although only a distant relative of the Fischers—would be the one to take on this cause. "I cannot have lived, and not have been involved," he explained. "I cannot accept what happened in this case. I can accept that there was a murder, but I cannot accept the truth that I know so well being changed. It is like history being altered, and you knowing that what is being said is not true, and doing nothing about it."

Over and over he replayed the trial in his mind. "Why couldn't the jury see what Laura Brevetti was doing?" he wondered. "All that talk about Leah's window was irrelevant and meant to confuse, because it assumed there was an intruder. But there was absolutely no evidence to support it. This was an assumption, created and exploited by the defense."

As he dwelt on it, he developed the theory that perhaps this case was doomed to be lost. Nominally, it was a lone, defenseless Swiss girl who was being prosecuted. In reality, the District Attorney's office was pitted against the larger resources of a profitable au pair agency with far-reaching international business associations. E. F. Au Pair was under the same ownership as a network of language schools, E. F. Education Inc., which described itself as the world's largest private educational institution. According to Bill Fischer's research, the sole shareholder in these affiliated companies was a man with a financial interest in some forty other companies in Switzerland. Jan wondered whether this might explain the Swiss Consulate's unusual interest in Olivia's trial; he also speculated that forces beyond Laura Brevetti may have helped to secure Olivia's acquittal.

Carl Vergari, George Bolen's chief at the time of the trial, commented: "The Swiss authorities circled their wagons in this case. They were very self-protective and tight with information. They claim to have cooperated fully but we were unable to learn anything about this girl's background or history. For example, we had no idea until after the trial that her father was a fireman, and that may have had a bearing. Other free world societies are pretty wide open, but in Switzerland secrecy is a national characteristic."

Vergari had no doubt that the right person was accused of Kristie's murder. "But there was a lack of motive. There was the idea that a young woman could not possibly set fire to a baby. And I cannot recall a public rooting section for a defendant such as I saw at this trial."

At the Swiss Consulate Eric Dardenne observed that "to set three fires in a house you must have some experience of arson and burglary. And if you set them, you do not call the police." Otherwise he was noncommittal.

"I never asked Miss Brevetti the question: What really happened? Or whether she thought her client guilty or not. It is up to the prosecutor to do that, and I would not intervene. My job was to see that Olivia Riner got a fair trial."

Settled in their new home, Bill and Denise began to rebuild their lives, making slow progress. Her feelings were poignantly described in a letter written eighteen months after Kristie's death: "My mind has replayed those events over and over again like a broken record that cannot be repaired. My hands have written down words that appear to come from another world, from a wretched, tormented creature whose cries of agony can be heard in my sleep. I will never, ever lose sight of what happened. I have only learned to live with a higher level of pain."

Bill avoided discussing the murder. Like his father, he contained his grief. The pain etched on his face when he testified in court had, over ensuing months, softened a little, but only to become absorbed into the rest of his body, where it seemed to have lodged as a lasting part of him.

Leah lost the job she had held for three years. Her employer told her she had taken too much time off to attend the trial; she wondered whether the suspicion surrounding her was an unspoken factor. The shock of dismissal forced her to rethink her career, and she went back to college to train as a social worker.

"I'd like to do something to help people, like Marianne Walsh does," she explained. It was a new possibility which she was prepared to work hard for, and did: the one positive outcome of her long nightmare.

The stories which had been spread about her and John diminished, but did not disappear. "People still talk about it," Betsy remarked, months later. "They still think it was John. At day care, a new mother who didn't know of my connection with the case said, 'How good that the girl was acquitted. We all knew it was the boyfriend.' Mothers need to believe that their children are safe in another woman's care."

"When I think about what happened to me," John said, "I wonder if I shouldn't have stayed outside that night. But if it would have saved Kristie I would have gone through that experience many times over, not just the fire but everything that happened to me afterward, if only it would have made a difference.''

He added: ''I still hesitate before walking into strange places. I'm uneasy about meeting people I haven't seen in a long time, wondering what they think. The anger is still there but not the way it was.''

At family gatherings the Fischers began to make a conscious effort to talk about other things. Even so, these were no longer easy occasions. There was the Mother's Day party given by Leah for her mother and grandmother; Denise promised to come with Bill, but didn't, and was found in her room sobbing hysterically. And there was E.J.'s third birthday party, as sparsely attended as his second because of its proximity to Kimmy's and Kristie's birthdays. Every celebration seemed to be a reminder of pain.

''It's never going to go away,'' Bill's brother, Bob, acknowledged. ''It will go on and on and on. One day someone will make a movie about it. Ten years down the road when you think you have it over with, you will be sitting at home watching television, and the late show will come on, and there it will be all over again.''

''There are constant reminders,'' Jim agreed. ''Every time something happens to a nanny, the newspapers mention this case, and they still can't get the name right. The nanny trial and what's-her-name Fischer, instead of Kristie. It will never stop. It will haunt us. It will follow us to our graves.

''We are not a typical family, but we are close because of what we have been through. The average family doesn't have to deal with the kind of things that have happened to us. At some point maybe a mother or father dies, a marriage breaks up. That they can adjust to. But what we have been through is way above the average family's experience. And we survived.''

PART FOUR

THE CRIME

39

> "There is a motive, but we don't know what it is. Perhaps she was angry at me. Or she was angry at Bill. Perhaps she was insane, or manic depressed. Perhaps she was an abused child who had some crazy idea about wanting to save this baby from abuse. We may never know. But there *is* a motive."
>
> —DENISE FISCHER

It was the missing link in the chain of evidence, and without it none of the rest made sense. In the absence of a motive George Bolen was lost, and Laura Brevetti could weave a tale which won an acquittal. Her intruder theory did not bear close analysis, but it was easier for people to accept than the guilt of her client. Even in a society as violent as that of the United States, it was beyond imagining that a shy young girl who said she loved babies could do anything so calculated and terrible as to set an infant on fire.

It was not the kind of child abuse that comes out of anger or impatience. Medical examiners are all too familiar with the deaths of babies who have been dropped, or smacked, or fatally shaken by a parent or a baby-sitter who has lost control. These are impetuous acts which would probably not be committed if, in that moment of blind frustration, the perpetrator were rational enough to stop and think. But whoever murdered Kristie Fischer did think about it first, and intended to kill her.

Neither the police nor the district attorney's staff ever wavered in their assessment that Olivia Riner was that killer. The stumbling block for the prosecution, the public, and the press was the innocent appearance of the accused young woman and the naked horror of the act. Yet there was something wrong, something badly off kilter, about the absence of any perceptible reaction from her over the death of an infant in her care. No pain, no guilt, no grief that anybody could see. No regrets that she did not save the baby's life. No wishing that she had made more effort, or done something differently. There was also the way she stuck to a story which did not bear analysis. It was like a tale told by a child to explain a broken vase which "just fell off the table." The fires in the Fischers' home just happened: She didn't cause them, she didn't know who did, and although she was alone in the house with the baby, someone else must have walked from room to room lighting them. Like the child's explanation, it defied the accepted laws of physics. Yet it could not be disproved because there were no other witnesses.

Whatever happened in the Fischer household that winter afternoon was beyond comprehension. In his twenty-five years as Westchester County's district attorney, Carl Vergari had not encountered a crime remotely like it.

"This case is truly extraordinary," he said. "It is one of a kind, thank God. And why it happened I do not think we shall ever know."

It was hard to leave it at that. Months after Olivia's acquittal, the research for this book led down an unlikely avenue to the discovery of an extraordinary collection of old case histories, shockingly similar to the crimes with which she was charged. In light of her story they make astonishing reading, removing the case against Olivia Riner from the category of the unique to that of a known crime which was committed, time and again, by girls of her own ethnic background, long before Olivia was born.

These case histories form the basis of a medical thesis by Dr. Karl Jaspers, published in Germany in 1907. It was never translated into English, but can be found in major reference libraries of German-speaking Europe, including the Zentralbibliothek in Zurich. In it Jaspers discussed the eighteenth- and nineteenth-century phenomenon of young Central European girls, sent away from home to be live-in nursemaids, who set fires and murdered infants in their charge. Enough of these bizarre stories had been recorded for him to study their similarities and draw some conclusions. Jaspers was struck by the contrast between the naively innocent demeanor of the girls, and the diabolical kind of murders they planned: the same contradiction that puzzled the prosecution in the case of Olivia Riner. Jaspers summarized the girls' motives in his title, *Heimweh und Verbrechen* (*Homesickness and Crime*).

When it was first published, eighty-five years before Olivia's trial, his report was seen in professional circles as an unusual and important piece of research. It was written as the dissertation for his medical doctorate at the University of Heidelberg, in an era and place where psychopathology was a growing but fledgling science. As research became more sophisticated and life-styles changed, Jaspers's study of the homicidal loneliness of live-in nursemaids lost its relevance. With twentieth-century advances, the practice of hiring immature young girls to care for small children, unsupervised, virtually disappeared. There were no more known case histories because the cases had become history. Jaspers went on to become professor of psychology at Heidelberg and turned to a career in philosophy in which he achieved international renown as a leading existentialist thinker and writer. Nevertheless, he considered his early psychiatric work—including his unconventional study of murderous nannies—to be among his most significant. He spent the latter part of his life in Switzerland, as a professor at the University of Basel, and died there in 1969.

The old employment practice which he described in *Heimweh und Verbrechen* was risky and exploitive. The girls in Jaspers's study were essentially indentured labor, most of them little more than children themselves. The parents who hired them out were relieved to have one less mouth to feed, and may have seen this as a way of offering their daughters a better life. But the girls knew that if they ran away to go home, they would be punished by their parents and sent back to the same situation that made them so miserable.

The contemporary au pair system is much more free, yet there are strong parallels. In both instances, young women of limited worldly experience go to work as nannies in completely strange environments, cut off from the emotional support of families and friends. Often they are left for hours with the infants in their charge, with little to do and no one to talk to. For au pairs there is also the loneliness of an unfamiliar culture and a language not well understood.

The program, as it is currently structured in the United States, requires a one-year agreement on both sides. To a girl longing to go home, a year's commitment can seem like endless servitude. In theory, she need only contact her agency and say she wants to quit. In practice, that involves awkwardness with the host family, loss of face, and a sense of failure. It is not the kind of decision that a young woman of Olivia Riner's rigid and dutiful personality would easily make. She had made an agreement that she was expected to keep, and she would see that as binding. On her own admission Olivia was an unrelenting perfectionist.

"Even if I were perfect I would be dissatisfied," she confided to her diary. She also wrote that on the night of her arrival she was tempted to turn around and go back home, that she often cried herself to sleep, but felt bound to stay for the promised year because her father would be disappointed in her if she did not fulfill her contract. And her father's approval was all-important to her. Like the girls in Jaspers's study, she hid her homesickness and did not think she had any options.

These were her feelings on her third day as Kristie's nanny: "I am missing my home, my room, simply everything. Or nothing? What good is it, I am here and should make the best of it, or . . . ?" Leaving the question unformed, she continued angrily: "Sometimes I am sick of everything, the amiability, the badly pampered baby! All the baby has to do is to scream once and the whole family rushes to feed her, to change her diapers, to play with her or rock her to sleep, as she does not go to sleep otherwise. Damn!"

Karl Jaspers was fascinated by the pathology of those young nursemaids who, feeling homesick and hopelessly trapped, found their own terrible solutions. Their desire to return to their families was so overwhelming that they simply and permanently eliminated their own jobs, either by setting fire to their employers' homes, or by killing the infants in their charge. Some girls did both, with barely a qualm. In the scattered settlements of the old German Empire, none of these girls could have been aware of what the others had done, yet spontaneously and independently they committed dastardly crimes of startling similarity, as if in response to the same primitive impulse. In every case, they felt homesick from the day they took their jobs, and committed the crimes within the first few weeks of their employment.

Prior to these criminal outbursts, all the girls were perceived to be compliant, caring, and trustworthy: ideal nanny material. None of them had a criminal past. Most of them worked conscientiously and behaved affectionately toward the infants in their charge. In their new jobs some were living at a higher standard than they had known before, and were treated kindly. Most of them felt ashamed of being homesick and tried to conceal their unhappiness. Nevertheless, their overwhelming emotion was such a strong desire to get back home that all sense of proportion and morality was lost.

These girls murdered the infants they purported to love in a variety of vicious ways, such as scalding, choking, poisoning, and drowning. They set fires by such deliberate actions as dumping live coals in a hay barn, and carrying a lighted stick up a ladder to ignite a thatched roof. Although some of these crimes were impulsive, most were planned, often days ahead. But the consequences were usually left to chance. Lacking the sophistication to invent a credible alibi, most girls denied any knowledge of the crime, and told carelessly concocted stories which were transparently untrue. It was as though they could not think or plan beyond the action which set them free, or yet envisage the possibility of prison. Those who eventually confessed explained, with a child's imperfect logic, that it was necessary for them to do what they did in order to get back home. They could think of no permanent, face-saving way other than to burn the house or kill the baby. The motive was as simple as that, and from case to case it was identical. As Jaspers expressed it, these girls "felt driven in their bleak and unspeakable sadness."

Quoting from an earlier researcher, he told of one of the youngest perpetrators, an Austrian girl only nine and a half years old who, around the year 1840, murdered two children and set a house on fire in the space of five days. Eventually she confessed: "I longed for my parents, I knew that I would be allowed to go home after the little child's death, so I suffocated him with a cloth until he turned blue." This did not have the effect she planned. The infant's death was assumed to be accidental and, instead of welcoming the girl home, her mother sent her to another job even farther away. There, the girl related, "I set fire to the house . . . in the hope that once the house and the child were burned, they would not need a nanny anymore. But since that did not accomplish my purpose, I laid the little boy on the bed, covered his face with cushions, and sat on him until he stopped moving."

Jaspers's accounts make chilling reading. Although related in clinical language, the facts are so raw that they leave a haunting impression of generations of long-dead, deeply unhappy girls, and the babies whose lives they took. One of the more recent in his study, a girl named Apollonia, born in 1892, would have been known to him personally because as part of her punishment—also, no doubt, as an object of study—she was put to work as a servant in the Heidelberg psychiatric clinic while Jaspers was there. Thus he was able to learn her story in detail.

She was the daughter of a stonemason, one of nine children. In early teenage she had helped to care for her younger siblings, who were very much attached to her, and when both parents were working she managed the household. Her teachers described her as an average student, occasionally moody, but otherwise very shy, sensitive, and well behaved. Because of her parents' poverty she left school at fourteen and was immediately sent to work in the household of a well-to-do couple with three children. Like many a modern au pair, she took the job willingly, relishing the adventure.

Nevertheless, she was intensely homesick from her first day, wept a great deal, and showed symptoms of profound depression. She would have run away but for the memory of the beating that her father gave her brother Eugen when he ran home from his job. The idea of murdering the little boy in her care came to her when his mother warned her not to give him more than one spoonful of medicine; with two spoonfuls, she was told, he might never get up again. Apollonia gave him several spoonfuls, and lied about the missing medicine by saying she had spilled it. Several days later, seeing no ill effects on the infant, she decided to drown him. In the middle of the night she got up, dressed, crept into her employers' bedroom while they were sleeping, took him from his cradle, and in the darkness carried him down to the river. She threw him in, ran to the house, undressed, and went back to bed.

When the little boy's father awoke, crying out that someone had stolen his son, Apollonia joined in the search. The body was found and, in an unexpected turn of events, both parents were arrested on suspicion of doing away with their own child. Stricken by conscience, Apollonia confessed. Asked her reason, she stated: "I want to go home." It was all she would say about her crime.

Her behavior in the psychiatric clinic was observed as very timid, moody, and depressed, but hardworking and obedient. There had not been enough follow-up in any of the earlier cases cited by Jaspers to judge the long-term effect of their crimes upon girls like Apollonia, and he observed her only in the controlled conditions of the clinic. He noted, however, that few of the girls in his study seemed to have much consciousness of guilt. And he predicted that they were likely to present psychopathic symptoms in later life.

One of the vilest murders described in his report was committed in 1836 by a sixteen-year-old girl named Marie Katharina who was sent to work in a household several hours' journey from her home. There were two children, aged one and six; she was hired to care for the baby. Most days she was left alone with the children, confined to a stuffy room of the house where she was obliged to spend hours sitting by the baby's cradle, spinning.

She became increasingly miserable, but hid her feelings from her employers, giving a laughing explanation when asked about her glum expression. After being told that two of their previous children had died, she formed the idea of killing the baby. She thought about it for several days, overcoming her scruples by convincing herself that this child was probably marked for death anyway.

Jaspers related: "She remembered that she had once heard at home that oil of vitriol [sulfuric acid] made you die, and she wanted to give some to the child. Her memory of oil of vitriol was only dark and vague, she had absolutely no further knowledge of it; she thought it must be a way to make the child fall asleep peacefully and die."

She tried to buy the poison at a nearby pharmacy, was refused, but a second pharmacy sold her some. The following morning she poured this liquid into the baby's mouth, was horrified by the immediate effect of the corrosive acid, and screamed to neighbors for help. Nothing could be done; the child died in agony. Marie Katharina's explanation was the usual mixture of half-truth and unbelievable invention. She said that when the baby cried she gave the oil of vitriol in the belief that it was soothing medicine, but she had no explanation for this poison being in the house. Later, when she confessed to the crime, she said that her homesickness left her as soon as she killed the baby. It was assumed that the violence of her action gave her emotional release. Judged to be on the borderline of insanity, she was sentenced to four years in a house of correction.

In another case, a girl named Eva Barbara, aged fifteen and three-quarters, made three murder attempts on a baby of only a few weeks—first with a needle, then with hot oil, finally and successfully with boiling coffee. She, too, was judged as suffering from extreme homesickness, and given a two-year sentence.

These relatively mild sentences in a punitive era reflect both the extent, and the understanding, of criminal homesickness which developed in German-speaking Europe through the nineteenth century. It had been mentioned as early as 1795 when a researcher noted that most criminal fires were set by young girls given into servitude straight from their parents' home: a very different profile of an arsonist from that of the disaffected, underachieving young man who is the American stereotype of an arsonist today. The girls who committed arson did so by using materials in the house, usually a live coal or a brand taken from the fire, and they lit the places that would burn fastest: a hay loft, household furnishings, and in one instance, a hired hand's bed.

Over the next century, cases of murderous and arsonist nursemaids were documented in such high numbers that researchers, particularly in Germany, tried hard to find explanations. They began with the vague premise that some mysterious force within adolescent girls could cause them to commit strange and evil acts, even when there was no history of mental or behavioral disorders. They looked for the usual kind of motives—hate, envy, vindictiveness—but found none. Finally, a researcher writing in 1830 concluded that these girls wanted nothing more than to go home, and could think of no other way than to destroy their employers' domestic situations, and thus put an end to their jobs.

The debilitating effect of homesickness upon the human psyche had long been observed among European soldiers sent to serve in other countries. A researcher of 1774 noted that it was prevalent among the Swiss; it was presumed that the sickness was physical, caused by a deprivation of mountain air. Interestingly, the German word for homesickness, *heimweh*, comes from the Swiss dialect and expresses a more intense suffering than mere sickness: a profound and melancholic longing.

By the second half of the nineteenth century there had been enough research into the motives of murderous nursemaids for the law courts of the old German Empire to have reached a compassionate understanding of why certain well-behaved girls suddenly turned criminal. Several of the late-nineteenth-century cases quoted by Jaspers were evaluated by committees of medical experts, and the girls' prison sentences were often abbreviated as a result of the physicians' frequent findings: diminished accountability because of emotionally crippling homesickness. Jaspers commented that this was a huge advance over the forensic thinking of almost a century earlier when, according to a case recorded in 1801, a fourteen-year-old country girl was sentenced to death after committing arson (no other crime was mentioned) at the homes of two successive employers. She said it was the only way she knew to get home.

In an attempt to identify the girls most likely to be susceptible, Jaspers found one constant characteristic. In physical appearance and behavior, they were all very childlike for their years. Most of them appeared to be in sound mental health, were quite intelligent, and planned their crimes with a certain sophistication. But their reasoning processes had not kept pace with their intellectual development. They rationalized, and often looked, as though they were several years younger. In a case recorded in 1855, a thirteen-year-old girl, described as being in a good mental state but still very much a child, brutally battered a baby to death in order to get home. For her trial she memorized a hymn and recited it to the judge, in the naive belief that he would see her as a good girl and set her free.

Jaspers pointed out that in some of the early case histories, this childishness was probably misdiagnosed as retardation. But, he wrote, "What we find among homesickness criminals is not feeblemindedness but a horizon kept narrow by upbringing and environment; not immorality but feelings restricted to the childish aspects of life."

He made a differentiation between normal homesickness and the "pathological homesickness" of his study. What Jaspers understood, more clearly than any of the earlier researchers, was that homesickness of itself does not cause criminal behavior, but that it can be the trigger which makes some relatively benign preexisting condition become violently explosive.

Because the case histories predate modern psychiatry, none of them offers much insight into the girls' psychological state before they left home. However, some of the anecdotal descriptions suggest such prior disorders as depression, anxiety, and congenital abnormality. These girls might have gone through life without serious trouble if they had not gone, unsupported and unprepared, into a strange environment from which there seemed to be no escape. It was the confluence of the two conditions which caused the explosion, as of a lighted fuse introduced to a stick of dynamite.

Initially, some of the older girls looked forward to working away from home, but when the reality did not meet their expectations, they became desperate to return to the only security they knew. Many of their employers observed a moodiness and withdrawal which they had not seen at first; what they thought to be increasing laziness may have been depression. In his analysis of these symptoms, Jaspers showed psychological insights in advance of his time. He made the analogy between a child and a young plant, both completely dependent for survival upon the only environment they have ever known. When either of them is transplanted, all support systems are lost. A child can adapt to new conditions in the security of its family, but feels threatened, terrified, and cast adrift in unfamiliar surroundings. The homicidal nursemaids of Jaspers's study were not killing out of evil intent, but in a kind of life-and-death struggle for their own sanity.

Some observations about Olivia Riner may be relevant. She, too, had looked forward to spending a year away from home. Before applying for the position of au pair she considered going to Africa or South America as a Red Cross volunteer, but her parents dissuaded her, saying it was too dangerous. The United States was her next choice, colored by her memories of visits to Disney World and New York City. She imagined that a year in America would be a broadening experience, with no sense that the humdrum life of Thornwood had a lot less to offer her than the small Swiss town, within easy access of Zurich, where she grew up.

For the first month of her contract she had the constant company of Denise, who took her shopping and to restaurants, and showed her the neighborhood. After that, Olivia was to be alone all day with the baby, without a car, in a rural community where most of the neighbors were out at work. There was nowhere for her to go alone, comfortably, when she was free in the evenings, and no one to confide in but her diary. The fact that within that month she made five telephone calls, which she had to pay for herself, to relatives in Switzerland suggests how much she missed them. Her U.S. government-sponsored au pair agreement, imaginatively described as a student exchange program, required that she should take a continuing education course as well as supplying forty-five hours a week of child care. Olivia wanted to attend English classes, which would have given her an outside interest. But this was midterm, and after a month in Thornwood she had yet to find a suitable course. On the day before the fire she tried hard to think positive thoughts.

"I made a firm resolution to enjoy everything here fully," she wrote, "because it is only once in your lifetime that you get such an opportunity, and you have to grasp this opportunity, because otherwise it is gone and you will be sorry about it for the rest of your life."

The following day began the first full week of Denise's being back at work. Only then would Olivia have felt the full impact of her situation: that for the next eleven months she would be spending most of her waking hours confined to this house, alone with Kristie. This was very different from the American experience she had anticipated. The gloom of winter, and the bleak, incessant rain of that Monday would have added to her desolation.

In happier moments she seemed to have great affection for Kristie, and to delight in watching her development. This baby was, after all, her reason for being here. But she felt ambivalent about her, with feelings which ranged from caring protectiveness to outright resentment. The love showered upon Kristie underlined Olivia's own loneliness, and her diary entries indicate that she brooded about this. She was depressed from the time of her arrival at the Fischers' home.

"I turned twenty today!" she wrote on her fourth day there. "Actually a reason to celebrate, but who's celebrating? Not me. Kristie is a spoiled, pampered tyrant. Most of the times she cries for unknown reasons. I would just let her cry, but the mother won't. But so what? When she's at work I can just let her cry for a while. Nobody will hear it except me. Fine."

This festering anger, on her own birthday, surely came from her unfulfilled need to spend the anniversary with people who would make a fuss of her, as Denise was fussing over her daughter. "Why don't I have children? Why don't I have love?" she wanted to know.

Another clue to her thinking is that strange diary entry about her former employer, the Swiss doctor who she wished would have a fatal accident. ("If I believed in God I would even pray for that.") It was such an extreme reaction to an uncongenial situation. Surely she could have found another job. But she could not see this as a possibility, and felt hopelessly trapped. The only escape she could imagine was for the doctor to die, swiftly, even violently, so that her job as his assistant would cease to exist.

Since Olivia declined to be interviewed for this book, some of her recent handwriting was shown to Dr. Herry O. Teltscher, the New York clinical psychologist, psychotherapist, and handwriting examiner with more than fifty years' experience in Europe and the United States. He has testified at many trials; his expertise covers the research and utilization of handwriting as a diagnostic tool in mental and emotional disorders, in criminology, in questioned-document examination, jury screening, and court testimony.

Dr. Teltscher was asked to examine some recent samples of Olivia's neat, printlike writing in her native German. No information was given to him as to her identity. He was told only that the writer was a twenty-year-old German-speaking woman. These were his comments: "My overall impression is of her rigid personality, that of a young woman who would find it easiest to work in a prescribed, structured situation. If she is interested in her job she will do her best to manage. But secretly she rebels against some of the things she has to do. Outwardly she can be very friendly and polite, but what she expresses overtly, and how she really feels may be of a different order. For example, there is much anger which is controlled on the surface.

"Her writing shows many signs of emotional insecurity. She frequently incurs feelings of rejection, and anxieties. It would be important to explore her relationship with her mother in infancy. As a child she may have felt rejected, and those feelings remained. Her writing indicates, furthermore, that she is depressed: It does not appear like a temporary mood but seems to have existed for some time, particularly since she is outwardly controlled and fearful of articulating her anger.

"She is the type of girl who will tell you only as much as she wants to tell. Basically, she keeps things to herself.

"Even though she is intuitive and possesses a certain amount of creativity, she has remained emotionally immature. Her emotional growth has not kept pace with her intellectual ability."

Still with no knowledge of whose writing he was studying, Dr. Teltscher was asked: "Could this young woman's depression be profound?"

"I think it could be quite profound," he replied. "Especially when it is difficult for her to find a way out. Remember what I said about her rigidity."

"How would she try to find a way out? Suppose she was in a situation she couldn't tolerate."

"All of a sudden she is not twenty anymore. She is six. She would try to find an anchor in other people, because once again she has become a dependent child herself."

"What if there was nobody she could depend upon?"

"If she had a creative outlet, somewhere she could put her creative energy, that might help her."

"And if that kind of outlet wasn't available to her?"

"If she was completely alone, and there was no one to turn to, I think she might do something desperate. There is this tremendous amount of inner anger."

Long after the trial Maya Hess could not shake the memory of Olivia's tiny, twisting hands. She had watched them day after day in court from only inches away, hands that did not seem to belong to the rest of this girl's body, but to have been left behind from her childhood. "They were the only part of her that moved, as if they had a life of their own," Maya said. "The rest of her was catatonic."

It was tempting to wonder whether these were the hands that poured the accelerants and struck the matches, and if so, whether the deed was done by the child in her, with a child's imperfect understanding of the consequences.

Bill Fischer continued to speculate that Olivia had intended to play the heroine, and that Patricia Highsmith's short story could have given her the germ of an idea. It was tantalizing, the way that tale fit in so many respects, except for one important detail: Unlike the nanny in the story, Olivia did not attempt to enter the burning nursery.

Alone in the family, Jan Menting held on to the thought that came to him the morning after the fire, when he walked into the ruins of Kristie's nursery and saw the deeply etched circular scorch mark on the carpet, outlining the charred remains of an infant carrier. He did not know about Jaspers's research, but he did know what a powerful emotion homesickness can be; how a person can literally pine away and die from it.

"I had never met Olivia Riner," he said, "but none of the other theories, like her wanting to be a heroine, was plausible to me. That fire around the baby was an act of insanity. And homesickness can be such a profound psychological condition that your sanity might break. Then you could do something you would never contemplate in a normal state."

Others had raised this possibility, and it had quickly been dismissed. It was inconceivable that an unhappy employee would kill rather than quit.

"You mean that the motive they attribute to the nanny is that she was homesick?" Geraldo Rivera had sounded incredulous in the television program that turned the tide of public opinion in this case. "That's the best they could do?"

It was indeed. And whoever they were, they could have been right.

357

INDEX